THE NEW INTERNATIONAL CUISINE

THE NEW INTERNATIONAL CUISINE

Slimming Dishes

from the World's Great Chefs

By Armand Aulicino

A&W Publishers, Inc., New York

To the many talented cooks, in so many parts of the world, who generously shared with me their insights into cookery, their recipes, and their enthusiasm for fine cuisine.

Drawings by Ric Estrada

Published by
A & W Publishers, Inc.
95 Madison Avenue
New York, New York 10016

Designed by Fran Miskin

Library of Congress Cataloging in Publication Data

Aulicino, Armand.
    The new international cuisine.

    Includes index.
    1. Cookery, International.   2. Low-calorie diet—Recipes.   3. Low-cholesterol diet—Recipes.   I.   Title.
TX725.A1A75   641.5′635   79-53133
ISBN 0-89479-051-X

Printed in the United States of America

CONTENTS

THE NEW INTERNATIONAL CUISINE

THE NEW INTERNATIONAL CUISINE

Slimming Dishes
from the World's Great Chefs

By Armand Aulicino

A&W Publishers, Inc., New York

To the many talented cooks, in so many parts of the world, who generously shared with me their insights into cookery, their recipes, and their enthusiasm for fine cuisine.

Drawings by Ric Estrada

Copyright © 1979 by Armand Aulicino

Published by
A & W Publishers, Inc.
95 Madison Avenue
New York, New York 10016

Designed by Fran Miskin

Library of Congress Cataloging in Publication Data

Aulicino, Armand.
    The new international cuisine.

    Includes index.
    1. Cookery, International.   2. Low-calorie
diet—Recipes.   3. Low-cholesterol
diet—Recipes.   I. Title.
TX725.A1A75   641.5′635   79-53133
ISBN 0-89479-051-X

Printed in the United States of America

CONTENTS

ACKNOWLEDGMENTS

CHEFS, MASTER COOKS, AND DROW MAHRS

Christian Albino
Ettore Alzetta
Chuin Bao
Manfred Bertele
Paul Bocuse
Li Chen
Moon Chow
Joseph Curly
Michel Dufrenne
Mauro Ernesto
Augusto Farinetti
Omelia Giovenetti
Alfredo Guinci
Yuan Hung Kao
Bruno Kumin
Gaston LeNôtre

Amedé Lozach
Jacques Manière
Leonida Morini
Adelio Pagani
Cham Piu
Jean-Pierre Plet
André René
Joseph Seppi Renggli
Guiseppe Ruga
Albert Schnell
Wong Dong Shen
Shoh Chow Sheng
Marie-Louise Vaillant
Roger Vergé
Leo Waldmeier
Shih Check Wong

OUTSTANDING COOKS:

Roslyn Chvala
Alice El-Tawil
Humphrey Evans III
Dorothy Ewing
Paul Fitzwater
Paula Galusha
Silvana Giovenetti
Nicola Girola
Betsy Klein
Mrs. Lee Chin Koon

Dorothy Kunstadt
Cynthia List
Ellen Mollica
Gloria Palesa
Mario Robella
Rosalba Serreti
Florence Shields
Betty Silverman
Mark Wong

RESTAURATEURS AND HOTELIERS:

Robert M. Arnold
Joseph H. Baum
Paul Bocuse
Peter Bonfantini
Georges Cannellos
Robert Carrier
Maurice Casanova
Riccardo Damiani
Luigi Giovenetti
Bruce Ho
Terry Ko
Paul Kovi
George Lang
Peter Lee

Gaston LeNôtre
Alan Lewis
Luigi Lucchini
Rudolf Mack
Jacques Manière
Tom Margittai
Maurizio Rossi
James A. Smith
Henriette Spalter
Mastro Steffano
Ambroise Vaillant
Roger Vergé
Ming Wang
Yvonne Wong

CULINARY SPECIALISTS:

Anton (Toni) Aigner
John Arvonio
Joseph H. Baum
Charles A. Bell
Elaine Bissel
Clement Chan
Yannou Collart
Paolo Conti
Serena Di Lapigio
Ruth Epstein
Delio Franca

Vincenza Guinci
Barbara Kafka
George Lang
Lee Cheng-Ling
Guido Raimondi
Alan Reyburn
Gianpiero Rollini
Father John
  Romaniello
Luciano A. Rossi
Russel Wright

SPECIAL ARRANGEMENTS:

Antonio Del Balzo and CIGA Hotels
Jean Gillet and the Hotel Meurice
Nicola Girola, Alessandro Spicaglia, and
    Alitalia Airlines
Alan Gould and Hilton International
Mohamid Hamid, Davis Williams, and
    Olympic Airways
Don Rosendale, Jerry Cosley and Trans
    World Airlines

SPECIAL ASSISTANCE:

Mary LaPorta Aulicino
Anita Diamant
Larry Dorion
Ric Estrada
Terry Faye
Robert Gravallese
René Hénaff
Jim Hon
Bonnell Irvine

RECIPE TESTING:

Paula Galusha
Gloria Palesa
Rosalba Serreti
Catherine Van der Hude
Mark Wong

—and very special thanks to my personal
kitchen brigade: my daughter Leslie

Recipes marked with the symbol (*) can be prepared in advance and frozen for future use.

. . .

The recipe for any dish shown in boldface type is given in this book; see index for page number.

THE REVOLUTIONARY
NEW CUISINE

La nouvelle cuisine (the new cuisine) and *minceur cuisine* (the new "slimming" cookery) are widely acclaimed throughout the world today as revolutionary styles of cooking. *La nouvelle cuisine* was originated in France by Paul Bocuse and a closely knit band of *Michelin*-starred chefs, including the Troisgros brothers, Roger Vergé, Alain Chapel, Jacques Manière, and Michael Guérard. It was Guérard who branched out into *minceur cuisine* and its slimming concepts, which utilize low-calorie as well as low-cholesterol ingredients.

Both the new cuisines involve techniques by which the freshest of ingredients in season are prepared so that their natural flavors are enhanced, rather than being masked by traditionally overpowering sauces and garnishes. The new cuisine at its best—especially as more and more of it incorporates the principles of slimming cookery—is an imaginative and healthful approach to modern cookery, a concept both better suited to our contemporary lifestyle and more in accord with our increased awareness of nutrition. It is at once a deeply satisfying and creatively novel method of eating well and healthfully, insisting as it does on the use of natural ingredients, while minimizing unnecessary calories and saturated fats as well as other ingredients that can be damaging to our health. It is by no means a fad diet, but rather an exciting, sensible, and stimulating way of living well and eating well.

In a matter of a few years, millions of words have been written on the subject of the new cookery. Numerous cookbooks have appeared, including those by Michel Guérard and Paul Bocuse—and, of course, my own *The New French Cooking: Minceur Cuisine Extraordinaire,* which proved to be the first cookbook on the subject written in English specifically for the busy American homemaker. In spite of tremendous worldwide publicity, however, very few of those interested in the new cuisine had managed to taste authentic versions of the much-touted new dishes. As Bill Collins of the *Philadelphia Inquirer* (November 21, 1976) wrote, "I have dined with Bocuse and several of his colleagues, but I never tasted the new French cooking...until...I was part of a small group of journalists entertained by Armand Aulicino." Craig Claiborne of *The New York Times* (October 1, 1975) said much the same thing a year earlier, when he visited my home to first sample my *minceur* dishes.

Since that time, the wave of cookbooks on the new slimming cooking style have compromised some of its ideals. Almost without exception, they permit the use of minimal quantities of butter, saturated fats and oils, cream, egg yolks, and sugar. In so doing—although they stress the low-calorie benefits of the technique—virtually none of the major books on the subject have given any attention to the importance of its low-cholesterol benefits, which are an integral aspect of the true slimming cuisine. Many have succumbed as well to the use of potentially harmful sugar substitutes, like saccharine, the continued use of wheat flour, and minimal amounts of egg yolks, saturated fats, cream, and butter. But this is really like being "a little bit pregnant."

There is no need to compromise, however. As I have demonstrated in *The New French Cooking,* you can adapt most of the traditional ethnic recipes of the world, including your own favorites, to a more healthful and slimming cuisine without using *any* cream, butter, wheat flour, saturated fats or oils, or sugar (other than natural sugars found in fruits and vegetables). In addition to this original proven concept, I have incorporated into this book the latest ideas about the benefits of fructose (fruit sugar), including a large number of dessert and other recipes that utilize the fructose found in honey, pure maple syrup, and in date and other fruit sugars available in crystallized form. Fruit sugars are consistent with the basic premises of the new slimming cookery, inasmuch as their greater concentration of sweetness requires the use of smaller quantities, thereby reducing caloric intake; and, more important, fructose is easily digested. It does not tax the pancreas, causing increased insulin production, as does sucrose sugar, which also has other potentially harmful effects to the human body.

This book, therefore, represents a return to the advantages of the true slimming cookery: that marriage of strictly natural and healthy ingredients, improved cooking processes and techniques, and attractive presentation—the artful garnishing of each dish with carefully selected edibles in an imaginative composition of colors, shapes, and textures. I offer this book, also, as a complete guide to the new cuisine. You need not refer to my original book, *The New French Cooking,* or to any other book on the subject, to understand and prepare a wide variety of menus and recipes to meet your needs throughout the year.

But this book is also an extension of

the original concept of the new style of cookery. Since the idea had its inception in France, the recipes first developed by its originators were naturally drawn almost exclusively from *la grande cuisine,* or *haute cuisine* (the cuisine of the experts), and *la cuisine bourgeoise* (the cuisine of the people)—dishes that had been traditional French specialties. This book, instead, offers recipes adapted from the classic dishes of the foremost ethnic cuisines of the world; and since our focus now is broadly international rather than parochially French, we will henceforth call them *slimming* recipes, using the French designations only to refer to particular techniques as they originally were practiced by the famous French chefs. Here, then, you will find specialties from the enduring cuisines of Italy's northern, central, and southern regions—authentic dishes Italians savor in their homes, *trattorie,* and restaurants; and recipes drawn both from the classic *haute cuisine* of France and its *bourgeois* regional cookery, as practiced in the famous "three Bs": Bordeaux, Brittany, and Burgundy. There are recipes as well from Normandy, Provence, and neighboring Belgium. Here, too, are slimming adaptations of the great Mandarin, Szechuan, Hunan, and Cantonese dishes of China. The feast is extended with traditional as well as contemporary favorites from American cuisine—recipes that strongly reflect international as well as American Indian influences.

Before exploring our slimming and more healthful versions of these classic dishes, let's trace the development of the new techniques of cookery in relation to traditional cuisines, and examine the outstanding cuisines of the world as they continue to change. Since each cuisine is a reflection of the people, geography, climate, resources, and availability of ingredients in each country, we should not be surprised to find that the cuisine itself is subject to gradual or dramatic changes consistent with changes in any of the basic factors influencing that particular society.

In the case of the esteemed cuisines of France and China, particularly, as I will try to show presently, that is exactly what has happened, with the result that their status as great cuisines must now be reevaluated. But let's consider first the birth of the new cuisine in France.

The new concepts of cookery were an offshoot of Chef Paul Bocuse's decision to abandon the excesses of *haute cuisine* and originate a *nouvelle cuisine* in his renowned restaurant at Collonges, near Lyons, not so many years ago. Simply, he decided to emphasize the natural ingredients of each dish, and to avoid masking the natural essences of fresh meats, fish, and vegetables with the traditionally overly rich and superfluous sauces of *la grande cuisine.* Although other well-known French chefs, such as the Troisgros brothers and Jacques Manière, were already experimenting along similar lines, it was Bocuse who was to be, almost instantly, acclaimed as one of the best and most influential chefs of the world. He attracted a group of talented *Michelin*-starred colleagues, and the group became known as the "young bulls," or the *bande à Bocuse.* Soon each of them was experimenting further, outdoing each other in advancing the techniques of *la nouvelle cuisine.*

Michel Guérard at first developed recipes eschewing the use of cream, butter, egg yolks, wheat flour, and sugar (other than natural sugars found in fruits and vegetables). However, with the passage of time, and finally with the writing of his book on *minceur* cookery, Guérard elected to disregard his earlier concern with low-cholesterol recipes and began to use small quantities of these ingredients, as well as some artificial ingredients. His new book, *Michel Guérard's Cuisine Gourmande,* was described by the author (in an interview in *The New York Times,* August 3, 1977) as the "antidote" to his first cookbook. Obviously, the renowned chef has returned to his first love: the complex and inventive but higher-calorie dishes that have won him three stars from *Michelin.* I discussed both of Guérard's cookbooks with Jacques Manière in Paris. "I liked his first book on *minceur cuisine,"* Manière confided, "but not his new one on *cuisine gourmande.* It is too much a book about cooking and recipes, which mean nothing. If a book is good, it must be because of its *esprit* and its concepts, not the recipes. The *esprit* of cooking is always more important than mere recipes!"

La nouvelle cuisine was not so much an innovation as it was a dramatic departure from the overindulgences of *la grande cuisine.* Paul Bocuse surprised me recently when he confided, "There is no *nouvelle cuisine;* there is only good or bad cuisine." Manière adds, "Unfortunately, in life there are both good workers and bad workers, which explains perhaps why there is both good and bad cuisine. You know, there is no one more difficult—I would even say more wicked—than one who doesn't understand the *esprit* and will not develop a taste for good cuisine."

Actually, in many other countries, particularly the United States, fine cooks and nutritionists had been advocating, for many years before Bocuse, a sensible cookery that avoided the use of superfluous sauces and potentially harmful ingredients. Still it was the impetus of the world-famous Paul Bocuse and his highly publicized announcement that *haute cuisine* was dead and *la nouvelle cuisine* was born that brought the new style of cookery into focus.

Jacques Manière, who is now the acclaimed *cuisinier* of the Dodin Bouffant restaurant in Paris, put it succinctly in an interview with Susan Heller Anderson for *The New York Times* (October 5, 1977): "There is no *nouvelle cuisine*—it's the same old cuisine thought out for the needs of our day." In the early 1970s Manière began steaming foods, thus reviving *la cuisine à la vapeur,* which is an important *nouvelle* cooking process. "Of course it was nothing original," he said. "The Chinese did it ages ago, the Persians and Moroccans, too. At first I steamed chickens, then fish. Suddenly, everyone followed. It was light and amusing. We must battle against the pretension of *haute cuisine."*

The *bande à Bocuse* was soon to include such other master chefs as Roger Vergé, the Troisgros brothers, Alain Chapel, and Alain Senderens. However, neither *la nouvelle cuisine* nor *minceur cuisine* could have had the revolutionary impact on the world's contemporary cuisines without the tremendous publicity and coverage by the media. Jacques Manière put it bluntly in his interview with Ms. Anderson: "Chefs are made by journalists. If it weren't for them, Guérard would still be a pastry chef at the Lido, Chapel would be peeling potatoes in Lyon, and I'd be in Pantin."

An interesting factor contributing to the widespread influence of the new cuisine is the tendency of today's outstanding chefs to travel to other countries. This is not a new development: in the last century, Antonin Carême traveled to Czarist Russia, while Auguste Escoffier spent most of his career at the prestigious Savoy Hotel in London. Today's chefs are even more willing to leave their restaurants periodically and travel abroad. Paul Bocuse is often in Japan, where he teaches and is involved with restaurant ventures; Michel Guérard has created the food service for Régine's private clubs throughout the world; and Alain Chapel, the Troisgros brothers, and others make periodic visits to the United States and other countries preparing their cuisine in the finest restaurants (and wealthy homes). There have been mixed reactions to these travels of the famous chefs. On the one hand, the greater exposure of the chefs' talents has encouraged their freely sharing their techniques and recipes with other international chefs and welcoming the influences of other ethnic cuisines on their own.

But on the negative side, there is the old problem: Who is watching the store? "There are times when the great chefs of France bounce about like a troupe of Wallendas," Gael Greene wrote in *New York* magazine (October 11, 1977), "and are hailed as national heroes ... ambassadors of civilization. For that we owe a debt (and a tear) to Paul Bocuse. . . . Ten years ago, the great Lyonnaise chef decided that success ought to mean more than just noble captivity in the kitchen. That was the debut of the chef as superstar. He persuaded a band of culinary chums to fly jet stream with him—a brilliant kitchen Mafia, whisks-for-hire. And many restaurants suffered." Many culinary experts have cautioned us about the inferior fare produced by the "ghost chefs" who take over the kitchens while the superstars are on tour. Later in the year in the same magazine, Julia Child complains about "a certain sameness of menu" in the new-cuisine restaurants, and of sauces that taste like "liquified bouillon cubes." Ms. Child adds, "Not every chef is a creator, and those who cannot create will copy those who can."

I find this situation particularly unfortunate, since those tasting *nouvelle* or *minceur* dishes for the first time, even in the finest restaurants, can easily be disillusioned by a dish improperly prepared. During an interview by Sherman Kaplan on station WBBM in Chicago, he surprised me by saying, "Your book *The New French Cooking* is excellent and exciting, but I must confess that I have tasted *minceur* cuisine and found it interesting but not truly satisfying." My response was, "It really depends on where and how you tasted it. I must assume the *minceur* dishes were not well prepared." After the program, I learned that Kaplan had dined in an outstanding *haute cuisine* restaurant in Chicago, one of the most expensive spots in town, and a true gourmet's delight, that was publicizing its avant-garde inclinations by offering the new cuisine. That evening, my daughter and I dined at this restaurant; each of us ordered the *minceur* specialties with great anticipation, and our tab at the end of the evening was staggering. But the meal was absurdly inadequate. The sauces were watery and bland, the food flavorless and unevenly cooked, and the vegetables were not even

THE REVOLUTIONARY NEW CUISINE

properly *al dente*. A few carrot squiggles, occasional green peppercorns, and a touch of parsley or watercress provided the unimaginative and unappealing garnishing. It was truly appalling. Yet most of the diners, including the very knowledgeable Sherman Kaplan, went away assuming they had tasted the revolutionary new *slimming* cuisine. Certainly not!

Jacques Manière told me in a recent interview: "It's not possible to achieve a *plat génial* (a completely satisfying dish) every day. Even the best cooks," he apologized, "cannot be *sure* how a dish is going to turn out." Other chefs blame poor cuisine on the tremendous pressures of a professional kitchen trying to serve hundreds of patrons. Says Executive Chef Jean-Pierre Ferraro of La Crémaillère in Banksville, New York (as quoted by Mimi Sheraton in *The New York Times,* October 12, 1977): "I like my wife's cooking. Like all good home cooks, she does everything more quickly and more naturally than we do in a professional, classic kitchen. The true *pot de femme* always results in food that is personal—it reflects the personality of the cook."

But it is not only the new cuisine that can prove to be a disappointment to adventurous diners. In France, one finds that neither *la grande cuisine* nor *la cuisine bourgeoise* has maintained the standards that one used to associate with fine French cuisine. As I reported in the Gannett Group newspapers on September 3, 1978, "Anyone returning to the 'culinary capital of the world' after a year or so will find dramatic changes; the formerly coveted *haute cuisine* and *la cuisine bourgeoise* are in an obvious state of flux, most notably in Paris. The *nouvelle cuisine* initiated by

Paul Bocuse and his band of chefs appears to be overtaking traditional French cooking, but only on a superficial level. The citadels of *haute cuisine* are slowly and reluctantly making some concessions to the new cuisine; and restaurants specializing in ethnic cuisines—especially Middle Eastern and Far Eastern cookery—are becoming increasingly more fashionable and popular." Mimi Sheraton, reevaluating the *Michelin* three-star restaurants in France for *The New York Times* on June 7, 1978, found many disappointments, including the restaurants of Paul Bocuse, Michel Guérard, Alain Chapel, and Alain Senderens. Pointing out that all of the restaurants had received high ratings both by *Guide Kléber* and *Gault & Millau,* Ms. Sheraton wrote, "It was disappointing to note the enormous differences in the quality of food. . . . It is hard to understand why at least one of those prestigious guides does not break ranks and seriously downgrade at least one of that supposedly august group." In my own travels recently, I found that the only concession to *nouvelle cuisine* in most of my favorite traditional restaurants and bistros in Paris was in featuring more fish and seafood, including a terrine of fish reportedly invented by every chef I met—and the increased tendency to serve salads as appetizers (shades of California) or before the entrée, which is a startling innovation in France, where salads traditionally were served at the end of the meal.

Regarding the confused status of *la cuisine bourgeoise,* Jacques Manière told me in a recent interview: "The French housewives are themselves in a period of transition; they are a bit confused by the challenge to their habitual recipes, and we have to give them time to adapt. Many wives also work, as do their husbands, so they don't have time to shop and cook as they used to, preferring fast foods or a simple plate of spaghetti. Also, the household where the grandmother would be cooking all day—alas, that's passé! There's an evolution of society going on; the society of fifty years ago and the society of today are completely different. It's a new way of thinking—and, of course, a new way of cuisine!"

This brings us to the subject of the relative merits of the great cuisines of the world. Has the time come to revise our former opinions? I think so, and my own updated judgment is reflected in this book. As you proceed, you will note that I have featured the cuisines of Italy, France, China, and the United States, with appreciably more emphasis on the Italian. I believe this is appropriate for a number of important reasons

Until recently, I was in complete agreement with most culinary authorities that the three finest cuisines of the world are the Chinese, the French, and the Italian—and in that order. These titans of the culinary world developed cooking into an art through the imaginative and expert use of fresh and deftly blended ingredients, appropriate cooking processes, and an ability to suit the cuisine to the particular needs and living patterns of the populace in each country. Also, each of these cultures has made major contributions to ethnic cuisines throughout the world.

This is still true, and what I have to say is not intended to minimize those contributions. However, I am now convinced that the rating of the three most outstanding cuisines has changed. There can be lit-

tle question that Italian classical and regional cuisines, particularly of northern Italy, are now by far the most outstanding of the world's cuisines. How can this be so? Well, let us see what has happened in recent years in China, France, and Italy.

As I show later in the historical section on China, the cuisine of that vast country was heavily influenced from the earliest times not only by practical necessities (like shortages of food and fuel) but by political and even philosophical considerations. Confucius, for example, established a protocol for serving and appreciating fine food; and Lao-Tze, in seeking a harmony with nature, emphasized the nutritional value of food and advocated the use of natural foods, plants, and herbs.

Just as political and philosophical factors were instrumental in establishing the roots of Chinese cuisine, these identical factors are now responsible for minimizing the glory of what for centuries was heralded as the finest cuisine of the world. For the Communist government revolutionized virtually every aspect of Chinese life, including its cuisine. By isolating itself from the Western world and its imports of food ingredients for two decades, China has had to make do with the limited items available within the country. Therefore, the ten thousand or more incredibly artful and delectable Chinese recipes of earlier days have now been reduced to a repertoire of several hundred; and only the older chefs trained in the spirit of the past are expert enough to accomplish these with any degree of success. As it will become apparent during our tour of China, fuel is still a scarcity and gas, so necessary to fire the woks for stir-frying, is

THE REVOLUTIONARY NEW CUISINE

not readily available; this alone has resulted in changed cooking processes, with inferior results.

Philosophers and political leaders in China are still influencing its cuisine. The still omnipotent Mao, in spite of the more liberalized policies of his successor, Vice-Premier Teng Hsiao-p'ing, still determines what and how foods will be cooked and who will be assigned, in the interests of the state, to its preparation and serving. As George Lang (whom we will meet later) wrote in *The New York Times* on May 1, 1977, "In today's China, the old rules of aesthetics and concern about gastronomy are looked upon with suspicion."

When a cuisine begins to deteriorate in its native environment, the remnants of its glory can be found among expatriates in other countries, where the initial standards for excellence are zealously maintained. In Hong Kong one can still discover superb interpretations of Chinese cuisine; and often in the restaurants and homes of Chinese expatriates in other countries, including America, one can still find that attention to detail, to concept, and to the important ritualistic approach which marks fine Chinese cookery. But in China today, the culinary glories that once were unchallenged have become a thing of the past. Political revolutions that strive to change or reduce the role of the family can also be culinary revolutions; that was the case in Russia, reportedly in Cuba, and certainly in the People's Republic of China.

Political revolution, however, is not the only catalyst affecting the change of a country's cuisine. Even demographic changes can be a factor. In France, cities like Strasbourg, Lyons, and Marseilles are approaching the million mark in population, rivaling Paris, which used to dwarf all other French cities, not only in numbers but importance. As Sanche de Gramont put it in his book *The French,* "It has always been taken for granted that excellence in all fields is Parisian." No longer.

It is interesting to note that the death knell to Parisian *haute cuisine* was sounded by Paul Bocuse in Lyons, not in Paris. Although *la nouvelle cuisine* is being embraced by an increasingly larger number of restaurants in Paris, this is a matter of their getting on the bandwagon —too often, as I have already pointed out, with disastrous results.

And the poor quality is not confined to new-cuisine restaurants. After a frankly sybaritic tour of celebrated restaurants in France, Gael Greene wrote in *New York* magazine, October 11, 1977: "Yes, there was disenchantment. . . . Costly dinners at mighty three-star temples sadly flawed. . . . And money is merely paper. Dinner in the celebrated restaurants will run at least $100 for two." She adds: "How *la grande cuisine* has bloomed and barbed in just a decade. The once Young Turks of French cooking are middle-aged. The great chefs [of *la nouvelle cuisine*] have become court jesters . . . and superstars. The desperate pressure to 'create' has driven some otherwise talented chefs over the edge into sheer silliness."

Beyond this, other factors further the decline of French cuisine. The new cookery, for one thing, is chef oriented. Both Paul Bocuse's and Michel Guérard's new cookbooks are beyond the everyday practical needs of the busy homemaker in today's world. Many critics wrote that the recipes were often too complicated or hard to follow, and that ingredients called for were difficult or impossible to get. Unlike Escoffier's *Ma Cuisine* or Pellegrino Artusi's classic on Italian cuisine, the Bocuse and Guérard cookbooks seem unlikely to become a part of the daily repertoire of the average French homemaker. While the old *haute cuisine* is reported to be dead in France, the new cuisine has not quite come into its own.

Furthermore, anyone who truly knows France and has lived there for a while knows that the Frenchwoman's reputed prowess in the kitchen is truly a myth. Frenchwomen I have observed in the kitchen might have been able to turn out a few traditional specialties expertly, but generally were more adept at assembling a meal by drawing on the excellent local *pâtisserie* and *charcuterie* for ready-made dishes. And even today, private kitchens are poorly equipped by conventional American standards.

Is this shocking? Perhaps, but the evidence is clear. Recently, on Beverly Sills's television interview program, *Lifestyles,* her guests included Craig Claiborne and Gael Greene. At one point, Craig mentioned "fine French cooking," whereupon Beverly Sills, in her inimitably blunt way, interrupted, "Please, let's not promote that nonsense. I've been deathly ill with bad food in France!" Gael Greene then added: "Let's face it, Frenchwomen appreciate fine food but are not fine cooks. They buy breads and cakes in *pâtisseries,* and pâtés in *charcuteries*—and don't labor with love over dishes."

At another point in the same program, Craig advanced the idea that "the Chinese love good food." Beverly Sills remarked,

"But with the new regime, we don't know!" All of which sums up my own contention that both the Chinese and French cuisines have slipped in their ratings as outstanding cuisines to points well below that of the Italian classical and regional cuisines as practiced today. During our tours of these countries, the facts will be documented further.

Like all fine cuisines, Italian cookery draws on the fresh produce and ingredients available locally; it is essentially a cuisine of popular origin, evolving from the family and its needs. The distinctive feature of Italian cuisine is that the men of the country still play an important role—more often establishing and maintaining standards of fine cookery than the women who may actually do the cooking. For centuries, the same situation obtained in China and France. Confucius, for example, held that a true Chinese gentleman was necessarily an enthusiastic gourmet who prepared menus and served as an intelligent critic to the prized chefs of the household. He believed in the importance of culinary skills to the point that, reportedly, he left his own wife, whom he considered to be an inferior cook. In France, dedicated gourmets like Brillat-Savarin would oversee the culinary activities of servants, demonstrating their direct interest in the matters of the table. As de Gramont tells us in his book *The French,* "Gastronomy developed a distinct species, the gourmet, the man who gives priority in human affairs to the discriminate enjoyment of food."

In Italy today, virtually every waiter in any restaurant or family-style *trattoria* can tell you precisely how a specific dish is made; they are as knowledgeable as the chefs. Men in every walk of life are connoisseurs of fine food and familiar with the art of cooking. Nico Girolla, formerly an executive with Alitalia Airlines, often tells stories most characteristic of Italy of how the gourmet-minded men of his native Mantua (near Bologna) travel hundreds of kilometers to savor a special dish that one of them had experienced in an out-of-the-way *trattoria* or country home.

Italian cooking is nourishing and sensible. Sauces are used to complement, not mask, basic foods. Vegetables are popular ingredients: the Italian loves his *orto* (vegetable garden), and freshly harvested produce finds its way into each meal whenever possible. In addition, the imaginative creativity of Italian cooks, coupled with the diversity of produce from the various regions of this captivating country, make for a cuisine that is healthful, interesting, and delicious. These foundations are so strong that even in a changing world, the fast-food and self-service establishments in Italy (unlike those in France and other countries, including our own) have not bastardized the roots of Italian cookery. Instead, they provide good food by means of the *tavola calda* (hot table), which offers traditional specialties consistent in quality with the Italian concept of eating carefully and well within the parameters of one's needs, preferences, and pocketbook.

The single most important secret ingredient in Italian cuisine is *amore:* the loving touch and care that go into the preparation and serving of fine food, especially for loved ones. After all, cooking for family and friends is a love gesture, a projection of one's desire to please and satisfy those who are important to us. Cooking can provide a tremendous sense of gratification—the sum of one's need to provide pleasure, satisfaction, and fond memories. And there is always an enthusiastic response to food lovingly prepared and served. Many of us have sensed this without expressing it; but the feeling has also been expressed. Food has been called the language of love. As the Arabs say, "Our eating shows our love."

We must return to an awareness of these values. Betty Freidan, the noted exponent of women's liberation, finally got around to such an awareness in her article for *The New York Times,* January 5, 1977. After years of forgoing the pleasures of cooking for loved ones, she confesses to having rediscovered its gratifications. "No, I am not announcing public defection from the women's movement," she writes. "I think in fact I'm just coming out on the other end of women's liberation. I mean, why should I deprive myself or be ashamed of the sensuous joy I have been secretly snatching, scrambling ambrosial eggs for a man I specially love, or plying my long lost son with chicken soup?"

Today, men are increasingly more active in the kitchen. Whether sharing the cooking regularly with their wives or cooking on weekends for family and friends, men are discovering the satisfactions of their loving efforts as cooks. Robert Carrier wrote, "Cooking can be a game in which you and the whole family can participate. . . . My mother kept her family together with the wonderfully simple expedient of making her three sons as well as her husband join in to make the family meals both inexpensive and pleasurable. . . . Few things in life give more real pleasure than sitting down with family and friends to a dish one has cooked with care and attention. Such a dish demands to be tasted, talked about, compared with other dishes, other meals."

The renewed awareness of *amore* as the secret ingredient applies also to professional chefs. In an interview with Flora Lewis (*The New York Times,* August 3, 1977), Guérard said, "We don't want to be fashionable. I don't like people who come in blasé . . . For them, I spoil the kitchen. I ignore them . . . Ah, but the ones who come with *gourmandise* in their eyes, I see it right away. For them, we'd chop ourselves in four to please them, do anything they want, bring them the moon. If they only knew. . . ." Now that's a love gesture by a professional!

"I've always associated cooking and love," Guérard continued, "because my grandmother was a very good cook and she loved me very much. You can't cook for people you don't love, and the more you love them, the better you cook." Perhaps that is the best dictum for fine cookery.

With these precepts well in hand, let's proceed with our own preparation of menus and recipes of outstanding dishes of the new cuisine adapted from the classic dishes of the world.

To facilitate the planning and preparation of exciting slimming meals for virtually any occasion, I have included menus and recipes from the foremost ethnic cuisines of the world. You can prepare and present to your family and friends complete, delectable Chinese, French, American, or Italian meals, or those from any other great ethnic cuisine. However, as I point out in "Getting a Head Start," in addition to preparing a menu of entirely Chinese or French dishes, or menus from additional outstanding ethnic cuisines, I prefer to vary my menus by incorporating dishes from different countries, including our own. In that chapter, therefore, I present a group of menus that incorporate dishes from different ethnic sources for each meal, utilizing the various cooking processes essential to the new cuisine.

It's all a matter of taste, preference, and your own individual approach to cooking and serving. Some of you may wonder whether a Ukrainian borscht appetizer would appropriately precede a French or Brazilian main course, possibly followed by a Greek dessert. Of course, it depends on the sensible balancing of the respective dishes you select, particularly in terms of their ingredients and the heartiness of the individual dishes you elect to make. In devising any menu, you must give consideration to the harmony of the individual dishes with each other. It is unlikely that you would want to serve Swedish Sill Salad (potato, beet and herring salad) followed by Southern Potato and Ham Croquettes, or begin with a hearty, virtually one-course meal such as Cioppino, which has been described as our American bouillabaisse, then expect to follow with an equally robust dish such as Brunswick Stew, topped off with a dessert of delicious but filling cheesecake!

From the earliest days when man began to travel to other regions and countries, he has been influenced by and adopted the concepts, ingredients, recipes, and cooking processes of other cuisines. Thus the Arabs of the Middle East have influenced Italian cuisine, which in turn, particularly through Catherine de Medici (who went to France in 1533 to marry the

future King Henry II), is credited with providing the initial spurt to *la grande cuisine* of France. The Portuguese seafarers influenced the cuisine of Japan and introduced stockfish (dried cod) to such faraway and seemingly unlikely places as Malaysia and Indonesia, not to mention France, where it is called *morue;* Italy, where it is called *baccalà;* and Holland, where it is called *stokvis.* The interaction among cuisines is still going on. Superstar Chef Paul Bocuse admitted to adopting a vegetable soup from American black soul food for his restaurant in Collonges, and Jean Troigros serves a raw spinach salad he discovered at the "21" restaurant in New York City.

You will note that most of the menus in this book call for full-course dinners, including appetizer or hors d'oeuvre, the main course and an accoutrement or side dish as applicable, and a dessert. These, of course, can be varied for luncheons or lighter meals, when fewer courses can be served. In many countries abroad, the midday meal is the main one of the day; more courses are served then than at the evening or nighttime meal. Although most of the menus include a dessert, many ethnic cuisines do not usually complete a meal with dessert. The Chinese, as we know, do not eat desserts, preferring savories, which are special piquant dishes. The Italians and the French prefer fruit and cheese to end their meals, indulging in pastries and other tantalizing sweets on special occasions, Sundays, and festive holidays.

As mentioned previously, "bonus" recipes are also included, particularly in the large number of dessert recipes that the reader can use at his option. These, incidentally, utilize fructose (fruit sugars), which is consistent with the basic premises of slimming cuisine, inasmuch as its greater strength requires smaller quantities, thereby reducing caloric intake. More important, fructose is easily digested and, unlike sucrose, does not harm the human body.

I leave it to the reader to adjust the menus accordingly; in fact, as I have said earlier, I encourage the mixing and blending of particular dishes from any menu, regardless of the country of origin (as suggested in "Getting a Head Start"). Also, with the exception of specific international holidays, such as Easter and Christmas, I have not tied these menus to parties, birthdays, or other occasions. My aim is to provide menus, recipes, and ideas sufficient to satisfy the individual preferences and lifestyle of virtually any cook or homemaker among my readers.

Lastly, don't feel overwhelmed by the often exotic-sounding herbs and spices we must expect to find in varying ethnic cuisines. You needn't go out and buy a comprehensive set of every available herb and spice. Where possible, alternates will be suggested that may be more readily available in your larder or on your shelves. Select recipes for your menus that appeal to you, and slowly add to your collection the specific herbs and spices essential to the particular specialties you will be making. In this way, you will be sensibly building a store of these ingredients as well as enlarging your repertoire of delicious dishes. Remember that while each cuisine has its characteristic herbs and spices, these are becoming increasingly international and more easily available.

Herbs and spices should be purchased

in small quantities and stored in a cool place in airtight containers, preferably made of tinted glass (to avoid the direct rays of the sun). Most of the ingredients for our recipes of the new cuisine will be found in local markets, shops, and health-food stores. Special or hard-to-get items are generally available in the gourmet shops of local department stores, in ethnic markets and shops in your immediate area, or from sources indicated at the end of this book. Shopping in ethnic markets can be a great deal of fun and stimulation, very much like being on a "cook's tour" of that particular cuisine.

The cuisines of the world have hun-dreds of specialties waiting to be adapted with our slimming techniques and new processes of cookery, and included in your personal repertoire of fine dishes that are not only eminently satisfying, but far more suited to our contemporary lifestyle and nutritional ideas than was conceivable in the past. Recipes marked with the symbol (*) can be prepared in advance and frozen for future use.

In the next section, we take a closer look at the basic principles of the new techniques and cooking processes and provide you with specific instructions and suggestions for applying them to your own kitchen.

COOKING IN
THE NEW STYLE

Most of the readers of this book will realize that they have been using some of the principles of the new slimming cuisine all along. Do you avoid saturated fats and oils, eliminate or reduce the quantities of cream and butter in your sauces, and eschew fried foods? Do you dislike overcooked meats, fish, and vegetables? If so, you are already approaching cookery in the new style. Here, however, we use these approaches in a systematic and consistent way. But remember that we must not lose our sense of focus: the new cuisine is a rethinking of traditional culinary techniques; it has been called "the same venerable cuisine, thought out for the needs of our day." It involves the simple and honest preparation of each dish, bringing out the essences of its basic ingredients and presenting the dish in an attractive manner. Our constant aim is to avoid superfluous and potentially harmful ingredients and to achieve dishes that are at the same time delectable and low both in calories and in cholesterol—more suitable to contemporary needs.

To create your own personalized concept of slimming cuisine, it is important that you become thoroughly familiar with all of its basic ideas, and with the specific cooking processes and techniques necessary to carry them out. Here, then, are the basic principles and cooking instructions:

Begin with the freshest ingredients possible at the peak of their flavor, whether meat, poultry, seafood, vegetables, or fruits. When such ingredients are not available at their peak, frozen foods harvested and processed at the peak of their flavor are preferable to so-called fresh items of inferior quality. As Paul Bocuse told me recently, "Freezing is not the problem; it is a matter of the quality of the ingredients that are frozen." He proved it by serving a delectable dinner he had prepared with chefs Roger Vergé and Gaston Le Nôtre: the entire meal had been prepared and frozen in advance.

Eliminate high-cholesterol saturated fats and oils, judiciously using instead small amounts of polyunsaturated margarine or such polyunsaturated oils as safflower, corn, soybean, cottonseed, or peanut. Small amounts of olive oil may be used alone or blended with the preferred polyunsaturated oils.

The judicious use of spices and herbs, carefully measured, enhances the natural ingredients without overpowering their flavors. Little salt is required, but larger quantities of pepper are used, depending on individual taste. For those of my readers who prefer not to use any salt at all, I recommend using 2 tablespoons of lemon juice and ⅛ teaspoon of dried lemon peel for each tablespoon of salt called for in the following recipes.

Appropriate sauces to complement the basic ingredients are bound with egg whites, vegetable purées, potato flour, cornstarch, or arrowroot. Sauces are often made with *fromage blanc* (low-calorie and low-fat white cheeses, such as ricotta, Iceland, or farmer cheese) or with yogurt mixed with lemon juice and thickened with purées of vegetables.

When not using polyunsaturated margarine or oil in cooking, Teflon cookware or nonstick cookware sprays are used. Many recipes in this book call for cookware spray. For those who prefer to use neither spray nor Teflon, however, small quantities of polyunsaturated oil can be brushed onto the pan to avoid sticking.

Wines and brandy (or consommé) are used for deglazing particles of food in the pan *(déglaçage)* or for reducing sauces over high heat until the alcohol content has evaporated. Dry vermouth may be used whenever dry white wine is called for in any recipe.

Sautéing is accomplished by using (in place of oil) small amounts of water, stock or broth, consommé or bouillon, and/or wines or dry vermouth, depending on the amount of natural moisture contained in the ingredients, and the pot is shuffled occasionally during cooking to avoid sticking. Cooking *au sec* is the cooking of ingredients without added water in tightly covered cookware. Vegetables are cooked only until they are *al dente,* or firm and crisp—as if they had just been harvested. Applying moistened paper toweling between the lid and pan assures a tight seal when cooking on the range, and aluminum foil is used in the same manner when cooking in the oven.

Meats and poultry are browned on the range or in the oven without fats or oil. It is the high heat, not the fats, that browns the meat. Simply dip the meat in cold water; drain, but do not pat dry, and place immediately in a previously heated pan on the range or in the oven at high temperatures. Ingredients that have been marinated are browned in the same manner, using the marinade instead of water.

Excessive fat should be trimmed away from all meats before cooking. Remove the concentration of fat under the skin and near the rear cavity; then further defat poultry by wrapping in tinfoil and placing in an oven set at 450° F for fifteen minutes. Soups and stews made in advance can be chilled to facilitate skimming away any layer of fat that has risen to the surface.

Steaming, borrowed from Chinese cuisine, is an important cooking process in the slimming technique. Tightly covered pans or casseroles are used, so that the ingredients, resting on a trivet or rack slightly above the level of boiling liquid, are cooked by steam *à la vapeur*. Cooking *en vessie* (in a bag), *en papillote* (paper-wrapped), or using a pressure cooker are variations of this ancient process.

Stir-frying is another process borrowed from Oriental cuisine. Most easily accomplished in a wok, a small amount of consommé or polyunsaturated oil is heated before stirring in and constantly tossing ingredients that are thus rapidly cooked. Additional ingredients or sauces are added before the completion of cooking. Whenever desired or appropriate for a recipe, frying can be accomplished in a similar manner with a minimal amount of polyunsaturated oil, heated on the range or in a hot oven until the oil reaches a temperature of 375° F, which has been reached when a cube of bread dropped into the hot oil turns golden brown. This technique avoids the use of the large quantities of oil called for in standard deep-frying techniques.

Many slimming dishes freeze well, and the recipes for these are marked with an asterisk (*). Dishes may be prepared in advance, refrigerated or frozen at specific steps in the recipe, and reserved until you are ready to complete the cooking and garnishing.

Many special dishes are mentioned in the text of this book; the recipes for these appear later in the appropriate recipe sections. The titles of special dishes for which recipes are provided are printed in boldface type, and you can find the recipes by referring to the Index. For your convenience, however, dishes mentioned within this chapter, the recipes for which appear elsewhere, are immediately followed by the specific pages on which the recipes appear, so that you do not have to consult the Index.

To prepare new-cuisine dishes, there is no need to buy special or expensive equipment beyond what is generally found in the average kitchens of American homemakers. With a little bit of imagination, you will find that it is fun and rewarding to adapt existing cookware and kitchen utensils to the new slimming processes. As is fundamental in Chinese cuisine, the new technique utilizes the most suitable cooking process for any particular dish, and this is determined by the ingredients in each recipe. Nonetheless, the majority of the international recipes in this book can be prepared on top of the range, in an oven, in a microwave oven, in pressure cookers or electric skillets, or by using steamers, woks, clay pots, or crockery pots, and in some instances on outdoor grills.

COOKWARE, EQUIPMENT, AND UTENSILS

For those whose kitchens are less than reasonably equipped, or for homemakers in the process of setting up their kitchens, the following is a list of basic equipment you will find helpful in preparing your new-cuisine recipes. Again, I want to emphasize the advantages of beginning slowly and carefully in adding equipment to your kitchen, experimenting first with the many imaginative and creative ways you can adapt existing equipment to slimming processes you may elect to use only occasionally. Of course, you will want to have on hand the most suitable cookware and utensils for the basic processes that are used here consistently.

PRIMARY COOKWARE:
(Glass or nonlead appropriate cookware should be used in microwave ovens.)
A 5-quart, or larger, stockpot with lid
A large (5-quart), and a small (3-quart) heavy-based skillet with covers
A 5-quart enamel, heavy-based metal or glass casserole, with cover
A 5-quart and a smaller enamel heavy-based iron pot, with covers
A 2¾-quart enamel or glass saucepan and two 1½-quart saucepans, with covers
A Chinese or French three-tier steamer with cover
A Chinese wok
A 5-quart and 2-quart Dutch oven
A double-boiler

SECONDARY COOKWARE:
A 4-quart, or larger, pressure cooker
A 3-quart unglazed, nonlead clay casserole, with cover
A fish poacher adequate for a 3-pound fish, or larger
An electric skillet

A slow-cooking crockery pot with high and low adjustments

BASIC KITCHEN EQUIPMENT:
An electric blender and/or food mill. Food processors can be helpful in many recipes, but generally have the limitation that they have only a 1-pint capacity for liquids
Mixing bowls, preferably ceramic or glass for marinades
An 8-inch ceramic or porcelain quiche dish
Charlotte or soufflé dishes, both 2-quart and 4-ounce (for individual servings) sizes
Baking sheet, rolling pin, pastry bag and tubes, and pastry brush
Baking dishes and 9-inch pie plates, preferably glass
Sharp knives for efficient cubing and mincing of meats and vegetables
Mortar and pestle
Domed glass lids to cover standard pot sizes
Cylindrical-type cheese grater for soft cheese
All-purpose grater, preferably flat, for grating vegetables
A vegetable peeler, preferably with a swivel blade
A *chinois*-type sieve with wooden pestle
Cheesecloth and kitchen twine
Long-, medium-, and short-length skewers
Measuring cups, 1-, 2-, and 4-cup sizes
Measuring spoons
Ladles and spatulas, preferably wooden
A heatproof pad for electric ranges, such as the "Flame Tamer"

Metal trivet and adjustable vegetable
steamer

A scale registering ounces and pounds as
well as grams and kilograms

An efficient oven thermometer. It's better
to know! Most ovens do not regularly
generate even temperatures consistent
with the dial setting.

Waxed paper, aluminum foil and/or
parchment available through your
butcher.

STAPLES:

Corn, peanut, safflower, olive, or other
acceptable oils

Polyunsaturated margarine

Cookware spray or brush for thinly
layering pans with polyunsaturated oil
to avoid sticking of ingredients

Fresh or canned chicken or meat stock,
consommé, or bouillon

Canned Italian-style plum tomatoes to be
used when fresh vine-ripened
tomatoes are not available. Use 1 cup
of the canned for ¾ pound of fresh
tomatoes called for in the recipes.

Dry white wine or dry vermouth, sherry,
Madeira, cognac or brandy

Light and dark soy sauce, available in
Oriental markets, commercial brands
are generally light soy sauce.

Salt, preferably coarse kosher or sea salt

Pepper mill with black peppercorns,
and/or ground black and white
pepper, and green peppercorns

Herbs and spices, either fresh, freeze-
dried, or dried (stored in a cool place
away from direct sunlight)

Shallots or onions, garlic, raisins, pine
nuts *(pignoli),* and almonds

Since wheat flour is not used, stock up
on white rye flour, rice flour, cornstarch,
potato starch, and baking powder. These
ingredients are available at supermarkets,
ethnic shops, and health-food shops.

• • •

These can be considered the essentials
for a reasonably equipped new-cuisine
kitchen. Since we will be preparing specialties from varying ethnic cuisines, there
will of course be some special ingredients,
such as unfamiliar herbs and spices, that
are traditionally used in specific cuisines.
These can be obtained from neighborhood
ethnic markets, from gourmet shops in
large department stores, or from the
sources indicated at the end of the book.

Fine cooks and professional chefs
make a point of recommending that you
read each recipe carefully and line up all
of the necessary ingredients, cookware,
and utensils you will need before you sart
cooking. I have found that when everything is ready and available during the actual cooking processes, it helps avoid
chaos in the kitchen and reduces pressure.
Professionals also dress comfortably, with
special attention given to their shoes. Be
sure to do the same, and it will help you to
relax and enjoy the excitement of preparing these delicious and more healthful recipes.

A word about introducing new cuisine
menus to your family. Most of us have a
number of favorite ethnic dishes that already are a part of our personal repertoires of recipes. Whether originally
French, Italian, Scandinavian, Polish, or
whatever, these have become standbys for
family and friends and have been so well
integrated into our own concepts and

preferences that they have become our very own specialties.

The intent of this book is to expand your repertoire, encouraging you to be even more familiar with a wide range of ethnic dishes from the outstanding cuisines of the world—and to demonstrate how simply these recipes of the new international cuisine can be prepared right in your own kitchen.

As popular as many ethnic dishes already are with many of us, one often hears distraught homemakers saying things like: "My husband is just a meat and potatoes man," or, "My children don't like fancy foods," or, "I wish I had more time to experiment, but...." Of course, each of us has to take the members of our households, as well as our guests, into consideration in planning menus; still, there are many things we can do to help. The most successful ingredient, I have found, in combating resistance to trying new foods is to make a game of discovery and participation by stimulating the inherent sense of adventure in all of us.

I am reminded of the days in our own household when my three daughters were under ten years old. Although both my wife and I enjoyed a variety of foods, we found that our children's tastes were limited. As a result, we were preparing two meals many evenings, one for the children and one for the adults. Occasionally, we overcame the problem with a family meal —generally some form of chicken or veal which was acceptable to all, particularly the children.

Finally, in desperation, I approached the youngsters with the idea that the family make a "tour of the world" through cuisine. Living in the New York City area at the time, we decided to visit one of the many ethnic areas of the city each month. In preparation, we would go to the library and read about that particular ethnic group, its country of origin, culture, history, and so on. I had obtained a large map of the city and marked off a number of ethnic centers: Chinatown, the neighboring Jewish and Italian sections, and those parts of the city that were German, Czech, Indian, Greek, or Puerto Rican.

On our ethnic excursions during the subsequent months, we did much the same things that tourists do in visiting other countries. We tried restaurants, browsed through shops, took photographs, walked the streets asking directions and meeting people, and excitedly pointed out to each other various places of interest. In Chinatown, cooking utensils such as the wok and the multiple-tiered steamer became visual realities, and exotic foods such as winter melon and bamboo shoots became familiar. I must confess that my wife and I ordered simply and carefully, easing our children into their first adventurous experiences with each cuisine. But their palates developed rapidly, becoming refined and broadened; and the inevitable result was that we adopted many ethnic specialties into our family repertoire. I hope you will have as much fun with your own family.

To assist you in initiating yourself, your family, or your guests into the new cuisine, I have provided five menus in the following chapter, with alternate main-course recipes for three or more weekends from each of the great cuisines. In this connection, a point I made earlier is worth repeating: homemakers tend to think that the entire meal must be devoted to a single ethnic cuisine. But need a meal be entirely French, Chinese, Mexican, or whatever? I think not. Isn't it more creative and adventuresome at times to select different dishes from a number of ethnic groups in devising a menu? You might want to try it, particularly with the youngsters in mind. And since the new cuisine utilizes a number of specific processes, I have provided a section to help you become more familiar with them and have indicated which of these processes are involved in the preparation of specific recipes.

GETTING A HEAD START

The following menus have been carefully selected in terms of utilizing one or more of the fundamental techniques and cooking processes necessary to the new international cuisine, as well as to initiate you into the pleasure of preparing these dishes with ease and presenting them attractively. If you are a novice, I suggest that you consider devoting the first week or several weekends to familiarizing yourself with the techniques described here. You may wish to share your "head start" with a close friend or member of the family, or delve into this low-calorie and low-cholesterol cuisine by yourself and then surprise your family or guests with your new accomplishments.

Throughout this book I encourage you to make any variations you wish to suit your own particular needs and preferences. Many gourmet cooks will not want to serve all four courses at every meal; rather they will select a main dish and an accoutrement, then elect whether they wish to serve an appetizer or dessert. Increasingly, this has become the tendency in outstanding culinary capitals, such as Paris, where the French now prefer eating *très léger* (lightly); or Milan and Rome, where *cucina magra* (lean cookery), is in order, since this approach is more adaptable to contemporary modes of living. Most of the individual recipes can be adapted as well for lighter luncheons or suppers.

These five menus, therefore, are intended as a guide for your first several weekends of cooking in the new healthful style. In fact, all the recipes in this chapter, as well as throughout the book, surpass the *Dietary Goals for the United States,* the report of January 1977 by the Select Committee on Nutrition and Human Needs of the United States Senate. This report emphasizes the dangers of overconsumption of saturated fats, sucrose, and salt—all of which are minimized or eliminated in our recipes, as are wheat flour and artificial ingredients.

I also suggest that you take the time to write out a shopping list for each recipe you plan to use. This should include the staples you will want to keep on hand and a checklist of the cookware and kitchen utensils you will need. Making these simple preparations ahead will prevent confusion and unnecessary pressure while you follow the directions for completing each recipe.

The recipes for each dish included in the following menus will be found in subsequent pages, as indicated. In addition, I have provided suggestions for garnishing and, for your further consideration, Bonus Ideas drawn in every case from the foremost cuisines of the world, including our own.

COOKING PROCESSES FOR THE NEW INTERNATIONAL CUISINE

<u>Sauté:</u> Derived from the French verb *sauter* (to jump), the word "sauté" refers to the movement of food when cooked in a pan over medium heat. We no longer believe this process must be done with fats and oils, as considered standard in the past. Instead, in the new cuisine, sautéing is accomplished simply by adding small amounts of water, stock or broth, and/or white wine to the items to be cooked. Our preferred recipes are **Salmi of Duck** (page 45), **Creole Jambalaya** (page 33), and/or **Seppi's Linguine and Zucchini with Pesto** (page 57).

Au sec (Étuver à sec): This process of the new international cuisine involves cooking food dry *(au sec),* without added water, utilizing the natural moisture of the ingredients. Vegetables particularly are washed and drained, but not patted dry, before cooking over medium-to-low heat in tightly covered cookware, which is shuffled occasionally. Our preferred recipes are **Green Beans Biarritz** (page 42) and/or **Purple Onion and Beet Marmalade** (page 47).

<u>Browning meats (Searing):</u> In the new cuisine we stress the fact that it is the high heat, not fats or oils, that browns meats, or sears them. This process assures that the natural juices are sealed in rather than permitted to be released into the cooking liquid. Therefore we simply dip the meat into cold water or a marinade, drain but do not pat dry, and place in a nonstick treated pan on the range or in an oven set at high temperatures. An alternate method for browning meat is to place it in a dry pan, over high heat, which has been sprinkled with salt. Our preferred recipes for browning moistened meat are **Country Captain** (page 54), **Stir-Fried Beef in Curry Sauce** (page 46) and **Ham Steaks with Madeira Sauce** (page 41). Recipes for browning with salt are **Steak Diane** (page 55) and **Peppered Steak** (page 57).

<u>Steaming:</u> This efficient and economical cooking process, borrowed from Oriental cookery, involves cooking items resting on a trivet or rack that is slightly above the level of boiling liquid, in tightly covered cookware; hence the food is cooked by steam, or *à la vapeur.* The use of a pressure cooker permits even greater time and energy savings. In China, a variation of this process is smoking, whereby the vapors of aromatic ingredients, like tea, are used to flavor the foods. Our preferred recipe for steaming is **Asparagus Salad with Lemon Sauce** *El Toulà* (page 52). A recipe for pressure-cooking is **Beet Cups with Caviar** (page 32), and a recipe for smoking is **Cantonese Smoked Fish** (page 50).

<u>En papillote:</u> Paper-wrapped cookery,

a variation of the steaming process, is used in many of the great cuisines of the world. Quickly cooked or partially cooked ingredients are wrapped and sealed in parchment or other suitable types of paper, then cooked until the steam inside puffs up the envelope and the ingredients are done with all of their aroma sealed inside. The individual *papillotes* are generally served closed, to be opened by each diner at the table. Our preferred recipes are **Pompano Cooked in Parchment** (page 39), **Japanese Chicken Baked in Foil** (page 51), and/or **Paper-Wrapped Steak** (page 51).

Stir-frying: Although a heavy-based skillet will do, this process is accomplished most easily by using a wok, probably the most efficient cookware invented. The wok holds heat well, and its spherical shape facilitates the constant stirring required of ingredients at varying temperatures: the closer to the base and heat source, the higher the temperature. Small amounts of polyunsaturated oil, consommé, or basic sauces are heated to high temperatures before stirring in and constantly tossing the ingredients, which cook rapidly. Additional ingredients, such as other sauces and condiments, are added before the completion of cooking. Our preferred recipes are **Stir-Fried Beef in Curry Sauce** (page 46), **Lamb with Broccoli** (page 46), and **Minced Squab Wrapped in Lettuce Leaves** (page 38).

Frying: In the new cuisine, a variation of the above Oriental cooking process can be used instead of deep-frying with excessive amounts of fats and oils. Instead, a thin coat of polyunsaturated oil is heated in a pan over the range or in an oven at very high temperature (until the oil reaches 375° F) before the ingredients are added for frying. Our preferred recipes are **Shanghai Mock Smoked Fish** (page 50), **Betsy's Fried Okra** (page 35), and **Italian Soup with Rice Dumplings** (page 53).

Puréeing: Cooked ingredients are converted into a smooth consistency by mashing, sieving, or using food mills or mechanical blenders. Vegetable purées are used to thicken sauces instead of wheat flour, cream, butter, and egg yolks. Our preferred recipes are **Ligurian Pesto Sauce** (page 58), **Brandade of Stockfish** (page 44), and/or **Cantaloupe Pie with Meringue** (page 53).

Cooking in a mold: A mold is a container that shapes chopped or puréed foods into a desired form. During cooking, the filled mold is placed in a pan of water reaching a little more than halfway up the depth of the mold. This is a variation of the steaming process. Natural molds, like the hollowed-out shell of an eggplant, may be used. Our preferred recipe for cooking in a mold is **Island of Snow in a Mold** (page 48); and the recipes for natural molds are **Cantaloupe Baked Alaska** (page 42) and **Beet Cups with Caviar** (page 32).

Reduction: This process is used to reduce cooking liquids by boiling them down over high heat. Through evaporation, stocks and sauces become more concentrated and thickened. Our preferred recipes are **Sauce Duxelles** (page 40), **Creole Jambalaya** (page 33), and/or **Ham Steaks with Madeira Sauce** (page 41).

Deglazing (Déglacer): A process often preceding reduction in which the particles or glazes that stick to a pan are diluted with broth or wine in the preparation of sauces. Brandy, Madeira, and other heavy wines are generally used, the alcoholic content of which evaporates during the cooking process. Our preferred recipe is **Steak Diane** (page 55).

Garnishing and Presentation: Garnishing is an integral part of every dish prepared in the new cuisine, which prizes the need to satisfy the eye as well as the palate. Decorative edibles are added to complement the basic flavors, textures, and colors of the food served. Portions of any dish should be pleasingly arranged on large plates, without overcrowding, and garnished appropriately.

You are now ready for your "tour" of the great ethnic cuisines of the world. Begin by preparing any of the following menus of your choice, modifying them as you desire. However, do be sure to include at least one of the preferred recipes in each category: these have been carefully selected to assist you in understanding the basic techniques and cooking processes involved in the new cuisine. The recipes for the dishes included in the menus will be found on the pages previously indicated. In addition, I have provided suggestions for garnishing, Bonus Ideas, and alternate recipes for your further consideration.

Have a happy head start!

HEAD START MENUS OF THE NEW INTERNATIONAL CUISINE

MENU #1

Appetizer: Beet Cups with Caviar *(American, Alaska)*
Main Dish: Veal Scallops in Tomato Sauce *(Italian)*
Alternate Main Dish: Creole Jambalaya *(American, New Orleans)*
Accoutrement: Betsy's Fried Okra *(American, Quaker)*
Dessert: Honey Pie, Sifnos Style *(Greek)*

MENU #2

Appetizer: Mince Squab Wrapped in Lettuce Leaves *(Chinese)*
Main Dish: Pompano Cooked in Parchment *(American, New Orleans)*
Alternate Main Dish: Ham Steaks with Madeira Sauce *(Italian)*
Accoutrement: Green Beans Biarritz *(French)*
Dessert: Cantaloupe Baked Alaska *(American, International)*

MENU #3

Appetizer: *Brandade* of Stockfish *(French)*

Main Dish: Salmi of Duck *(American, New Orleans)*
Alternate Main Dish: Stir-Fried Beef in Curry Sauce *(Chinese)*
Accoutrement: Purple Onion and Beet Marmalade *(American, Baton Rouge)*
Dessert: Island of Snow in a Mold *(Italian)*

MENU #4

Appetizer: Rustic Cheese Tart *(French)*
Main Course: Cantonese Smoked Fish *(Chinese)*
Alternate Main Dish: Japanese Chicken Baked in Foil *(Japanese)*
Accoutrement: Asparagus Salad with Lemon Sauce El Toulà *(Italian)*
Dessert: Cantaloupe Pie *(American, North Carolina)*

MENU #5

Appetizer: Italian Soup with Rice Dumplings *(Italian)*
Main Course: Country Captain *(Indian/Pakistani)*
Alternate Main Course: Steak Diane *(French)*
Accoutrement: Seppi's Linguine and Zucchini with *Pesto (American, International)*
Dessert: Neapolitan Ricotta Cheesecake *(Italian)*

BEET CUPS
WITH CAVIAR

Alaskan
The beet root is both colorful and versatile, and a staple of many of the cuisines of the world. Although many of us are not likely to consider the beet for gourmet dishes, this simple use of a beet cup as a natural mold for caviar—probably introduced to Alaska by the early Russian settlers—results in a memorable appetizer or hors d'oeuvre. For other exciting dishes using beets, see the recipes and Bonus Ideas for **Stuffed Beet Cups** (page 317).

It is important to note that beet roots should be cooked in their skins, which are then easily removed, in order to maintain their rich color during cooking.

12 small cooked or canned beets
1 teaspoon coarse salt
1 tablespoon white wine vinegar
2-ounce jar (56 grams) black caviar or
    lumpfish
1 tablespoon lemon juice
6 sprigs of parsley
1 head of curly endive
YIELD: Six servings

1. If using fresh beets, wash them in their skins in cold water, then cook in salted boiling water, with the vinegar, for 45 minutes, or until tender. If cooked in a pressure cooker, the beets will be tender in about 12 minutes. Cool slightly, and remove the skins using your thumb and forefinger. If using canned beets, drain well.

2. Cut a thin slice from the root end of each beet so that it will stand, then scoop out part of the center of each beet. Fill each cup with equal portions of the caviar, flavor with some lemon juice, and garnish with a sprig of parsley. Serve 2 to each diner on a bed of curly endive as an appetizer, or on a platter as hors d'oeuvres.

Bonus Ideas: Other appetizers or hors d'oeuvres using beets include **Beet Cups with Herring and Cucumber,** which is prepared by filling the cavities of small beets with herring or anchovy and garnishing with diced cucumbers that have been marinated with **French Dressing** or **Pennsylvania Boiled Dressing** (page 317).

I find that oranges, apples, celery, endives, and cabbage all have a special affinity to beets. **Beet Cups with Oranges** are made simply by filling 6 medium-size cooked or canned beets with 2 diced oranges mixed with 3 tablespoons of minced onion or scallion. This dish is served over a bed of lettuce with a spoonful of **Slimming Mayonnaise** (page 152).

SCALOPPINE
AL POMIDORO
(Veal Scallops in Tomato Sauce)

Italian
Italians are very partial to tender, young veal that is pinkish white in color. To ensure getting the best quality and the proper cutting of veal—especially for *scaloppine*—in the United States, one would be wise to find a butcher in an Italian section if at all possible. For information on the cutting of veal and instructions on preparing scallops, see **Scaloppine al Marsala** (page 93).

1½ pounds veal scaloppine, pounded thin
⅓ cup white wine, dry vermouth, or
    bouillon
1 teaspoon cornstarch or potato starch
1 onion, chopped
1½ pounds fresh tomatoes, or 2 cups
    Italian-style canned plum tomatoes
1 teaspoon coarse salt
6 twists of a pepper mill
1 tablespoon fresh sage leaves, or 1
    teaspoon dried
2 sprigs fresh oregano, or 1 teaspoon dried
2 tablespoons unsalted capers
Cookware spray
YIELD: Six servings

1. If your butcher hasn't already done so, cover the scallops with waxed paper and pound them with a mallet or the side of a cleaver until very thin, about ¹⁄₁₆ inch. Discard the waxed paper; dip the scallops into cold water; drain, but do not pat dry.

2. Apply cookware spray to a large skillet and sear the scallops on both sides quickly over very high heat. Sprinkle ¼ cup of the white wine and the cornstarch over the scallops and continue cooking over medium heat until most of the wine evaporates—about 3 minutes. Remove the scallops and set them aside between 2 warm plates.

3. Sauté the onions in the balance of the white wine until the onions are translucent. Core the tomatoes and cut into quarters or eighths, depending on size. Add the tomatoes, salt, pepper, and sage leaves to the onions; bring the mixture to a boil; then simmer over medium heat for 5 minutes. Return the scallops with their juices to the skillet and sprinkle with the oregano. Stir the scallops until they are completely covered with the sauce. Tightly cover the skillet, and let stand for 5 minutes away from the heat before serving garnished with the capers.

Bonus Ideas: Veal Rolls in Tomato Sauce (*Rolatini al Pomidoro*) can be prepared to serve six by following the directions for tomato sauce in the basic recipe above. While the sauce is simmering, trim the pounded scallops into approximately 4- by 5-inch rectangles, reserving the trimmings. Cover each scallop with a thin slice of Canadian bacon or prosciutto, the trimmings from the scallops, and a dot of margarine; sprinkle with 1 tablespoon of Parmesan cheese. Tightly roll the scallops and skewer the ends with toothpicks, forming *rolatini*. Dip the *rolatini* into water, then sear them quickly over high heat. Reduce the heat, sprinkle the veal rolls with ¼ cup of white wine or dry vermouth, and cook several minutes until the wine evaporates. Add the tomato sauce, cover, and simmer for about 3 minutes, turning the *rolatini* occasionally. Remove from the heat and let stand, covered, for 5 minutes before serving.

CREOLE JAMBALAYA*

New Orleans

This classic Creole dish reflects both the intermingling of ethnic influences and the abundant variety of natural produce, especially seafood, in New Orleans. It is believed to originally have been a Spanish *paella*, utilizing principally rice and ham as ingredients; eventually it was adapted by Creole cooks, who added shrimp and seafood from the surrounding bayous. A wide variety of meat and seafood ingredients can be added to jambalaya, but the secret of this immensely satisfying stew is the harmonious blend of all of its ingredients, which has made the dish a masterpiece of American regional cuisine.

2 onions, chopped
1 clove garlic, mashed
2 tablespoons white wine or bouillon
1 tablespoon polyunsaturated margarine
1 tablespoon cornstarch, potato starch, or
    arrowroot
2¼ pounds fresh tomatoes, or 3 cups
    Italian-style canned plum tomatoes
2 cups chicken broth or water
1 teaspoon each, coarse salt and
    Worcestershire sauce
½ teaspoon each, cayenne pepper and
    dried thyme
1½ cups raw rice
¼ pound Canadian bacon or ham, cut into
    strips
1½ pounds shrimp, peeled and deveined
1 dozen oysters, drained (optional)
2 tablespoons each, parsley and celery
    tops, chopped
Cookware spray
YIELD: Six to eight servings

1. Apply cookware spray to a large heavy-based pan; over moderate heat, sauté the onions and the garlic, which has been skewered with a toothpick, in the white wine until the onions are translucent. Combine the margarine and cornstarch into a roux.

2. Move the vegetables aside in the pan, add the roux, and cook until it begins to change color. Remove the stem ends of the tomatoes; cut into quarters or eighths, depending on the size of the tomatoes; and add them to the pan with the broth,

salt, Worcestershire sauce, cayenne, and thyme.

3. Bring the mixture to a boil; after 5 minutes of cooking, reduce the heat, stir in the rice and Canadian bacon, and simmer covered over the lowest possible heat for about 25 minutes (adding additional water as necessary) until the rice is almost cooked to taste and the liquid is virtually absorbed. Remove the garlic and stir the shrimp and oysters into the stew; cover and simmer for about 3 minutes until the shrimp are light pink in color. Remove from the heat and let stand for 5 minutes before sprinkling with the parsley and celery and serving hot.

Bonus Ideas: Other versions of jambalaya use chicken, breakfast sausage, or crabmeat—alone or in combination. One of my favorites is **Crabmeat Jambalaya***, using 1½ cups each of diced cooked ham or Canadian bacon, cooked chicken, and cooked and flaked crabmeat. This is prepared by following the above recipe, except that the ham, chicken, and crabmeat are added to the tomato mixture with the rice. Cover and simmer over low heat for about 30 minutes, until the rice is cooked to taste, and the liquid virtually absorbed. Serve with chopped parsley, chopped celery tops, and ¼ bay leaf that has been crumbled.

Creole Shrimp* is prepared in a similar manner, with 2 stalks of celery added to the vegetables being sautéd in the first step. Cook the rice separately and set aside while the tomato mixture is simmering for 30 minutes. Blend in 3 pounds of peeled and deveined raw shrimp and continue simmering for 3 minutes. Stir in 1 teaspoon of filé powder and serve immediately over the boiled rice. Filé (dried sassafras leaves and such spices as sage, allspice, and coriander, powdered in a mortar with a pestle) can be purchased in gourmet shops and is also used in preparing **New Orleans Chicken Gumbo*** (page 325). However, 1½ pounds of fresh okra pods, sliced into ¼-inch wheels (or 2 10-ounce packages of frozen sliced okra), can be used instead. In no case should the okra and filé powder be used together as thickening agents in any recipe. The okra is cooked with the other ingredients, while the filé is always added during the very last minute of cooking and must never be permitted to boil.

BETSY'S FRIED OKRA

Quaker
This popular Southern dish is both simple to prepare and delicious. It is an excellent accompaniment to many meals, but you will find it an addictive snack as well. Betsy Klein, who introduced me to this recipe, says she eats it "like it was ice cream!"

1½ pounds fresh okra pods, or 2 10-ounce packages frozen sliced okra
1 cup fine white or yellow cornmeal
1 teaspoon coarse salt
4 twists of a pepper mill
¼ cup polyunsaturated oil or margarine
YIELD: Six servings

1. Wash and trim the okra and cut into ¼-inch wheels. If using frozen okra, drain well. Combine the cornmeal and seasonings in a paper bag, add the sliced okra, and shake until thoroughly coated.

2. Line a baking pan with the oil; heat in an oven set at 400° F, until the oil has reached 375° F. (When a cube of bread dropped into the hot oil turns golden brown, the oil is ready.) Add the coated okra, and "fry" until crisp and golden on each side. If you prefer, the okra can be sautéed in margarine in a large skillet over high heat for 2 minutes on each side, or until golden brown. Drain on paper toweling, and serve warm.

Bonus Ideas: Some Southern cooks prefer to dip the okra wheels in 4 tablespoons of cornstarch first, then in 2 egg whites lightly beaten with 1 tablespoon of water, before coating them with the seasoned cornmeal. Once prepared, they are sautéed (in margarine) as above. If necessary, the cooked okra can be kept warm in an oven set at 200° F, before serving it warm.

MELOPITTA*
(Honey Pie, Sifnos Style)

Greek
Pastry made with honey is a classic delicacy of various ethnic cuisines, including the Italian, Ukrainian, Persian, Jewish, and particularly the Greek. In Greece, honey puffs were awarded to winners of sports festivals for centuries.

Melopitta is a favorite dessert on the island of Sifnos at Easter time. Traditionally, it is made with *mizithra* (Greek unsalted cottage cheese), which you can purchase at local Greek groceries; low-fat cottage cheese would be a most satisfactory alternate.

2 pounds *mizithra* **or low-fat cottage
cheese**
½ cup fruit sugar or pure cane syrup
2 cups honey
10 egg whites
3 tablespoons olive or corn oil
**1 9-inch Wheatless Pie Crust (page 37) or
purchased pie shell**
½ cup dry beans
1½ tablespoons powdered cinnamon
YIELD: Eight servings

1. In a large bowl, combine the
mizithra, fruit sugar, and honey; mix thoroughly. Lightly beat the egg whites with
the olive oil, add to the mixture, and blend
well.

2. Prepare the Wheatless Pie Crust, or
use a completely thawed frozen pie shell,
and line a quiche dish or cake pan with
the pie shell. With a fork, make a series of
holes in the shell; layer with waxed paper
and ½ cup of beans to prevent puffing,
and prebake in an oven set at 450° F for
10 minutes. Remove the waxed paper and
beans and set aside to cool.

3. Spread the *mizithra* and honey mixture into the cooled pie crust, and bake in
an oven set at 350° F for 30 minutes, or
until golden brown. Sprinkle with the cinnamon, cool, then cut into squares or triangles before serving.

Bonus Ideas: *Phyllo,* the Greek pastry
available fresh in Greek grocery stores or
frozen in many supermarkets, can be used
instead of a pie shell. It is preferable to
use the fresh *phyllo,* which is easier to
work with; but the frozen, when thoroughly thawed, can be used as well. You
will need 5 sheets of *phyllo* pastry; each
sheet should be brushed with melted margarine before placing the next pastry sheet
over it when lining the quiche dish. One of
the "tricks of the trade" I learned from
Chef Joseph Seppi Renggli of The Four
Seasons restaurant in New York is to
sprinkle each margarine-brushed sheet of
phyllo with one or more tablespoons of
bread crumbs or wheat germ, which keeps
the pastry from becoming soggy. After lining the dish with all 5 sheets, spread the
filling into the pastry, and proceed with
the rest of the above recipe.

At Christmas, Italians serve **Strufoli***
(honey balls), which are similar to a delicacy of Jewish cookery called *Teiglach*
(honey balls and nuts), served during the
Rosh Hashanah holidays. To prepare
Strufoli for 8 servings, sift together 6 times
(to properly aerate) 2 cups each of rice
flour and white rye flour with 8 teaspoons
of baking powder. Make a well in the
center, and add 8 egg whites lightly beaten
with 5 tablespoons of olive or corn oil, ¼
teaspoon salt, 4 tablespoons polyunsaturated margarine, and the grated rind
of ½ lemon and ⅓ orange. Blend into a
smooth dough and knead vigorously. Let
the dough rise, covered with a moist cloth,
for about 1 hour. Line a baking dish with
a thin layer of olive or corn oil and place
in an oven set at 400° F. Roll out the
dough to a ¼-inch thickness; then cut into
½-inch strips. Using the palms of your
hands, roll each strip; then cut into ¼-
inch pieces, each of which is rolled into a
ball. When the oil is very hot (375° F),
add a few pastry balls at a time and fry
until golden brown on all sides. While the
pastry balls are draining on paper toweling, combine ⅔ cup honey, 3 tablespoons
fruit sugar, and 2 tablespoons water in a
large saucepan. Bring to a boil, then simmer over low heat until the mixture is

clear. Add the *Strufoli* balls to the mixture, stir briefly, then pour onto a circular platter. With wet hands, shape the *Strufoli* into a ring or mound and sprinkle with colored candy sprinkles. I find it difficult to keep members of my family from tasting the *Strufoli* while it is standing for several hours, which is recommended before serving.

If you prefer, you can add ⅓ cup of **Candied Fruits** (page 91) to the honey mixture; an additional ⅓ cup may also be added to the final garnishing with the colored candy sprinkles.

If ½ cup of blanched and finely ground almonds are added to the dough in the above recipe, you can prepare Ukrainian **Verhuny** (honey puff balls). While the golden-brown honey balls are draining, heat 1 cup of honey and 3 tablespoons of fruit sugar until the mixture is clear. Mix the pastry balls and honey mixture in a large bowl, then transfer to a 10-inch pan spread with margarine to cool. Place the pan in hot water for about 5 minutes, before inverting and cutting the *Verhuny* into squares or slices.

WHEATLESS PIE CRUST*

American

A versatile and light pie crust, especially suitable for quiches and desserts with fruit and sweet fillings, as well as for a number of other recipes you will find in this book. It is important that the combination of flours be well sifted for proper aeration, and that the margarine and cottage cheese be chilled.

⅓ **cup each, rice flour and white rye flour**
2 teaspoons baking powder
½ **teaspoon coarse salt**
½ **cup dry nonfat cottage cheese or part-skim ricotta, drained and chilled**
½ **cup polyunsaturated margarine, chilled**
½ **cup dry beans**
Cookware spray
YIELD: One 9-inch crust

1. Sift the combined flours, baking powder, and salt 6 times into a bowl; add the chilled cottage cheese and margarine. Work the mixture until a smooth ball is formed, adding several drops of cold water as necessary. Wrap the ball of dough in waxed paper or aluminum foil and refrigerate at least 2 hours or preferably overnight.

2. When removed from the refrigerator, let the dough rest for 30 minutes. Cover a work area with a pastry cloth or waxed paper, then press the dough into a flattened circle. Roll the dough from its center to the outer edges into a ⅛-inch thick circle that is about 2 inches larger than the pie pan you intend to use.

3. Apply cookware spray to a pie pan; then invert the pie shell into the pan. Peel off the top layer of pastry cloth or waxed paper. Trim the overhanging edges, leaving about 1 inch of the dough beyond the rim of the pan. Anchor the edging to the underside of the rim of the pan to prevent shrinkage; then flute the border of the crust with a fork or make decorative edges.

4. Prick the pie shell with a fork and layer with ½ cup of dry beans to prevent puffing during prebaking. Place in an oven set at 450° F for 10 minutes. Set aside to cool before filling.

Bonus Ideas: The combined flours may also be aerated in a food processor or electric blender for 2 minutes at moderate speed. As an alternative to flouring your rolling pin to prevent sticking when rolling the dough, try placing a second layer of waxed paper over the flattened circle of dough. Always roll from the center of the dough to its outward edges, and lift, do not roll, the rolling pin back to the center each time. Leftover trimmed strips can be used for joining any tears in the pie shell as necessary by simply moistening the ends of the strips and pressing together. Leftover trimmings can also be rerolled, cut into ½-inch strips with a knife or pastry cutter, and crisscrossed, or latticed, over the top of the filling. Of course, if 2 pastry crusts are required for a covered pie, simply double the above recipe.

BOK OPP SOONG
(Minced Squab Wrapped in Lettuce Leaves)

Chinese

This delightful Chinese appetizer is a personal favorite. I think you'll also find its contrast of the spiced, minced meat and refreshing lettuce leaves a distinctive combination.

As we will see in greater detail during the Chinese section of our tour, the government of the People's Republic of China has sought to reduce the tremendously wide repertoire of Chinese dishes by publishing a more limited list of recipes approved for use by the Mainland Chinese. The most recent list of approved recipes does not include any *soong* (minced)

dishes. This one, also known as Phoenix Nest, is considered a dish that assures good fortune when eaten in celebration of the New Year.

1 chicken liver
1 teaspoon polyunsaturated margarine
1¾-pound squab or Cornish hen, cleaned, boned, and minced
1 teaspoon coarse salt
2 tablespoons cornstarch
2 tablespoons soy sauce
3 tablespoons of peanut or corn oil
½ cup diced bamboo shoots
1 slice ginger, diced
2 scallions, white part only, diced
1 shallot, diced, or 1 tablespoon chopped onion
2 teaspoons oyster sauce
4 teaspoons water
2 tablespoons finely chopped Chinese parsley
1 tablespoon *hoisin* sauce
1 head lettuce, washed, leaves separated and chilled
YIELD: Six servings

1. Sauté the chicken liver in the margarine over high heat until it loses its pink color and is firm. Mince and add to the minced squab meat. Toss the meat mixture with the salt and half the cornstarch and soy sauce.
2. Heat the oil in a wok or skillet, and stir-fry the meat mixture for 1 minute before adding the bamboo shoots, ginger, scallions, and shallot. Add the oyster sauce and the balance of the soy sauce, and sauté for 3 minutes longer.
3. Mix the balance of the cornstarch with the water and add to the wok, stirring well. Transfer the *soong* mixture to a platter and sprinkle with parsley. Spread

small amounts of the *hoisin* sauce (a bean paste sauce; see Hard to Get Ingredients) on the lettuce leaves, add about 1½ tablespoons of the *soong* mixture to each leaf, wrap envelope style, and serve. You should have about 18 Phoenix Nests, 3 for each portion.

Bonus Ideas: I prefer the *soong* completely wrapped in the lettuce leaves, but often provide the cooked ingredients and leaves at the table for each diner to wrap as he or she wishes. Phoenix Nests is also served with the *soong* in a lettuce leaf cup. In any case, spread the *hoisin* sauce on the lettuce leaves judiciously. Because of its concentrated flavor, I recommend that you use less, rather than more, the first time you prepare this dish.

Personally, I am not partial to iceberg lettuce, preferring instead Boston and other lettuce varieties. However, after trying *soong* dishes with a number of varieties of salad greens, I must concede that iceberg lettuce provides an excellent texture to balance the *soong* mixture.

Whenever squab is not easily available, I have successfully used Cornish hens; and according to Bruce Ho of the Seven Seas restaurant in New York, minced beef, pork, chicken, turkey, or rabbit can be used as the main ingredient.

POMPANO EN PAPILLOTE*
(Pompano Cooked in Parchment)

New Orleans

Cooking *en papillote,* or in a parchment or aluminum foil envelope, is a simple and elegant way to prepare delicate fish dishes. Pompano is probably the most popular favorite in this category—a specialty of New Orleans.

6 lengths of parchment or aluminum foil, 16 by 12 inches
6 1-pound whole pompano, red snapper, halibut, or haddock, or 6 fish filets
1 teaspoon coarse salt
6 twists of a pepper mill
24 button mushrooms
6 tablespoons polyunsaturated margarine
3 tablespoons *Sauce Duxelles* (page 40)
3 tablespoons olive, corn, or peanut oil (optional)
Cookware spray
YIELD: Six servings

1. Fold each length of parchment or aluminum foil in half and cut into the shape of a heart about 8 inches long. Apply cookware spray to the inside of the aluminum foil. If using parchment, use the optional oil to brush the inside of the *papillote.*

2. Place one portion of the cleaned and washed fish or filets on one side of each heart, and sprinkle with ¼ teaspoon of the salt and 1 twist of the pepper mill. If using filets, fold them in half. Sauté the mushrooms for 2 minutes in the margarine; then transfer 4 to each *papillote* and top each portion with ½ tablespoon of the *Sauce Duxelles.*

3. Fold and crimp the edges of each *papillote* heart to seal in the ingredients. If using parchment, you may wish to use a paste of flour and water placed on the crimped edges to ensure proper sealing. Allow several minutes for the paste to dry. Apply cookware spray to a baking dish large enough to contain the filled *papil-*

lotes, and bake in an oven set at 425° F for 15 minutes. Serve each envelope on individual hot plates to be opened at the table by each diner.

Bonus Ideas: Interesting variations I have tried have included the addition to each envelope of 2 tablespoons diced Canadian bacon, 2 chopped shrimp, or 2 tablespoons of sautéed crabmeat and 2 or more clams, oysters, or mussels. I think you will find this both an elegant and imaginative method of preparing fish and seafood. Also I generally provide 2 lemon wedges when serving each *papillote.*

In addition to baking in the oven, you can bake the *papillotes* in a microwave oven for about 10 minutes or, as the Italians do, you can fry the well-sealed envelopes on each side for about 10 minutes in hot oil. Whichever method you elect, you will know that the contents are cooked when the *papillotes* are puffed up.

SAUCE DUXELLES*
(Minced Mushroom Sauce)

French
Duxelles is believed to have originated in the town of Uxel on the French Riviera. Many fine cooks keep a reserve of *duxelles* on hand in the freezer for use whenever a mushroom flavor is desired in dishes or sauces.

¾ cup white wine or dry vermouth
¾ cup fish stock, clam juice, or consommé
2 tablespoons chopped shallots, onions, or scallions

3 tablespoons melted polyunsaturated margarine
3 tablespoons cornstarch or potato starch
½ cup of concentrated fish or meat stock
½ cup tomato purée
3 tablespoons *duxelles*

Duxelles:
½ pound mushrooms, minced
1 medium onion, minced
2 tablespoons white wine, dry vermouth, or consommé
5 tablespoons polyunsaturated margarine
1 teaspoon minced parsley
⅛ teaspoon grated nutmeg
½ teaspoon coarse salt
3 twists of a pepper mill
Cookware spray
YIELD: About one cup

1. First prepare the *duxelles.* Press the minced mushrooms, including stems, in a cloth to extract as much moisture as possible. Apply cookware spray to a skillet, and sauté the onions until translucent in the white wine. Add the margarine and mushrooms and cook over medium heat until the mushrooms are virtually a paste. Add the balance of the ingredients and continue cooking until there is no longer any moisture in the pan. Set aside 3 tablespoons, and reserve the balance of the *duxelles* in tightly capped jars in the refrigerator, or freeze for future use in convenient 1-tablespoon quantities.

2. Prepare the sauce, combining the wine, fish stock, and shallots in a saucepan. Bring to a boil, then reduce to half over high heat. Combine the melted margarine and cornstarch in a skillet and cook over moderate heat until lightly brown in color. Gradually stir in the additional ½ cup of concentrated fish stock, the tomato purée, and the reduced wine and stock mixture. Blend well, then add the reserved *duxelles;* blend again and correct for seasoning. Serve hot.

Bonus Ideas: Consider keeping reserves of this sauce in the refrigerator or freezer, since it lends itself admirably to a wide variety of fish dishes. If using clam juice, which tends to be salty, it is rarely necessary to add any salt when correcting for seasoning.

When storing *Sauce Duxelles,* I cover the sauce with paper spread with margarine before capping the container.

PROSCIUTTO COTTO CON MADEIRA
(Ham Steaks with Madeira Sauce)

Italian

The famous Parma ham is internationally known as Italian *prosciutto,* but Italians use other ham, including *prosciutto cotto* (boiled ham), in their cooking as well.

2 precooked or cured ham steaks, each 1 inch thick
½ cup each, chopped onions and carrots
¼ pound chopped mushrooms
1 bay leaf
¼ cup Madeira or Marsala wine
Cookware spray
YIELD: Six servings

1. Dip the ham steaks into cold water; drain, but do not pat dry. Apply cookware spray to a skillet and brown both sides of the steaks over high heat.

2. Place the balance of the ingredients, except the wine, into a baking dish. Arrange the steaks on top of the vegetables and pour in the wine. Bake in an oven set at 400° F for 30 minutes; baste the steaks occasionally.

3. Remove the steaks, cut each into 3 or more pieces, and set aside on a warm platter. Skim the Madeira sauce, and reduce to ⅓ over high heat before ladling the sauce over the ham. Serve hot.

Bonus Ideas: I usually serve this dish as part of **Crochette di Polenta con Prosciutto Cotto** (Polenta Croquettes with Ham). The polenta croquettes can be cooked in the oven until golden brown during the last 10 minutes that the ham steaks are baking.

Another favorite accoutrement is **Corn Sticks*** (also known in the Caribbean as *Surrullitos de Maiz*). To prepare 1½ dozen corn sticks, sift together 6 times ¼ cup each of rice flour and white rye flour, 3 teaspoons baking powder, and ½ teaspoon salt, then stir in 1½ cups of cornmeal. Lightly beat 2 egg whites and 1 tablespoon of corn oil in a separate bowl; then blend in ¼ cup of melted margarine, ¾ cup of milk, and 1 teaspoon honey. Combine the flour and egg mixtures; blend into a batter, then spoon into cornstick pans or muffin tins that have been lightly greased with margarine. Bake in an oven set at 375° F for 20 minutes, or until a toothpick inserted in the center comes out dry.

For **Corn Bread***, prepare the same batter with only 2 tablespoons of melted margarine, pour into a greased 8-inch square pan, and bake in an oven set at 425° F for 20 minutes.

HARICOTS VERTS À LA BIARRITZ
(Green Beans Biarritz)

French
A delightful dish to accompany many main courses, but also one that I find a particularly refreshing end to a satisfying meal.

1½ pounds green beans
½ teaspoon coarse salt
1 large Bermuda onion, thinly sliced
½ cup *Sauce Vinaigrette*

Sauce Vinaigrette: (French Dressing)
2 tablespoons olive or corn oil, or in
    combination
1 tablespoon wine or rice wine vinegar
½ teaspoon coarse salt
6 twists of a pepper mill or 4 mashed
    green peppercorns
½ teaspoon dry mustard
YIELD: Four to six servings

1. Trim off the tips and strings of the beans, wash and drain, but do not pat dry. Cook *au sec* over low heat in a tightly covered pan with the salt for about 10 minutes until *al dente,* shuffling the pan occasionally. Drain in a colander, adding cold water to stop the cooking process. Pat dry with paper toweling and set aside on a platter with a thin layer of the sliced onions over the beans.
2. Prepare the *Sauce Vinaigrette* by combining all the ingredients in a bowl or electric blender. Whisk or blend until smooth; or simply place the ingredients in a covered jar and shake well. Toss green beans and onions in sauce and serve.

Bonus Ideas: If using this dressing with fruits, use either grapefruit or lemon juice instead of vinegar.

A satisfying variation using green beans and onions is **Haricots Verts à la Bretonne** (Green Beans, Breton Style). Sauté 1 small chopped onion in 2 tablespoons of margarine for 3 minutes. Add 3 tablespoons tomato sauce, 4 twists of a pepper mill and 1½ pounds of green beans cooked *au sec.* Cover the pan and simmer over medium heat for 5 minutes. Transfer to a serving dish and sprinkle with 2 tablespoons of chopped parsley.

CANTALOUPE BAKED ALASKA*

American/International
This spectacular and easy-to-make dessert is one of my favorite variations of the internationally popular **Baked Alaska.** In this version, the cantaloupe shell and the meringue covering insulate the cold ingredients inside from the high heat during baking.

4 cantaloupes
1 quart commercial or homemade Frozen
    Yogurt (page 43)
Meringue:
5 egg whites, at room temperature
¼ teaspoon cream of tartar
1 teaspoon vanilla extract or ½ teaspoon
    grated lemon rind (optional)
¾ cup pulverized fruit or date sugar
YIELD: Eight servings

1. Cut the cantaloupes in half, scoop out the fruit, and dice to 1-inch cubes. Chill the melon cubes in the freezer, in which the frozen yogurt should also be reserved until ready for use. Set the cantaloupe shells aside.

2. Prepare the Meringue by beating the egg whites, cream of tartar, and optional vanilla extract or lemon rind until foamy. Gradually stir in the sugar and continue beating until the egg white mixture is glossy and forms stiff peaks.

3. Remove the melon cubes and frozen yogurt from the freezer and quickly fill each cantaloupe shell, first with the diced melon, then with scoops or slices of the frozen yogurt. Spread the Meringue over each shell, completely covering the filling and the rim of the shell to provide an effective seal. Decorate by swirling the Meringue into a pattern of peaks, and bake in the center of an oven set at 475° F for 5 minutes, or until slightly browned. Serve at once on chilled dishes.

Bonus Ideas: For an even more festive touch, you can flambé the Baked Alaska with 1 tablespoon of heated Cognac or other brandy which has been ignited immediately before serving.

FROZEN YOGURT*

American/International
Yogurt is increasingly popular, both as an ingredient for desserts and a refreshing dessert in its own right. Excellent frozen yogurt is available commercially, but it is simple to make at home—either in an ice cream maker, following the instructions for preparing ice cream, or in an ice cube tray after removing the dividers.

2 teaspoons powdered gelatin
¼ cup water or skimmed milk
½ cup fruit sugar, honey, or pure maple syrup
2 cups each, commercial or Homemade Yogurt (page 307) and puréed fruit
⅓ teaspoon coarse salt
2 egg whites
YIELD: One quart

1. Dissolve the gelatin in the water in a double boiler over low heat, stirring well. Add the sugar and salt and let the mixture cool before adding the yogurt and puréed fruit of your choice.

2. Pour the mixture into ice cube trays, having removed their dividers, and freeze for 2 hours, or until firm. Remove from the freezer and let stand for 1 hour, or until sufficiently thawed to be beaten with an electric beater until creamy. Beat the egg whites until soft peaks form and fold into the frozen yogurt. Refreeze for 2 hours, or until firm. Except when preparing Baked Alaska, soften the frozen yogurt at room temperature for about 15 minutes before serving.

Bonus Ideas: A wide variety of fresh or unsweetened frozen fruits may be used for flavoring frozen yogurt. Try strawberries, blueberries, peaches, and more exotic variations such as kiwi, papaya, or melons. If the natural fruit sugars are not sufficiently sweet, add honey or pure maple syrup.

BRANDADE DE MORUE*
(Brandade of Stockfish)

French

Stockfish, or dried salt cod, has been called "the poor man's friend" because of its low cost, high nutritional value, and versatility. Originated by the Portuguese, salt codfish became a staple on ships before the innovation of refrigeration, and was quickly adopted by virtually every major cuisine throughout the world.

In spite of its humble beginnings, stockfish now appears on the menus of notable and expensive restaurants in many countries. In France, stockfish is called *morue,* and this creamed salt cod purée is a national favorite suitable as an appetizer, light entrée, or snack.

1 pound stockfish, or dried, salt cod
½ cup each, skim milk and olive, corn or peanut oil
1 clove garlic, mashed
4 twists of a pepper mill
2 truffles (optional)
2 tablespoons melted polyunsaturated margarine (optional)
YIELD: Four servings, or one dozen canapés

1. If not already presoaked, place the dried cod in cold water and soak for at least 12 hours, changing the water several times; if possible, soak in a basin under a trickle of running water.

2. Drain the cod and place in a large pot with cold water to cover. Bring to a boil over medium heat, but permit boiling for no longer than 2 minutes; then remove pot from heat and soak the cod for an additional 30 minutes. When cool, drain; remove the skin and cut the cod into small pieces. Flake the fish and remove and discard all bones.

3. If using an electric blender, purée all of the ingredients except the truffles until the mixture has the consistency of mashed potatoes. The puréeing can be accomplished with a mortar and pestle, or you can purée all the ingredients in a heavy saucepan over very low heat, stirring the mixture with a wooden spoon until it is mashed into a paste of the proper consistency.

4. Shape the *brandade* into a dome in the center of a warm platter, and serve surrounded by toasted bread or Melba toast. For canapés, spread the puréed fish on crackers or toast. Garnish the *brandade* or canapés with thin slices of the optional truffles, which have previously been tossed in melted margarine.

Bonus Ideas: The Italians purée stockfish using a rolling pin, as in the preparation of **Baccalà Mantecato** (page 75). For a richer *Brandade de Morue,* many French cooks remove the scales while soaking the dried fish, and then use the skin—since they believe that incorporating the skin into the purée assures a smoother *brandade.*

Morue Antonin Carême*, or Stockfish Antonin Carême, can be prepared to serve 6 by soaking 2 pounds of dried cod and following the first two steps of the above recipe. Drain, flake the fish, and place in an oven set at 250° F until completely dry. Apply cookware spray to a pan and sauté 3 large onions, minced, in 3 tablespoons of white wine or consommé. When the onions become translucent, blend in ¼ pound of margarine and simmer until the onions are golden. Add the dried flakes of fish, and when brown, add the juice of 1 lemon, 5 twists of a pepper mill, and grated nutmeg to taste. Serve hot with toasted bread or crackers.

SALMI OF DUCK

New Orleans
Salmis of wild fowl or domesticated poultry are dishes that resulted from the influence of French classic cuisine on the Creole cooking of New Orleans. Credited by some to the fourteenth-century Taillevent, and by others to Carême centuries later, they are dramatic dishes to serve, since the final stages of cooking are done in a chafing dish at the dining table (the first two thirds of the cooking having been done in the kitchen).

1 5-pound duckling
1 lemon, cut in half
1 teaspoon coarse salt
5 twists of a pepper mill
1 onion, peeled, spiked with 2 cloves
1 teaspoon each, chopped parsley, diced
    carrot, chopped celery
⅓ cup minced onions or scallions
2 cups duck stock or chicken consommé
3 tablespoons diced Canadian bacon
    (optional)
1 bay leaf, chopped
1 teaspoon each, fresh parsley and thyme,
    or ½ teaspoon each, dried
3 tablespoons cornstarch or potato starch
3 tablespoons polyunsaturated margarine
⅛ teaspoon each, mace, ground pepper,
    and cayenne
1 cup claret or dry white wine
2 dozen pitted olives
½ pound button mushrooms
½ cup croutons and 2 tablespoons chopped
    parsley (optional)
YIELD: Four to six servings

1. Prepare the duckling for roasting by removing all excess fat from the cavity and neck area and the fat glands at the base of the tail. Prick the skin with a sharp fork to let remaining fat escape during roasting. Rub the inside of the cavity with lemon juice; truss the duckling.

2. Place the duck on a rack in a roasting pan, breast side up, and roast for 15 minutes in an oven set at 425° F. Continue cooking, removing the fat in the pan occasionally, with the duckling turned first on one side and then the other, for about 1 hour, or until it is about two thirds cooked. Set aside to cool.

3. Remove and reserve the breasts, remove and discard the skin, and cut the meat away from the bones. Set the meat aside or refrigerate until ready to use.

4. Simmer in water to cover the carcass, wings, giblets, and bones, a **Bouquet Garni** (page 164), salt and pepper to taste, 1 onion spiked with 2 cloves, and 1 teaspoon each of chopped parsley, diced carrot, and chopped celery. After 30 minutes, strain, discarding the bones and other ingredients; and set the duck broth aside.

5. Sauté the onions in 2 tablespoons of the broth, or water, until they become translucent. Add the optional Canadian bacon, bay leaf, parsley, and thyme, and cook for 1 minute longer. Stir in the cornstarch and let it brown before adding the margarine and covering to simmer for 10 minutes.

6. Add the balance of the ingredients except the olives and mushrooms; cover and simmer for 10 minutes. Arrange the reserved pieces of duckling, surrounding the breasts, in a chafing dish. Garnish with the olives and mushrooms, and pour in the sauce to continue simmering at the table, over boiling water, for about 20 minutes. Serve hot with croutons and additional parsley, as desired.

Bonus Ideas: I have found that a bulb baster is excellent for sucking up the fat in the pan during roasting. Also, standing the duckling on one end for at least 1 hour of cooling time encourages the fat to run off.

The ancient Chinese technique of inserting metal spoons in the cavity of the duck, or other poultry, intensifies the heat and decreases cooking time.

As additional garnish, black truffles may be added, but this is more contemporary French than New Orleans. You can achieve a similar effect with sliced black, pitted olives.

GAI LEI, SEE DIK
(Stir-Fried Beef in Curry Sauce)

China

During the many centuries that it has existed, Chinese cuisine has influenced many other ethnic cuisines, including our own. On the other hand, the Chinese have also adopted ingredients from other countries —as is evident in the use of Indian curry in the preparation of this dish.

1 pound lean beef, preferably London broil or flank steak

Marinade:
2 egg whites, lightly beaten
2 tablespoons cornstarch

¼ **teaspoon ground white pepper**
1 clove garlic, mashed
1½ tablespoons each, curry powder and peanut or corn oil
¼ **teaspoon honey or pure maple syrup (optional)**
2½ tablespoons peanut or corn oil
1 clove garlic, minced
2 slices ginger, shredded
⅛ **teaspoon coarse salt**
1 large onion, thinly sliced
2 tablespoons chopped parsley or coriander leaves
YIELD: Four to six servings

1. Trim the meat of excess fat and, with a sharp knife, lightly score both sides with crisscross slashes; then thinly slice it. Combine the ingredients for the Marinade, add the beef strips, cover, and let stand for 15 minutes.

2. Heat 1½ tablespoons of the oil in a wok or skillet. Over high heat, stir-fry the garlic and ginger with the salt, until the garlic is golden brown. Drain, but do not pat dry, the beef strips, reserving the Marinade. Again over high heat, stir-fry the beef in the wok for about 1 minute, searing it well. Remove the meat and set aside.

3. Add 1 tablespoon of the oil to the wok, and stir-fry the onion slices until translucent. Add the reserved Marinade, and stir-cook until the sauce has thickened. Return the beef to the wok, and toss until the slices are evenly coated and heated through. Serve garnished with the chopped parsley or coriander leaves.

Bonus Ideas: Stir-Fried Lamb with Broccoli can be prepared in a similar manner, using 1 pound of lamb, cut into thin slices, instead of beef. A teaspoon of sherry or rice wine is substituted for the curry and oil in the marinade; the lamb is seared, stir-fried in the above manner, but not removed from the pan; the florets from 1 bunch of broccoli are added and stir-fried for about 15 seconds. Two teaspoons of cornstarch, blended with 2 tablespoons of soy sauce, are added to the wok, and the meat strips and broccoli are stir-fried until the sauce is thickened and has coated all the ingredients thoroughly. If the heavier broccoli stems are used, they should be cut diagonally into 1½-inch pieces, then parboiled for 2 minutes, before stir-frying.

A wide variety of your favorite vegetables can be combined with either beef or lamb slices in a similar manner; try Chinese cabbage, cauliflower, mustard greens, asparagus tips, celery stalks, or spinach.

PURPLE ONION AND BEET MARMALADE*

Baton Rouge

This accoutrement is a favorite of mine for game, poultry, and many other meat dishes. Since it takes about two hours for the natural sugar in the onions to caramelize, I find it prudent to prepare the marmalade in large batches, reserving extra quantities in the freezer for future use or for distinctive gifts to friends.

6 large purple onions, about 2 pounds
¾ cup raisins
1 teaspoon coarse salt
1 tablespoon lemon juice
2 pounds fresh or canned beets
3 slices each, fresh lemon and orange
2 whole cloves, crushed
Cookware spray
YIELD: One quart

1. Peel and slice the onions; apply cookware spray and cook *au sec* in a tightly covered skillet over moderate heat, stirring and shuffling the pot occasionally to avoid burning. After 1 hour, remove the cover and continue cooking about 1 hour longer, or until onions are caramelized.

2. Meanwhile, soak the raisins in ½ cup of warm water about 20 minutes, or until puffed. If using fresh beets, wash in cold water, then partially cook in boiling water with the salt and lemon juice for ½ hour, or in a pressure cooker for 7 minutes at 15 pounds of pressure. Cool slightly, and remove the skins using your thumb and forefinger. Julienne the beets by cutting into thin strips, about 3 inches long. If using canned beets, drain well and julienne if necessary.

3. Combine the beets, the raisins and their soaking water, the lemon and orange slices, and the crushed cloves in a saucepan with an additional ½ cup of water. Cook for about ½ hour (7 minutes in pressure cooker), or until the beets are tender.

4. Add the stewed beet mixture to the caramelized onions in the skillet, blend well, and cook for an additional 10 minutes. Cool and serve at room temperature.

Bonus Ideas: Instead of the beets, you may wish to try fruits, such as 1½ cups of currants (for **Purple Onion and Currant Marmalade**) or 2½ pounds of fresh plums that have been pitted, then stewed as in step 3 above for an hour (**Purple Onion and Plum Marmalade**).

When freezing, I use small glass jars, leaving space for expansion and topping the marmalade with a slice of lemon or orange before capping. I like to serve portions of the marmalade on a bed of fresh or stewed orange slices. This is an excellent accompaniment to many duck dishes, especially with the additional accompaniment of **Seppi's Fried Grapes,** an innovation of Chef Renggli of New York's Four Seasons restaurant. For each portion, dip 6 large seedless grapes, or white Malagas with their pits inside, into lightly beaten egg white, coat with wheat germ or bread crumbs, and fry in a thin layer of oil heated to 375° F until golden brown. Drain and serve.

ISOLA ALLA NEVE IN STAMPO*
(Island of Snow in a Mold)

Italian
Budini, or puddings, reportedly were created by Italian cooks to satisfy the British craving for custards, as a gesture to the flood of tourists visiting the country. Such classic French desserts as **Oeufs à la Neige** (Eggs in Snow) are also imaginative recreations of the basic custard: islands of meringue attractively surrounded by a velvety custard sauce.

1 meringue recipe (page 42)
1 tablespoon polyunsaturated margarine
2 tablespoons pulverized fruit or date
    sugar

Vanilla Custard Sauce:
2 cups skim milk
6 egg whites
¾ cup pulverized fruit or date sugar
2 teaspoons grated lemon rind
⅛ teaspoon coarse salt
1 teaspoon vanilla extract
YIELD: Six servings

1. Prepare the meringue batter and beat until glossy and peaks form. Grease the inside of a heavy 1-quart round or oval mold, then sprinkle as much as necessary of the 2 tablespoons of fruit sugar to coat the inside of the mold completely. Spoon all but 2 tablespoons of the meringue batter into the mold, then tap the mold against a hard surface to release any air pockets in the meringue.

2. Cover the mold tightly with aluminum foil that has been slashed with several steam vents, then place the mold in a pan with enough hot water to reach no more than two thirds the height of the mold. Bake in an oven set at 350° F for 30 minutes, or until the meringue is firm.

3. Remove the mold from the pan in the oven; remove the foil and let stand for 5 minutes. Unmold the meringue island onto a platter and let cool to room temperature.

4. Meanwhile, prepare the Vanilla Custard Sauce by first scalding the skim milk in a glass or enamel pan. Combine and beat together the balance of the custard ingredients, except the vanilla extract, until well blended and light in texture. Transfer to a heavy saucepan and cook over low heat (never boiling), stirring constantly until the custard is thick enough to coat a spoon. Remove from the heat, stir in the vanilla, and leave to cool. Continue to stir the custard, so that it does not form a skin on the surface. Blend in the reserved 2 tablespoons of meringue batter, then pour the sauce around the meringue island, and chill in the refrigerator for about 2 hours before serving.

Bonus Ideas: To prepare **Eggs in Snow,** the French poach 1-tablespoon "rounds" of meringue batter in scalded milk for 4 minutes, turning them once. The meringue rounds are drained, then arranged on top of the cooled custard before chilling and serving.

With either version of this dessert, you may wish to try **Custard Sauce Praline,** which is a variation of Vanilla Custard Sauce using only ¼ cup of pulverized fruit or date sugar and ¾ cup of **Praline Powder.** Praline Powder, which is popular with pastry cooks in many countries, is prepared by browning ¾ cup of shelled almonds in an oven set at 400° F. In a heavy-based enamel pan, combine ½ cup of fruit or date sugar, ½ pod of vanilla bean or 1 teaspoon of vanilla extract, and 1 tablespoon of warm water. Stir over medium heat until the mixture is golden brown and the texture of caramel. Allow to cool and harden, then mash with a rolling pin or mallet; or pulverize a few pieces at a time in an electric blender or food processor. The powder can be stored for future use in an airtight and moisture-proof container.

QUICHE DE CAMPAGNE*
(Rustic Cheese Tart)

French

A tangy appetizer, this tart can be served as a light luncheon entrée or sliced as an hors d'oeuvre. It is made with goat cheese, such as French chèvre or Scandinavian mysot, or with Italian pecorino, which is made with sheep's milk, and can be prepared quickly with a frozen homemade **Wheatless Pie Crust** (page 37) or with a commercially available frozen pie shell that meets our slimming standards.

½ pound goat cheese (chèvre or mysot) or pecorino
¼ pound Camembert cheese, softened

Basic Quiche Mixture:
5 egg whites, lightly beaten
3 tablespoons polyunsaturated oil or margarine
½ cup each, skim milk and low-fat ricotta, cottage cheese, or plain yogurt
¼ teaspoon each, coarse salt and dried chives
⅛ teaspoon each, white pepper and grated nutmeg
¾ teaspoon fresh dill or ¼ teaspoon dried
1 9-inch Wheatless Pie Crust (page 37) or purchased pie shell
YIELD: Six to eight servings

1. Combine and mix well the goat cheese, Camembert, 4 of the egg whites, and oil. Add the balance of the ingredients and blend in an electric blender or food processor for several seconds until slightly puréed.

2. Line a quiche dish or pie plate with the pie shell, cover with waxed paper, and fill with dry beans (the French use small pebbles) to prevent puffing. Bake in an oven set at 350° F for 5 minutes. Remove the paper and beans, and brush with the remaining egg white before baking an additional 3 minutes.

3. Spread the thoroughly blended cheese mixture into the pie shell and bake in an oven set at 400° F for 20 minutes. Reduce the heat to 350° F and bake an additional 10 minutes, or until a knife inserted into the center of the quiche is withdrawn clean. Cut into wedges; serve hot.

Bonus Ideas: Before baking, you may wish to sprinkle the surface of the quiche with 2 tablespoons of additional grated cheese, wheat germ, or bread crumbs.

As indicated in the recipe for **Tarte à l'Oignon** (page 156), a repertoire of distinctive quiches can be developed by the addition of favorite vegetables, meat, and seafood to the above Basic Quiche Mixture. Try adding 1 pound of precooked fresh or frozen chopped spinach that has been squeezed dry for **Spinach Quiche,** or ¼ pound of shredded smoked salmon for **Smoked Salmon Quiche,** and serve sprinkled with 2 tablespoons of chopped parsley or chives.

SHWIN YU
(Cantonese Smoked Fish)

Chinese
The Chinese have mastered the fine art of using aromatics in steaming or smoking fish and other ingredients, as indicated in the recipe for **Tsen Yu** (Steamed Sea Bass, page 241). Smoking is done in a steamer, with the principal ingredient elevated on an upper rack to absorb the aromatic vapors of the tea mixture steaming on a rack below. We will see later how Chef Renggli of New York's Four Seasons restaurant has adapted this smoking technique to oven cooking—for **Four Seasons Smoked Duck** (page 300).

1 3-pound carp, sea bass, or other white-
    fleshed fish, cleaned, boned, and scaled
1 tablespoon each, sherry and light soy
    sauce

1 teaspoon coarse salt
2 scallions, chopped
2 slices ginger, shredded
¼ cup raw rice
¼ cup oolong or other dark tea leaves
2 tablespoons fruit sugar
YIELD: Six to eight servings

1. Cut the fish into 3½-inch squares; sprinkle with the sherry, soy sauce, and salt; and marinate for at least 15 minutes.

2. Place the moist fish in a heat-proof dish, over the scallions and ginger, on the upper tier of a steamer. On the lower tier of the steamer, place a pan lined with aluminum foil sufficient to overlap the edges. Combine the rice, tea, and fruit sugar and sprinkle over the foil; then completely seal the foil with the smoking ingredients inside.

3. Tightly cover the steamer pan, adding a layer of additional foil over the lid if necessary to ensure a proper seal. Place the steamer without any water over medium heat, and steam the fish for 10 minutes. Turn off the heat, open the foil wrapping to release the smoke, then recover the steamer pan, and smoke the fish at least 10 minutes. Remove and cool the fish, which is served cold.

Bonus Ideas: Instead of tea, you may blend 1 tablespoon of honey or pure maple syrup with the fruit sugar to smoke the fish in the same manner as above.

Shanghai Mock Smoked Fish to serve six to eight is prepared first by cutting carp, or other white-fleshed fish, into ½-inch slices. Air-dry the fish in a cool place for 30 minutes; then marinate it for at least 2 hours, or preferably overnight, in a mixture of ¼ cup each of sherry and soy sauce, 3 chopped scallions, 3 shredded slices of ginger root, and ½ teaspoon each of coarse salt and powdered anise. Drain and dry the fish and bring the marinade to a boil. Turn off the heat and add several drops of sesame oil. Heat enough peanut oil to 375° F to fry the fish several pieces at a time. Drain and dip the pieces into the warm sauce; serve hot or cold after chilling in the refrigerator overnight.

TORINIKU NO SHICHIMI-YAKI*
(Japanese Chicken Baked in Foil)

Japanese
Cooking *en papillote* is common to many of the world's outstanding cuisines. Probably influenced by the Chinese and the Portuguese, the Japanese have made it a distinctive process in their own cuisine.

2 tablespoons sesame seeds
4 scallions, white parts only, minced
½ cup light soy sauce
2 teaspoons honey or pure maple syrup
1 3-pound chicken, cut into serving pieces
4 12-inch squares of aluminum foil
1 teaspoon equal parts of black pepper, poppy seeds, and dried orange peel
1 lemon, sliced
Cookware spray
YIELD: Four servings

1. Toast the sesame seeds in a skillet and heat until they begin to jump. Remove and crush the seeds with a mortar and pestle. Combine the sesame seeds, scallions, soy sauce, and 1 teaspoon of the honey, and marinate the chicken in the mixture for 30 minutes, turning frequently so that all parts are coated.

2. Apply cookware spray to 1 side of each square of foil. Place a piece of chicken in the center of each square of foil; sprinkle with the combination of black pepper, poppy seeds, dried orange peel, and the balance of the honey; then cover with 1 or 2 lemon slices before wrapping each *papillote* tightly. Bake in an oven set at 350° F for 30 minutes, or until the chicken is tender. Serve the *papillotes* on individual warm plates, to be opened at the table by each diner.

Bonus Ideas: In China, a wide variety of ingredients are deep-fried wrapped in cellophane or waxed paper. In Canton, **Tze Bao Ngo Pa*** (Paper-Wrapped Steak), is prepared with 2 pounds of sirloin or shell steak cut into 1½-inch cubes. (If you like your meat rare, place the cubes in the freezer for 30 minutes before cooking.) Marinate the cubes for 15 minutes in a combination of 2 tablespoons each of soy sauce, peanut oil, and gin or vodka, ½ teaspoon of honey or pure maple syrup, and ⅛ teaspoon each of coarse salt and pepper. Place 3 cubes of meat on each of 8 6-inch squares of waxed paper or lightly oiled parchment, and cover with ¼ slice of shredded ginger, 1 presoaked dried mushroom, and 2 1½-inch lengths of scallion. Spoon on some of the marinade, then fold each square of waxed paper into an envelope, with the flap tucked in. Heat enough peanut oil (375° F) to fry several *papillotes* at a time for 3 minutes, or until the paper is lightly browned. Drain, while frying the balance of the *papillotes;* then return all to the hot oil and fry for 2 minutes before serving immediately.

INSALATA DI ASPARAGI CON SALSA EL TOULÀ

(Asparagus Salad with Lemon Sauce El Toulà)

Italian

A simply prepared yet distinctive salad that is an excellent accompaniment to many main dishes. The piquant lemon sauce is extremely versatile, lending itself especially to a variety of fresh vegetables. The outstanding El Toulà restaurant in Milan serves this sauce as a dip with crisp vegetables, such as celery stalks, carrot sticks, fresh fennel stalks, sweet pepper strips, and cauliflower florets—which make wonderful appetizers or hors d'oeuvres.

3 dozen asparagus stalks, about 2½ pounds
1 teaspoon coarse salt

Salsa El Toulà:
¼ cup lemon juice
½ teaspoon coarse salt
4 twists of a pepper mill
¾ cup olive or corn oil, or a combination of both
½ teaspoon anchovy paste
⅛ teaspoon each, Worcestershire sauce and dry mustard
YIELD: Six servings

1. Wash and scrape the asparagus; then cut off and discard the tough ends. Steam the asparagus with the salt for about 12 minutes, or until *al dente*. Set aside.

2. In a jar with a cover, combine the lemon juice, salt, and pepper; cover and shake briefly. Uncover, then add the balance of the ingredients. Shake until thoroughly blended, then lightly coat the asparagus with the sauce and serve at room temperature.

Bonus Ideas: Another simple variation is **Insalata di Carote** (Shredded Carrot Salad). To serve six, shred 6 medium carrots on the largest holes of a grater, and toss with ½ cup of Lemon Sauce El Toulà. Also try **Avocado with Lemon Sauce El Toulà**. For each serving, fill the cavity of half an avocado with the lemon sauce and sprinkle with additional freshly ground black pepper.

CANTALOUPE PIE*

North Carolina

I learned this recipe from Betsy Klein, who is originally from Asheboro, North Carolina, and now lives in New York and Connecticut. Betsy's mother, now in her seventies, has, like many fine cooks, forgotten where she first learned some of her favorite recipes, including this one. Although Betsy's mother and grandmother were Quakers, this is not a Quaker recipe, nor did any of their neighbors make this delectable pie, which has been a family favorite over the years.

2 9-inch Wheatless Pie Crusts (page 37), or purchased frozen pie shells
½ cup dry beans
1 medium-size cantaloupe, as ripe as possible
½ cup fruit sugar
¼ teaspoon each, ground cloves and ground cinnamon, or ½ teaspoon allspice
2 tablespoons cornstarch dissolved in ¼ cup water

2 tablespoons polyunsaturated margarine
YIELD: Six to eight servings

1. Prepare the 2 Wheatless Pie Crusts, or thaw the purchased frozen shells. Line a quiche dish or pie pan with 1 shell; prick the shell all over with a fork; then layer with waxed paper and ½ cup of dry beans and prebake in an oven set at 450° F for 10 minutes. Remove the waxed paper and the beans, and set the shell aside to cool.

2. Remove and discard the seeds from the cantaloupe. Scoop out the fruit with a large melon scoop. (Make 1¼-inch balls, or trim away the skin and neatly cut the melon into 1¼-inch rectangular pieces.) Arrange the melon balls or pieces attractively on the cooled pie crust. Blend well the fruit sugar, spices, cornstarch, and water. Add all but 1 teaspoon of the sugar mixture to the melon balls, spreading it evenly, and dot with 1 tablespoon of the margarine. There should be sufficient liquid to be visible; if not, add up to several tablespoons of water, so that the mixture is moist and juicy.

3. Place the second pie shell over the filling, adjusting well to the shape of the melon pieces. Trim away any excess pastry as necessary and flute the edges with a fork. Make several gashes in the top to permit steam to escape. Melt the reserved margarine, brush the surface of the pie, then dust with the reserved fruit sugar. Bake in an oven set at 350° F for 45 to 50 minutes. Remove from the oven and let stand to cool up to 1 hour before serving.

Bonus Ideas: A Midwestern version of this pie, **Cantaloupe Pie with Meringue,** calls for cooking the scooped-out pulp in the top of a double boiler until it is soft and can be mashed with a fork. Remove from the heat and blend in ¾ cup of fruit sugar, ⅛ teaspoon coarse salt, 2 egg whites and 2 tablespoons corn oil beaten together, and 2 tablespoons cornstarch dissolved in ¼ cup of water. Return to the top of the double boiler, and cook to the consistency of a thick custard. Add 1½ tablespoons of vanilla extract, then pour the filling into a prebaked pie crust. Instead of using a second pie shell, the filling is covered with **meringue** (page 42) and baked in an oven set at 350° F, until the meringue is lightly browned. Remove from the oven, let the pie cool to room temperature, and serve cold.

ZUPPA CON GNOCCHI DI RISO
(Italian Soup with Rice Dumplings)

Italian
Italians are extremely fond of soups, which they prepare, beginning usually with clear chicken stock, with a wide variety of ingredients. The addition of dumplings proves to be a most gratifying touch.

2 quarts chicken broth, or consommé
2 cups long-grain rice
5 cups water
2 teaspoons coarse salt
½ pound Fontina cheese (preferably the skim milk variety), diced
3 tablespoons melted polyunsaturated margarine
2 tablespoons olive oil
4 egg whites, lightly beaten
¾ cup grated Parmesan cheese
½ cup rice flour or potato starch

¼ cup peanut or corn oil
1 each, carrot, turnip, and celery root or
    base, julienned
2 tablespoons parsley
YIELD: Eight servings

1. Simmer the chicken broth; meanwhile, boil 2 cups of rice in the water and salt for 20 minutes until *al dente*. Drain and place the rice over the diced Fontina cheese in a bowl. Blend well, then add the melted margarine, olive oil, beaten egg whites, and ½ cup of the grated Parmesan cheese. Shape the blended mixture into ½-inch dumplings and roll in the rice flour.

2. Add the peanut oil to a baking dish and place in an oven set at 400° F. When the oil is hot, about 375° F (reached when a cube of bread dropped in the oil turns golden brown), brown the dumplings all over. When golden brown, remove and drain on paper toweling.

3. Cook the julienned vegetables in the simmering broth for 10 minutes, or until *al dente*. Add the drained dumplings and cook for about 3 minutes longer. Serve 6 dumplings per portion in warm plates with the vegetables and broth. Sprinkle each serving with the parsley and the reserved Parmesan cheese, or let each diner garnish the soup at the table.

Bonus Ideas: Passatelli (Meat Dumplings), a specialty of Umbria, is an intriguing variation. Mix well 1 pound of uncooked beef finely ground into a paste, ¾ pound of cooked spinach that has been squeezed dry, 2 ounces of minced beef marrow, 2½ cups of soft bread crumbs, 5 egg whites, ¼ cup of olive oil or melted margarine, 1 cup grated Parmesan cheese, ⅛ teaspoon grated nutmeg, and 1 teaspoon coarse salt. Blend the mixture into a smooth paste and place in a colander. Bring 2 quarts of chicken stock or consommé to a boil, then press the dumpling mixture through the holes of the colander into the consommé. Simmer for 5 minutes, then serve the soup and *passatelli* hot with additional grated Parmesan cheese to taste.

COUNTRY CAPTAIN*

Indian/Pakistani
This easy-to-make dish owes its interesting name to the Moslem corruption of the English word "capon." It has become a favorite in the United Kingdom as well as in most Commonwealth countries. I find this dish pleasantly hot in taste; however, if you are not inclined to spicy dishes, I suggest you reduce the ginger root and chilies by one third to one half the quantities listed in the recipe.

1 3-pound chicken, cut into serving pieces
2 tablespoons dry vermouth, consommé,
    or water
5 slices ginger root, shredded
1 large onion, thinly sliced
3 green or red chilies, or 1½ teaspoons
    bell pepper
3 twists of a pepper mill
1 teaspoon coarse salt
YIELD: Four to six servings

1. Dip the chicken pieces into cold water; drain but do not pat dry. Place the chicken in a large skillet over very high heat and brown on all sides; remove and set aside.

2. Add the vermouth to the skillet; deglaze the pan; then sauté the ginger, onion, and the chilies (cut lengthwise) with the black pepper until the onion is translucent. Return the chicken to the skillet; add the salt and ½ cup of water; cook over medium heat for 30 minutes, or until tender. Serve hot over rice, if the accoutrement recommended in the menu is not used.

Bonus Ideas: You can use leftover chicken, or any leftover meat, to prepare this Indian dish: **Kobi Keema*** (Cabbage and Minced Meat). Sauté 2 minced onions in 2 tablespoons of dry vermouth or water until translucent; then add 1 pound of the minced meat, 1 teaspoon salt, 2 ounces of margarine, 2 cloves of minced garlic, ½ teaspoon each of ground ginger and chilies, ¼ teaspoon each of turmeric, ground coriander, and ground cumin seeds, and ⅛ teaspoon each of ground cloves and ground cinnamon. Sauté for 20 minutes, then add 1 small cabbage, shredded, and cook until tender. Blend well and serve.

STEAK DIANE

French
Festive dishes needn't be difficult to prepare; nor need they be time consuming. This dish is easy to make and has the added advantage that the entire preparation can be carried out at the dining table with the use of a very hot chafing dish. If you wish, the steaks can be flambéed, which adds to the dramatic presentation of this classic dish.

4 12-ounce sirloin, club, or porterhouse
    steaks, 1 inch thick
2 teaspoons coarse salt (optional)
4 tablespoons polyunsaturated margarine
4 tablespoons scallions, chopped
4 teaspoons chives, minced
2 tablespoons Worcestershire sauce
1 tablespoon dry mustard
1 teaspoon coarse salt
6 twists of a pepper mill
4 tablespoons Cognac or other brandy
    (optional)
3 tablespoons chopped parsley
YIELD: Four servings

1. If the steaks have bones, remove them; trim off all excess fat and score the edges of the steaks. Place them between waxed paper and pound with a mallet or the side of a cleaver until about ½ inch thick.
2. Dip the steaks in cold water; drain but do not pat dry; then brown both sides quickly in a skillet or chafing dish over very high heat. If you prefer, sprinkle the optional salt into the pan, and when the salt begins to lose color over the high heat, sear the steaks on both sides. Remove the steaks to a serving platter.
3. Melt the margarine in the pan, then add the balance of the ingredients except the Cognac and parsley; simmer over low heat, without boiling, until the sauce thickens and becomes brown. Return the steaks to the pan and cook 2 minutes on each side, or until done as desired. Preheat the optional Cognac, pour into the pan, deglaze, and ignite. Remove the steaks and place on the serving platter, garnish with the chopped parsley, and serve with the sauce.

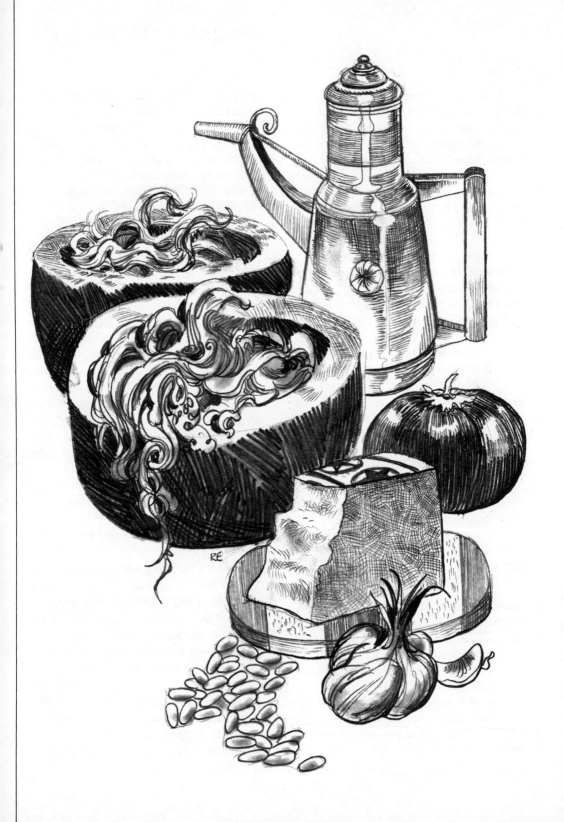

Bonus Ideas: Steak au Poivre (Peppered Steak) can be prepared in a similar manner with 3 tablespoons of black peppercorns, coarsely crushed in a mortar with a pestle, or 3 tablespoons of mashed green peppercorns. Bone and trim the steaks, then pound the peppercorns into both sides of the steaks before searing them in a very hot skillet that has been sprinkled with the salt. Reduce the heat and continue cooking until done as desired. Remove the steaks to a covered serving platter; heat ¼ cup of beef broth or consommé, to which ½ teaspoon of Bovril or other meat extract has been added. Add ¼ cup of white wine or dry vermouth and simmer the mixture for 5 minutes until it is reduced slightly. Stir in 4 tablespoons of margarine and blend thoroughly. Pour the sauce over the steaks, and flambé with heated Cognac or other brandy before serving garnished with chopped parsley.

SEPPI'S LINGUINE AND ZUCCHINI WITH PESTO

American/International

This imaginative accoutrement is an example of how a chef's personal preferences can influence the menu of a fine restaurant. Chef Renggli of The Four Seasons restaurant in New York City resists serving the standard accompaniment of potatoes with many of his entrées. As a result, he has conceived this intriguing combination of ingredients, which can also be served as an appetizer or luncheon main course.

½ pound zucchini squash
4 quarts water
1 tablespoon each, coarse salt and polyunsaturated oil
1 pound linguine
2 tablespoons polyunsaturated margarine
½ cup *Ligurian Pesto Sauce* (page 58)
Parmesan cheese, grated (optional)
YIELD: Eight servings as an accoutrement or appetizer

1. Wash the zucchini thoroughly, pat dry, then cut into quarters about 4 inches long. Cut the quarters into ⅛-inch thin sticks or into thin shreds about 4 inches long; for shredding in this manner, use a French *mandoline* or similar cutting device which will produce uniform pieces.

2. Bring the water to a boil in a large pot; then add the salt, the oil (to prevent sticking), and the linguine. Continue boiling, uncovered, for about 13 minutes, or until the linguine is *al dente*.

3. Meanwhile, melt the margarine in a skillet, and sauté the zucchini sticks until *al dente*. Transfer the zucchini to a large serving bowl or tureen. When the linguine is ready, drain in a colander and sprinkle with cold water to halt the cooking process. Pour the linguine over the zucchini, blend well, then ladle with half of the *pesto* sauce. Serve with additional *pesto* and grated Parmesan cheese, as desired, at the table.

Bonus Ideas: I find I can eliminate sautéing the zucchini sticks, with excellent results. Instead, after the linguine is boiling for 10 minutes, I add the zucchini, and after 3 minutes of boiling, both ingredients are cooked *al dente.* The mixture is drained in a colander, sprinkled with cold water, and then transferred to a large serving bowl containing the margarine. Toss well before blending with the *pesto,* and serve with additional sauce and grated Parmesan at the table.

For another variation, substitute spaghetti squash for the linguine and zucchini, using no pasta of any kind. I was first introduced to this unusual vegetable by Roslyn Chvala, who served it with **Italian Bolognese Sauce** (page 109). I find, however, that I prefer the spaghetti-like strands of the squash with basil sauce. Although the squash can be boiled 20 minutes, I prefer baking it in an oven set at 350° F for about 1 hour. In either case, be sure to puncture the squash with a fork to permit steam to escape during cooking. When cooked, cut in half, scrape away the seeds, then scrape out the pasta-like strands with a fork. Ladle with basil sauce and serve with additional sauce and grated Parmesan cheese at the table.

PESTO LIGURE*
(Ligurian Pesto Sauce)

Italian

This is one of the most distinctive sauces in Italian cuisine, and a personal favorite. Mamma Omelia, whom we will meet on our tour of Italy, adds potato slices to the cooking pasta; the potato is then added to the basil sauce for additional texture. Chef Ettore Alzetta of the Casanova restaurant in Milan adds a Venetian touch—*petit pois,* peas cooked *al dente.* You may wish to try

adding thin slices of water chestnuts to the pasta during cooking, a pleasant variation of Mamma Omelia's technique.

2 cups shredded fresh or frozen basil leaves
2 tablespoons pine nuts, almond slivers, or sunflower seeds
2 cloves garlic, mashed
⅛ teaspoon coarse salt
½ cup grated Parmesan cheese
2 tablespoons grated Romano-style pecorino cheese
4 tablespoons olive oil
1½ tablespoons polyunsaturated margarine
1 tablespoon hot water
1 russet potato, thinly sliced (optional)
YIELD: One cup

1. Using a mortar and pestle, grind the basil, nuts, garlic, and salt to form a paste. Add the grated cheeses, and continue grinding the mixture. Add the oil and blend it into the paste; then add the margarine and water until the mixture has the smooth consistency of mayonnaise.

2. If using an electric blender or food processor, combine all of the ingredients except the cheeses, margarine, water, and optional potato. Blend at high speed until a paste is formed, then transfer to a bowl. Blend in the cheese and margarine to a smooth consistency. Thin with the hot water (preferably water in which pasta is cooking) before serving.

3. If using the potato slices, cook them first in the salted water to be used for cooking the pasta. After 10 minutes of boiling, when the potatoes are not quite tender, add the pasta and cook uncovered until both the pasta and potatoes are *al* *dente.* Using a slotted spoon, transfer the potato slices to the *pesto* sauce to absorb its flavor.

Bonus Ideas: If freezing basil sauce, do not add the cheese and margarine before freezing, but do so after the sauce is thawed and ready for use. To avoid discoloration in the refrigerator or freezer, brush the top, or thinly layer, with oil.

If fresh basil leaves are not available, you can prepare **Instant Pesto*** using 2 cups of chopped parsley and ½ teaspoon dried basil and proceeding with the basic recipe.

TORTA DI RICOTTA*
(Neapolitan Ricotta Cheesecake)

Italian

This Bonus Recipe is a traditional favorite at Easter time and during other special holidays in Italy. Its ingredients include **Candied Fruits,** prepared with fruit sugar. The use of fruit sugar permits us to use a smaller quantity (with fewer calories) than would be the case with conventional sucrose sugars, which many doctors consider potentially harmful to the human system.

⅓ cup golden seedless raisins
1 tablespoon lemon rind, grated
½ cup granulated fruit sugar
1 pound low-fat ricotta cheese, sieved
8 egg whites
¼ cup each, rice flour or cornstarch and
    white rye flour
1 teaspoon baking powder
½ cup Candied Fruits, minced (page 91)

⅓ cup wheat germ or crumbled graham
    crackers
Cookware spray
YIELD: Eight to ten servings

1. Soak the raisins in warm water for 15 minutes, drain, and set aside. Gradually blend the lemon rind and all but 1 tablespoon of the fruit sugar into the ricotta. Lightly beat 5 of the egg whites and fold in 1 tablespoon at a time.
2. Combine the rice flour or cornstarch, rye flour, and baking powder, and sift 6 times; then add to the cheese mixture with the raisins and the minced Candied Fruits. Beat the balance of the egg whites until they form peaks; then fold into the mixture.
3. Apply cookware spray to a quiche or deep pie dish, or layer the pan with a thin coat of polyunsaturated margarine. Blend the wheat germ with the reserved fruit sugar, and coat the pan. Pour in the batter and bake in an oven set at 375° F for about 30 minutes. Remove from the oven and let cool before serving.

Bonus Ideas: Instead of wheat germ, you can line the pan and decorate the surface with **Italian Pastry Dough** (*Pasta Frolla,* page 60). Place 1 of the pastry shells into the quiche dish, so that the inside is completely covered; then make a series of small holes in the dough with a fork. After pouring in the ricotta mixture, arrange on top 1-inch rippled strips of dough, which have been cut with a pastry wheel from the balance of the dough. You can weave a lattice pattern by placing a row of the strips about ¾ inch apart, then weaving additional strips crisscross over and under the first layer of strips. If they break, moisten the edges with water and pinch together. Moisten the extreme ends of the strips and stick them to the edges of the pie, removing any lengths that extend beyond the edge of the pie. Brush the top strips with a mixture of 1 lightly beaten egg white mixed with 1 teaspoon of water. Bake in an oven set at 350° F for about 30 minutes; then cover lightly with aluminum foil and bake about 1 hour, or until an inserted toothpick comes out dry. Remove from the oven and let cool before serving.

PASTA FROLLA*
(Italian Pastry Dough)

Italian
This versatile sweet pastry dough is excellent for desserts with sweetened fillings. It can be used for pie crusts or tart shells; and if rolled into a ¼-inch thickness, the dough can be cut into various shapes for delicious **Italian Cookies***, which can be served on festive occasions, as is done in Italy at religious festivals.

**1 cup each, rice flour or cornstarch and
  white rye flour**
4 teaspoons baking powder
⅛ teaspoon coarse salt
½ cup granulated fruit sugar
2 egg whites
3 tablespoons low-fat or skimmed milk
½ cup polyunsaturated margarine, soft
1 tablespoon Armagnac or other brandy
1 tablespoon grated lemon rind
**YIELD: Two 10-inch pie crusts or 12 tart
  shells**

1. Combine the rice flour or corn-

starch, rye flour, and baking powder, and sift 6 times to aerate properly. In a large mixing bowl, blend the flour mixture with the salt and fruit sugar. Beat the egg whites with the milk for about 1 minute.

2. Make a well in the center of the flour mixture; pour in the egg mixture and the balance of the ingredients. Work the wet ingredients gently into the flour and pat into a large ball. If too dry, add additional milk, but the dough must not be too crumbly. Wrap in aluminum foil or waxed paper and refrigerate for 3 hours or longer.

3. Remove from the refrigerator, and let the dough rest for 30 minutes. Form into 2 balls and roll out on floured waxed paper into 2 10-inch circles for pie crusts, or into large sheets for tart shells.

Bonus Ideas: Italian Pastry Dough will keep in the refrigerator for about 1 week, and can be frozen for months. If freezing, shape into the quantity and form you plan to use and completely thaw before using. When the dough is removed from the refrigerator or thawed after freezing, let it rest for 30 minutes before rolling it out.

• • •

Join me now as we set off on a slimming cook's tour of the world's foremost culinary centers. We will visit typical ethnic kitchens in Italy, France, China, and the United States, gaining a firsthand knowledge of each cuisine by chatting with chefs and outstanding cooks and restaurateurs and observing them at work. For an in-depth understanding of each cuisine, we will also place it in its proper historical setting. We will sample dishes familiar and unusual; we will explore menus; finally, our appetites whetted, we will prepare our own recipes for the many specialties we will discover. Our first stop is Milan, the culinary center of superlative northern Italian classical and regional dishes.

ITALY

"Don't ever let the farmers find out how delicious pears and cheese are when served together."
—old Italian proverb

THE CUISINE IN PERSPECTIVE

During the Middle Ages, the peninsula we now call Italy was inhabited by a disparate mixture of Romans and Longobards, Greeks and Latins, Mohammedans, and, of course, Christians. This diversity caused all kinds of political, military, and social havoc. By the first century A.D., however, economic realities and the inevitable intermingling of peoples resulted in the fundamental mixture we now call Italian. These influences were naturally reflected in concepts of cooking and the formation of a national cuisine.

In addition to political and economic factors, the varying geographical characteristics of the peninsula obviously had a bearing on the development of Italian cuisine. Broadly, the north, with its abundant water and lands suitable for pasturage, favors butter as a basic ingredient, while oil is used in southern Italy, where the olive tree flourishes. Rice, grown in the north, is also abundant in many of its dishes, while the tomato (after its introduction from the New World in about A.D. 1500) became a staple of the southern part of the peninsula.

Both politically and in terms of its cuisine, Italy can be said to have flowered after the seventeenth century. Although Italians have great national pride, regional individuality is extremely strong. The Roman, the Neapolitan, the Piedmontese, and the Venetian have different regional characteristics. These pronounced local differences are also reflected in the various regional types of cooking that constitute what we generally consider Italian cuisine.

These regional cuisines developed about the time that new ingredients were discovered abroad, brought back, and incorporated into the Italian culinary repertoire. Among the new items were maize or cornmeal, the tomato, and, of course, the celebrated Chinese (or Indonesian) noodles that Marco Polo introduced to Italy in 1292.

Since pasta is the basic Italian dish, common throughout all of Italy, there is inevitably a controversy involving its origin. Although the popular story is that Marco Polo brought a form of pasta back from China, dry noodles were part of Indian and Arab cuisines well before Marco Polo's discovery; it is well known that strands of noodles were introduced into Sicily at the time of its conquest by the Arabs. Other historians claim that pasta was used by the early Romans, that it was one of the legacies developed during the Middle Ages after the collapse of the Roman Empire.

In any case, pasta is certainly a staple of Italian cuisine today—even in the north, where rice and *polenta,* made with cornmeal, are equally popular. While the origin of pasta is subject to considerable interpretation and conjecture, there is, for the record, a piece of indisputable evidence: in 1279, one Ugolino Scarpa, a Genoese notary, prepared a last testament for Pozio Bastone, a soldier from Genoa, who left his heirs, among other items, *"una barisella plena de macaronis,"* or a basket of dry pasta.

For me, what is significant is the fascinating interplay of influences—Roman, Indian, Arab, Chinese—which established pasta as a staple in Italy and eventually throughout the world. Similarly, other typically Italian dishes are reflected in other cuisines. Pizza, for instance, now considered typical of southern Italy, especially Naples, is also popular in Marseilles and other Mediterranean French port cities, where it is called *pissaladière.*

Other notable foreign influences in Italian cuisine are smoked bacon, known as *speck* (from Austria); almond paste and *cassata,* the soft ice cream typical of Sicily (legacies of the Arab conquests); and, of course, saffron (used in **Risotto alla Milanese**), which was adopted from Valencia as a result of the earlier Spanish domination of Lombardy.

Fundamentally, Italian cuisine is of popular origin, having evolved from the family, its needs, and available ingredients. As I pointed out earlier, Italians of both sexes are excellent cooks, the men significantly knowledgeable about food and its preparation. Cooking schools for the nonprofessional have only recently appeared in Italy; more often than not, they are frequented by foreigners wishing to learn Italian cuisine, and not by the Italians, who are proud of the excellent cooking schools they have in their own kitchens. The standard authority on Italian cooking is *The Science of Cooking and the Art of Eating Well,* written by Pellegrino Artusi around 1900 and still considered a masterpiece. More recently, Luigi Carnacina has become the popular authority on Italian cuisine.

Italian cooking is simple and nourishing: sauces never overpower basic ingredients; vegetables are generally served whole, and puréed foods are uncommon. The Italian loves his *orto,* or vegetable garden; its freshly harvested produce provides ingredients for meals when possible.

The most dramatic example of the influence of one cuisine on another results from the journey of the fourteen-year-old Catherine de Medici to France in 1533, when she married the future King Henry II. She brought with her not only many of the treasures of the Italian Renaissance but also outstanding chefs with their inventive cooking processes and many new ingredients, such as the artichoke and green bean. Catherine's trip resulted in the introduction of the dramatic new *sauce espagnole,* or basic brown sauce, which Escoffier called the most fundamental of the French "mother sauces." These provided the initial impetus to *la grand cuisine.*

As in many other countries, the style of contemporary life has changed in Italy, and there is more awareness of the caloric and cholesterol content of foods. Polyunsaturated oils are used more often, instead of or in combination with the traditional monosaturated olive oil. Although the pace of daily living has quickened with the growing industrialization of the country, whenever feasible the Italian still returns to his home for luncheon with his family; it is still the main meal of the day. More than likely, however, it will no longer be a four- or five-course meal, as in the days of Pellegrino Artusi. A Roman friend said recently, "Today anyone subscribing to Artusi's recipes religiously would probably die of high cholesterol within a month!" Nonetheless, the processes of Italian cookery are sound, and as adapted to slimming cuisine, become even more so, as well as more suited to our contemporary mode of life and knowledge of nutrition.

Italians rarely drink cocktails or hard liquor before a meal. Occasionally, they serve apéritifs such as vermouth or Campari, and invariably drink wine and mineral water with the meal. Every region has its local wine, or *vino del paese;* frequently, however, the outstanding wines of other regions are served, for instance, the famous Tuscan Chianti Classico. Types of this vintage wine are identified with such emblems as *il gallo nero,* a black rooster, or *il punte,* a young child against a Wedgwood blue background. Of these two, I find Chianti Classico Il Punte smoother and milder, as do many of my Italian friends, especially those who spent their youth working in the vineyards. Others of my personal favorites in red wines are Bardolino, Valpolicella, and especially Merlot from Veneto; Barolo and Grignolino from Piedmont; and from Sicily, Corvo di Casteldaccia, often referred to as Salaparutta, after the duke who founded this fine house in 1824. Among the white wines, I have enjoyed the white Salaparutta from Sicily, Orvieto from Umbria, Soave from Verona, and the ever popular Pinot Grigio (made with the same grapes used for champagne). Asti Spumante, an effervescent sparkling white wine, is popular for special occasions and is considered the champagne of the country.

A COOK'S TOUR OF ITALY

Our tour begins in Milan, which together with Genoa and Turin is part of the industrial triangle of the north. Milan has become the industrial design capital of the world, and, in recent years, I have visited and worked in this bustling and gracious city many times. In addition to the famed La Scala opera house, the Duomo, and the Galleria, Milan offers the finest concentration of excellent *ristoranti* and *trattorie* available anywhere in Italy.

Among the numerous internationally renowned restaurants are Giannino, St. Andrew, Savini, El Toulà, La Bagutta, and Casanova. However, I have explored literally hundreds of smaller, family-oriented restaurants and *trattorie* that feature not only distinctive food but also the personal touch of their owners and amazingly knowledgeable waiters.

Let me take you along to visit several such restaurants. You can meet their personnel and explore their kitchens. It is early in May, the weather is lovely, and the inevitable winter *nebbia,* or fog, that can envelop the Milan area is all but forgotten for another year. The Milanese are already beginning to migrate for long weekends to favorite resorts or summer homes at Lake Como or the Italian Riviera. We will take the Autostrada to Genoa and then east to Lerici.

This ancient town is built in the hills surrounding the Bay of Lerici, on the eastern side of the Gulf of La Spezia bordering on the Ligurian Sea. Known as the Coast of Poets, this picturesque basin with its lovely houses and villas was a magnet to such famous poets and painters as Dante, Petrarch, Shelley, Byron, D. H. Lawrence, and Turner. As might be expected, the surrounding hills have numerous hotels and *pensioni* suitable to meet the budgets of the Italian and foreign visitors who come each spring through fall for a day, a weekend, or a longer vacation.

Upon arriving in Lerici, one is ex-pected to promenade along the quay and the bordering public park, absorbing the view of the bay. Beyond the park is a rim of buildings with a continuous succession of shops, restaurants, and hotels. Some English is spoken, especially in the larger hotels; however, if one speaks Italian it helps immeasurably, for one can chat with the shopkeepers and inquire about the restaurants and *trattorie* in the area.

A young woman adjusting the vegetables on display outside of her shop recommended a *trattoria* called La Cucina Emilia, situated near the park. I found it attractively decorated and immaculately clean. The waitress recommended spaghetti with clams, the house specialty; when it arrived, however, the aroma of garlic was overpowering, and though a first taste proved to be delicious, it confirmed the heavy use of garlic. When the waitress returned, I mentioned jokingly that the dish had more garlic in it than I had tasted in months. I expected an apology or some explanation to the effect that they had a new chef, or whatever. Instead, she smiled triumphantly and said, "I'm pleased you noticed, because the heavy use of garlic in our fish dishes is our specialty!"

The next day, the effects of the garlic had worn off before my next meal at the Ristorante il Parma, a small restaurant also near the public park. Considering the locale, it was not surprising that most of the dishes on the menu featured fish and seafood, with only one or two items for those who might prefer other fare. My friends and I, surveying the menu and sensing that this was a distinctive restaurant, decided on different dishes for each of us, so that we could sample a larger range of the specialties of the house. With the help of a most knowledgeable and cooperative headwaiter, we ordered *assaggio di tutto,* which proved to be a sampling of antipasto specialties. Other offerings included **Insalata Frutti Di Mare,** or mixed seafood salad, and spiedini di gamberi, or shrimp brochettes. The brochettes were prepared by alternating on skewers shelled mussels and shrimp, wrapped in *prosciutto* or thin slices of Canadian bacon. The skewers, turned and grilled until done, were then sprinkled with salt and a little olive oil before being served with a garnish of chopped parsley. The antipasto was followed by two pasta dishes: *trenette al pesto* and *penne all'arrabbiata,* the former with basil sauce and the latter with a hot red pepper and tomato sauce. Another choice was **Muscoli Alla Marinara,** or mussels fisherman style. All of our dishes were accompanied by an excellent Merlot wine, *vino tipico del Veneto.* To complete the meal, which cost less than half of what it would be in a similar restaurant in Milan, we had the delicious combination of the **Pears with Parmesan Cheese** and the **Espresso Coffee.**

The headwaiter was named Walter (pronounced "Valter," since there is no letter *W* in the Italian alphabet), and during the meal, whenever Walter was not too rushed with other patrons, I asked him about the preparation of some of the dishes. I was particularly surprised that the basil sauce, which is a favorite of mine, contained several slices of boiled potato. Walter explained that the thinly sliced potatoes were cooked with the pasta and then blended into the *pesto* sauce before

serving. He was so pleasant and cooperative that I asked if it would be possible to be present in the kitchen the next morning to observe the preparation of the dishes for that day. He graciously accepted, and it was arranged that I would return at 10:30 A.M. the next morning. I returned to my room at the Hotel Shelley e delle Palme, with its small balcony facing the Bay of Lerici and affording a superb vista.

There had been a violent storm during the night. After a brisk walk on the next morning, I made my way to the Ristorante il Parma for my appointment to visit the kitchen. When I arrived, the restaurant was neatly set up, with all the tables ready. My first impression of the relatively large kitchen was one of consummate neatness and orderliness. It was dominated by a professional range in its center. Although the restaurant might be referred to as a "Mamma and Poppa" operation, as my visit progressed I soon realized how much more it was a family-coordinated effort under the quiet and loving but unmistakable dominance of Mamma Omelia, who is the master cook.

In a corner of the kitchen, Poppa Arturo Giovenetti was busily cleaning a huge pile of mussels. Walter introduced me to his sisters, Laura and Silvana, who were busily but effortlessly assisting in the preparation of various ingredients required that day. Silvana was blending parsley and garlic in a mortar with a pestle, explaining that this was added to virtually all of their dishes during preparation. The specialties were to be roast duck. **Risotto Alla Milanese,** and pasta and bean soup.

Mamma Omelia, who was preparing

the large duck for roasting, explained that she first boils the duck in water flavored with rosemary and garlic; after the duck is parboiled and removed, the broth is left to simmer. Walter termed the process *"occhioso,"* since during boiling two circular "eyes," formed by the natural oils of the duck released into the broth, appear on the surface. Mamma said that the duck broth would be used in preparing her *risotto* dishes. This came as no surprise: Italians reserve virtually every type of cooking liquid when preparing meat, poultry, seafood, or vegetable dishes for use in *risotto*. In another large stock kettle, minestrone was simmering—and would continue cooking all day.

Mamma Omelia willingly explained how she prepared basic sauces, such as Italian tomato sauce and bolognese meat sauce, continuing her preparations for the specialties of the day as she spoke. I was fascinated by the *pesto* with potato: very thinly sliced peeled potatoes are cooked with the *trenette*, which are similar to flat linguine noodles, then removed and added to the already prepared *pesto* to marinate and absorb its delightful basil flavor. Like many knowledgeable cooks, she adds a thin layer of oil to the surface of the *pesto,* which keeps it from darkening while stored in the refrigerator. The sliced potatoes provide a memorable texture to the dish—like water chestnuts in many Chinese dishes. In fact, I have since made this *pesto* with thin slices of water chestnuts, cooked simultaneously with the particular pasta I am using, and found this to be a most satisfying combination.

Perhaps the most remarkable thing about this busy restaurant was the ab-

sence of any sense of pressure. Walter glided back and forth from the kitchen like a ballet dancer, ordering, serving, always smiling and in complete control; Silvana also had her mother's deftness, ease of movement, and a great sense of pride in her work. Even when the fisherman did not arrive until afternoon, because of a storm the night before, and then with only a small catch of sardines, Mamma Omelia announced calmly that they would be able to manage with their reserve of fish from the day before. (I must confess that privately I thought serving day-old fish in this locale and particular restaurant a breach of integrity. However, as I was to learn later, this was not the case at all.)

At this point I noticed a large bowl of honey-colored "sticks" in water, and was told that these were *datteri di mare,* or "dates of the sea," so called because these shellfish look like dates and are sweet. *Datteri,* special to the Gulf of Spezia, are found in underwater caves and can be prepared in the same way as clams or mussels; because they are relatively expensive, however, they are served as **Zuppa Di Datteri** (datteri soup). Mamma, who gave me the recipe, said that the dish can be made with clams, mussels, or periwinkles, since *datteri* are not available in the United States. To serve four, two cups of fish broth or clam juice, one minced garlic clove, two tablespoons of chopped parsley and one-half cup of drained canned Italian-style plum tomatoes are placed in a heavy pot with a tightly fitting cover. The *datteri* are added and allowed to cook, covered, over medium to high heat until they are steamed open, in a matter of minutes. The soup is served in bowls with *crostini,* which are triangles of bread that have been rubbed with a cut clove of garlic and toasted. Additional parsley can be used as a garnish.

It was now slightly past 11:30 A.M., and as is the custom in most Italian restaurants, the cooks and staff were about to have their own lunch, so that they could be free to serve the patrons who would begin arriving about an hour later. I declined an invitation to join the family at their meal, since I felt my presence would be an imposition on their tight schedule. I left with a sense of the remarkable warmth and respect these wonderful people have for one another. Whenever I prepare any of the recipes that Mamma Omelia gave me, invariably I think back to that memorable morning in Lerici.

Further investigations in Lerici, incidentally, produced a surprising answer to the question of serving day-old fish—and some fascinating information about the harvesting and preparation of *datteri.*

In nearby Marina di Carrara, I was told that *datteri* are harvested by divers from underwater caves in great masses, the *datteri* still clinging to pieces of underwater rock; there is concern that if too much rock is chipped away from any underwater cave, a cave-in could occur. Originally, the divers brought up the rock pieces with *datteri* attached and separated them on the surface. Now, I was told, with the improvement and greater accessibility of underwater diving equipment, the fishermen perform the necessary separation underwater, bringing only the *datteri* to the surface. Each inch of their sticklike brown shells indicates one year of age.

From Vincenza, the young daughter of Alfredo and Lucia Guinci, owners of Lerici Vecchio, another restaurant, I learned that *datteri* could not only be served as a soup but eaten raw with fresh lemon juice. She said that *datteri* are also found in the waters of Venice and Naples, rarely, however, in such large quantities as in those of Lerici. During a cholera scare in the Bay of Naples, they had stopped serving raw *datteri* all along the coasts of Italy; but Vincenza still liked them raw!

On the subject of fresh fish, Vincenza insisted that large fish are better after they have been cleaned and stored in a refrigerator for one or two days, "to properly mature." I registered surprise and admitted that I had never heard of maturing fish, remembering that the Scandinavians do not consider fresh any fish that has been out of the water for several hours. But now I began to realize what Mamma Omelia meant when she said that they could manage with yesterday's catch: smaller fish, Vincenza explained, are best when served the same day they are caught, but larger fish like bass are best after maturing one or more days. With a knowing air, she added that all fish are best when caught in September and October.

She also recommended that *datteri* should never be refrigerated, but simply left in seawater, in which they will keep for several days, and that their size and age have no influence on their taste. Visitors come from all over the world to have *datteri* at Lerici, she told me.

Vincenza then revealed that at the Lerici Vecchia, **Zuppa Di Datteri** is made with white wine instead of fish broth or clam juice. When I asked whether diced onions might be sautéed in her combination of ingredients, she said definitively, "Never use onions with seafood!"

It is probably because of the unusual element of seasoned authority in one so attractively young that many of Vincenza's words remain with me, and were certainly on my mind when I returned to Milan the next day.

After a delightful dinner at the Casanova restaurant in Milan's Hotel Palace, beginning with **Baccalà ai 4 gusti,** or Stockfish—4 Venetian Styles, I arranged to obtain some of Chef Ettore Alzetta's recipes and to visit his kitchen the following morning. My host and guide was Gianpiero Rollini, assistant manager of the hotel. This is an expensive, attractively designed restaurant with a large staff catering to affluent patrons. Although it is well operated, the restaurant must be evaluated for what it is: a major business enterprise. Its style, however, is set by the dominating influence of its owner, Dr. Arrigo Cipriani, the famous Italian restaurateur whose family originated Harry's Bar and Torcello della Laguna in Venice, and Villa Cipriani in Asolo, near Padua. Ettore Alzetta grew up and worked most of his life with the renowned owner-gourmet. Signor Rollini told me that he specialized in *"la cucina di Cipriani, una cucina artiginale e Veneta,"* which could be interpreted as the style of Cipriani, or regional Venetian cooking brought to its apex.

The absolute freshness of ingredients, particularly of its fish and seafood, was the claim to fame of the Casanova restaurant. I was told that Cipriani's assistant in Venice selects and ships only the best and freshest fish and seafood, which are dispatched from Venice to Milan each day by truck or via the *rapido* (express train). During the two-hour trip, the fish are kept fresh in plastic bags containing ice.

Still curious about Vincenza's observations about maturing large fish, I asked the chef's opinion. The emphasis on freshness by everyone connected with the Casanova restaurant prepared me for an answer that would refute young Vincenza. I was all the more surprised to hear Chef Alzetta agree with her completely: "By all means, large fish like sea bass are better after maturing several days in a refrigerator set between 6° and 7° Celsius [approximately 43° F and 45° F]. It is the small fish that should be cooked right away."

Before beginning our tour of the kitchen, I asked the chef what a typical day in the restaurant was like. Ettore, as I soon learned to call him, prided himself on the fact that there was no special routine for preparing the food each day. He arrived at 7:00 A.M. each morning, preceded by the pastry chef, and personally selected all the food in "the line," which means items on the menu. If he saw that *osso buco,* for example, looked especially good in the market, he would make that dish the specialty of the day.

Ettore began his day by preparing the sauces. A sauce for that particular day was to be green peas with *pesto.* In this case, the fresh green peas were cooked with the *trenette,* or flat noodles, in the way that potatoes were added to the noodles at Ristorante il Parma in Lerici.

We finally made our way into the kitchen, which was huge and practical from a working point of view, and had, somewhat incongruously, beautiful marble floors. Among the dishes being prepared were **Zuppa Di Pesce,** or *bouillabaisse,* and bolognese meat and tomato sauce. On a counter behind the range were huge platters of stuffed tomatoes, roast peppers, anchovies, cooked zucchini, shrimp, crawfish, and sea bass—all ready to be served as **Antipasto all' Italiano.**

All the baking and the making of pasta were done in another part of the kitchen. I also noticed large dried *baccalà,* or stockfish, soaking in a bucket of water under a running faucet.

It was now almost 11:30 A.M., and the upstairs kitchen was beginning to serve the kitchen and hotel staffs, both of which were sizable. (Ettore's staff consisted of an assistant chef, or *sous-chef,* who chops, prepares, and cooks, a pastry chef, eight additional cooks, and six part-time dishwashers and floor cleaners.) There was a surprisingly relaxed atmosphere in the kitchen; apparently everything was under control. Although this was not a rushed or crowded restaurant, most dishes were prepared to order, and I wondered how smooth the patrons' luncheon service would be. However, the main dish of the day, *osso buco alla milanese,* was already prepared; only the accompanying *risotto* remained to be cooked. Since the tomato and Bolognese sauces were simmering and ready for use, it was just a matter of cooking pasta when these dishes were ordered. (Casanova makes all of its own pasta, which generally cooks more quickly than the commercially made variety.) Before leaving the kitchen, I took a quick inventory: the artichokes were almost ready, needing only a few more minutes of final cooking; the mushrooms were cooked and

being kept warm; the zucchini had been parboiled; the salad greens had been washed, cut, and set up in various combinations; and the fish soup was ready to go. The secret is obvious: the more time given to preparation and organization in the kitchen, the faster, smoother, and more gracious is the service. We homemakers may have far more modest menus and no staff to help us prepare them; still, the basic principles do apply to our kitchens.

Another secret of efficient service involves the maître d', who can suggest specials of the day that are almost ready to serve. At the Ristorante il Parma in Lerici, Mamma Omelia told me that whenever the house is very busy, she invariably makes extra portions of popular dishes knowing that the maître d' can promote that dish. I remember such an instance at one of my favorite restaurants in Milan, La Bagutta. When I ordered *trenette con pesto,* I was advised that the dish was prepared only for two or more persons. I was alone, but my disappointment was such that the maître d' shrugged his shoulders and said, "All right, we'll make it just for you." Shortly thereafter, another lone diner arrived and asked, *"Che cosa c'è di buono?"* In a most confidential manner, the maître d' replied, "If you like, although usually we serve it only for two persons, I have a portion of *trenette con pesto* ready to go." He gestured toward me, I smiled, and the newly arrived diner ordered it.

As I was leaving the kitchen at Casanova, Ettore showed me the sea bass appetizer to be served with lemon and oil, saying, "Now this is *the* real sea bass; it is absolutely fresh and matured to perfection!" Reminded of Vincenza's strictures on the freshness of seafood—and of the regional pride of Italy—I thanked the chef and returned to my hotel.

Now let's prepare our own slimming versions of the dishes we've discovered on our tour—as well as other traditional regional dishes that are classic of Italian cuisine.

MENUS AND RECIPES

MENU

Carciofi alla Romana
Baccalà ai 4 Gusti
Zucchini Cotti con Pastella
Pere e Grana
Caffè Espresso

Roman Artichokes
Stockfish—4 Venetian Styles
Zucchini Cooked in Batter
Pears with Parmesan Cheese
Espresso Coffee

CARCIOFI ALLA ROMANA
(Roman Artichokes)

Fresh mint provides a refreshing flavor to this popular Italian delicacy. Since the artichoke stems are an integral part of the dish, the artichokes are cooked upside down and served with the stems attached. A versatile appetizer or luncheon dish, it is equally delicious served hot or cooled to room temperature.

6 large artichokes
½ lemon
1 teaspoon fresh mint leaves, or ½ teaspoon dried
3 tablespoons minced parsley
1 clove garlic, minced
½ teaspoon coarse salt
4 twists of a pepper mill
½ cup olive oil or corn oil, or a blend of both
2 cups water
YIELD: Six servings

1. Remove all the tough outer leaves from the artichokes, and cut or simply snap off the upper third of all the inner leaves, removing all prickly tips or blemished parts. With a knife or vegetable peeler, scrape off the fibrous skin of the stems; spread the center petals and scoop out the choke. Wash under running water and rub all cut parts with lemon juice to avoid discoloration.

2. Crumble the mint leaves, or if using dried mint, soak in warm water for several minutes. In a bowl, mix the mint with the parsley, garlic, salt, and pepper. Set aside a third of the mixture and spoon the balance into each cavity, rubbing it well along the inner sides of the artichoke.

3. Place the artichokes upside down in a tightly covered, deep casserole; you may have to trim the stems slightly to properly fit the lid on. Rub the balance of the mint mixture on the outer sides of the artichokes. Add the oil and about 2 cups of water, which should cover the artichokes to about a third of their height. Place 2 thicknesses of damp paper toweling under the lid of the casserole and cover the pot tightly. Cook over medium heat for 45 minutes, or until tender.

4. After removing the artichokes to a serving dish, reduce the liquid in the casserole, over high heat, to a quarter of its original volume. Pour this sauce over the artichokes before serving them warm or at room temperature.

Bonus Ideas: I like to place a whole fresh mint leaf into the cavity of each artichoke, using less of the crumbled mint in the mixture. If cooking in a microwave oven, arrange the artichokes in a large, deep baking dish, leaving space in the center of the dish. Cover with waxed paper and cook 7 minutes. Baste the artichokes and cook for 14 additional minutes, basting once again. Remove from the oven and let stand for 10 minutes before serving with the reduced liquid. Artichokes Roman style can be cooked in a pressure cooker at 15 pounds pressure with 2 cups of water for about 6 minutes, depending on their size.

BACCALÀ AI 4 GUSTI*
(Stockfish—4 Venetian Styles)

Baccalà—dried salt codfish—was developed by the seafaring Portuguese and quickly spread to become a staple in the cuisines of most Mediterranean countries. Stockfish, or *stoccafisso,* prepared in the same manner as *baccalà,* is fresh cod that has been air-dried without salt.

Stockfish—4 Venetian Styles is a renowned luncheon specialty of the Casanova restaurant in Milan: for each serving, Chef Ettore Alzetta arranges samples of each of four delicious versions of the fish around a toasted slice of **polenta.**

You may wish to serve the combination for a special occasion—or to try each style individually first. If planning to serve a combination of styles, you may wish to use only 1 pound of dried cod, halving the quantities of all other ingredients for smaller portions of each style. Whatever your combination, *polenta* is a perfect accoutrement. You can save time and effort by purchasing the dried cod (available in many ethnic markets) either partially or completely presoaked. Once soaked and restored to its original texture, the fish can be frozen for long periods and kept available for future use.

BACCALÀ MANTECATO*
(Creamed Stockfish)

2 pounds stockfish or dried salt cod
½ cup olive, corn, or peanut oil
2 cloves garlic, minced
2 tablespoons minced parsley
4 twists of a pepper mill
8 anchovy filets, mashed
½ teaspoon coarse salt (optional)
YIELD: Six servings

1. If not already presoaked, place the dried cod in cold water and soak for at least 12 hours, changing the water several times; if possible, soak in a basin under running water.

2. Drain the cod and place in a large pot with cold water to cover. Bring to a boil over medium heat, but permit boiling for no longer than 2 minutes; then remove pot from the heat and soak the cod for an additional 30 minutes. When cool, drain;

remove the skin and bones and cut the cod into small pieces.

3. Using waxed paper on a sturdy flat surface, pound the cod with a mallet or rolling pin for several minutes, until the fish becomes a paste; add small quantities of the oil to be absorbed by the fish. Separately, combine the balance of the ingredients, including any oil left over, and beat until well blended.

4. Combine the fish paste with the oil mixture; beat with a balloon whisk or in an electric blender, until the mixture has the texture of whipped cream. Place the creamed cod in a pan and simmer over medium heat for 5 minutes; add additional seasoning as necessary. Allow to cool, then chill before serving with sliced *polenta* (which can either be cold or toasted).

Bonus Ideas: This has become my favorite of the several styles of preparing dried codfish, and is essential to any combination of styles served together. Especially adaptable to light luncheon meals, creamed stockfish is also a distinctive appetizer to many main course.

BACCALÀ ALLA VICENTINA*
(Stockfish Vicenza Style)

2 pounds stockfish or dried salt cod
2 tablespoons white wine, dry vermouth,
    or consommé
1 onion, thinly sliced
1 clove garlic, mashed
2 tablespoons minced parsley
8 anchovy filets, mashed

½ cup white wine (optional)
2 cups hot skim milk
½ teaspoon coarse salt
5 twists of a pepper mill
1 pinch of cinnamon or nutmeg (optional)
2 tablespoons cornstarch
3 tablespoons grated Parmesan cheese
Cookware spray
YIELD: Six servings

1. If not already presoaked, place the dried cod in cold water and soak for at least 12 hours, changing the water several times. If frozen, thaw before using.

2. Drain the cod and place in a large pot with cold water to cover. Bring to a boil over medium heat, but permit boiling for no longer than 2 minutes; then remove the pot from the heat and allow to cool for about 30 minutes. Drain the cod, remove the skin and bones, and cut into serving pieces.

3. Apply cookware spray to a skillet, add the wine or broth, and sauté the onion and garlic until the onions are translucent. Add the parsley, mashed anchovies, and optional white wine. Cook over high heat until the liquid has almost evaporated; then add the hot milk.

4. Sprinkle the salt, pepper, and optional cinnamon or nutmeg over the cod and dust each piece lightly with the cornstarch. Apply cookware spray to a large casserole and place the cod snugly into it in a single layer. Pour the hot milk mixture over the fish and bring to a boil.

5. Sprinkle with the grated Parmesan cheese, place the casserole in an oven at 350° F, and bake for 1½ hours. Serve with hot or toasted slices of *polenta*.

Bonus Ideas: Instead of the grated Parmesan cheese, you may try sprinkling the fish mixture with 2 tablespoons of wheat germ or bread crumbs. If cooking in a microwave oven, cook covered with waxed paper for 15 minutes; let the casserole stand for 5 minutes, rotate 90°, and cook an additional 10 minutes, or until tender.

BACCALÀ ALLA LIVORNESE*
(Stockfish Leghorn Style)

2 pounds stockfish or dried salt cod
2 tablespoons white wine, dry vermouth, or consommé
1 medium onion, minced
2 cloves garlic
½ teaspoon coarse salt
5 twists of a pepper mill
1½ cups white wine or dry vermouth
2 cups skinned fresh tomatoes, remove stem ends and cut into quarters, or 2 cups Italian-style canned plum tomatoes, drained
12 capers in vinegar, drained
12 pitted black olives (optional)
Cookware spray
YIELD: Six servings

1. If not already presoaked, place the dried cod in cold water and soak for at least 12 hours, changing the water several times. If frozen, thaw before using.
2. Drain the cod and place in a large pot with cold water to cover. Bring to a boil over medium heat, but permit boiling for no longer than 2 minutes; then remove the pot from the heat and allow to cool for about 30 minutes. Drain the cod, remove the skin and bones, and cut into serving pieces.

3. Apply cookware spray to a heavy-based pan or Dutch oven, add the wine or broth, onion, and garlic; sauté over medium to high heat for several minutes. When the garlic cloves have turned golden in color, remove and discard.
4. Add the cod and the balance of the ingredients; cook, covered, over medium heat for 1½ hours, or until tender. Serve with hot or toasted slices of *polenta*.

Bonus Ideas: If you prefer, transfer the sautéed onions to a casserole to which cookware spray has been applied. Then add the cod and the balance of the ingredients and bake, covered, in an oven at 350° F for 1½ hours. You can also complete the cooking in an electric skillet set at 350° F for the same length of time. If using a microwave oven, transfer the sautéed onions to a casserole. Add the cod and the balance of the ingredients, cover with waxed paper, and bake for 15 minutes; let stand for 5 minutes, rotate 90°, and cook for an additional 10 minutes, or until tender.

BACCALÀ ALLA CAPPUCCINO*
(Stockfish Capuchin Style)

2 pounds stockfish or dried salt cod
1 cup olive, corn or peanut oil
4 twists of a pepper mill
½ teaspoon coarse salt (optional)
1 clove garlic
3 tablespoons minced parsley
YIELD: Six servings

1. If not already presoaked, place the

dried fish in cold water and soak for at least 12 hours, changing the water several times. If frozen, thaw before using.

2. Drain the cod and place in a large pot with cold water to cover. Bring to a boil over medium heat but permit it to boil for no longer than 2 minutes. Remove the pot from the heat and allow to cool for about 30 minutes. Drain the fish, remove the skin and bones, and cut into serving pieces.

3. Place the fish and the balance of the ingredients in a large heavy-based pot or Dutch oven. Skewer the garlic clove with a toothpick so that it can be removed easily before serving. Cook over medium heat, covered, for about 1 hour, or until fork tender. Serve warm with hot or toasted slices of *polenta*.

Bonus Ideas: This dish can also be cooked in an electric skillet, an oven, or a microwave oven, following the directions given in the previous recipe.

It is said that the Portuguese have more than a thousand ways of preparing their *bacalhau*. Of these, my favorite is **Bacalhau a Gomes de Sá:** For six servings, soak and boil the cod, as in the above recipes; then skin and bone it and cut into 1-inch strips. Place the fish strips in a pan and pour over them 1¾ cups of skim milk that has been brought to a boil; let soak for about an hour. Meanwhile, boil, peel, and quarter 2 pounds of potatoes. In a casserole to which cookware spray has been applied, sauté 4 thinly sliced onions and 2 cloves of minced garlic in 2 tablespoons of white wine or consommé. When the onions are translucent, add the potatoes, ½ teaspoon of salt, 5 twists of a pep-

per mill, and the cod and milk mixture. Bake in an oven at 350° F for 15 minutes; serve hot, garnished with slices of pitted olives and minced parsley.

POLENTA

Polenta, made with cornmeal, has been a mainstay of the Lombardian and Venetian regions for centuries and has gradually become popular in other parts of Italy. This porridge-like dish is incredibly versatile. It can be used as a main dish or as an accoutrement, served soft and hot or cooled and hardened. Cut into serving pieces, it makes an ideal accompaniment to *baccalà,* meat, poultry, and especially wild game.

Traditionally, *polenta* is cooked in a *paiolo,* an unlined copper pot with a rounded bottom; but it can be done in any heavy kettle, and most easily in an enameled or glass double boiler. *Polenta* is usually made with finely milled white or yellow cornmeal, sometimes with a coarser-grained variety that produces a heavier texture. However, it can also be made with chestnut flour or *grano saraceno* (buckwheat), resulting in *polenta nera,* or dark polenta.

1 cup cornmeal
1 cup cold water
3 or more cups boiling water
1 teaspoon coarse salt
YIELD: Six servings

1. To avoid lumping, mix the cornmeal with the cold water and place in a large, heavy kettle or double boiler over moderately low heat.

2. Stir in the boiling water and salt, adding additional boiling water if necessary as the *polenta* thickens. If using a kettle, stir constantly for about 25 minutes, until the thickened cornmeal easily comes away from the sides of the pot. If using a double boiler, it is only necessary to stir regularly at 5-minute intervals. Cover and cook over boiling water for about 30 minutes, until the cornmeal separates from the sides of the pot. Serve hot or cold.

Bonus Ideas: When hot, polenta is delicious eaten alone with a dab of polyunsaturated margarine and sprinkled with grated Parmesan or soft Gorgonzola cheese. It is also a marvelous alternative to potatoes and blends well with numerous sauces and stews. To cool *polenta* and reserve for future use, place on a platter or wooden surface for a few minutes until it hardens. Using a taut string, saw the hardened *polenta* into ½-inch-thick slices, or into 2-inch squares. These can be kept between layers of waxed paper in the refrigerator for weeks at a time.

A traditional specialty is **Polenta alla Ciociara,** or *Polenta* Country Style. For four to six servings, puncture 6 sweet Italian sausages with a fork and cook in a skillet with ¼ inch of water until the water is absorbed. Using 2 tablespoons of olive, corn, or peanut oil, sauté ¼ cup of fresh or presoaked dried mushrooms with the sausages, which have been cut into ¼-inch slices. Season with coarse salt and pepper, then add 1 cup of tomato sauce. Apply cookware spray to a large baking dish and arrange in it several slices of *polenta* in crisscross fashion. Cover each layer with spoonfuls of the sauce and up to ¼ pound

of thin sliced, part-skim mozzarella cheese; sprinkle with grated Parmesan cheese. Bake in an oven at 400° F for about 15 minutes and serve with additional grated Parmesan cheese.

ZUCCHINI COTTI CON PASTELLA
(Zucchini Cooked in Batter)

Like onion rings, artichoke hearts, and other vegetables, zucchini can be fried in batter, resulting in a delicately crisp and delicious dish. This traditional Italian frying technique lends itself to marvelous variations: sliced yams, green beans, scallions, and (a childhood favorite) zucchini or squash blossoms can be similarly batter-fried.

1 pound zucchini
⅔ cup rice flour
6 tablespoons cornstarch
½ teaspoon baking powder
¼ teaspoon coarse salt
1 cup cold water
1 teaspoon olive, corn, or peanut oil
 (optional)
1 cup or more corn, olive, or peanut oil
YIELD: Four to six servings

1. Scrub the zucchini clean in cold water; remove and discard the extreme ends, and cut into ½-inch sticks, about 4 inches long.

2. In a medium bowl, stir together and sift well the flour, cornstarch, and baking powder. Add the salt and stir in the water gradually, with the optional oil, until the mixture is smooth and has the texture of pancake batter.

3. Heat enough of the remaining oil to fill no more than a third of the skillet; the oil should be very hot (about 375° F). To test it, drop a small cube of bread into the hot oil; when the bread turns golden brown, the oil is ready. Dip the zucchini sticks in the batter, allow the excess batter to drip off, and drop them into the oil, frying only as many as will not overcrowd the skillet. When both sides have a golden crust, remove the zucchini, drain on paper towels, and sprinkle with salt to taste. Repeat the process with the balance of the zucchini and serve hot.

Bonus Ideas: In some parts of Italy, 2 beaten egg whites are added to the batter, and Pellegrino Artusi suggests adding 1 tablespoon brandy. Some cooks prefer cutting the zucchini into thin slices rather than thin sticks. When using onions or yams, peel and thinly slice before adding to the batter. Another favorite recipe uses 3 medium artichokes cut into wedges, or 1 10-ounce package of frozen artichoke hearts, well thawed. Green beans, with the ends snapped off, and the whole white parts of scallions can be similarly fried. But if you have them in your garden or can find them in ethnic markets, you must try zucchini or squash blossoms prepared in this batter: simply remove the hard pistil from the flower, and wash and pat dry before dipping into the batter. Edible nasturtium flowers are a very satisfactory alternative.

If you prefer not to deep-fry, you can make:

ZEPPOLINE NAPOLETANE
(Neapolitan Patties)

2 large potatoes
⅔ cup rice flour or cornstarch
2 teaspoons powdered yeast
¼ cup warm water
1 teaspoon coarse salt
2 medium zucchini, about 1 pound, unpeeled
10 scallions
2 tablespoons white wine or consommé
1 tablespoon olive, corn, or peanut oil
4 twists of a pepper mill
1 tablespoon Parmesan cheese
Cookware spray
YIELD: Six servings

1. Boil the potatoes in their jackets for about 30 minutes, or until tender; peel, then rice or mash the potatoes while they are still warm, dusting your hands with flour to avoid scorching. Place the puréed potatoes in a bowl and add the rice flour.

2. Dissolve the yeast in the warm water; then combine with half of the salt and the potato and flour mixture, kneading the dough until it is elastic and has a smooth finish. Shape into a thick, circular loaf and make 2 crisscross cuts on the top surface. Cover with a damp cloth, remove to a warm place, and leave to rise about 1 hour.

3. Cut the zucchini into ½-inch sticks, about 4 inches long, and thinly slice the white parts only of the scallions. Apply cookware spray to a skillet, add the white wine, and sauté the vegetables for several

minutes, or until the vegetables are *al dente.* Season the vegetables with the balance of the salt, the pepper, and the Parmesan cheese.

4. Apply cookware spray to a large baking dish; then brush the inside with some of the oil. Spread a thin layer of the dough onto the palm of one hand and add several sticks of the cooked zucchini and some scallions. Cover with a second thin layer of dough, and press down to seal in the cooked vegetables.

5. Place the filled *zeppoline* in the baking dish and brush the surfaces of each with additional oil. Bake in an oven at 350° F for about 20 minutes. When the bottom of the patties are crisp, place the baking dish under the grill for several minutes, until the tops of the *zeppoline* are golden brown. Pat dry on paper toweling and serve warm.

Bonus Ideas: If the dough is rolled into a ⅛-inch thickness and cut into circles about 8 inches in diameter, you can prepare the famous Neapolitan specialty **Calzone Imbottito,** or Stuffed Calzone. Simply brush the circles of dough with oil and place in the center of each a slice of mozzarella cheese and diced pieces of prosciutto, Canadian bacon, or salami. Moisten the edges of each circle with beaten egg whites to properly seal them; then fold the dough over the filling, and press the edges. Brush each of the pouches with a bit of oil, line a baking sheet, cover the *calzones* with a damp towel, and then remove them to a warm place for approximately 1 hour. Put them in an oven set at 350° F and bake for about 40 minutes. Serve the stuffed *calzones* hot.

PERE E GRANA
(Pears with Parmesan Cheese)

Some years ago, while dining at the famous Ristorante Giannino in Milan, I overheard an American complimenting the maître d' on the *grana* (Parmesan cheese) he was enjoying. He asked how it was possible that here he could cut the cheese with a table knife, whereas in America, Parmesan is so dry and hard it can only be grated. The maître d' with obvious pride, responded, "Well, of course, in America the Parmesan comes from Argentina. Here we use only the genuine *parmigiano reggiano* that is made in Parma." I couldn't resist suggesting to my American neighbor that he try the balance of his cheese with a fresh pear. He did, and when he left the restaurant, he could still be heard extolling the excellent combination of flavors.

Surprisingly, most cookbooks on Italian cuisine do not include this overwhelmingly popular Italian dessert; perhaps their authors do not consider a recipe necessary, since the dish is so simple. But for those who do not know about the perfect harmony of pears and Parmesan, I offer the recipe below. It is essential that genuine, aged Parmesan cheese be used and that it be freshly cut and not dry, but still glistening with its natural moisture. The pears must be of excellent quality, such as a Bartlett, Anjou, or the russet-skinned Bosc, mature and at the peak of ripeness.

½ pound aged, genuine Parmesan cheese
6 ripe pears, at peak of flavor
YIELD: Four to six servings

1. Serve the whole pears in a bowl, and the cheese (cut into chunks) on a platter. The traditional after-dinner ritual calls for each person to cut and trim his pear, eating it alternately with chunks of cheese. If you prefer, however, you may quarter the pears lengthwise, remove the core sections, and serve on individual plates to each diner with several pieces of the Parmesan cheese freshly cut into 2-inch chunks.

Bonus Ideas: Italians enjoy many cheeses—with other fruits, such as apples or grapes, or crusty bread—at the end of the meal. Fontina, Bel Paese, and Gorgonzola are favorites.

Tuscan smoked mozzarella is served sliced in thin strips, sprinkled lightly with olive oil and freshly ground black pepper to taste.

Pears Stuffed with Provolone make an interesting summer dish. To serve six, halve 6 ripe pears and remove the peels and cores; brush with lemon juice to avoid discoloration. Blend 6 ounces of low-fat cream cheese with 4 ounces of shredded provolone, adding several tablespoons of part-skim ricotta or yogurt to achieve the texture of whipped cream. Spoon the cheese mixture into 6 of the pear halves, and cover each with another pear section. Chill and serve the stuffed pear upright over a bed of lettuce or watercress. Garnish with cherries, strawberries, or Mandarin orange sections, and serve separately with **Creamed Italian Dressing.** To prepare a scant cup, blend ½ cup of olive or corn oil, 3 tablespoons of vinegar or lemon juice, ¼ teaspoon of coarse salt, 3 twists of a pepper mill, and 2 tablespoons of grated Parmesan, Gruyère, or aged Cheddar cheese. Fold in up to 2 tablespoons of part-skim ricotta or yogurt, and serve.

CAFFÈ ESPRESSO
(Espresso Coffee)

Traditionally, every meal in Italy culminates with the inevitable cup of espresso coffee. It can be served double strength *(doppio)* or *lungo,* with the coffee diluted with extra water. Espresso can be flavored with a liqueur or steamed with hot milk and cinnamon for a *cappuccino.* These variations are generally relegated to the ubiquitous bars in Italy, or served on special occasions at home. Normally, espresso is served black in demitasse cups, slightly sweetened to taste.

Contrary to the custom in American restaurants, *Caffè Espresso* in Italy is not generally served with a zest of lemon *(una buccia di limone).* Some devotees of *Caffè Espresso* prefer to add a few drops of rose water instead of the zest of lemon.

Italian coffee is made with double-roasted coffee beans, finely ground to a powdery texture, and is available in bags or cans. Preferably, the unground roasted beans can be obtained in gourmet shops; for additional freshness and flavor, the beans can be finely ground just before using.

Espresso is best brewed in a *macchinetta* (espresso machine), which utilizes steam pressure in the preparation of the coffee. In Italy, either the Napoletana or the more modern Moka are favorite *macchinette* for brewing *Caffè Espresso.* These are also available in specialty shops or in ethnic markets here. However, you can make satisfactory espresso with any drip-type coffee pot, provided you use the specially pulverized double-roasted coffee.

2 tablespoons Italian-roast espresso coffee
6 tablespoons fresh water
1 lemon twist, honey, or liqueur to taste
YIELD: One serving

If using the *macchinetta* Moka:

1. Place the water in the lower chamber, but in no case higher than the safety valve near the top of the unit. Insert the coffee filter, put in the coffee (but do not pack it), then screw on the filter top.

2. Screw on the upper chamber of the unit, and place the pot over medium heat with the lid left open. When the coffee begins to steam through, lower the heat until the upper chamber is nearly filled. Close the lid, and when you hear a spluttering sound, turn off the heat and serve.

If using the *macchinetta* Napoletana:

1. Fill the bottom section of the pot with the water, but in no case higher than the escape vent near the top of the bottom unit.

2. Fill the metal filter with the pulverized coffee, but do not pack it. Tightly screw on the top of the filter. Since you will later be turning the entire pot right-side up, now place the empty half of the pot upside down, and with its spout pointing downward over the filter, and snap the two halves of the pot together.

3. Place the pot over medium heat until you see the steam escaping from the side vent. Protecting your hand with a heat-resistant pad, invert the pot so that the spout is now pointing upward. Allow several minutes for the water to filter through it to the bottom chamber before serving.

Bonus Ideas: Try not to leave the kitchen or become distracted while espresso is brewing: the pot must never be left over heat once the water in it has been utilized. If using drip or other types of coffee pots, follow the manufacturer's directions. Serve in demitasse cups with a twist of lemon, a few drops of rose water, or a dash of such liqueurs as Anisette, Cognac, Strega, or Tia Maria. For sweetening, if desired, use small amounts of honey or fruit sugar.

Many Italians prefer **Caffelatte** (the French *café au lait*) or coffee with hot milk with their breakfast croissants. To prepare *Caffelatte,* brew the *Caffè Espresso* and heat skim milk separately. Blend the two hot liquids by pouring equal amounts of each into the cup.

Caffè Cappuccino, or Espresso Capuchin Style, is another traditional favorite. Prepare equal portions of *Caffè Espresso* and hot skim milk; combine as with *Caffelatte,* but add a dash of ground cinnamon or nutmeg and honey or fruit sugar.

MENU

Spaghetti con Whiskey
Triglie al Cartoccio
Insalata Mista
Budino di Pesche

Spaghetti with Whiskey
Red Mullet *en Papillote*
Italian Mixed Salad
Peach Pudding

SPAGHETTI CON WHISKEY
(Spaghetti with Whiskey)

I obtained this recipe—with difficulty—from a deservedly popular restaurant in the Skyscraper Building in Milan, Il Ristorante Grattacielo. The dish was so unusual that I badgered the well-informed but busy waiter for the recipe, and each time he came by my table, whether serving me or a neighboring group, I got a bit more information about the ingredients and cooking process. Perhaps I should have been more aware of how busy the waiter was; and though I must confess to having tried his patience, I think you'll find that the recipe justified my persistence.

2 carrots, peeled and grated
2 onions, minced
1 clove garlic, minced
¼ cup olive and corn oil, combined
½ cup white wine or dry vermouth
2 tomatoes, cut into quarters
1 green pepper, diced
3 stalks celery with leaves, finely chopped
2 leeks or 6 scallions, white part only
1 medium zucchini or ½ pound eggplant, diced
4 tablespoons minced fresh parsley
1 teaspoon coarse salt
6 twists of a pepper mill
1 teaspoon each, fresh thyme, basil, and oregano, or ½ teaspoon each, dried
2 tablespoons rye or bourbon whiskey
⅛ teaspoon grated nutmeg (optional)
Parmesan cheese, grated
YIELD: Six servings

1. In a heavy pot, sauté the carrots, onions, and garlic in the oil for approximately 5 minutes, or until the onions are golden brown.

2. Add the wine, then the balance of the ingredients, except for the seasonings and the whiskey. Cook covered over medium heat for 20 minutes.

3. Add the seasonings and the whiskey, and cook uncovered over medium heat 10 minutes longer. If a smooth sauce is preferred, pass the mixture through a food mill to purée, or purée at low speed in an electric blender for about a minute.

4. Bring the mixture to a boil; then simmer uncovered about 15 minutes until reduced to a thick concentrate. Adjust the seasonings, adding the optional nutmeg if desired, and up to an additional tablespoon of whiskey, as necessary. Serve hot over spaghetti or your favorite pasta, adding grated Parmesan cheese to taste.

Bonus Ideas: This dish is a gardener's delight since a wide range of fresh summer vegetables can be substituted for or added to those in the recipe, producing what Italians call *"sugo da tutto l'orto,"* or "sauce from the entire garden"; pumpkin, cabbage, radishes, and peas are popular additional ingredients. For those who prefer not to use alcohol, ¾ cup of chicken broth or consommé can be substituted for the wine and whiskey. One tablespoon per serving of polyunsaturated margarine may be blended into the pasta before adding the sauce.

Since tomatoes, incidentally, were not brought to Italy until after Columbus's voyage in 1492, it can be assumed that before that date the Italians made a gravy similar to this one for their many indigenous pastas and those that Marco Polo brought back from the Far East in 1292.

TRIGLIE AL CARTOCCIO*
(Red Mullet *en Papillote*)

The mullet has had a long history as a culinary specialty, dating as far back as Ancient Egypt and Rome. Although Europeans prefer the red mullet, we are more likely to use the striped, silvery mullet found in our southern Atlantic and Pacific coastal waters.

These average about 2 pounds; however, for this recipe and whenever possible, select the smaller ½-pound fish, which are more delicate and delicious. Italians often add anchovies when cooking mullet.

1 cup skinned fresh tomatoes or Italian-style canned plum tomatoes
4 16-inch lengths aluminum foil or parchment
8 small mullet, about ½ pound each
1 teaspoon coarse salt
8 twists of a pepper mill
3 tablespoons olive, corn, or peanut oil (optional)
½ cup polyunsaturated margarine, soft
1½ tablespoons mashed unsalted anchovy filets
1 teaspoon fresh thyme, or ½ teaspoon dried
1 tablespoon fresh parsley, finely chopped
Cookware spray
YIELD: Four servings

1. Remove stem ends and chop the tomatoes, then boil in a pan for 15 minutes, reducing to a concentrated sauce. Fold each of the lengths of foil or parchment into halves; cut each half into the shape of a heart, large enough to contain a serving of 2 fish.

2. Clean and wash the fish thoroughly, and season the insides with salt and pepper. If using aluminum foil, apply cookware spray to the inside of the foil *papillotes,* and place 2 mullets in each, adding additional seasoning to taste. If using parchment, then use the optional oil to brush the insides of each parchment envelope.

3. Prepare **Anchovy Butter** by creaming the ½ cup of polyunsaturated margarine with 1½ tablespoons of mashed unsalted anchovy filets. For each serving, place 1 tablespoon of the anchovy butter under the fish, and spread another tablespoon on top. Sprinkle with the thyme and parsley.

4. Fold and crimp the edges of each *papillote* to seal in the ingredients. If using parchment, you may want to use a paste of flour and water, placed on the crimped edges, to ensure proper sealing. Allow several minutes for the paste to dry.

5. Apply cookware spray to a baking dish large enough to contain the filled *papillotes,* and bake in an oven at 350° F for 20 minutes. Serve the fish in their envelopes, to be opened at the table by each guest, on individual warm plates. Serve the tomato sauce separately, to be ladled over the fish as desired.

Bonus Ideas: For those who prefer not to use anchovy filets, creamed soft margarine alone may be used; or such seasonings as fennel seeds or crushed capers may be substituted. The anchovy butter, however, adds a delightful flavor. A few grains of cayenne and ⅛ teaspoon of lemon juice will enhance the flavor of anchovy butter.

A delightful variation is **Almond Butter***. To prepare, blanch ½ pound of shelled almonds by pouring boiling water over the almonds and letting them stand for about 1 minute. Pour cold water over them and remove their now-loosened skins by rubbing them between the thumb and index fingers. Pound the skinned nuts into a paste, adding 2 teaspoons of water. Blend the paste well with ½ cup of soft polyunsaturated margarine and use as an *amandine* with fish and poultry dishes.

Another alternate is **Sauce Béchamel** or **Sauce Velouté** (velvety white sauce) which can also be used in a number of other dishes. To prepare 1 cup, combine 2 tablespoons of cornstarch or potato starch with 2 tablespoons of polyunsaturated margarine; cook over moderate heat until slightly brown (roux blond). Gradually add 1 cup of milk that has been brought to the boil, with salt and white pepper to taste. Cook for 10 minutes. To prepare enriched **Sauce Velouté**, which has a creamy consistency, add 1 cup of part-skim ricotta or yogurt, ⅛ teaspoon lemon juice, and 4 egg whites, slightly beaten until foamy, to produce 2 cups of sauce. For **Sauce Velouté au Currie,** or Velvety Curry Sauce, add ¼ cup of part-skim ricotta or yogurt and curry powder to taste to 1 cup of **Sauce Velouté. Sauce Mornay** is made in a similar manner, using ⅓ cup of ricotta or yogurt and several grains of cayenne powder, with ⅓ cup of grated Gruyère cheese to 1 cup of **Sauce Velouté.** Cook the sauce until thickened, then stir in the cheese, and continue stirring until the cheese is melted. Add the ricotta and cayenne, and season to taste with a dash of coarse salt and pepper.

Sauce Velouté for Seafood is prepared by substituting fish stock or clam juice for the hot milk. However, do not add salt if using clam juice, which is naturally salty.

INSALATA MISTA
(Italian Mixed Salad)

Italians love their gardens, as I have said. Inevitably, they also love colorful salads, which are served usually as a *contorno,* or side dish, eaten either with the main course or directly afterward. When wine is being served with the meal, Italians, like the French, use lemon juice instead of vinegar in their *salsa vinaigrette* sauce.

Depending on availability, a variety of greens can be used: our own Boston lettuce, or romaine, Bibb, or for a touch of color, red-tipped lettuce. For a delicate touch of bitterness, watercress, chicory, escarole, arugola, lamb's tongues, or dandelion leaves can be added. However, the bitterish greens are rarely included in an *Insalatona Mista,* or Italian Medley Salad, which is a meal in itself with the addition of vegetables and possibly meat, fish, or fruit.

Italians have a traditional saying: "Four types of people are required to prepare a salad: a wastrel for oil, a miser for vinegar, a moderate person for salt, and a madman to toss it well."

1 pound Boston, Bibb or romaine lettuce, or in combination

Bruschetta:
**1 Italian breadstick or toasted crust of
bread**
1 clove garlic, halved

Salsa Vinaigrette:
6 tablespoons olive, walnut, or peanut oil
**1½ to 2 tablespoons wine vinegar, rice
wine vinegar, or lemon juice**
¼ teaspoon prepared Dijon mustard
**¼ teaspoon each, fresh thyme, basil, and
oregano or ⅛ teaspoon each dried
(soaked in few drops of oil)**
5 twists of a pepper mill
1 teaspoon grated Parmesan cheese
YIELD: Four to six servings

1. Thoroughly wash the greens and
dry completely in a salad basket or spin-
ner, or roll in an absorbent towel and refrigerate for about an hour before
dressing.

2. Prepare the *Bruschetta* by brushing
the breadstick or crust of bread with oil
before rubbing with the cut clove of garlic.
Place the *Bruschetta* and the greens in a
salad bowl.

3. Prepare the *Salsa Vinaigrette* by
blending the oil and wine vinegar, rice
wine vinegar, or lemon juice, depending
on taste. Add the mustard and herbs, then
mix into the *vinaigrette* sauce the pepper
and grated Parmesan cheese. Pour over
the greens and *Bruschetta* before serving.

Bonus Ideas: Italians also enjoy the ritual of dressing their salads individually.
Cruets of oil and vinegar, together with
the ingredients required for the *Salsa Vinaigrette,* are made available at the table,
the salad already served on individual
plates. Fresh tomatoes, cut into wedges,

are often added to the green salad after it
has been dressed.

One of my favorite Italian green salads
is **Indivia con Rugola,** or Belgian Endive
and Arugola Salad. To serve four to six,
cut the ends of 3 endives, separate the
leaves, and wash with ½ bunch of arugola.
Cut the leaves of both greens into ½-inch
pieces and dry thoroughly. Pour *Salsa
Vinaigrette* over the greens and toss well
before serving. Should arugola not be
available, use ½ bunch of watercress and
10 chopped walnuts to prepare **Watercress, Endive, and Walnut Salad.** Do not
cut the endives, but place the separated
leaves on 6 individual plates, and garnish
with sprigs of watercress and chopped
walnuts before adding the dressing. Serve
immediately.

You may wish to try the above-men-
tioned **Insalatona Mista,** or medley of
cooked vegetables. For six servings, boil
and peel 3 medium potatoes, then cut into
¼-inch slices, and place in a salad bowl.
Prepare 1 large green and 1 yellow or red
sweet pepper by skewering them and
roasting in a broiler or on top of the
range. Rotate the peppers until the skins
are blistered all over, but not charred. Peel
off skins, core, remove the seeds, and cut
into 1-inch strips. Place ½ pound of green
or waxed beans in 2 tablespoons of water
in a pan to which cookware spray has
been applied; sauté until tender but still
firm. Drain thoroughly, add beans, with
the pepper strips, to the salad bowl. Drain
and cut into quarters 1 cup of canned
whole beets; mix with the other ingredients. Pour *Salsa Vinaigrette* over the vegetables, adding coarse salt and freshly
ground pepper to taste, and toss gently.

Serve as a *contorno* with meat and fish dishes, or add chopped pieces of cooked meat or fish for a light one-course meal.

BUDINO DI PESCHE*
(Peach Pudding)

Probably influenced by the hordes of British tourists who have visited Italy over the years, the Italians have imaginatively adopted this dessert as one of their own. It can be made just as easily with fresh apricots, berries, pineapple, or bananas.

8 large peaches
2 tablespoons honey or pure maple syrup
¾ cup white wine
3 egg whites
Cookware spray
YIELD: Four servings

1. Peel and pit the peaches and cut them into ½-inch pieces. Apply cookware spray to a skillet and add the peaches, honey, and wine. Sauté over moderate heat for about 15 minutes, or until tender.

2. Sieve the peaches in a food mill or purée in an electric blender until they have the consistency of jam; set aside and cool.

3. Using a balloon whisk or electric beater, whip the egg whites until they form peaks. Fold into the peach mixture.

4. Apply cookware spray to a 2-quart metal or ovenproof mold and add the mixture. Set the mold in a shallow pan with warm water to a depth of 1 inch. Bake in an oven at 325° F for about 30 minutes. Remove and cool for about 15 minutes. Unmold and serve warm or slightly chilled, as you prefer.

Bonus Ideas: Instead of baking in the oven, you can use a double boiler, cooking for 30 minutes. To chill quickly, set the mold in ice water.

The Italians have devised puddings in many fascinating variations. Try **Budino di Ricotta***, or Ricotta Cheese Pudding. For six servings, force 1½ pounds of low-fat ricotta or cottage cheese through a fine sieve and set aside in a bowl. Soak 2 tablespoons golden seedless raisins and 5 tablespoons **Candied Orange and Lemon Peel** in ⅓ cup of rum. Apply cookware spray to a deep circular baking dish and coat it with wheat germ, finely grated bread crumbs, or graham crackers. Beat 6 egg whites until they form peaks. Combine the ricotta with 4 teaspoons arrowroot and 4 tablespoons honey, maple syrup, or fruit sugar; add the raisin and rum mixture, 1 teaspoon of grated lemon rind, and a pinch of cinnamon. Blend thoroughly, then fold in the egg whites. Pour the mixture into the baking dish up to ½ the depth of the dish. Bake in an oven at 375° F for about 1 hour, or until the surface of the pudding is lightly golden in color. Let stand in the oven with the heat turned off until it is cooled. Unmold and serve at room temperature or thoroughly chilled with **Praline Powder.**

Try using Praline Powder to prepare **Salsa di Nocciole,** or Custard Sauce Praline, an ideal accompaniment to **Torta di Frutta** (Fresh Fruit Cake). To prepare this imaginative recipe for eight servings, stir gently 6 egg whites into a large bowl with ½ cup of pulverized fruit or date sugar. Add ⅛ teaspoon of coarse salt and stir in 2 cups of scalded skim milk, a very little at a time. Skim off any foam; then add

½ pod of vanilla bean or 1 teaspoon of extract.

CANDIED CITRUS PEEL

Both candied fruit and candied citrus peel can be prepared without using potentially harmful sucrose sugars.

1 cup of orange, lemon, lime or grapefruit peels
1¼ cups water
⅓ cup honey, pure maple syrup, or fruit sugar
YIELD: One cup

1. Gently grate the skin of the fruit before peeling; then peel and cut into thin strips. Place the peels in a heavy enameled pan, and cover with 1 cup of the water. Bring to a boil; then simmer for 10 to 15 minutes, depending on the bitterness you prefer. Drain well and repeat this process 3 or more times.

2. Using the same pan, add the balance of water and the honey; stir until the mixture boils, add the citrus peels, and continue boiling until they are transparent and the syrup has been absorbed. Place on a baking tin in an oven set at 200° F for up to 1 hour to dry thoroughly. Store in airtight and moisture-proof jars in a cool place.

Bonus Ideas: To prepare **Candied Fruits,** simmer in water until *al dente* 3½ cups of pitted cherries, peaches, apricots, or plums that have been peeled, cored, and sliced. Sections of quince, pineapple, citron, or whole figs or kumquats also can be candied. Drain the cooked fruit thoroughly while you combine 1¼ cups of fruit or date sugar, ⅓ cup of pure maple or corn syrup, and 1 cup of water. Bring to a boil, add the fruit, and simmer until the fruit is translucent; when adding the fruit, take care not to overcrowd the pan. Skim the fruit from the syrup and drain on paper toweling. Dust with pulverized fruit sugar and dry thoroughly on racks in sunshine, or on baking tins in an oven set at 250° F. Store between layers of waxed paper in a tightly covered, moisture-proof container.

MENU

Risotto con Asparagi
Scaloppine al Marsala
Cipolline Agrodolce
Insalata Caprese
Pere al Vino Rosso

Risotto with Asparagus
Veal Scallops with Marsala
Italian Sweet and Sour Onions
Capri-Style Mozzarella and Tomato Salad
Pears in Red Wine

RISOTTO CON ASPARAGI
(Risotto with Asparagus)

In Italy, as in other European countries as well as the United States, young, slender asparagus stalks are a harbinger of spring. These delicate vegetables are served steamed until *al dente,* then sprinkled with grated Parmesan cheese. When combined with a fine *risotto*, however, they are a rare delight. At an annual dinner of the prestigious Accademia Italiana della Cucina in New York City, a guest speaker paraphrased the old Italian adage about cheese and pears: "Don't let the farmers know how magnificent rice and asparagus are together, or they will keep them all for themselves!"

Whenever possible, round-grained Italian rice (available in ethnic shops and markets) should be used for *risotto;* the more generally available long-grained Patna or Carolina rice can also be used with minor adjustments in the length of cooking time. Brown rice is an excellent alternate to Italian rice, but should be presoaked in water for about 2 hours and will require longer cooking time.

Whichever type of rice you select, unless using a pressure cooker, you must stir the rice mixture constantly with a wooden spoon, adding additional broth as necessary. Cook only until just *al dente*. And a word of caution from those experts in rice cookery, the Chinese, whose New Year's greeting is, "May your rice never burn."

7 cups chicken bouillon or canned
    consommé
2½ pounds asparagus
1 teaspoon coarse salt
2 quarts boiling water
½ cup chopped onion
1 tablespoon water or dry vermouth
1 cup white wine or dry vermouth
2 cups rice
1 tablespoon polyunsaturated margarine
    (optional)
1 cup grated Parmesan cheese
Cookware spray
YIELD: Six servings

1. In a saucepan, bring the bouillon to a boil and let simmer until ready for use. Wash and scrape the asparagus with a knife or vegetable peeler; cut off and discard the tough ends. Add the salt to the water and bring to a boil. Steam or boil the asparagus for about 12 minutes, or until tender but firm. Drain thoroughly and set aside.

2. Apply cookware spray to a heavy pan or casserole and sauté the onions with 1 tablespoon of water until translucent. Add the wine and cook over high heat until reduced by one half.

3. Add the rice and stir constantly for about 3 minutes, until the grains are coated and have become transparent. Add 5 cups of hot bouillon and stir well over high heat until the rice absorbs the liquid. Add 1 cup of bouillon, cover, and cook over low-to-medium heat, continuing to stir and adding small quantities of additional bouillon until the rice is tender and firm. Depending on the type of rice you use, the cooking time will be between 20 and 35 minutes.

4. About 3 minutes before the rice is *al dente*, add the cooked asparagus; remove from the heat after 3 minutes, add the optional margarine and ½ cup of grated Parmesan cheese. Mix well and serve immediately on a heated platter, with the balance of the Parmesan in a separate bowl.

Bonus Ideas: Italy has literally hundreds of *risotto* dishes, variously combined with vegetables, seafood, meats, poultry, game, fruits, nuts, and other delicacies. Cooking liquids are reserved daily for use in future *risotto* dishes. Some restaurants, like the Splugen Bräu on the Corso Europa in Milan, feature a different *risotto* specialty each day—with seemingly endless variations.

Risotto alla Milanese, or Risotto Milanese Style, is probably the most renowned. You can make it by adding 2 ounces raw beef marrow or 2 tablespoons margarine and 5 twists of a pepper mill when sautéing the chopped onions in step 2 of the above *risotto* recipe. In step 3, after the grains of rice are coated and transparent, soak ½ teaspoon of saffron or turmeric in 2 tablespoons of bouillon and add to the 5 cups of hot bouillon in which the rice is stirred.

Risotto ai Funghi, or Risotto with Mushrooms, is made simply by adding 1 ounce of presoaked dried mushrooms, chopped, to the pan after the grains of rice are coated and transparent.

If you use ¼ pound of asparagus, ½ pound of sliced zucchini or summer squash, and ¼ pound each of peas and lima beans, you can prepare **Risotto alla Paesana,** or Rustic Risotto. Cook the asparagus and set aside. Sauté the zucchini, peas, and lima beans with the onions; then add 1½ cups of Italian-style canned plum tomatoes instead of the white wine. Bring the mixture to a boil, add the rice, and continue cooking, stirring constantly for about 20 minutes or until the rice is almost *al dente.* Add the cooked asparagus and cook for several minutes more. Season with margarine and grated Parmesan and serve on a heated platter, with additional Parmesan in a separate bowl.

If using a pressure cooker, you can avoid the constant stirring and cook the *risotto* in about 6 minutes, if using Italian or Carolina rice, or 10 minutes or more, if using brown rice. Remove the trivet from the cooker and sauté the onions until translucent; then proceed with the directions until the rice is coated and transparent. Pour in the boiling bouillon, cover, and cook at 15 pounds pressure for 6 minutes. Remove from heat and allow the pressure to reduce before removing the lid; the rice should have absorbed the liquid and be almost *al dente.* If it is not, allow to cook in the open pan. Stir in the cooked asparagus and add ½ cup of grated Parmesan cheese before serving.

SCALOPPINE AL MARSALA
(Veal Scallops with Marsala)

Veal is undoubtedly the most favored meat in Italy. Young, pinkish white, and very tender, it is cut from 2- to 3-month-old milk-fed calves; since its flavor is so delicate, veal dishes are generally enhanced by piquant and other sauces. American veal is either formula fed (and thus more expensive) or naturally fed with cow's milk. Although the latter type is far less costly, it can be very satisfactory, provided you find a butcher expert in the proper cutting of veal. You can usually find such a butcher in Italian sections throughout the country.

Especially for *scaloppine* dishes, be sure that your butcher cuts ¼-inch slices from the rump, leg, or from the top round, across the grain of the meat. Have him flatten them into 1⁄16-inch-thin scallops of solid meat, without fat or membrane tissue. Alternatively, you can do this at home by covering the veal slices with waxed paper and pounding them with a mallet or the side of a cleaver. The same procedure is used for veal cutlets, which are ½-inch slices of the same cuts of meat.

There is virtually no fat or waste with veal, and because it is low in calories and cholesterol, it is an extremely good value despite its generally high cost. If veal is dark reddish in color, it is not milk fed, but older and already baby beef. This type can be improved by blanching quickly with cold water, marinating in lemon juice for an hour, or marinating in milk overnight in the refrigerator. Should satisfactory veal not be available, you can substitute pounded chicken breasts in any *scaloppine* dish.

1 tablespoon olive, corn, or peanut oil
2 tablespoons polyunsaturated margarine
1½ pounds veal *scaloppine*, pounded thin
2 tablespoons corn flour
½ teaspoon coarse salt
6 twists of a pepper mill
¾ cup dry Marsala or Madeira
4 tablespoons polyunsaturated margarine
12 sprigs fresh parsley
6 lemon wedges
YIELD: Six servings

1. Heat the oil and 2 tablespoons margarine over a medium flame in a heavy-based skillet. Dredge the scallops in a mixture of the flour, salt, and pepper, shaking off any excess.
2. When the oil is hot, brown the scallops quickly (about 3 minutes) and transfer to a warm platter. Pour the Marsala into the skillet, deglaze the particles on the bottom, and boil over high heat for about 30 seconds. Lower the heat, add the 4 tablespoons of margarine and juices from the platter of *scaloppine*, and simmer until the sauce is thickened. Return the scallops to the skillet only long enough to coat them with the sauce on both sides.
3. Serve the *scaloppine* with the Marsala sauce on a warmed platter, garnished with sprigs of parsley and lemon wedges.

Bonus Ideas: Equally popular and simple to make is **Scaloppine al Limone,** or Veal Scallops with Lemon, also known as Veal *Piccata.* Instead of using wine, once the scallops have been browned quickly and transferred to a warm platter, add ¼ cup lemon juice, 2 tablespoons margarine, and ¼ cup of finely chopped parsley to the juices in the skillet. Stir the mixture well and pour over the hot scallops before serving. Garnish with thinly sliced lemon and sprigs of parlsey.

Another variation is **Scaloppine ai Funghi,** or Veal Scallops with Mushrooms. Once the scallops have been browned quickly in the skillet, remove the meat, add 3 tablespoons of dry white wine or sherry, and cook over high heat until the liquid is reduced to a third. Add ½ cup of bouillon or consommé and ½ pound of thinly sliced mushrooms. Cover the skillet and simmer gently over low heat for about 10 minutes before serving.

Two simple-to-make internationally renowned variations are **Scaloppine alla Milanese,** or Milanese Veal Scallops, and **Saltimbocca,** or Veal Scallops with Prosciutto—which are so delicious they "jump right into your mouth," as the Romans say. For each serving of *Saltimbocca,* use 2 pounded veal scallops. Cover each with 1 slice of *prosciutto* or Canadian bacon, 1 tablespoon each of grated Parmesan cheese and peeled, seeded, and chopped tomato,

1 fresh sage leaf or ¼ teaspoon dried sage, and 3 twists of a pepper mill. Bake in an oven at 375° F for 15 minutes in a baking dish coated with olive, corn, or peanut oil. *Saltimbocca* can also be rolled, skewered with toothpicks, and cooked until golden with 2 tablespoons each of margarine and oil. Remove the meat to a warm platter and deglaze the pan with ¼ cup of white wine or Marsala. Pour the sauce over the *Saltimbocca* before serving.

For Milanese Veal Scallops: use 6 pounded *scaloppine;* press coarse salt and pepper to taste into both sides of the scallops; coat with 2 beaten egg whites, then dredge with ½ cup of unsweetened wheat germ or bread crumbs. Sauté 3 minutes on each side in a combination of oil and margarine; drain on paper toweling, and serve with wedges of lemon. This recipe is also the basis for **Scaloppine San Giorgio,** or Veal Cordon Bleu. Simply place 1 slice each of Gruyère cheese and boiled ham between 2 scallops of equal size, and seal the edges with whisked egg whites. After they have set for 10 minutes, coat and cook the stuffed *scaloppine* as above. The great chef, Albert Stockli, of Restaurant Associates fame, ingeniously added the grated rinds of 2 lemons to the bread crumb mixture, a variation that I heartily recommend.

CIPOLLINE AGRODOLCE
(Italian Sweet and Sour Onions)

One of the first vegetables to be cultivated by man, onions are used extensively in Italian cuisine: incorporated into various dishes, enjoyed as an accoutrement with meat and poultry, and served as an entrée in their own right. Although sweet and sour dishes are more often associated with Chinese cuisine, this Italian favorite, with its combination of sweet and tart, is well worth the long simmering period required to prepare it.

2½ pounds small white onions
2 teaspoons fruit sugar, honey, or pure maple syrup
½ cup white wine vinegar
¼ teaspoon coarse salt
4 twists of a pepper mill
YIELD: Six servings

1. Blanch the unpeeled onions in boiling water. Peel the outer skin only and remove any sprouts, but do not remove the root. Cut crisscross notches in the root end.

2. Arrange a single layer of the onions in a large skillet or casserole and cover with a 1-inch depth of water. Add the balance of the ingredients, cover, and simmer over low heat for 30 minutes, turning the onions frequently.

3. Uncover and continue to simmer until the onions are golden brown and fork tender. Depending on the size of the onions, this will require up to 60 minutes. Turn the onions frequently, and add 1 tablespoon of warm water as necessary. Serve hot.

Bonus Ideas: A quicker variation is **Zucchini Agrodolce,** or Sweet and Sour Zucchini. Sauté 2 pounds of sliced zucchini in a skillet with 3 tablespoons each of margarine and olive, corn, or peanut oil. When browned on both sides, drain the slices on paper towels and set aside.

Deglaze the skillet with 2 teaspoons each of wine vinegar and lemon juice, and add ½ teaspoon coarse salt and 4 twists of a pepper mill. Blend thoroughly and set aside. Slice 2 purple onions and sauté in 3 tablespoons margarine until slightly softened. Rub 1 cut clove of garlic on the inside of a 2-quart baking dish or casserole and layer with half of the cooked zucchini. Cover with the cooked onions; then top with a layer of the balance of the zucchini. Pour the vinegar mixture over the top and sprinkle with 2 tablespoons grated Parmesan cheese. Bake in an oven at 350° F for about 15 minutes, and serve garnished with fresh basil or mint leaves.

My personal favorite, as a luncheon entrée, is **Cipolle Farcite Napoletane,** or Neapolitan Stuffed Onions. For 6 servings, slice off both ends of 6 large, unpeeled onions. Cook in boiling water for about 10 minutes. Remove, drain, and peel the onions when cool. Meanwhile, combine 1 cup skim ricotta cheese, 2 egg whites, 1 tablespoon oil, 1 tablespoon minced parsley, 1 teaspoon coarse salt, and 4 twists of a pepper mill. Gently remove the centers from the onions, leaving a ½-inch-thick shell. Cover the bottom hole of each onion with part of the center. Chop ½ cup of the balance of the centers and blend into the ricotta mixture. Preheat the oven to 350° F, simultaneously melting 1 tablespoon margarine. Fill the onion cavities with the mixture and place in a large baking dish or casserole. Brush with the melted margarine and bake for 20 minutes. Serve hot.

A heartier version is **Cipolle Farcite all' Italiana,** or Italian Stuffed Onions. Prepare 6 onions as in the above recipe, but retain and cook the top slices as well. Sauté the chopped onion centers and ¼ pound sliced mushrooms with 2 tablespoons of wine or consommé until the onions are translucent. Add 1 cup cooked minced veal or beef and season with a dash each of coarse salt, freshly ground pepper, and nutmeg. Spoon the stuffing into the cavities of the onions and replace the cooked tops. Apply cookware spray and 4 tablespoons margarine to a heavy-based pan. Cook over medium heat until the margarine is melted; then gently place the stuffed onions into the pan. Pour heated bouillon or consommé to cover the lower halves of the onions. Cover and simmer for 25 minutes or until fork tender, basting occasionally.

INSALATA CAPRESE
(Capri-style Mozzarella and Tomato Salad)

Often after a particularly rich dish, Italians will request something light—*"qualche cosa di leggiero."*

A popular favorite in this category is this delicate salad combining the flavors and textures of mozzarella cheese, tomatoes, and oregano. These colorful ingredients appeal equally to the eye and the palate, lending themselves to creative arrangements, and may be served as an antipasto or summer luncheon dish.

3 large ripe tomatoes
1½ pounds mozzarella cheese
Salt, pepper, and oregano to taste

¼ cup olive oil, or olive combined with
   corn or peanut oil
Sprigs of fresh basil or mint
YIELD: Six servings

1. Wash and dry the tomatoes and cut
2 of them into slices. Slice the third tomato up to the base, leaving the slices attached. Spread the slices gently, giving the
tomato a fan effect.

2. Slice the mozzarella and place the
slices between each section of the tomato-
fan. Place the stuffed tomato as the centerpiece on a circular platter, and alternate
slices of the cheese and tomatoes in a circle around it. Season with salt, pepper,
oregano, and oil, and garnish with fresh
basil or mint leaves.

Bonus Ideas: For individual servings,
use 6 smaller tomatoes cut into fan shapes.
Adjust the arrangement of the ingredients
to the shape of the platter you use,
whether circular, rectangular, or boat
shaped. I like to garnish the outer rim of
the platter with individual basil leaves and
use small sprigs to decorate the top of the
centerpiece.

PERE AL VINO ROSSO
(Pears in Red Wine)

You will need firm pears for this recipe.
The variety, of course, will depend on the
season: In spring, Sekels are available, followed by Bartletts in late summer; in the
fall, you will find Comices, and in winter,
Boscs and Anjous. Whatever the variety,
be sure to leave the stems on while cook-

ing and to avoid overpuncturing when
testing for doneness, which will mar the
attractiveness of the dish.

1½ cups red wine
½ cup of fruit sugar, honey, or pure maple
   syrup
6 large pears with stems, whole and
   unpeeled
3 tablespoons unflavored gelatin
1 tablespoon lemon juice
2 tablespoons port wine
YIELD: Six servings

1. Prepare a syrup by boiling 1 cup of
the red wine with half the sugar for about
5 minutes. Add the pears to the mixture
and cook over low heat until tender.

2. Sprinkle the gelatin over 1 cup of
cold water in a saucepan, and cook over
low heat for 3 minutes, stirring constantly.
Add 1 cup of boiling water, the balance of
wine and sugar, and the lemon juice.

3. Boil the gelatin mixture for 5 minutes, then pour into a ring mold. Cool and
refrigerate for about 2 hours, or until firm.

4. Remove the cooked pears from the
heat and add the port wine. When the
pears are cooled and the liquid set, dip the
chilled mold briefly into hot water and
turn the gelatin ring onto a serving platter.
Arrange the pears in the middle of the ring
and coat with some of the syrup, serving
the balance as an accompaniment.

Bonus Ideas: For individual servings,
prepare the gelatin, then chill and chop
into squares. Surround each pear with
chopped gelatin before coating the pear
with syrup. You can easily adapt this recipe to any other favorite fruit, except fresh
pineapple, which counteracts the jelling.

MENU

Antipasto all' Italiana
Gnocchi di Zucca
Bistecca alla Fiorentina
Crocchette di Patate E Prosciutto
Pan di Spagna
Macedonia di Frutta

Italian Antipasto
Pumpkin Gnocchi
Florentine Broiled Beefsteak
Potato Croquettes with Ham
Italian Sponge Cake
Medley of Fruit

ANTIPASTO ALL' ITALIANA
(Italian Antipasto)

Although antipasto is closely associated with Italian cuisine, Italians reserve this dish for special occasions only—unlike the French, who habitually have *hors d'oeuvre variés* before lunch. As a rule, the Italian will prefer to start his meal with lean slices of prosciutto, served with freshly ground pepper or with a slice of melon, fresh figs, or persimmons, when they are in season. Nevertheless, many restaurants in Italy feature a variety of antipasto, and one could make a meal of this one dish alone.

When *antipasto* is served at the beginning of a meal, I recommend an assortment combining no more than 3 items, which are sufficient for a colorful appetizer. When you are serving a large group

buffet style, then a wide variety of ingredients, as found in restaurants, is more appropriate.

Following are recipes for a number of appetizers that you can combine judiciously to suit any main course. Adjust the number of servings according to the combination you decide upon. All of these dishes can be used as luncheon entrées.

MELANZANE RIPIENE
(Italian Stuffed Eggplant)

4 small eggplants, unpeeled
½ teaspoon coarse salt
½ cup olive, corn or peanut oil
1 cup skinned fresh tomatoes or Italian-style canned plum tomatoes
1 onion, sliced
1 clove garlic, minced
3 tablespoons white wine or consommé
½ pound ground beef, veal, or lamb
1 dash cayenne pepper
3 fresh basil leaves, or ¼ teaspoon dried
1 tablespoon polyunsaturated margarine
1 sprig fresh mint, or ¼ teaspoon dried
Cookware spray
YIELD: Four servings

1. Trim the ends from the eggplants and cut in half lengthwise; scoop out the soft pulp and set aside. Sprinkle half the salt and 1 tablespoon of oil into the eggplant shells. Mash the pulp, or purée through a vegetable mill or in an electric blender.

2. Remove stem ends and chop the tomatoes; bring them to a simmer in a

saucepan over medium heat; cook for 30 minutes. Sieve or purée the tomatoes; return to the pan and simmer with the balance of the salt and 1 tablespoon of oil for 5 minutes longer.

3. Apply cookware spray to a skillet and sauté the onion and garlic with half the wine or consommé, until the onion becomes translucent. Increase the heat to medium, add the ground meat, and cook until it loses its pink color. Add the cayenne pepper, then blend in the pulp, basil, and the balance of the wine or consommé. Bring to a boil, cover, and simmer over low heat for 15 minutes, stirring frequently.

4. Coat a baking dish or casserole with the balance of the oil. Fill the eggplant shells with the meat mixture; arrange them in a single layer in the dish to which ¼ cup of water has been added. Dot the stuffed eggplants with the margarine or brush the tops with oil. Bake in an oven at 350° F for about 30 minutes, or until fork tender. Serve hot or at room temperature, with the tomato sauce ladled over the stuffed eggplants and garnished with the mint.

Bonus Ideas: If you prefer not to use meat in the stuffing, try substituting ½ pound of mozzarella cheese, cut into cubes. Eliminate the onions and combine the tomatoes with the cheese and mashed eggplant pulp instead of preparing the tomato sauce. Bake and serve.

Italians also serve stuffed zucchini and stuffed tomatoes, dishes not unlike the Greek *dolmathes,* which are served as *mezes,* or appetizing snacks, with wine before a meal.

INVOLTINI DI PROSCIUTTO ED ASPARAGI
(Prosciutto Rolls with Asparagus)

24 asparagus, about 1½ pounds
1 tablespoon coarse salt
4 large slices prosciutto, thinly sliced
3 tablespoons polyunsaturated margarine, melted
¾ cup grated Parmesan cheese
Cookware spray
YIELD: Four servings

1. Scrape the asparagus stalks with a knife or vegetable peeler, and trim off and discard the tough ends. Tie into bundles of 6; place standing upright in a tall covered pot with about 2 inches of salted water. Steam for 10 minutes, or until *al dente.* If you prefer, bring 4 quarts of water to a boil; then add the salt and cook the bundles of asparagus for about 10 minutes, or until tender but still firm.

2. Drain, untie, and let the asparagus cool. Place 6 stalks on each slice of *prosciutto,* brush with 1 teaspoon of melted margarine, and sprinkle with 1 tablespoon of Parmesan cheese. Roll the slices and secure with toothpicks.

3. Apply cookware spray to a baking dish and gently arrange the rolls in a single layer. Sprinkle with the remaining grated cheese; pour the balance of the melted margarine over the rolls and bake in an oven at 350° F for about 10 minutes. Serve hot.

Bonus Ideas: If necessary, lean ham or thinly sliced Canadian bacon may be used instead of *prosciutto.* Although I don't think it necessary, Italians often serve these *involtini* on trimmed slices of bread toasted or browned in margarine.

CROSTINI DI FEGATINI DI POLLO
(Chicken Livers on Toast)

½ pound chicken livers
½ onion, thinly sliced
2 tablespoons olive, corn, or peanut oil
2 tablespoons polyunsaturated margarine
1 sprig fresh sage, or ⅛ teaspoon dried
1 teaspoon coarse salt
4 slices bread or 8 cocktail crackers
1 tablespoon lemon juice or vinegar
2 tablespoons grated Parmesan cheese
   (optional)
Cookware spray
YIELD: Four servings

1. Pat the chicken livers dry, and chop into small pieces. Apply cookware spray to a skillet; sauté the onion with the oil and margarine combined until translucent. Add the chicken livers, sage, salt, and the wine, and sauté over medium heat for 10 minutes, or until they lose their pink color. Remove from the heat when cooked.

2. Toast the bread and cut into triangular halves. Add the lemon juice and grated Parmesan cheese to the livers; then spread on the toast. Place under a broiler briefly to heat through before serving.

Bonus Ideas: I like to prepare these *crostini* using chicken giblets cut into small pieces. Since gizzard and heart require longer cooking, I sauté them first until almost tender before adding the chicken livers. Before adding the lemon juice and grated cheese, remove the pan from the oven and stir two egg whites into the giblet mixture. In Milan, the superb Trattoria Da Me serves this dish made with the innards from veal or lamb on toasted *polenta,* a memorable variation.

INSALATA FRUTTI DI MARE*
(Mixed Seafood Salad)

This Italian favorite is also one of mine. When serving antipasto, I almost invariably include a delicious combination of seafood; and since this salad freezes well, I generally prepare large quantities, reserving portions in the freezer for future use. This dish can be varied to suit your personal preferences as well as the availability of fresh seafood in your market. However, to get a blend of tastes and textures, use as many seafoods as you can.

1 dozen each, mussels and baby clams
½ cup olive oil
7 tablespoons vinegar
2 teaspoons coarse salt
¾ pound small shrimp, unshelled
½ pound sea scallops
1 pound octopus
½ pound squid
2 each, carrots, celery stalks, and onions
2 sweet red peppers
6 each, black and green olives
¼ cup lemon juice
2 tablespoons minced parsley
5 twists of a pepper mill
1 clove garlic, mashed
½ teaspoon fresh marjoram, or ¼
   teaspoon dried
1 head of Boston lettuce
YIELD: Six servings

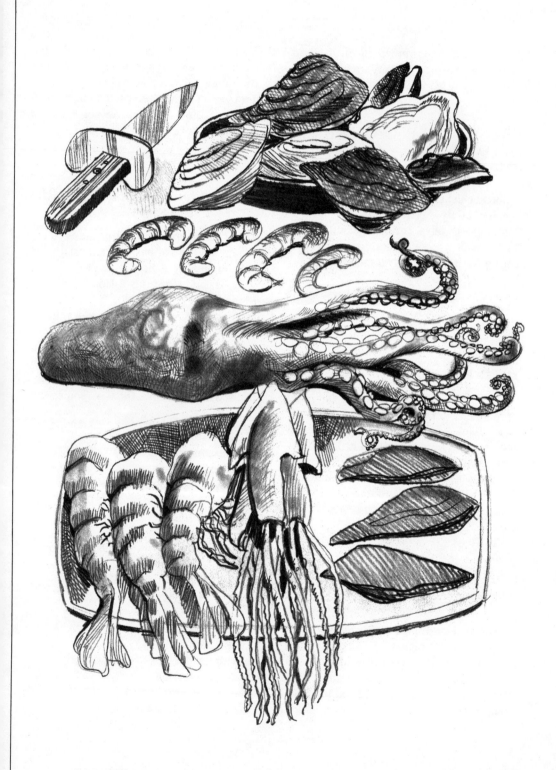

1. Place the thoroughly scrubbed mussels and clams in a large pan with 1 tablespoon of oil; cook, covered, over high heat for 10 minutes, or until the shells open. Remove the meat from the shells, rinsing and removing any sand. Strain the juices and cooking liquid and set aside.

2. Bring to a boil 2 quarts of water to which 2 tablespoons vinegar and ½ teaspoon salt have been added. Wash the unshelled shrimp in cold water, then cook for about 2 minutes. Drain, cool, peel, and devein the shrimp. Leave the small shrimp whole, but cut any larger ones into ½-inch pieces and set aside.

3. Thoroughly wash the scallops in cold water. Bring 2 cups of water to a boil, having added 1 tablespoon vinegar and ½ teaspoon salt. Cook the scallops in the boiling mixture for 2 minutes. Drain, cool, and cut into ½-inch cubes. Set aside.

4. It is preferable to purchase the octopus and squid already cleaned, peeled, and ready for use. If not, invert and remove the inside bag of the octopus; discard the eye, the beak or mouth, and the extreme ends of the tentacles. Wash thoroughly and beat the octopus vigorously with a kitchen mallet to tenderize it. In a similar manner, clean the squid by removing its ink sac, entrails, eyes, and bone; wash thoroughly. Place in a large pot under running cold water and peel off the outer skin.

5. Peel but leave whole the carrots, celery stalks, and onions. Place one of each into 2 separate pots, each containing 2½ cups water, half the reserved liquid from the mussels and clams, 2 tablespoons vinegar, and ½ teaspoon salt. Bring both pots to a boil; then place the octopus in one pot and the squid in the other. Cover and simmer over low heat until fork tender. The squid will cook in about 20 minutes, and the octopus in about 45 minutes. Drain, cool, and cut the octopus into ⅜-inch circular slices. Set both aside, discarding the cooked vegetables.

6. Place the peppers under the broiler and rotate them frequently until roasted and blistered on all sides. Peel and discard the charred skins. Cut the peppers lengthwise into 1½-inch strips, discarding cores and seeds. Pat strips dry with paper toweling.

7. Arrange all the pieces of seafood in a large mixing bowl. Pit and slice the olives; add to the bowl with the red pepper, lemon juice, parsley, and oil. Mix thoroughly; add additional salt if necessary, then the freshly ground pepper, mashed garlic, and marjoram. Cover the bowl and let the mixture stand for 2 hours. Remove the garlic, and mix gently before serving on a bed of lettuce.

Bonus Ideas: If refrigerated or frozen beforehand, allow sufficient time for the *insalata* to come to room temperature. Mix gently and serve.

FUNGHI TRIFOLATI
(Sautéed Mushrooms)

1 pound whole mushrooms
4 tablespoons dry white wine or bouillon
1 teaspoon minced garlic
½ teaspoon coarse salt
4 twists of a pepper mill
1 teaspoon lemon juice (optional)
2 tablespoons minced parsley
Cookware spray
YIELD: Four servings

1. Gently brush the mushrooms clean with a damp cloth. Cut off and discard the ends of the stems. Cut the mushrooms lengthwise into ¼-inch slices.

2. Apply cookware spray to a large skillet, add some of the wine, and sauté the garlic until soft. Turn the heat to high, add the mushrooms and the balance of the wine, and cook for 3 minutes. Reduce to low heat, add the salt and pepper, and cook for 7 minutes more, stirring frequently. Stir in the parsley and remove from the heat.

3. Sprinkle with lemon juice; add salt if necessary. Serve at room temperature.

Bonus Ideas: Italians are very fond of mushrooms, especially the renowned field mushrooms called *porcini.* You can use whole, small buttom mushrooms in the above recipe. If you have large mushrooms with 2-inch caps, you can use 12 to serve six and prepare **Funghi Ripieni,** or Lombard Stuffed Mushrooms. Remove the stems from the cleaned mushrooms and mince fine. Apply cookware spray to a skillet and sauté 2 tablespoons minced onion with 2 tablespoons white wine or bouillon until translucent. Add 3 tablespoons of chopped *prosciutto* or Canadian bacon and cook over medium heat for about 1 minute. Add the chopped stems, salt, and pepper and sauté for 3 minutes, stirring frequently. Prepare a **Béchamel Sauce** with 1½ tablespoons corn or potato flour, 1½ tablespoons margarine, and 1 cup of skim milk. Transfer the contents of the skillet to a bowl; add the warm sauce and ¼ cup grated Parmesan cheese. Mix thoroughly. Rub a baking dish with margarine, and add in a single layer of mushroom caps filled with the stuffing. Sprinkle with bread crumbs or unsweetened wheat germ and dot each cap with margarine. Bake in a preheated oven at 375° F for 15 minutes (use the upper third of the oven). Let stand for 10 minutes before serving.

Of course, many other items can be included in *Antipasto all'Italiana.* Crisp, fresh vegetables—finocchio, celery hearts, radishes, and carrot sticks—are often used. Anchovy filets, marinated artichoke hearts, roasted sweet peppers, and wafer-thin slices of *prosciutto* and salami are other favorites. However, keep in mind that in Italy, cheese (with only one exception I know of) is never served as an antipasto; rather it is reserved for the end of the meal. The exception is the recipe that follows for an Italian cheese fondue, which is served as the only appetizer before the meal.

FONDUTA ALLA PIEMONTESE
(Piedmontese Fondue)

This appetizer is as popular in the region of Piedmont as *fondue neuchâteloise* is in Switzerland. However, unlike the Swiss, the Italians do not serve their fondue still simmering at the table, to be used as a dip. Rather, it is prepared beforehand in the kitchen, then served hot in deep plates.

¾ cup skim milk
¾ pound Piedmontese Fontina cheese,
    diced
2 egg whites
2 tablespoons olive or corn oil
½ cup polyunsaturated margarine

¼ teaspoon white pepper
1 white truffle, thinly sliced, or ¼ pound
   mushrooms, minced
8 slices bread, toasted
YIELD: Six servings

1. Heat the milk and combine with the diced cheese in a bowl. Let the mixture steep for several hours, preferably overnight.

2. Place the mixture in the top of a double boiler, over hot, but not boiling, water. Cook over low heat, stirring constantly with a wooden spoon, until the cheese melts. Beat the egg whites for about 1 minute until foamy, and add with the oil and margarine to the mixture. Continue to cook, stirring constantly, until the fondue is smooth, thick, and shiny. Add pepper.

3. Pour into deep plates, sprinkle with the sliced truffles, and serve with the toast, which has been cut into triangles or finger sticks.

Bonus Ideas: If you prefer to serve the fondue still simmering at the table, you can use an electric skillet or any casserole with a heat source for cooking. However, the fondue will require constant stirring and must never reach the boiling point. In this case, serve the truffles and pepper separately.

If you are unable to find Fontina, you can use Gruyère or Edam—but you will be sacrificing both authenticity and taste. As we learned in Lerici, the Italians have adopted from the French and the Swiss **Fondue Bourguignonne.** For six servings, Mamma Omelia cuts 2 pounds of filet or sirloin of beef into ¾-inch cubes. She sprinkles 1½ teaspoons coarse salt over the meat, wraps it in a cloth towel, and re-frigerates it for 24 hours, permitting the meat cubes to absorb the salt. You may then preheat 1½ cups of olive, corn, or peanut oil and keep it bubbling hot in a casserole over a heat source at the table. Serve the meat cubes on a platter with long forks. Each diner can spear the cubes and cook them to taste in the hot oil for 1 or more minutes. The cooked meat can be dipped into each of several dipping sauces provided in separate bowls at the table. Mamma Omelia's suggestions for sauces are ready-made ketchup; barbecue sauce or mayonnaise; **Salsa Indiana,** which is mayonnaise blended with minced onion and a dash of curry powder; **Salsa Fantasia,** which is mayonnaise blended with minced garlic and finely chopped parsley; or **Salsa Andalusa,** which is mayonnaise combined with grilled and diced pepperoni or Canadian bacon, tomato sauce, and minced parsley.

GNOCCHI DI ZUCCA*
(Pumpkin *Gnocchi*)

This is a specialty Italians favor, and one you will enjoy making and serving. I first savored *gnocchi* made with pumpkin at a pleasant and convenient restaurant in Milan, Il Ristorante del Grisi, which is near the Hotel Principe e Savoia. Surprisingly, I have never seen a recipe for it in any cookbook of Italian cuisine, including those which claim to be comprehensive. Neither Luigi Carnacina, Pellegrino Artusi, or the other well-known writers on Italian cookery even mention pumpkin gnocchi, much less have a recipe for this distinctive dish. The following recipe is adapted from one used by Il Ristorante del Grisi and from another by Rosalba Serreti, an excellent cook in the Italian tradition, who also provided the variation for *Lasagne di Zucca Rosalba* (included in the Bonus Ideas).

1¾ pounds fresh or canned pumpkin
1 teaspoon coarse salt
5 twists of a pepper mill
1 dash saffron or turmeric powder
4 tablespoons polyunsaturated margarine
9 ounces semolina or potato flour
2 egg whites
2 tablespoons olive, corn, or peanut oil
¾ cup grated Parmesan cheese
YIELD: Six servings

1. If using fresh pumpkin, cut the flesh into 1-inch pieces and place in a pan with salt, pepper, and saffron. Cook the mixture, covered, until the natural moisture of the pumpkin is released. Uncover and boil for about 1 minute, or until fork tender. Mash with a fork, or purée through a food mill or in an electric blender. If using canned pumpkin, simply blend in the seasonings.

2. Melt half the margarine in a pan. Add the pumpkin and heat through; add the semolina in small quantities, or "as if it were raining," as the Italians say. Stir the mixture into a smooth consistency.

3. Remove from heat and add the egg whites, oil, ½ cup of grated cheese, and the balance of the margarine. Blend until smooth.

4. On an unfloured board, knead the mixture into a dough with a rolling pin, and form the dough until it is ½ inch thick. Using the rim of a liqueur glass or egg cup, cut the dough into circles of 1½-inches in diameter.

5. Arrange the *gnocchi* in parallel lines in a baking dish; sprinkle with the balance of the Parmesan cheese and dot with margarine. Bake in an oven at 400° F for several minutes to gratinée, until the surface is browned.

Bonus Ideas: Instead of preparing a gratinée, let the *gnocchi* set, then simmer 2 to 3 minutes in boiling water until they float. Drain, serve with **Marinara Tomato Sauce** or **Bolognese Sauce.** A tantalizing variation is to serve Pumpkin *Gnocchi* with **Salsa di Cannellini.** Cannellini Bean Sauce is prepared by thoroughly rinsing 1 16-ounce can of white cannellini beans, draining and puréeing through a food mill or in an electric blender, and mixing with several tablespoons of Marinara Tomato Sauce. Serve the *gnocchi* with the *Salsa di Cannellini,* grated Parmesan cheese, and dabs of low-fat ricotta cheese. Remember that fresh pumpkin has its own moisture, depending on its freshness. When necessary, add small quantities of skimmed milk while cooking the pumpkin to a smooth consistency.

To prepare Rosalba's Pumpkin Lasagne, or **Lasagn di Zucca Rosalba*,** use 1 pound of semolina flour and only ½ pound of pumpkin, together with the balance of ingredients listed in the above recipe. Proceed as directed above to form the dough. Roll the dough into a ¼-inch thickness and cut into strips 2 inches wide by 8 inches long. If using a rectangular pan, crisscross the strips over alternating layers of meatballs, ground meat, mozzarella, or ricotta cheese, and top with

Salsa di Cannellini. You may wish to note that Italians also use purée of pumpkin, instead of ground meat or ricotta cheese, to stuff ravioli.

BISTECCA ALLA FIORENTINA
(Florentine Broiled Beefsteak)

The excellence of Tuscan beef is matched only by the simple and direct method used by the Florentines to broil it—preferably over hot coals. It can also be prepared with a gas or electric broiler, only, however, at the highest temperatures possible. Traditionally, 1½-inch-thick T-bone steaks are used, but other cuts of young beef can be used as well.

Some Italians prefer to marinate the steak in oil for an hour before cooking; some brush with oil while broiling; while others prefer adding a few drops of oil or margarine when the steak is served. I find it preferable to bring steak to room temperature and then season with freshly ground pepper and 1 tablespoon of oil before broiling.

2 T-bone steaks, 1½ inches thick
1 clove garlic (optional)
4 twists of a pepper mill
1 teaspoon coarse salt
4 tablespoons olive, corn, or peanut oil
8 lemon wedges
YIELD: Four servings

1. Trim the steaks of excess fat, cut each into 2 serving pieces, and bring to room temperature. If using the garlic, cut the clove and rub both sides of the steaks with it. Season each side with some of the salt and 1 twist of a pepper mill and brush with 1 tablespoon of oil. If using a gas or electric broiler, preheat at highest temperature for about 15 minutes.

2. Broil over a hot charcoal fire for 5 minutes on each side for rare and 7 minutes on each side for medium steaks. Serve immediately with 2 wedges of lemon for each serving.

Bonus Ideas: This dish can be prepared with shell or Porterhouse steaks, after the tougher tails have been removed and ground for other use. The same cuts, as well as rib steaks, can be pan-broiled to prepare **Bistecca Arrabbiata,** or Piquant Ruby Beefsteak. For four servings, have 2 large steaks cut to about ¾ inch thick, then sliced in half. Cover with waxed paper and flatten with a mallet or the side of a cleaver. Dip the steaks into cool water; drain, but do not pat dry. Apply cookware spray to a large skillet and place over high heat. When the skillet is very hot, add the steaks and sear 3 minutes on each side for rare and 5 minutes for medium steaks. Transfer to a warm platter, and season each side of the steaks with ⅛ teaspoon salt and 1 twist of a pepper mill. Using ½ cup each of red wine and Marsala, deglaze the skillet over high heat for about 1 minute. Add 2 minced cloves of garlic and 1 teaspoon fennel seeds. Lower the heat to medium and add 1 tablespoon tomato paste diluted in 1 tablespoon red wine and ¼ teaspoon chopped red pepper or chili pepper. Stir the mixture and cook 1 minute, or until the sauce has the consistency of a ruby-red syrup. Return the steaks and their juices to the skillet, turning the steaks in the sauce for about 2 minutes. Serve them with the sauce on a hot platter, and sprinkle with minced parsley.

Another variation is **Bistecche alla Siciliana,** or Sicilian Beefsteak. Prepare the steaks for four servings in the same manner as above. After heating the skillet to very hot, add 1 teaspoon minced garlic; then place the moist steaks into the skillet. Sear for 2 minutes on each side; then add 1 cup of peeled, seeded, and chopped tomatoes, ⅓ cup pitted black olives, ⅓ cup pimiento slices, and 2 tablespoons each of unsalted capers and diced celery. Season with 1 teaspoon salt, 5 twists of a pepper mill, and 1 teaspoon minced fresh oregano or ½ teaspoon dried. Cook for about 10 minutes; then cover the steaks with the sauce and serve on a warm platter.

CROCCHETTE DI PATATE E PROSCIUTTO COTTO*
(Potato Croquettes with Ham)

The genesis of this recipe is one of my favorite stories. Originally, it was given to me by an excellent cook in Virginia, who specialized in traditional Southern specialties. The recipe was named Southern Ham Croquettes and called for 2 cups of hominy grits. One day I served this dish to some visiting friends from Italy, and for one reason or another I substituted mashed potatoes for the grits. "*Crocchette fatte proprio come le faceva mia madre!*" exclaimed one of my guests. "I must have this recipe. They are exactly like those my mother used to make in Campania!" And

that's how I happened to make a "southern Italian–southern American specialty."

These croquettes can be served as an accoutrement, a main course, or, if made in small balls, as tantalizing appetizers.

2 cups mashed potatoes
3 egg whites
2 cups minced, cooked ham or Canadian bacon
2 tablespoons yogurt or sour cream
2 tablespoons melted polyunsaturated margarine
⅛ teaspoon cayenne pepper
½ teaspoon coarse salt
5 twists of a pepper mill
1 tablespoon olive, corn, or peanut oil
½ cup wheat germ or toasted bread crumbs
Cookware spray
YIELD: Four to six servings

1. Blend and beat together the potatoes, 2 of the egg whites, the ham, yogurt, margarine, cayenne pepper, and seasonings. Form into 8 or move oval-shaped croquettes, depending on the size preferred.

2. Apply cookware spray to a large baking dish and add a thin layer of oil, just enough to cover the bottom of the dish. Place the dish in an oven heated to 400° F.

3. Beat the remaining egg white for about 1 minute until foamy. Dip each of the croquettes into the egg white, then into the wheat germ until completely coated.

4. Drop a cube of bread into the hot oil in the oven. When the bread turns golden brown, the oil is about 375° F and ready. Cook the croquettes about 5 minutes on each side until golden brown. Drain on paper toweling and serve hot.

Bonus Ideas: In the United States, these croquettes often are served with warmed ketchup. However, I prefer serving them Italian style with wedges of lemon, **Salsa di Pomidoro** (Marinara Tomato Sauce), or **Salsa Bolognese** (Bolognese Sauce).

Croquettes can also be made with 2 cups of **polenta** or hominy grits, instead of mashed potatoes, and prepared in precisely the same manner. A striking variation—especially for serving as an appetizer or hors d'oeuvre—is **Crocchette Spinose,** or Potato Thistles. For six servings, blend and beat together 2 cups mashed potatoes, 2 cups minced ham, 2 tablespoons yogurt or sour cream, 2 tablespoons melted polyunsaturated margarine, ¼ cup grated Parmesan cheese, ½ teaspoon coarse salt, 5 twists of a pepper mill, 2 egg whites, and ⅛ teaspoon ground nutmeg. In a separate dish, combine 1 cup of crushed *vermicelli* (thin noodles) or shredded wheat with ⅓ cup of potato or rice flour. Form the potato mixture into 1½-inch balls and roll into the noodle mixture until completely coated. Apply cookware spray to a baking dish and pour a thin layer (about ¼ cup) of olive, corn, or peanut oil into the dish. Place in an oven at 400° F until the oil is very hot, about 375° F (or when a cube of bread inserted in the oil turns golden brown). Slip the Potato Thistles into the hot oil, and cook on all sides until they turn golden brown. Drain on paper toweling, and serve hot with lemon wedges.

Croquettes, of course, can be deep-fried, but I prefer the above method, which has the advantage or using less oil. The same technique, incidentally, can be used in preparing French-fried potatoes.

Italians, as mentioned previously, flavor croquettes with either of two of their fundamental tomato sauces.

SALSA DI POMIDORO*
(Marinara Tomato Sauce)

2 medium onions, chopped
1 clove garlic, minced
1 medium carrot, scraped and grated
2 tablespoons white wine, consommé, or water
3 pounds fresh tomatoes, chopped, or 1 35-ounce can of Italian-style plum tomatoes
1 teaspoon coarse salt
4 twists of a pepper mill
¼ teaspoon each, dried thyme and oregano
½ teaspoon honey or pure maple syrup
Cookware spray
YIELD: One quart

1. Apply cookware spray to a heavy saucepan and sauté the onions, garlic, and carrot in the wine. Cover and simmer for several minutes over medium heat until the onions are translucent.

2. Add the plum tomatoes and the balance of the ingredients; simmer gently over low heat, stirring frequently, for about 30 minutes, or until the sauce thickens. If you prefer a smooth sauce, force mixture through a fine sieve or food mill, or place in an electric blender at high speed for 15 seconds.

Bonus Ideas: To prepare 1 quart of **Salsa Bolognese*** (Bolognese Sauce), after sautéing the vegetables until the onions are translucent, add 1 pound of ground beef, or ½ pound of beef and ¼ pound each of Canadian bacon and chicken livers. Continue sautéing over medium heat until the beef has lost its pink color. Add ½ cup of red wine and cook 5 minutes longer. Add the tomatoes and the balance of the ingredients for Marinara Tomato Sauce, plus 1 bay leaf and 1 tablespoon of tomato paste or ketchup, and simmer for about 20 minutes over low heat, stirring occasionally. Press the sauce through a fine sieve or food mill, or place in an electric blender at high speed for 30 seconds until smooth. Return the sauce to the pan and simmer gently over low heat for 30 minutes. Longer simmering enhances the flavor of the sauce, although small amounts of boiling water should be added if it becomes too thick. For a richer sauce, you may wish to add 1 stalk of celery, minced; ½ green pepper, diced; and/or ⅓ cup of fresh or canned mushrooms, when first sautéing the vegetables. A pinch of ground nutmeg is optional when cooking the meat.

Either of these tomato sauces can be used with one of my mother's favorites: **Crocchette con Mozzarella e Prosciutto***, or Croquettes Stuffed with Mozzarella and Ham. To serve six, follow the recipe for **Potato Thistles** replacing the 2 cups of ham with ½ cup of *prosciutto,* minced cooked ham, or Canadian bacon and 1 cup of cubed mozzarella cheese. When the potato mixture has cooled, place on a lightly floured board and roll into a long loaf, 3 inches wide. Slice the roll into about 1 dozen 2-inch slices. Combine 2 tablespoons minced parsley with the ham and mozzarella, and place a spoonful in the center of each of the slices. Overlap the slices and roll into a ball with the stuffing encased. Dust with potato or rice flour, dip into a lightly beaten egg white, then roll in wheat germ, bread crumbs or crushed *vermicelli.* Allow to set for about 10 minutes while heating a thin layer of oil in a baking dish in an oven at 400° F. When the oil is about 375° F (when a bread cube dropped into the oil turns golden brown), cook the croquettes until golden on all sides. Drain on paper toweling and serve hot with lemon wedges or a spoonful of tomato sauce.

PAN DI SPAGNA*
(Italian Sponge Cake)

In Italy, sponge cake is referred to as being "in the Spanish style," implying an influence from earlier Spanish conquests. Nevertheless, it is used in a typically Italian manner as the base for many imaginative desserts, especially as an accoutrement to chilled **Macedonia di Frutta,** or Medley of Fruit, with which it makes what has become a traditional combination.

12 egg whites
6 tablespoons melted polyunsaturated
    margarine
¾ cup pulverized fruit sugar
1 tablespoon orange juice
½ teaspoon salt
1 cup potato or rice flour
1½ teaspoons baking powder
1 teaspoon grated lemon rind, yellow part
    only

**1 teaspoon vanilla or almond extract
(optional)**
YIELD: Two 9-inch layers

1. Beat 6 of the egg whites and the margarine for about 1 minute, until foamy. Combine with ½ cup of the fruit sugar and the orange juice; continue to beat until light and fluffy. Set aside.

2. Place the balance of the egg whites in a bowl, add the salt and the remaining sugar, and beat with a wire whisk for about 30 minutes, or with a rotary electric beater for about 5 minutes, until soft peaks have formed. Set aside.

3. Sift the flour and baking powder together 3 times; stir in the orange juice and egg white mixture. Slowly blend in the lemon rind and the optional vanilla extract.

4. Fold in the peaked egg white mixture until thoroughly blended. Line 2 9-inch cake pans with waxed paper sprinkled with potato flour, and pour the mixture evenly into the pans. Bake in an oven at 350° F for about 30 minutes, or until a cake tester comes out clean and the cake springs back when pressed gently. Allow to cool, remove from the pans, and peel off the waxed paper. Dust with **Praline Powder** before serving.

Bonus Ideas: *Pan di Spagna* may not only be served with *Macedonia di Frutta,* but also lends itself admirably to recipes calling for ladyfingers or **Angel Food Cake.** Try preparing **Torta di Frutta,** or Fresh Fruit Cake. Cut 1 of the sponge cake layers in half and sprinkle the lower half with Grand Marnier or your favorite liqueur. Spread with a filling of **Custard Sauce Praline.** Arrange ½ cup of pitted cherries around the outer rim, and cover with the second layer. Sprinkle additional liquer over the surface, then spread with another layer of Custard Sauce Praline, garnishing the top with a cluster of pitted cherries.

A strikingly imaginative variation is **Budino Etna*,** or Mount Etna Pudding. To serve six, rub polyunsaturated margarine into a 1½-quart mold and sprinkle with fruit sugar. Fill the mold with alternate layers of sponge cake, 1 cup of **Candied Fruits,** and ½ cup of golden raisins that have been steeped in rum. When the mold is slightly more than ¾ full, gradually add, in small quantities, 2 cups of **Custard Sauce Praline.** Place the mold in a pan with 1 inch of hot water. Bake in an oven at 350° F for 30 minutes, or until the *budino* is set. Cool thoroughly before turning the pudding onto a decorative serving dish. Pour ¾ cup of additional Custard Sauce Praline over the *budino* and decorate the center with a "mountain" of Candied Fruit (½ cup) surrounded by a ring of frosted grapes interspersed with frosted mint leaves.

MACEDONIA DI FRUTTA
(Medley of Fruit)

The ancient kingdom of Macedon, in the Balkan Peninsula, which was noted for its varied racial mixtures, has lent its name to this colorful and delicious medley of fruit. Affectionately called "Signora Macedo-

nia" by Pellegrino Artusi, this versatile dessert can be varied according to the fruits available in season, or can be made satisfactorily with frozen or canned fruit when necessary.

1 pound cherries
1 pound seedless grapes
1 cup each, raspberries and strawberries
2 bananas
4 peaches
2 tablespoons lemon juice
¼ cup honey or pure maple syrup
2 tablespoons fruit or date sugar (optional)
¼ cup kümmel, maraschino, or other liqueur
YIELD: Six servings

1. Wash and clean all the fruit and place until ready for use in 2 quarts of cool water acidulated with the lemon juice to avoid discoloration.
2. Pitt the cherries and cut each into 3 sections. Cut the grapes and raspberries in half and quarter the strawberries. Thinly slice the bananas and cut the peaches into thin wedges. Other fruits, if used, should be similarly cut or diced.
3. In a bowl, gently blend the fruit with the honey and optional fruit sugar; chill, tossing the mixture occasionally. Just before serving, add the liqueur.

Bonus Ideas: Fresh red currants, blueberries, pineapple, plums, pears, orange or tangerine sections, and ripe melon balls are often used as part of the medley of fruit. If using fresh currants, place them in a bowl with a combination of honey and fruit sugar, and let them marinate for 2 hours before adding to the medley.

A stunning variation is Macedonia in a Mold*, which uses 5 cups of any combination of fruit pieces to serve four. Marinate the fruit in a bowl with the juice of 1 lemon and ½ cup of honey or pure maple syrup for about 30 minutes. Press the fruit firmly into a 1½-quart ice cream mold, a melon mold, or any pan or mold with a tight-fitting lid suitable for steaming. Cover tightly and place in the freezer for several hours. When ready to serve, unmold, dipping the mold briefly into hot water if necessary. Serve the marbleized macédoine at room temperature on a chilled platter in its own glory, or thoroughly chilled with either Praline Powder, or Custard Sauce Praline.

For the ultimate pièce de résistance, try Macedonia Baked Alaska*, using the frozen molded fruit instead of frozen yogurt over Pan di Spagna, topping with meringue as in Baked Alaska.

MENU

Zuppa di Vongole alla Marinara
Pollo alla Cacciatora
Insalata di Fagiolini
Cannoli alla Siciliana

Clam Soup, Fisherman's Style
Chicken, Hunter's Style
Green Bean Salad
Sicilian Stuffed Pastry Horns

ZUPPA DI VONGOLE ALLA MARINARA*
(Clam Soup, Fisherman's Style)

A popular soup that is easy to make, and

one that may be varied to suit individual preferences. In fact, each of the self-proclaimed experts on fish cookery in Italy insists that his is the only authentic method of preparing this dish, a boast that applies as well to the more elaborate **Zuppa di Pesce,** or Italian Fish Soup. In Lerici, Mamma Omelia uses a little onion, while others insist that onions are never used with fish or seafood. At Il Ristorante di Parma, neither water nor wine is added when preparing the broth, although Luigi Carnacina and Pellegrino Artusi recommend both white wine and white wine vinegar. Obviously it is all a matter of taste.

**48 clams or mussels, or a combination of
  both**
1 medium onion, chopped
1 clove garlic, minced (optional)
1 cup white wine or dry vermouth
6 cups fish stock or bottled clam juice
**1½ pounds fresh tomatoes, chopped, or 1
  16-ounce can Italian-style plum
  tomatoes (optional)**
5 twists of a pepper mill
**¼ teaspoon fresh oregano or ⅛ teaspoon
  dried**
1 tablespoon minced parsley (optional)
**6 slices Italian bread or English muffins,
  toasted**
Cookware spray
YIELD: Six servings

1. Scrub the clams thoroughly under running water. If using mussels, thoroughly wash, scrub, and beard; set aside to soak in cool water

2. Apply cookware spray to a heavy-based pan with a tightly fitting lid, and sauté the onion and optional garlic in 2 ta-blespoons of white wine or fish stock, until the onion is translucent.

3. Stir in the balance of the wine and cook, uncovered, over high heat until the wine is reduced by half. Add the fish stock and the seasonings. Bring to a boil. If tomatoes are used, use only 4 cups of fish stock, add the tomatoes, and bring the mixture to a boil. Add the clams and/or mussels and the optional parsley, cover the pot tightly, and cook for about 10 minutes, or until the shells open, shuffling the pan occasionally. Discard any clams or mussels that have remained closed.

4. Arrange a slice of toasted Italian bread or English muffin in each of 6 bowls, and cover with 8 clams or mussels. Strain liquid in pot through several layers of cheesecloth; pour into bowls.

Bonus Ideas: Zuppa di Pesce*, Italian Fish Soup, is a heartier version of the above recipe, using as many varieties of fish as possible to enhance the richness of the dish. In Tuscany, it is called *cacciucco,* or fish stew, and is served as a one-course meal. To serve six, you will need 5 pounds of assorted fish and seafood, including firmly fleshed fish, such as sea bass, snapper, halibut, or haddock; tender-fleshed fish such as cod, perch, or mullet; and clams, mussels, shrimp, or squid, as you prefer. In a tightly closed pot, steam the clams and mussels until they open and set aside with their strained liquid. In an earthenware or enameled pan or casserole, apply cookware spray and sauté 1 tablespoon chopped onion, 2 cloves minced garlic, ¼ teaspoon each of dried thyme and sage, 1 bay leaf, and ¼-inch hot chili pepper in 2 tablespoons of fish stock or clam juice until the onions are translucent. Add ½ cup white wine or dry vermouth and continue cooking until the wine is almost evaporated. Add 1½ pounds of fresh tomatoes, chopped, or one 16-ounce can of Italian-style plum tomatoes, 1 teaspoon salt, 5 twists of a pepper mill, and 2 tablespoons white wine vinegar diluted in 2 cups of water. Bring to a boil and simmer over medium heat for 10 minutes. Sieve, return to the pot, and add the firmly fleshed fish. Cover, bring to a boil, then simmer over low heat for 10 minutes before adding the tender-fleshed fish and continuing to cook for 7 minutes longer. Transfer the pieces of fish to a covered tureen, pour in the soup, and just before serving add the mussels and clams and their strained juices. Serve in bowls, sprinkled with parsley and garnished with triangles of toasted bread.

When reheating the broth, remove the fish and seafood to avoid overcooking; return to the hot broth to heat through before serving. This dish is similar to bouillabaisse marseilles and other Mediterranean fish soups. To prepare **Brodo di Pesce con Pasta,** or Fish Broth with Pasta, reserve any excess broth, strain, and reduce it over high heat to the consistency of a thickened sauce. Add your favorite pasta or noodles; serve hot, sprinkled with grated Parmesan cheese.

POLLO ALLA CACCIATORA*

(Chicken, Hunter's Style)

Although the Greeks taught the ancient Romans how to fatten the scrawny chickens that were kept mainly for their eggs, it wasn't until the Renaissance that Italians began to appreciate and use this now popular meat in their cuisine.

Chicken, Hunter's Style, is really a *spezzatino,* or stew, which is generally prepared in Italy using young and tender frying chickens.

3½ pounds frying chicken, cut into serving pieces
1 teaspoon coarse salt
6 twists of a pepper mill
¾ pound fresh mushrooms, or 2 ounces dried
1 medium onion, minced
2 tablespoons chicken broth or white wine
2 teaspoons arrowroot or cornstarch
½ cup white wine or dry vermouth
2 tablespoons Cognac
1 cup chicken broth or consommé
1 cup fresh tomatoes, skinned and both stem ends removed, or Italian-style canned plum tomatoes, drained
2 tablespoons each, chopped parsley and basil or 1 tablespoon each, dried
10 ounces fresh or frozen peas, cooked (optional)
Cookware spray
YIELD: Six servings

1. Bring the chicken pieces to room temperature before washing in cool water. Season the moist chicken, which has not been patted dry, with salt and freshly ground pepper. Apply cookware spray to a large skillet or Dutch oven and brown the chicken on all sides over high heat for about 20 minutes. Remove and set aside in a warm place, wrapped in aluminum foil if necessary.

2. If dried mushrooms and herbs are used, soak in warm water for 20 minutes and drain before using. Add the onions and mushrooms to the skillet with 2 tablespoons of broth or wine and sauté for 5 minutes until the onions are translucent, stirring and scraping the pan to loosen and browned particles. Add the arrowroot and stir constantly over low heat for 2 minutes longer.

3. Add the wine, Cognac, chicken broth, tomatoes; bring to a boil, then cover, and simmer over low heat for 10 minutes.

4. Add the browned chicken pieces, cover, and simmer over low heat for 30 minutes, or until the chicken is tender. Transfer the chicken to a platter, sprinkle with the cooked peas, and keep warm in an oven at 250° F.

5. When ready to serve, reduce the mushroom sauce over high heat for about 15 minutes. Remove from heat and add half of the parsley and basil. Pour the sauce over the chicken pieces and garnish with the balance of parsley and basil. Serve hot with **polenta** or rice.

Bonus Ideas: Instead of using chicken, you can prepare **Veal Hunter's Style*** in the same way with 1½ pounds of lean veal, cut into ½-inch cubes. Or, using the same quantity of veal, you can prepare **Sauté de Veau Marengo*** (Veal Marengo), or use 3½ pounds frying chicken, cut into serving pieces, for **Sauté de Poulet Marengo***. For either *Marengo,* use only ½ pound mushrooms; add 1½ tablespoons tomato paste, 4 tablespoons parsley, 24 pearl onions, and 12 pitted black olives when sautéing the mushrooms for 5 minutes. Transfer the veal or chicken parts and other ingre-

dients to a casserole; sprinkle with 1 tablespoon of brandy and heat through in an oven set at 350° F for 30 minutes before serving. You may also wish to try another Italian chicken stew, **Spezzatino di Pollo con Peperoni***, a Roman specialty. To prepare Chicken Stew with Peppers for six, prepare and brown the chicken as for *Pollo alla Cacciatora,* transfer to a hot platter, and keep warm. Roast 1 pound of sweet red, green, and yellow peppers, and cut into 1-inch strips. Add to the pan used for browning the chicken the peppers and 1½ pounds fresh tomatoes or 1 16-ounce can of Italian-style plum tomatoes that have been sieved. Stir over medium heat for 3 minutes; then add 1 cup of chicken stock or consommé, 1 teaspoon salt, and 5 twists of a pepper mill. Bring to a boil, then lower the flame. Simmer, tightly covered, for about 1 hour or until fork tender. **Veal Stew with Peppers*** can be made by substituting 1½ pounds of cubed veal and halving the cooking time.

A family favorite is **Pollo alla Zingara** (Chicken, Gypsy Style). For six servings, prepare and brown the chicken pieces as for *Pollo alla Cacciatora,* then add 1 tablespoon paprika and ½ cup red wine. Cover and simmer for about 30 minutes until the chicken is fork tender. Transfer the chicken to a hot platter and keep warm. Add to the pan ¼ cup of Port or Madeira wine, 1 cup reduced **Brown Sauce,** 2 thinly sliced onions, 1 tablespoon each of minced Canadian bacon and minced boiled tongue, 1 tablespoon each minched mushrooms and sliced truffle or black pitted olives. Simmer, uncovered, for 5 minutes. Pour over the chicken and serve with boiled rice. Instead of chicken, 1½ pounds of veal may be used for this recipe.

INSALATA DI FAGIOLINI*
(Green Bean Salad)

A typical *insalata,* simple and refreshing.

1½ pounds green beans
1 teaspoon coarse salt
¼ cup olive, corn, or peanut oil
2 tablespoons lemon juice
Cookware spray
YIELD: Six servings

   1. Snap off both ends of the beans, wash in cool water, shake off the excess, but do not pat dry.
   2. Apply cookware spray to a heavy pot with a tightly fitting cover; add the moist beans with 1 tablespoon of water and the salt. Cover and sauté *au sec* over low heat for approximately 20 minutes, shuffling the pot occasionally and checking periodically to determine when the beans are *al dente.*
   3. Place the crisp but tender beans in a salad bowl; add the oil and toss until the beans have a thin glossy coating. Add the lemon juice and toss again before serving warm or at room temperature. Garnish with fresh mint leaves.

   Bonus Ideas: For special meals, a more elaborate salad can be prepared: **Cannellini con Caviale** (White Bean and Caviar Salad). For six servings, use 1 pound dry *cannellini* (navy beans) or kidney beans, or 1 pound canned *cannellini* or kidney beans. If dry beans are used, cook uncovered with 2 quarts of water and bring to a boil; set aside, still covered, to soak 1 hour. Drain and add ¼ cup sliced celery, 1 teaspoon salt, and 2 quarts of water. Bring to a boil once again; then simmer for about 30 minutes. Drain thoroughly. If using canned beans, wash and drain thoroughly. Halve 1 large purple onion and thinly slice 1 lemon. Mix the beans in a salad bowl with the sliced onion, ¼ cup chopped parsley, and 2 ounces of black or red caviar. Add 1 cup **Salsa Citronette** (Italian Lemon Sauce) and toss well. Garnish the rim and center of the salad with alternating halved slices of onion and lemon and sprinkle with parsley before serving.

   To prepare 1 cup of **Italian Lemon Sauce,** combine in a jar ¼ cup lemon juice with ½ teaspoon coarse salt and 4 twists of a pepper mill. Cover and shake briefly; uncover and add ¾ cup of olive, corn, or peanut oil.

CANNOLI ALLA SICILIANA*
(Sicilian Stuffed Pastry Horns)

Cannoli take their name from the pipes around which the *scorza,* or pastry dough, is wrapped, forming the traditional horn shape of this delicacy. You can purchase 5-inch metal *cannoli* tubes, but most Italians cut their own from aluminum piping (1-inch diameter), wooden dowels, or even broomstick handles.

Cannoli, like so many of the sweet pastries that resulted from Turkish and Arabic influences of Sicilian cookery, are rarely served at the end of a meal in Italian households—except on special family occasions or religious holidays. Generally, as we noted earlier, an Italian meal culminates with fruits, cheeses, or puddings. But for those who would like to add more slimming versions of imaginative southern Italian pastries to their repertories, for use on such special occasions, I am presenting this and other pastry specialties (in the Bonus Ideas).

Pastry Dough:
½ cup cornstarch or rice flour
¾ cup white rye flour
2¼ teaspoons baking powder
⅛ teaspoon salt
1 teaspoon each, expresso or instant
    coffee, and carob powder
3 tablespoons polyunsaturated margarine
½ cup Marsala or Madeira wine
1 tablespoon pure maple syrup, honey, or
    fruit sugar
4 *Cannoli* tubes, or 1-inch-thick wooden
    dowels, 5 inches long
1 cup olive, corn, or peanut oil

Filling:
2 cups low-fat ricotta
4 tablespoons pure maple syrup, honey, or
    fruit sugar
1 teaspoon flower water or vanilla extract
¼ cup diced Candied Fruits
¼ cup coarsely chopped pistachio nuts
YIELD: One dozen

1. Combine the cornstarch, rye flour, and baking powder, and sift 6 times. Blend in the salt, coffee, and carob powder, and cut in the margarine. Make a well in the center of the mixture and add to the center the wine and maple syrup; then work the flour mixture into the liquids until a firm dough is formed. Transfer to a floured board and knead vigorously for 15 minutes, adding additional wine as necessary, until the dough is smooth and elastic but not sticky. Form into a ball, cover

with a slightly damp cloth, and let the dough set for 2 hours.

2. Roll the dough into a very thin layer, about 1/16-inch thick, and cut into 12 5-inch squares. Place a *Cannoli* tube diagonally on each square and wrap the sides over the tube, moistening the overlapping ends with water and pressing together.

3. Layer a baking dish with half of the oil and place in an oven at 400° F until the oil is very hot, about 375° F (when a cube of bread dropped into the oil turns golden brown). Slide the *Cannoli* into the hot oil, 4 at a time. Cook, turning often with tongs, until all sides are golden brown. Remove with tongs, drain on paper toweling, and continue to cook the balance of the *Cannoli,* adding additional oil as necessary.

4. While the *Cannoli* drain and cool, prepare the filling. Beat the ricotta with a wire whisk or an electric beater until smooth and creamy. Blend in the maple syrup and beat until velvety. Mix in the flower water and **Candied Fruits,** blending well. Fill the cooked shells using either a spoon or a pastry bag.

5. Garnish the ends of the *Cannoli* by dipping into chopped pistachio nuts before serving.

Bonus Ideas: You can use cocoa instead of espresso coffee or carob powder. If preparing the filling ahead, chill in the refrigerator before using, or freeze both the ricotta filling and the pastry horns separately.

Another popular Italian dessert, particularly during the Mardi Gras carnival (when it is served decorated with paper confetti), is **Chiacchiere,** or Ribbons and Patches. This Tuscan delicacy is also called Lover's Knots because of the knot-like effect of its tied strips of dough. These can be served alone at the end of a meal or as an accompaniment to fruit or pudding desserts. To serve six, combine 1¼ cups cornstarch, 1½ cups white rye flour, and 7 teaspoons baking powder, and sift 6 times onto a board, making a well in the center. Add to the center 3 egg whites, 2 table-spoons soft margarine, ¼ cup pure maple syrup or fruit sugar, ⅛ teaspoon salt, 1 grated orange rind, ½ grated lemon rind, and ¼ cup of white wine or dry vermouth. Using the tips of your fingers or a fork, work the flour gently into the other ingredients until the dough is stiff but pliable. Cover with a slightly moist cloth and let the dough set for 2 hours, then roll into a thin, ⅛-inch layer and cut into 1-inch strips about 8 inches long. Knot these as you would ribbons and set aside. Cut the balance of dough into 3- or 4-inch squares and rectangulars. Line a baking dish with a thin layer of olive, corn, or peanut oil and place in an oven at 400° F. When the oil is very hot, cook the pastry until golden brown on both sides. If you prefer to deep-fry the Lover's Knots or the *Cannoli Scorze,* use enough oil to cover the pastry and fry a few pieces at a time when the oil has reached about 375° F, or after a cube of bread has turned golden when placed in it. Drain, cool on paper towels, and serve piled high on a platter, sprinkled with Vanilla Fruit Sugar or Citrus Zested Fruit Sugar.

Vanilla Fruit Sugar is prepared by adding about 1 inch of a vanilla bean to a cup of fruit sugar and storing it in a tightly closed canister in a cool place. If the flavor is too concentrated, blend with additional fruit sugar to taste when using. **Citrus**

Zested Fruit Sugar is prepared by adding 1½ tablespoons of orange, tangerine, lemon, or lime zest to 1 cup of fruit sugar and storing in a tightly closed canister in a cool place.

MENU

Risi e Bisi
Cima alla Genovese
Pan di Carruba
Gorgonzola Calda

Venetian Rice and Pea Soup
Genoese Stuffed Veal
Italian Carob Bread
Gorgonzola Cheese Spread

RISI E BISI*
(Venetian Rice and Pea Soup)

This is one of the most popular soups in Italy, where soup cookery is a fine art. Considered by the Venetians as a harbinger of spring, it was the first dish served to the Doges each April 25, the religious holiday set aside to honor St. Mark, the patron saint of the Venetian Republic.

Risi e bisi is a dish that is subject to creative interpretation. Ideally, it is very thick, but can still be eaten with a spoon; often, however, it is prepared so that it is thick to the consistency of a *risotto,* in which case it is eaten with a fork. Like pasta and *risotto,* soup is often the first course of a typical Italian meal.

1 medium onion or 2 scallions, chopped
4 ounces Canadian bacon, cut into strips
4 tablespoons white wine or beef bouillon
3 cups fresh of frozen peas
1 teaspoon coarse salt
4 twists of a pepper mill
6 cups beef broth or bouillon
1½ cups raw long-grain rice
⅔ cup grated Parmesan cheese
4 tablespoons chopped parsley
Cookware Spray
YIELD: Six Servings

1. Apply cookware spray to a heavy-based pan or Dutch oven; sauté the onions and Canadian bacon in 2 tablespoons of the wine for about 5 minutes, or until the onions are translucent.

2. Add the peas, salt, and pepper, and sauté with 2 tablespoons of additional wine or bouillon for 3 minutes, stirring frequently. Add 5 cups of the beef broth, cover, and bring to a boil.

3. Blend in the rice, half of the parsley, and the balance of the broth. Cover and simmer over low heat for 15 minutes, or until the rice is *al dente* and still moist. Add more broth or water, as necessary, while cooking the rice. Top with the Parmesan cheese and serve garnished with the balance of the chopped parsley.

Bonus Ideas: This dish should be made with fresh, young spring peas, if at all possible; otherwise use frozen *petits pois*.

Rice with Peas and Asparagus Tips*, which omits the Canadian bacon, is a Roman variation. Proceed as above, using 2 cups shelled peas and 1 pound asparagus that has been scraped, trimmed of tough ends, and cut into 1-inch lengths. After the peas and rice have simmered in the broth mixture for 10 minutes, add the asparagus pieces and simmer 10 minutes longer, until the rice is *al dente*. Remove from heat and blend in ¼ cup of grated Parmesan cheese and 2 tablespoons polyunsaturated margarine. Stir well and serve hot with additional Parmesan cheese if desired.

Stracciatella* (Italian Egg Drop Soup) —one of the simplest of the popular Italian soups—is reminiscent of its Chinese counterpart. To serve six, bring 6 cups of chicken broth or bouillon to a boil; then lower to a simmer. Separately, combine 3 egg whites with 3 tablespoons of bread crumbs, stir in ¼ cup each of grated Parmesan and Gruyère cheese, ⅓ teaspoon salt, and ⅛ teaspoon ground nutmeg. Ladle several tablespoons of the simmering broth into the egg mixture; then stir it into the broth. Reduce heat to low, stirring constantly for about 3 minutes, until thickened. Serve with croutons of toasted bread and garnish with chopped parsley.

Probably the most renowned Italian soup is **Pasta e Fagioli,** or Italian Pasta and Bean Soup. (Many have associated this delicious rustic soup with Italians who migrated to America.) To serve six, cover 1 pound of white kidney beans with water and bring to a boil. Remove from heat and let stand, covered, for 1 hour. Put 3 tablespoons each of beef broth or bouillon, chopped onion, celery and carrot in a stockpot and sauté until the onions are translucent. After 5 minutes, add 1 cup undrained Italian-style canned plum tomatoes and continue cooking for 10 minutes. Add 3 cups of beef broth, or a combination of broth and water, and cook over medium heat for 1 hour, or until the beans are tender. Add 1 teaspoon salt and 6 twists of a pepper mill. Bring the soup to a boil and add ¾ cup of *ditalini* or *tubettini* pasta; boil the pasta only until still firm but not quite cooked. Remove pot from heat and let stand for about 10 minutes before serving hot, sprinkled with grated Romano cheese.

CIMA ALLA GENOVESE*
(Genoese Stuffed Veal)

This is a festive rustic dish, excellent as part of a buffet; it can be served hot in its own broth or chilled during summer months. Ideally, this Ligurian specialty is prepared using a cleaned calf's stomach; however, since you will have difficulty finding one of these in most sections of the United States, the dish can easily be made with either boned breast of veal or boned shoulder of veal. (The stomach forms a natural pouch, while the breast or shoulder has to be slit horizontally, forming a bag for the stuffing.)

¼ **pound fresh sweetbreads**
½ **pound calf's brains (optional)**
¼ **cup veal bone marrow (optional)**
1½ **teaspoons coarse salt**
1 **medium onion, minced**
1 **clove garlic, minced**
2 **tablespoons white wine or bouillon**
¼ **pound lean *prosciutto* or Canadian bacon**
½ **pound veal, finely chopped**
1 **cup fresh or frozen peas**
5 **egg whites, lightly beaten**
3 **tablespoons olive, corn, or peanut oil**
⅓ **cup grated Parmesan cheese**
1 **teaspoon fresh marjoram or ½ teaspoon dried**

2 **ounces shelled pistachio nuts, pine nuts, or sunflower seeds**
2 **pounds breast or shoulder of veal, boned**
2½ **quarts water or veal or chicken stock**
Cookware spray
YIELD: Eight to twelve servings

1. Soak the sweetbreads and brains in cold water for at least 1 hour. Drain, place with the marrow in a pan of cold water, and bring to a boil. Drain again and bring to a boil in fresh water, adding ½ teaspoon salt; lower the heat and simmer for 10 minutes, or until tender. Drain, remove and discard the surface skin and membranes, and cut into 2-inch cubes.

2. Apply cookware spray to a skillet and sauté the minced onion and garlic with the wine or bouillon until the onions are translucent. Add the *prosciutto* and finely chopped veal and cook over medium heat until the veal loses its pink color. Add the sweetbreads, brains, and marrow, and continue sautéing until golden brown. Remove the mixture from the skillet and place in a bowl with the peas, beaten egg whites, oil, grated Parmesan cheese, marjoram, pistachio nuts, and balance of salt. Blend the mixture thoroughly.

3. Press the stuffing into the veal pouch, leaving room for expansion during cooking. Sew up the open end of the pouch and place veal in a large kettle covered with water or stock. Cook uncovered for 1 hour over moderate heat, then an additional hour covered. Remove from heat and let the veal cool in the liquid. Drain, place on a board, and cover with a cloth or aluminum foil. Place a heavy weight over the covered meat to compress the veal and stuffing until ready to serve.

4. If serving hot, remove the threads and cut the meat into slices. If serving cold, place the wrapped meat (with the weight) in the refrigerator to chill. Remove the thread and cut the slices before serving.

Bonus Ideas: Reserve the cooking liquid to prepare *risotto* or use as a basis for soup. You can cook *Cima* in an oven at 375° F, instead of in water or stock. Wrap the stuffed veal in aluminum foil and seal it well; place in a baking dish, and bake for 2 hours. Remove the foil and threads, slice, and serve either hot or cold.

Genoese Stuffed Veal lends itself to a number of other cooking processes. If using a microwave oven, place the stuffed veal in a baking dish on an inverted ovenproof saucer or casserole lid; cover with waxed paper and cook each side 9 minutes to the pound, or about 15 minutes. Turn and cook 15 minutes longer. The internal temperature should be 160° F, which will increase by 10° F while standing; cover with aluminum foil and let stand about 20 minutes before serving. Allow 1 or 2 minutes longer per pound for cooking if the stuffed veal has been refrigerated and is not at room temperature.

If using a clay pot, presoak for 15 minutes and place the stuffed veal inside without wrapping in foil. Cover and cook in an oven at 450° F for about 1 hour. Check the internal temperature; when slightly below 175° F, remove the stuffed veal and wrap in aluminum foil.

If using a pressure cooker, place the stuffed veal on a trivet and fill cooker with hot water or stock up to half its capacity. At 15-pound pressure, once the valve is engaged, cook 13 minutes to the pound, or about 40 minutes. Reduce the pressure with cold water, lift out the stuffed veal and wrap in aluminum foil.

An Italian variation of *Cima* utilizing an inexpensive cut of veal is **Petto di Vitello Ripieno*,** or Italian Stuffed Breast of Veal. To serve six, have your butcher dress the veal to remove the bones, which can be reserved for preparing broth. Pound the boned veal as you would in preparing **scaloppine.** Sprinkle with 1 teaspoon coarse salt and 6 twists of a pepper mill. The stuffing is made by blending in a bowl 2 egg whites, 2 tablespoons presoaked raisins, 2 tablespoons each, pine nuts and chopped parsley, 5 tablespoons wheat germ or bread crumbs, ¼ pound lean *prosciutto* or Canadian bacon, and ½ cup of diced apple or pear. Spread the stuffing over the meat and roll tightly before tying it securely. Dip the rolled veal into cool water; drain but do not pat dry. Apply cookware spray to a heavy-based skillet or Dutch oven and brown the moist meat on all sides over high heat for about 15 minutes. Add ½ cup of white wine or dry vermouth and cook for 10 minutes, turning the meat occasionally. Lower the heat, adding additional wine as necessary, and simmer partially covered for about 2 hours, or until fork tender. Remove the stuffed veal and let it set for 10 minutes before untying and cutting into ½-inch slices. Deglaze the pan with wine or brandy and pour the sauce over the sliced veal before serving. If using a pressure cooker, add ¾ cup of wine, and after the valve is engaged, cook for 13 minutes to the pound at 15-pound pressure.

PAN DI CARRUBA*
(Italian Carob Bread)

Carob flour or powder is milled from the pods of the tamarind, a Mediterranean tree; the pods are also known as locust beans or St. John's bread, and the dried leaves are used in curries. Although carob powder has only recently been discovered by health-food faddists, it has been known and used since biblical times. In some parts of Italy, the tree is so common that the pods literally litter the countryside—to the extent that in Bologna they are fed to horses. (Originally, *mortadella*, the large sausage from Bologna, was made with horse flesh and was noted for the distinctive flavor derived from the carob-fed horses.)

During the deprivation of World War II, many Italians rediscovered carob powder and used it as a substitute for unavailable wheat and chestnut flours. Carob powder can be used in any recipes calling for powdered chestnut or chocolate; in fact, toasted carob powder has a flavor remarkably like that of chocolate. Half the quantity can be used in recipes calling for chocolate; however, since the powder burns at higher temperatures, always use a slow oven, between 300° and 325° F.

2 tablespoons dry yeast
2 cups warm water
4 tablespoons carob powder
4 cups potato flour
3 tablespoons molasses
1 teaspoon coarse salt
1 egg white
Polyunsaturated margarine
YIELD: One loaf

1. In a mixing bowl, dissolve the yeast in 1 cup of warm water and let it set for about 10 minutes. Meanwhile, blend the carob powder and flour on a board and form a well in the center.

2. Add the balance of warm water, the molasses, and salt to the dissolved yeast; stir well and pour into the center of the flour. Using your fingers or a fork, blend the flour into the yeast mixture. Knead for about 5 minutes, until the dough is smooth but still elastic.

3. Shape the dough into a flattened ball, place in a bowl greased with polyunsaturated margarine, and make 2 crisscross cuts on the surface. Cover with a dampened cloth and set in a warm place to rise, until the cuts have closed and the dough has doubled in bulk. Punch down the dough with your fist, cover, and let sit for about 20 minutes, until it rises to approximately 1½ times its volume.

4. Shape the dough into a loaf and place on a baking tin greased with polyunsaturated margarine, or in a greased 9-inch loaf pan. Brush the surface of the loaf with lightly beaten egg white and bake in an oven at 300° F for about 45 minutes, or until a toothpick comes out clean after piercing the loaf. Cook for 15 minutes before slicing. It is excellent when served with **Gorgonzola Cheese Spread.**

Bonus Ideas: If a more chocolaty taste is desired, toast the carob powder in an oven at 300° F for several minutes before blending with the flour. If freezing for future use, let the loaf cool and set, then place in a plastic bag. When ready to use, thaw thoroughly and warm through in an oven at 300° F.

GORGONZOLA CALDA
(Gorgonzola Cheese Spread)

Although Italians rarely indulge in bread and butter during a meal, they make an exception of this tantalizing *spalmato di Gorgonzola*, which is a spread eaten on freshly baked **Italian Carob Bread** or another bread at the end of the meal, often accompanied by fresh fruit. When the Gorgonzola is heated briefly, its flavor is tremendously enhanced.

½ pound Gorgonzola cheese
¼ pound polyunsaturated margarine
1 tablespoon white wine (optional)
6 slices fresh carob, Italian, or French
   bread
YIELD: Six servings

1. Combine the Gorgonzola cheese, margarine, and optional white wine, mashing into a paste.

2. Wrap the cheese mixture in aluminum foil and heat in an oven at 250° F for 3 minutes before serving with the bread.

Bonus Ideas: Of course you may use Roquefort instead of Gorgonzola, but I find Roquefort subtly sharper than the Italian blue cheese, which I prefer.

Try making a **Gorgonzola Sauce**—ideal over any *pasta,* especially *gnocchi.* To serve six, mash ½ cup Gorgonzola cheese and blend into a paste with 1 tablespoon white wine or skim milk. Combine the paste with 3 tablespoons polyunsaturated margarine, ¼ cup skim milk, and 1 teaspoon salt. Cook over medium heat in a glass or enameled double boiler or *bain-marie* for several minutes, stirring with a wooden spoon until creamy. Cover, remove from heat, and serve with the pasta of your choice. The addition of 1 tablespoon of brandy, a touch borrowed from the French, provides a special accent to this sauce. Just before serving, heat and ignite the brandy and pour into the mixture.

• • •

For those of us who care, however, French cuisine has a vast repertoire of memorable and exciting dishes, many of which we will want to adapt to today's lifestyle. So now, like Catherine de Medici centuries ago, we must leave Italy for France and nearby Belgium, this time for a more contemporary cook's view of the land, its restaurants, and recipes.

FRANCE

> *"Great cooking is when things taste of what they are."*
> *—Curnonsky, president Académie des Gastronomes*

THE CUISINE IN PERSPECTIVE

During the period of the Roman Empire, the Gauls, who inhabited the region now known as France, already had their own cuisine: they cultivated vegetables and grains, drew on fish and seafood from the bordering waters, and created excellent cheeses, including Cantal (one of my favorites). Cooking then, however, was primitive and far from refined. It wasn't until the fourteenth century, with the appearance of Guillaume Tisel (known as Taillevent), head cook to Charles VI, that the semblance of a sophisticated French cuisine began to take form. Taillevent, as the author of one of the oldest cookbooks, *Le Viandier,* initiated the important task of codifying the then known dishes—a task essential to the future development of any fine cuisine.

But even this early gastronomy was predominantly for the privileged few and had little effect on the humble efforts at cookery or the eating habits of the ordinary people. It was not until 1533, when Catherine de Medici went to France to marry the future King Henry II, that a dramatic change took place. the fourteen-year-old bride-to-be was determined to captivate not only the royal court but the ordinary people of France as well. She brought with her many of the riches of the then flowering Renaissance in Italy, including Venetian chefs, new foods and ingredients, and new cooking techniques. Some of the new foods and techniques, drawn from other cultures, had in turn been brought back to Italy as a result of the exploratory voyages of Genoese and Venetian seafarers. It was young Catherine who established the Frenchwoman's right to eat at the same dining table with men. *La sauce brune* (also called *sauce espagnole)*, the basic brown sauce of *la grande cuisine,* was the creation of one of Catherine's chefs and proved to be an important turning point in the development of *la grande cuisine:* it soon became the most fundamental of the "mother sauces," as Escoffier was to call them many years later.

By the end of the eighteenth century, many other cuisines of the world had contributed to French cooking. Spices, and recipes for using them in aromatic dishes, had been brought back from the East by the returning Crusaders. While the artichoke, the tomato, and a Florentine recipe for sherbet (originally an Arab creation) were introduced by Catherine, the now famous French croissant came from an Austrian recipe introduced by Marie Antoinette. An eighteenth-century Polish king gave France *baba au rhum,* and Brillat-Savarin returned from America with tales of feasting on turkey.

It was Brillat-Savarin, who wrote *The Physiology of Taste,* and Antonin Carême, author of masterly twelve volumes on cookery, who achieved the necessary codification of the French *haute cuisine.* As *Larousse Gastronomique* points out, "Carême should be regarded, even today, as the founder of '*la grande cuisine*' . . . his practical work as an inventor of sauces, as pastrymaker, designer and author of works devoted to cooking, place him at an immense distance from all those who preceded him in his career."

And Auguste Escoffier, the "Chef of Kings," in the late 1800s was to achieve the twin distinction of establishing himself as the dominant influence in the refinement of *la grande cuisine,* and of reaching a general audience with his masterpiece: *Ma Cuisine,* a book that was to have a tremendous influence for more than half a century on cooks both in France and throughout the world. Escoffier was to spend most of his sixty active years as an outstanding culinary authority at the Savoy Hotel in London, away from France (like La Chapelle, who was in the service of Lord Chesterfield and the Prince of Orange a century earlier). The mystique of *haute cuisine,* as *the* cuisine of France, was being exported around the world.

But the fact remains that *la grande cuisine* was conceived almost exclusively for royalty, the privileged, and the affluent. It had no relationship to *la cuisine bourgeoise,* the cuisine of the people, or to their needs and mode of living. Carême was chef to Talleyrand and later to the affluent Rothschilds. As illustrious as his recipes and techniques may have been, most of his dishes required a large staff in the kitchen and virtually an entire day to prepare. His works were designed for and read by other chefs—not the ordinary people of France. *Haute cuisine,* in fact, has never been the family cuisine of the French. It is too expensive to prepare, too involved in its techniques, and far too rich to be consumed on a daily basis. As Howard Hillman wrote in *The New York Times,* November 7, 1976, "Classic French cuisine is one of France's greatest glories, but it is not the true cuisine of the country —fewer than 1 percent of the dishes eaten by Frenchmen are prepared in the classic manner. Such rich and elaborate dishes are usually consumed in expensive gastronomic temples that the average Frenchman cannot afford to patronize.... Its critics say 'good riddance'—who needs so many calories, such a high cholesterol count and so much money spent on a meal ...?" Indeed, from the turn of the century, the ordinary people were developing their own *cuisine bourgeoise* with simple regional dishes, such as *coq au vin, petite marmite* and *bouillabaisse Marseillaise.* Instead of their adopting the much-touted *haute cuisine* specialties, just the opposite took place: the chefs adapted and refined honest regional dishes into more complicated versions for their restaurant cuisine. And with time, another factor entered into the picture: other countries, especially the United States, became concerned with nutritional considerations and their applicability to the more sedentary mode of contemporary life. We were already shunning harmful or superfluous sauces and ingredients.

Still, it was not until 1960s that Paul Bocuse and his "Young Bulls" gave the *coup de grâce* to *la grande cuisine.* As we saw earlier, Bocuse and his colleagues dramatically denounced the rich, masking sauces of the classic cuisine. Instead, they prized basic, fresh, and natural ingredients, simply and intelligently prepared. But old habits die hard. As a result, the cuisine in France's great restaurants and bistros is in a state of flux. The "temples" of *haute cuisine* are aware that their patrons are eating *très léger* (lightly), but many of their regular patrons expect to find favorite specialties of the old cuisine. *Chef de Cuisine* Jean-Pierre Plet of the Hotel Meurice said it best, as I reported in the Gannett's Westchester-Rockland newspapers in July 1978: "Although *nouvelle cuisine* is popular with those who want it, most Parisians are simply cutting out some courses from the traditionally large *haute cuisine* meals. People are eating more lightly, both at lunch and at dinner, and generally will omit the appetizer, salad, and dessert or cheese. Fish, of course, is particularly popular, and every chef including myself has invented a terrine of fish to accommodate the desire to dine in the new style. Still, our guests and regular customers expect the finest *haute cuisine,* and since they prefer to eat lightly, it is our function to satisfy their needs." Maurice Casanova, owner of Le Fouquet on the Champs-Elysées, said in the same article: "We have made a few concessions to *nouvelle cuisine,* since our clients keep coming back and want to find our specialties. Some return after ten or twenty years and want to taste the dishes they remember from their earlier visits. Therefore, we are obliged to have one section of our kitchen cooking all of our old specialties while the other prepares the new dishes on the menu. However, if I were to open a new restaurant today, I would concentrate only on the new and lighter cuisine!"

Not only are French restaurants changing to the new cuisine, but the new cuisine itself is continually evolving . The urge to experiment and create new dishes —especially those more suitable to our current way of life—has caught on with many chefs (with an assist from the media and the publicity-conscious *bande à Bocuse).* As Joseph Wechsberg notes in an article for *Gourmet* magazine in October 1977, the young and talented Christian Clément, chef at Le Meriadeck in Bordeaux, says that he isn't doing *la nouvelle cuisine* at all; he prefers to call it *"la cuisine d'aujourd'hui,"* today's cooking. Clément has gathered around him a second band of dissident chefs—"The Young Musketeers"—and so it goes.

Meanwhile, the cooking of the ordinary people, *la cuisine bourgeoise,* continues to be the main cookery of France, though it, too, is in a state of confusion. Our own James Beard calls it *"la cuisine simple."* In his introduction to Alvin Kerry's *Family Cookbook,* Beard says, "I am afraid that it does not thrive today as well as it once did."

If *la grande cuisine* no longer holds sway over France, it does continue its influence, like an elderly *grande dame,* in other parts of the world. Often, however, restaurants that serve it seem desperately to be trying to hold on to standards that no longer have validity. Journalist Sandy Seaver writes (in the *New York Post,* October 18, 1977) that in such out-of-the-way places as Guadeloupe and Martinique in the Caribbean, you can have "elegant meals prepared in the classic French manner, served impeccably and accompanied by excellent imported wines." Even at the Sheraton Hotel in Cairo, French cuisine is far better than one might expect. Yet if one looks closely at the Egyptian maître d' and waiters their desperation often betrays them, they are obviously emulating an alien culture and an alien standard of cuisine.

I found a striking example of this state of affairs in Athens, while researching this book. There I met Georges Cannellos, director general of the Grand Bretagne Hotel and president of the Fédération des Associations Hotelières de Grèce. When I asked permission to visit his kitchen, he replied, "Really, there are no great chefs left in the hotel field. There are pedestrian cooks who don't have an instinctive sense, but must be taught every little thing. Do you really want to watch and study how I have to teach them to make even a decent Hollandaise sauce? You are most welcome to the kitchen . . . but would it be worth your while?" And with that, he suggested that I would do better to visit an authentic Greek kitchen, which I did!

What will be the fate of the *grande dame* of French cuisine? We can't tell. She is still to be seen in noted restaurants in France and other countries, wherever the re-creation of classic French dishes is a status symbol. Many believe that the highest standards of *la grande cuisine* are still maintained in neighboring Belgium, though the new slimming cookery is making inroads even there.

Regardless of which type of cuisine is being practiced—*nouvelle, haute,* or *bourgeoise*—French cookery benefits from the vast supply of ingredients produced in the various regions of the country. As in the past, very little is imported today, although more and more snails now come from Eastern Europe and elsewhere, and goose livers from Israel. This is equally true of wines, which are invariably served with meals in France. On a daily basis, less expensive, common wines are consumed, while finer vintage wines are reserved for Sundays, holidays, and special occasions.

The "three Bs" of France are the major regions Bordeaux, Burgundy, and Brittany. Burgundy is considered by many to have the most distinctive regional cuisine (*à la bourguignonne),* as well as the finest produce and wines in all of France. It produces what is often called "the best poultry in the world," excellent cattle, fish, snails, bountiful vegetables and fruits, and, of course, such outstanding wines as Chambertin, Beaujolais, Pouilly-Fuissé, and Chablis. Brittany provides exceptional seafood, Nantes ducklings and turkey, the delicate *pré-salé* lamb raised on salt meadows, and the popular Breton beverage: cider. Bordeaux is acknowledged for its excellent fish and seafood and world-famous wines: Château-Lafite Rothschild, Margaux, Latour and Haut-Brion, Cheval and Yquem, among others. Additional notable regions of France include the following: Normandy, bordering on the English Channel, excels in fish and seafood, cattle, fruits (particularly apples), and dairy products. Although it produces no exceptional wines, Normandy is famous for Benedictine and Calvados, an apple-flavored liqueur. Provence, basking in the Mediterranean sunshine, is rich with many varieties of fish and seafood, tomatoes, olives, garlic, fruits, vegetables, and cheeses; and two wines: Blanc de Cassis and Muscat de Bandols.

Alsace and Lorraine, regions with a strong German influence, produce *charcuterie* (cooked and cured pork meats), sauerkraut, cheeses, beer, and kirsch. Neighboring Belgium provides produce for the French table, particularly *witlof* (Belgian endive), Brussels sprouts, salsify (oyster root), and such fresh herbs as chervil, tarragon, and chives. It also produces excellent *fromage blanc* (soft white cheese).

Generally, breakfast in France is simply coffee with a roll or croissant. The main meal of the day may be either the midday or the dinner meal and usually consists of three of four courses. Special meals begin with hors d'oeuvres, soup,

and/or a fish entrée, followed by a main course of meat, poultry, or game with vegetables and/or a salad. To end the meal, a light dessert, or fruit or cheese, and espresso or strong filtered coffee *(cafe filtre)* may be served. Family meals are generally simpler, omitting one of the courses, and are served with *vin ordinaire* (non vintage wine), mineral water, and, of course, the traditional crusted French bread—which is now often disappointing, since the introduction of electric ovens for baking.

Increasingly, with problems of urbanization and transportation, fewer of the French in sizable cities are able to return home for the midday meal. Hence, the dinner meal becomes the principal meal of the day. Numerous fast-food chains have mushroomed in French cities, especially Paris. Although some are along the lines of the Italian *tavola calda,* providing adequate versions of traditional French *bourgeoise* food on a self-service basis, an almost incredible number of Wimpys, McDonald's, Kentucky Fried Chicken and "Le Drug Store" establishments are contaminating the previously high standards of everyday French cuisine.

For those of us who care, however, French cuisine still has a vast repertoire of memorable dishes, many of which we will add, in their slimming versions, to our own menus. With this in mind, let's set off on our second cook's tour.

A COOK'S TOUR OF FRANCE

We are in Paris, the fabulous City of

Lights and one of the most beautiful cities in the world. It is the gastronomic capital of the world: What better starting point for our tour?

Paris is a city meant for leisurely strolling, for slowly absorbing sights, sounds, and atmosphere. One should, as the French say, *flâner les boulevards*—walk unhurriedly, if not aimlessly, taking in the city's myriad impressions. So we will stroll along the Seine or the Champs-Elysées. A must is the Tuileries, especially on Sunday mornings, when fathers take over the park with their enthusiastic children. Although the old Les Halles is gone, since the produce markets have been moved near Orly airport, most of the old restaurants are still where they were, and new ones have been mushrooming. Not far away is the old Jewish ghetto, worth meandering through. Montparnasse, Montmartre, and Pigalle provide other insights into the city. Of course we will want to make our way to Notre-Dame and the charming village atmosphere of Île St. Louis, eventually proceeding to the Latin Quarter, the Panthéon, and the colorful bustle of the Left Bank. One of my favorite walks is along the Rue Royale, with its marvelous shops and Maxim's; to the Madeleine, with its bordering flower market, and, of course, the inimitable Fauchon and all of its culinary delights. Perhaps because of the many photographs one has seen, or the movies set in Paris, one senses a wonderful *déjà vu* upon first arriving in this city. It seems so right, so familiar and enchanting—it simply lives up to its promise.

Most tourists enjoy Paris, but few ever really have an opportunity to know and understand it. It wasn't until I worked in Paris and was part of the daily routines of the French people that I truly began to understand the city. The French are very private, imbued with a very strong image of the importance of their culture and, at first, not easy to know. It is not surprising, then, that few foreigners have an opportunity to visit the homes of the French.

Outsiders who are invited into French homes are amazed to find that the average French kitchen is unbelievably tiny and usually ill-equipped by our standards—and this in a country heralded as having one of the finest cuisines in the world. The first kitchen I used in Paris, during the year and a half I worked there, measured 4 feet by 5 feet; it was fairly well equipped. But my daughter, who studied in Paris, had a kitchen that measured 3 feet by 4 feet, with hardly enough room to turn around. This kitchen boasted a two-burner gas range, a small refrigerator adequate for very little storage, and an outside metal box used for auxiliary refrigeration in cold weather. Even in larger and better-equipped kitchens, there is no kitchen table; one eats in the living room, where (if it has a fireplace) grilling and roasting occasionally are also done.

The French find such kitchens adequate because, as a rule, they had been accustomed to shopping every day or every other day in nearby markets. In Paris, one learns not to buy in large quantities. Rather than a pound of butter, a dozen eggs, and meats in bulk, one buys 100 grams of butter, a few eggs, and small quantities of meat, fish, and vegetables.

The kitchens described above are typical of present-day Paris and are considered improvements over those of prewar France. Before the war, the typical family kitchen was a tiny room with a window and, below the window, a *garde manger*—a rectangular hole cut through the wall and covered on the outdoors side with a heavy wire mesh, permitting fresh air to enter. This device opened inside into a cabinet. It was used for storage of vegetables, bread, and other perishables, and served as an auxiliary to the refrigerator (if there was one) or icebox. Such kitchens would also have two gas burners over a small oven, or a coal-burning stove. Generally, they would also include a washtub for doing laundry.

Since in France, until recently, one shops practically every day, each district has numerous markets close at hand, with wonderful displays of fresh produce, meats, fish and seafood, and bustling with activity. Formerly, these markets were open every day except Sunday. In recent years, however, most district markets function only on alternate days of the week. One must, incidentally, observe a certain protocol in the markets: never may one select or handle the produce; that is the sole prerogative of the vendor. Once, when I instinctively reached for a head of lettuce I wanted, the vendor brushed me aside, firmly informing me that *he* would select the lettuce.

As we noted earlier, there has been a change in French eating habits, owing to the increasing problems of urbanization that have beset all cities. Since in many families both the husband and wife work, daily shopping in the smaller local markets is difficult, and few can manage to return home for a major midday meal. As a result, in Paris particularly, larger supermarkets are taking hold, in which the busy homemaker can save time by taking advantage of one-stop shopping. Whereas

earlier one had to buy bread in a *boulangerie,* cooked items in a *charcuterie,* and dairy products and meats in other specialty shops, it is now common to buy most of these items in one huge market. Even the traditionally small neighborhood Potins have grown into supermarket status in most areas.

Most *quartiers,* nevertheless, still have their convenience shops, the most popular of which are the *charcuteries.* All over Paris and in most of the provinces, the ubiquitous *charcuterie* provides pre-cooked, ready-to-go items; pâtés, terrines, prepared salads, cooked vegetables, and other delicacies. Increasingly, they are adding low-fat cheeses and other items in demand by newly diet-conscious Parisians. Many a hostess will assemble a meal from these prepared foods—without any embarrassment that her guests might have expected the various courses to have been homemade. Indeed, Parisian hostesses will point with pride to these assembled meals, noting how carefully they shopped to find the very best ready-to-go pâté, or whatever, available in Paris. Thus French housewives, as hostesses, have become great assemblers. Whether for a family meal or for entertaining, they will stop by the local Potin to buy precooked items to fill in the menu around a possible home-cooked main dish. In Paris, incidentally, the *sine qua non* for quality delicacies is the fabulous Fauchon.

When I lived on Rue Gallande in Paris, there was a convenient smaller supermarket on the same street that had limited supplies of most items, including frozen foods and complete meals. However, I preferred the individual specialty shops both for quality and, I must confess, for atmosphere. I made it a point to invite guests on the evenings of the days when the open-air market was functioning in my area, knowing I would have access to fresh and interesting ingredients—and that poking around the market would give me ideas for my menu.

Paul Bocuse goes so far as to insist that no cook should prepare a menu without first exploring what is available in the market. With increased urbanization, this concept of *cuisine du marché,* or the cookery of the marketplace, is becoming increasingly difficult for the French and certainly for the average American homemaker. Yet even in France, I did what I recommend doing when shopping in the United States. One knows from the newspapers, advertisements on store windows, and so forth what items are available and what the good values are. I begin with a menu in mind, but keep it loose enough so that other items I might find in the market can be added to, or substituted for, those on my menu. If I am planning to serve fish, I may change my mind as to which type to serve depending on the quality and availability of what I see in the shops, but I will still prepare fish. This applies, also, of course, to meats, but perhaps it is with vegetables and fruits that one's menu can be most elastic. If it included **Carrots Vichy,** for example, and while shopping one found especially appetizing string beans or asparagus instead, these should be substituted for the carrots.

When shopping in Paris, I would sometimes become so intrigued with a previously unknown or untried ingredient that I would experiment with it almost endlessly. One night when I had returned to Paris quite late, I had supper with some business associates at a favorite restaurant. I ordered steak, but asked the maître d' if I could please have anything else but the *pommes frites* that inevitably come with grilled steak. He nodded that I could, and the steak arrived accompanied by unfamiliar oval items in place of the potatoes. (Recent visitors to Paris have noted with surprise that most of the restaurants and bistros, especially those specializing in *nouvelle cuisine,* will now ask if you want vegetables *or* French-fried potatoes with meat dishes.) When I tried them, I knew I had savored something unusual and delicious. Wondering what they could be, I asked my associates to try some. Each reacted favorably, but no one knew what the mysterious but delectable vegetable was. The maître d' told me that it was *salsifis.* He did not know its English name, but confided his simple recipe for preparing this root, available in most French markets in season. After peeling, the 2-inch pieces are parboiled, drained, and sautéed in olive oil with minced garlic and chopped parsley.

I was so fascinated with *salsifis* that I bought as much as I could find while in Paris and experimented with it; but still I didn't know what it was called in English or whether it would be available at home. It wasn't until I returned to New York and was lunching at The Four Seasons that I found out. Fortunately, James Beard was also in the restaurant that day, and a friend brought my question to him. As quick as a flash, James Beard called across to me, "It's called salsify, or oyster root here, and you can probably buy some at Balducci's on Sixth Avenue!"

Whether living in Paris or visiting, one must explore its many special restaurants.

If one can afford *Michelin*-starred establishments, and if *la grande cuisine* is still one's choice, many expensive restaurants are available. But no one, Frenchmen included, could possibly eat regularly in these much-touted establishments and survive gastronomically or financially. Instead, Paris offers many less expensive restaurants that people frequent on a more regular basis; as in Italy, friends are eager to tell you of their favorites. I have also found that Parisians are reluctant to travel very far from the *quartier* in which they live: they prefer to frequent the best of neighborhood establishments rather than travel across the busy traffic to another section of Paris. Many of these restaurants are not rated by *Michelin* and are hardly mentioned by some of the other culinary guides.

One of the smaller restaurants, which has since been highly rated, that I enjoyed regularly and always found dependable was Chez Max, a short distance from the Madeleine on Rue de Castellane. Since it was at Chez Max that I learned a great deal about wines, we will pause here—instead of visiting its kitchen—to consider the important subject of French wines, their relative merits and methods of service. For instance, I learned from the maître d' there that some red wines should be chilled. Whenever I ordered a Beaujolais, it was immediately opened to let it breathe, and in warm weather placed in an ice bucket. The maître d' felt the same about clarets like St.-Emilion.

Experts tell us that red wines should be served at room temperature, while white wines and champagne should be chilled to between 40° F and 45° F. However, room temperature is quite a variable, depending on geographic location and the season of the year. As we know, wine should be stored for best results in a dark, cool place at a temperature between 55° F and 60° F. In the *Joy of Cooking*, Irma S. Rombauer says that with few exceptions wines should be served at 45° F to 60° F, while *The Dione Lucas Book of French Cooking* states categorically: "Beaujolais within a year of its vintage date is preferred slightly cool." Raymond Oliver, in his *La Cuisine,* is most specific on this score. Under "Serving Temperatures for Wines," he lists the following: "Beaujolais: slightly chilled, or at 60° F; Côtes du Rhône and Burgundy: cellar temperature, or just warm at 62° to 65° F; Red Bordeaux and Touraine: *chambrès,* from 65° to 68° F." *Chambrer* means to transfer a bottle of wine from the cooler cellar storage area to a warmer room a day or two before serving. This traditional procedure, however, was based on room temperature that rarely exceeded 60° F in the days before central heating.

In spite of all this, I still find most waiters and maître d's (in overly warm restaurants) astounded by my request to slightly cool bottles of red wine I order. Such are the pretensions of assumed expertise in all matters pertaining to wine.

But France has marvelous wines, and everyone is full of information about the prospects of each new harvest each year. A memorable experience for me was the annual arrival of the young *Beaujolais nouveau,* which is the recently harvested but not fully fermented wine. Every year in late November and early December, Frenchmen cherish this delicious young wine; it is featured in restaurants, bistros, and markets, and everywhere there are announcements of its arrival and availability. For several weeks it is the most popular wine in Paris.

Vin ordinaire, of course, is the daily wine of France, and is available in bottles of all sizes in wine shops and supermarkets. I have heard many tourists talk and write home about the excellent and inexpensive *vins ordinaires* they have tasted. However, so few of them know that these daily wines are blends made predominantly with Italian wine, as well as those from Tunisia and other countries! Most people assume that the French are great producers and consumers of their own wine, yet statistics show that every year the French are by far the greatest importers of Italian wines, used specifically for blending with lesser French wines for *vins ordinaires.*

Another illusion concerning the gastronomic capital of the world is that French restaurants have huge, scrupulously clean and well-equipped kitchens. Although commercial kitchens in France are adequate for the professional preparation and serving of food, standards of size and equipment do not compare favorably with those in our country. In many cases, this is because of the architectural brilliance of Paris and the stringent regulations regarding the conversion of its old buildings. The vaulted "caves," or basement areas, of Paris are hauntingly attractive when renovated for public use. However, many restaurants, including the famous three-star Maxim's and Grand Véfours, have had to locate their kitchens in these caves, beneath the main buildings that house the dining rooms. The limitations and compactness of space result in cramped arrangements of the kitchen equipment.

As Chef Amedé Lozach of La Côte Basque in New York told me, "Restaurant kitchens in France are generally much smaller than those in the United States, except in hotels, where they tend to be large, since space is often not a problem. Most of the kitchens are in basements. Both in New York and in Paris...the rent...is so high that the kitchens become the areas most affected. Dining rooms, which are obviously more visible to the diners, have to be attractive and spacious; but the kitchens, generally unseen by the public, have to fit into cost limitations; hence the basement area is used often."

Some of the kitchens in renowned Parisian restaurants are not respected highly by culinary experts who have visited them, either in terms of space, equipment, or standards of cleanliness. Still, the kitchen in a fine restaurant like the Tour d'Argent, which has excellent standards, is not much larger than those of outstanding provincial restaurants, which serve considerably fewer diners at each sitting.

Tom Margittai, co-owner (with Paul Kovi) of The Four Seasons in New York, points out that one of the reasons for the differences in size between kitchens in French and American restaurants is that French restaurants tend to serve fewer dishes to fewer diners than their American counterparts. This is even more evident in the case of restaurants serving *la nouvelle cuisine.* Michel Guérard's seasonal menu at his restaurant Eugénie-les-Bains offers only a few alternate choices for appetizer, main course, and dessert, and is backed by a proportionately large kitchen staff.

Freddy Giradet in his restaurant in Crissier in Switzerland serves a menu of similar size—with a staff of 30 serving a dining room that accommodates only 60 diners, which may help explain the tremendous attention to detail and the superb success of this restaurant. As Arthur Gold and Robert Fizdale wrote in *Vogue* magazine (February 1977), " 'I aged ten years after eating my first meal at Giradet's,' Michel Guérard . . . grudgingly whispered to us. When we asked the great Paul Bocuse . . . what he thought, he exploded, *'C'est la bombe!* Giradet is the only chef who ever astonished me.' "

Traditionally, the major restaurants in various countries, regardless of their particular specialization in cuisine, have followed what has since come to be called the French pattern. This refers to the organization of the kitchen under the supreme authority of the executive chef. The "pattern" is followed not only in the temples of *la grande cuisine* but also in the more personal kitchens specializing in *la nouvelle cuisine.* As Tom Margittai puts it, "The *nouvelle* kitchens don't vary very much from the French or European pattern, except that they will have more steamers for *cuisine à la vapeur* and more *robots coupes."* (The latter are heavy-duty professional food processors.)

A French professional kitchen is run like a military establishment, under the unquestioned rule of the executive chef. Working under him in close collaboration are the *sous-chef* and the *chefs de partie,* who are in charge of the various departments responsible for the preparation of sauces, pastry, meat, fish, and vegetables. The *sous-chef* is senior, and in the executive chef's absence assumes total responsi-

bility for the kitchen. The *saucier,* in charge of preparing sauces, is considered the next most important member of the kitchen brigade. Following him are the *entremettier* (vegetables), the *rôtisseur* (roasting, grilling, and frying), the *pâtissier* (pastry), and the *garde manger* (provisions and supplies), who also prepares cold dishes and hors d'oeuvre and supervises the cutting and preparation of meat and fish for the cooks. Larger kitchen operations also will have a *chef tournant,* who takes over a different post each day, relieving the *chefs de partie* on a rotating basis. Each department will have one or more assistants, called *commis.*

Smaller, family-style restaurants are divided more simply into four principal divisions: roasting chef, fish chef, pastry chef and the commissary or storeroom for supplies, with one or more chefs in each of these categories, again depending upon the size of the operation. Of course, the bistro, specializing in *la cuisine bourgeoise,* is an extension of the family kitchen, and is simply a "Mamma and Poppa" operation, with the husband usually functioning as the chef, and perhaps doubling as bartender, and the wife at the *caisse,* or cash register, and handling in some instances the commissary.

An unusual and effective instance of the latter is the Restaurant Le Biarritz, specializing in *la cuisine bourgeoise,* in New York City. Marie-Louise and Ambroise Vaillant are a talented team, both as patrons and cooks. Although Ambroise Vaillant is the head chef, Madame Marie-Louise arrives several mornings a week at 7:00 A.M. to prepare sauces. Her husband arrives about 9:30 to start cooking for the day, and with the aid of a single dishwasher can handle all the cooking for 300 servings. Later, when the diners arrive, he doubles as bartender and takes over the *caisse,* while Madame greets the diners and functions as waitress. In the evenings they have a grill chef to assist them.

After closing each night, Marie-Louise also prepares all the pastry, in their apartment upstairs; and on Sundays, when the restaurant is closed, she polishes the copper pots, one of the major decorative items in the restaurant.

Another major difference between the outstanding *nouvelle* kitchens and those of the traditional *haute cuisine* concerns the preparation of sauces. In *nouvelle* kitchens, the sauces will be made daily with fresh ingredients, and only in quantities necessary for specific dishes. In *haute cuisine* kitchens, the stocks from which sauces are made are often kept simmering on the stove for days, even weeks!

Chef Alain Senderens of L'Archestrate, in an interview with James Villas in *Town and Country* magazine (April 1977), said: "For some fifty or sixty years there was not only an absolute halt in the evolution of our cuisine but, even worse, the quality of French cooking began to waver drastically. Take stocks, for instance, the very foundation of our classic sauces. For years chefs kept a stockpot simmering... throwing in anything from time to time, never degreasing the liquid and simply letting the *fond* (stock) become a disgusting mess. Today what stocks we do use contain only the finest fresh ingredients and are purified as much as possible."

James Villas continues: "At one point during my stay in Paris I had occasion to verify Senderens' insinuation by sneaking into the kitchen of one of the city's most famous three-star 'temples' and viewing the stockpots. Suffice to say, after the spectacle I observed, you could never drag me back into the place."

To truly appreciate the demands of time and energy required of the executive chef and his staff, one must spend some time in a typical professional restaurant planned and operated in the French pattern. Culinary specialists are aware of the fact that the concept of kitchen planning and the general organization of luxury restaurants serving French food in the United States was begun almost single-handedly by Henri Soulé, who served as the youngest maître d'hôtel at the French pavilion at the New York world's fair in the late 1930s. Encouraged by its huge success in serving fine and authentic French food, Soulé remained in this country and became patron of the famous Le Chambord, Le Pavillon, and La Côte Basque, as well as influencing the establishment of such other outstanding restaurants in the French pattern as Le Grenouille and La Caravelle. When Henri Soulé died in the 1960s, Madame Henriette Spalter took over La Côte Basque as *patronne,* with Albert Spalter as the manager; they still operate the restaurant maintaining Soulé's original high standards for the preparation and serving of fine French food.

Let's visit with Chef *Amedè Lozach* in the kitchen of New York's *La Côte Basque,* which is, like its counterparts in Paris, located in the basement of the building housing the elegant and well-appointed dining room above. The kitchen is considerably larger than those one would find in Paris for a similar establishment, but is representative of kitchens in the French pattern.

We arrive about 9:00 A.M. to find the first shift of the kitchen staff quietly and efficiently at work. The *saucier,* or sauce chef, has been working since 7:30, as has the vegetable man. The other staff members begin arriving at 8:00, and Executive Chef Lozach will arrive at about 10:00, having placed his orders for the produce and ingredients at 9:00 P.M. the night before. (He has also worked with the *sous-chef* and the second kitchen crew until about 10:30 P.M., when he regularly leaves the *sous-chef* in charge of the kitchen operations; the kitchen is closed at about 11:00 P.M., and everything is put in order for the first crew the next morning.)

La Côte Basque's kitchen is sprawling, even meandering—but efficiently designed. Dominating it is the huge professional stove, or *fourneau,* a long Vulcan gas range with ovens and two-tier grill; parallel to the range is the steam table, which also affords ample cutting surfaces and other work areas; and immediately overhead, an enormous rack with pans and skillets hangs within easy reach of the cooks. Surrounding this center of activity, but all in the main kitchen, are the pastry, salad, and dishwashing areas; adjoining the kitchen, in a small separate room, is the commissary or storeroom, which also serves as Chef Lozach's office. Above his desk and file cabinets are shelves containing canned items, coffee, sugars, packages of spaghetti, silver polish, and other cleaning items; it is not unlike the pantry in a well-stocked home. To the right of the commissary is the wine cellar. The kitchen also opens into a third room, the work center for the *garde manger* and his staff, responsible for the preparation of meats, fish, and vegetables.

One feels the heat of the *fourneau* and the intensely bright overhead lights; the chef and his staff all wear light cotton jackets. But the atmosphere is informal, with only the *saucier* wearing the traditional *toque blanche,* or chef's hat, jauntily on his head. It is also quiet. Everyone moves about confidently and with purpose; there is little chatter, and one senses a rhythm of accomplishment as the staff cooperates to meet the inexorable 12:30 P.M. "deadline," when everything has to be prepared and ready for the arrival of the luncheon diners.

The ordering procedure is equally efficient; the maître d' takes the order and gives it to the waiter, who in turn rushes down the flight of stairs to the kitchen and places it with the head cooks. The executive chef or *sous-chef* supervises and checks each completed dish before it is handed over to the waiter, who records the order formally with the *cassis,* then places the food on *la guéridon,* or serving table, which has an individual heating unit *(le réchaud).* The serving table is rolled into the dining room to the diner's table, where the food is heated, if necessary, before being served. Such reheating, incidentally, never applies to dishes containing sauces; these are brought from the kitchen in well-covered casseroles. Roasted or stuffed meats, the chief elements of some *plats du jour,* are placed in *la voiture,* the steam table, which keeps them covered and ready to be carved and served. And to facilitate ready service, Chef Lozach has the main element of some dishes prepared in advance. Take *poularde au champagne,* for example: since it takes about 45 minutes to roast these chickens, three or four will be roasted ahead; as these are used for orders, another group of chickens will be started, so that there is no unnecessary waiting. The restaurant has fixed price menus with nine *plats du jour,* which of course vary daily, plus ten specialties available daily at a supplementary charge.

It is now slightly after 11:00 A.M., and the morning kitchen crew of the restaurant is just about to have lunch. Their luncheon break is from 11:15 to noon, while the evening crew will have dinner from 6:15 P.M. to 7:00—in both instances, of course, before the dining room is open to guests. The dining room staff, except for the captains and maître d', eat in a separate room near the kitchen at the same time as the kitchen staff, and have the same food. The captains and maître d' will eat upstairs in the dining room at about 3:00 P.M. after the luncheon diners have left.

While the other members of his staff are busily performing their duties, Chef Amedé Lozach discusses the kitchen operation with us—between an occasional phone call or question from a member of the brigade. The chef considers his role to be organizational and executive; he must preside over each separate operation of the restaurant, be aware of costs, and be able to delegate work to others. However, we find him marvelously relaxed and pleasant with his staff. As he says, "Pressure doesn't help anyone in the kitchen. I have good people who know their job, and

most of them have been with the restaurant for many years." Only the *saucier* is new to the establishment, having arrived from France about three months ago.

The chef has been with La Côte Basque for nine years, originally as the *sous-chef,* or second in command. Before that, he worked in a restaurant in La Place de la République in Paris and attended the École des Hôteliers de Paris. Under him, the executive staff at La Côte Basque consists of the *sous-chef,* the *saucier,* and head cook. Ordinarily, the French pattern also calls for a pastry chef. The restaurant's former pastry chef, however, Guy Pascal, now operates its new retail shop, Délices La Côte Basque, which supplies the pastry requirements of the restaurant in exchange for pâtés and terrines that Chef Lozach prepares for the shop. Actually, in France, the pastry chef is usually located outside the kitchen proper.

The balance of his staff consists of three cooks in the morning and three (as the second crew) in the afternoon; plus a chef responsible primarily for the preparation of omelettes; hors d'oeuvres, fish, and meat chefs; a vegetable man; an oyster man; four dishwashers in the morning and five in the evening; and pot washers. This staff handles between 60 and 100 servings for luncheon and between 80 and 150 for dinner. Even with such an effective staff, and efficiently run as La Côte Basque's kitchen is, Chef Amedé Lozach devotes at least 13 hours to it each day except for Sunday, when the restaurant is closed.

One cannot help but notice, incidentally, that the restaurant business is primarily a man's world; with only a few exceptions, one finds very few women in operations like La Côte Basque's. The question is inevitably raised: Can women handle the demands of time and energy necessary to obtain training in professional restaurant kitchens? The new wave of *nouvelle* chefs, particularly Bocuse, have openly denigrated women as professional chefs, stressing that women simply do not have the necessary stamina.

Nevertheless, many women have successfully functioned as fine chefs in France and elsewhere in the world. We have already met Madame Marie-Louise Vaillant and noted her schedule and accomplishments at Le Biarritz; we might also consider the accomplishments of one of the most famous women chefs, Léa Bidault, who in her 70s still operates Chez Léa in Lyons. Robert Courtine has referred to her as "the *grande dame,* the Holy Mother, of our gastronomic capital." Paul Bocuse and other three-star chefs are regular customers in her restaurant, which has justly earned its own *Michelin* stars over the years. As part of her operation, Madame Léa begins the day at 7:00 A.M., shopping in the nearby markets, and is usually at the restaurant from luncheon to closing time, near midnight. Apparently, when one has the desire and dedication, the necessary stamina is forthcoming, whether the chef is male or female.

However, there is no gainsaying the fact that the preparation of food in restaurants is necessarily done under pressure. How many of us realize that cooking at home, even when preparing large festive meals, is always easier and yields more successful finished dishes than is possible in the best and most efficient of restaurant kitchens? As we have mentioned previ-

ously, Chef Jean-Pierre Ferraro of La Crémaillère has confessed that good home cooks can do everything more quickly and naturally than chefs working under the pressures inherent in a professional classic kitchen.

As we have seen, then, both *la grande cuisine* and *la cuisine bourgeoise* are in a state of flux; each is waning from formerly acclaimed high standards. And as James Beard has noted, French home cooking isn't what it once was. With reference to *la grande cuisine,* Jean Didier, director of *Guide Kléber,* was recently asked by Baron Andries de Groot about the quality of classic cuisine in *Michelin*-starred French restaurants. His blunt reply was, "The *grande luxe* restaurants of Paris are no longer the first tables of France. They represent nothing except *grande luxe*—maintained by wealthy amateurs who are in no way connoisseurs, who are simply drawn to a familiar and chichi name and are entirely unaware of the changes in history."

Yet the *nouvelle cuisine* chefs, as well as the younger chefs in the provinces expounding *cuisine d'aujourd'hui,* are aware of changes in history. What is their prognostication for the future of French cuisine? Perhaps Alain Chapel, who like Bocuse and the Troisgros brothers has journeyed to the United States, has the answer. "I came to look Americans over," Chapel confesses in an article in *Bon Appétit* magazine (November 1977); "I was very impressed by their eagerness to learn French cuisine. In France, traditions are slowly fading. Three-star restaurants are a luxury; we are not even an industry, but here I think we can keep traditions alive.... Yes," he concluded. "America

will be the new repository of French tradition."

With this encouragement, let's now explore our slimming adaptations of traditional French dishes that we can add to our international repertoire. Not only will we be aware of "changes in history," but we will keep Escoffier's tenet in mind: *"Surtout faîtes simple"* ("Above all, keep things simple"). As previously noted, Curnonsky, who was considered the prince of gourmets in the Paris of the 1920s, put it succinctly: "Great cooking is when things taste of what they are."

MENU AND RECIPES

MENU

Escargots à la Bourguignonne
Épaule d'Agneau Farcie
Haricots Verts
Salade de Tomatoes
Sorbet au Cassis
Café Filtre

Snails Bourguignonne
Stuffed Shoulder of Lamb
French Green Beans
Brittany Tomato Salad
Cassis Sherbet
French Filtered Coffee

ESCARGOTS À LA BOURGUIGNONNE*
(Snails Bourguignonne)

It wasn't until my initial trip to Paris that I ventured to order snails. I immediately become addicted to these delectable morsels and have remained a snail enthusiast ever since.

These terrestrial vegetarians lend themselves to a number of delicious variations and can be made easily with specially cultivated canned snails, which are generally used in most restaurants and home kitchens. For those who would like the experience of preparing fresh snails, I am including directions for their preparation in the Bonus Ideas below.

4 dozen each, canned snails and snail shells
1 cup white wine or dry vermouth
¼ pound polyunsaturated margarine
2 tablespoons minced shallots or 1½ tablespoons grated onion
2 cloves garlic, mashed
2 tablespoons chopped parsley
½ teaspoon coarse salt
½ teaspoon white pepper
⅓ cup grated Swiss or Parmesan cheese
YIELD: Eight servings

1. Remove snails from can, discard liquid, and drain the snails before placing in a saucepan with the wine; simmer for 10 minutes. Drain again and allow to cool, discarding the cooking liquid.

2. Combine the balance of the ingredients, except the grated cheese, and blend well. Place 1 teaspoon of the mixture into each shell, insert one snail into each, then fill the balance of the shell with the balance of the mixture, or additional margarine as necessary.

3. Dip the stuffed shells into the grated cheese and place on escargot plates or crinkled aluminum foil. Add a little water to the bottom of the plates and sprinkle the shells with additional grated cheese. Just before serving, place in a preheated oven at 400° F for about 10 minutes. Serve with croutons or French bread—preferably with the traditional tongs and fork made especially for eating snails.

Bonus Ideas: Escoffier recommends sprinkling the stuffed snail shells with bread crumbs, instead of grated cheese, before heating in the oven.

Ceramic snail dishes, with indentations for stuffing, are available in many specialty shops. And though I personally prefer using snail shells, which can be washed and reserved for future use, you can use mushroom caps, topping each cap with the snail and margarine mixture, which adds to the taste of the dish.

To prepare **Escargots au Vin*** (Snails Marinated in Wine) for six servings, place 18 drained snails in an earthenware bowl with 2 cups of dry white wine or champagne; marinate three hours or overnight. Drain and reserve the marinade. Prepare half the margarine mixture as for *Escargots à la Bourguignonne.* Using 18 large mushroom caps, fill each with 1 snail and some of the mixture. Prepare 6 *papillotes,* using 10-inch squares of aluminum foil. Spray the dull side of each with cookware spray. Place 3 filled mushroom caps on each square of foil and fold into a triangle. Add a proportionate amount of the reserved marinade. Seal the edges of the foil envelope and bake in a preheated oven at 350° F for about 15 minutes. Serve the sealed *papillotes,* to be opened by each diner, on individual plates.

The following recipe also uses mushroom caps.

ESCARGOTS AU CURRIE (Stuffed Mushrooms with Curried Snails)

18 large mushroom caps
6 tablespoons polyunsaturated margarine
18 canned snails
1 cup white wine or dry vermouth
2 teaspoons curry powder
1 cup *Sauce Mornay*
1 teaspoon coarse salt
3 twists of pepper mill
⅓ cup grated Parmesan cheese
Cookware spray
YIELD: Six servings

1. Sauté the mushroom caps in a skillet with half of the margarine for about 3 minutes. Remove the mushrooms and set aside, reserving the juices in the skillet. Add the snails and the balance of the margarine; sauté for about 2 minutes. Pour in the wine and stir well

2. Apply cookware spray to a baking dish and arrange the mushroom caps in it, leaving spaces between them; then place a snail on each cap.

3. Blend the curry powder with the wine and juices in the skillet, simmer over low heat for 3 minutes, add the **Sauce Mornay,** salt, and pepper, and bring to a boil. Spoon the sauce over the stuffed mushrooms.

4. Just before serving, sprinkle the stuffed mushrooms with grated Parmesan

cheese and place in an oven preheated to 450° F for about 5 minutes.

Bonus Ideas: Mussels can be used instead of snails in most recipes. To prepare **Moules à l'Escargot** for six servings, prepare 3 quarts of **Moules à la Marinière** (Mussels, Fisherman's Style). These are made by thoroughly washing, scrubbing, and bearding 3 quarts of mussels. Place 1 large diced onion, 4 sprigs of parsley, 1 bay leaf, and ½ teaspoon dried thyme in a heavy pot with cover. Add the mussels, 1 cup of dry white wine or dry vermouth, and low heat for about 12 minutes, or until the mussels have opened. Discard any mussels that have not opened. If serving as *Moules à la Marinière,* add 3 tablespoons of chopped parsley and serve hot in a tureen over slices of French bread or English muffins. If preparing *Moules à l'Escargot*,* remove the mussels; wash and dry half as many shells as you have mussels. Place one mussel on each shell, stuff with the margarine mixture for *Escargots à la Bourguignonne,* and proceed with the balance of instructions for that recipe.

Snails are considered a delicacy in many other countries besides France. The Romans and Chinese prized them centuries ago; and, in fact, most of the snails used in France today are imported from Middle Europe and such countries as Turkey, China, Greece, and Algeria. In Greece, **Saligaria** is prepared in the same manner as Snails Bourguignonne, except that they are dipped in a combination of bread crumbs and Parmesan cheese before baking in the oven.

In the first century A.D., Pliny the Elder held Sicilian snails to be the best in the world. Here is a Sicilian recipe for snails still popular today:

LUMACHE ALLA SICILIANA
(Snails Sicilian Style)

2 tablespoons chicken broth or white wine
1 onion, chopped
1 clove garlic, mashed
1 teaspoon fresh rosemary or ½ teaspoon dried
1 tablespoon tomato paste or ketchup
2 cups boiling water
3 dozen canned snails
1 teaspoon coarse salt
¼ teaspoon white pepper
1 tablespoon chopped parsley
Cookware spray
YIELD: Six servings

1. Apply cookware spray to large saucepan; add the broth and sauté the onions and garlic until the onions are translucent. Add the rosemary and tomato paste; simmer for 5 minutes, stirring constantly.

2. Gradually add the water and bring the mixture to a boil. Stir in the snails and simmer for 15 minutes. Season with the salt, pepper, and parsley, and simmer, covered, for 30 minutes.

3. Serve the snails with their juices in soup plates, accompanied by croutons or crusty bread. Provide additional chopped parsley or chives for further garnishing, if desired.

Bonus Ideas: Both the Romans and the

Milanese include anchovy filets in their recipes for snails. To prepare **Lumache alla Romana*** (Snails, Roman Style) for six servings, you will need 3 dozen canned snails. Apply cookware spray to a casserole and sauté *au sec* one minced clove of garlic, 2 tablespoons chopped parsley, 6 mashed anchovies, 1 chopped roast sweet red pepper, and 1 teaspoon chopped fresh mint. Add 1 teaspoon coarse salt and ¼ teaspoon white pepper and simmer over low heat for 30 minutes. Drain the snails, add to the sauce, and cook 5 minutes longer before serving hot in the casserole.

The Italians also have a delightful way of preparing snails with fritter dough.

BIGNÈ DI LUMACHE
(Italian Snail Fritters)

6 dozen canned snails
1 cup olive or corn oil
¼ cup lemon juice
3 tablespoons chopped parsley
½ teaspoon coarse salt
3 twists of a pepper mill

Pastella per Bignè (Fritter Dough):
¼ cup white rye or potato flour
⅛ teaspoon baking powder
¼ teaspoon coarse salt
5 egg whites
3 tablespoons corn oil
⅛ teaspoon cayenne
½ cup skim evaporated milk
½ cup olive, corn, or peanut oil
YIELD: Six servings

1. In an earthenware bowl, combine the drained snails, 1 cup of olive oil, lemon juice, parsley, and seasonings; marinate for 2 or more hours. Drain and pat dry before using.

2. Prepare the Fritter Dough by sifting the flour, baking powder, and salt 6 times and combining in an electric blender with the balance of the dough ingredients except the milk. Add the milk gradually as the mixture is blended at high speed for no more than 30 seconds. Refrigerate for 2 hours. When ready to use, beat the mixture lightly for 5 minutes.

3. Preheat the oven to 400° F, pour a thin layer of oil into a baking dish, and heat until the oil is 375° F (when a cube of bread dropped into the oil turns golden brown). Dip the reserved snails into the batter and brown on all sides in the hot oil. Drain on paper toweling, arrange on a hot serving platter with lemon wedges or preferably garnished with fried parsley and lemon wedges, and serve with **Marinara Tomato Sauce.**

Bonus Ideas: For those who wish to use fresh snails in these recipes, here are a few pointers that have been known ever since the ancient Romans cultivated snails on special farms. Many enthusiasts are now cultivating snails (on a smaller scale) by placing live snails in a barrel with a mesh wire cover. Being vegetarians, the snails can be fed fresh lettuce leaves or other greens.

Since uncultivated snails may eat vegetable matter not beneficial to humans, they are "purged" in various ways. Fortunately, the fresh snails in American markets generally are imported from North Africa and need little preparation. Simply soak them in tepid water until the membrane that covers the shell is broken and the head of the snail emerges; be sure to discard any snails shells from which the heads do not emerge. Boil in **Court Bouillon** for about 3 hours, and drain before using in any of the above recipes.

The Europeans, however, insist on a more complicated procedure to purge the snails found locally in their vineyards. Some experts say they should not be fed for at least two weeks or more; others recommend placing the live snails for several days in a covered wicker basket with heads of lettuce and slices of bread that have been soaked in water or milk and then wrung dry. If you follow this procedure, after 3 or more days, thoroughly wash the snails in running water; then soak them in an enamel basin with water to cover, seasoned with a cup of vinegar and 2 tablespoons coarse salt. Drain and place in a basin under running water until the water in the pan is clear. At this point, the heads of the snails should emerge from the shells; those that do not should be discarded. Place the snails in a pan with water to cover and bring to a boil; simmer for 10 minutes. Drain and cool; then remove the snails from their shells. Snip off the tips of their heads and the black tail ends and cook in **Court Bouillon,** simmering for 3 hours. Drain before using in any of the recipes.

But as we have said, most restaurants and home kitchens use canned, specially cultivated, and already purged snails.

ÉPAULE D'AGNEAU FARCIE*
(Stuffed Shoulder of Lamb)

Stuffed shoulder of lamb, breast of lamb, or breast of veal are all popular dishes in the French provinces. These are, of course, inexpensive cuts of meat which become marvelously festive when enhanced with stuffings of aromatic herbs and vegetables.

Hopefully, your butcher can supply you with a boned 3-pound shoulder of lamb cut from the shank end. If not, you might buy the whole shoulder, use the shank end for this recipe and the other half to prepare another favorite lamb recipe: **Agneau Glacé** (Glazed Lamb).

4 tablespoons white wine or dry vermouth
1 small onion, chopped
1 clove garlic, mashed (optional)
8 medium mushrooms, minced
4 ounces Canadian bacon, diced
¼ teaspoon each, dried rosemary and
   thyme
1 teaspoon chopped parsley
1 teaspoon coarse salt
4 twists of a pepper mill
3 pounds shoulder of lamb, boned
1 tablespoon corn or peanut oil
1 each, large carrot and large onion, sliced
1 cup meat stock or beef bouillon
3 sprigs of tarragon or parsley
Cookware spray
YIELD: Six servings

1. Apply cookware spray to a skillet, add half the wine, and sauté the onion and optional garlic until the onion is translucent. Add the mushrooms, Canadian bacon, herbs, and seasonings, and cook for 3 minutes, stirring occasionally.

2. Trim the excess fat from the boned lamb and lay flat, skin side down. Discard the garlic and spread the mushroom mixture evenly on the meat; then roll the meat into a long cylinder and tie with kitchen twine.

3. Preheat the oven to 350° F and

brush the rolled lamb with the oil. Place the carrot and onion slices into a roasting pan with 1 teaspoon of water. Insert a standing meat rack, place the rolled lamb on the rack, and roast for about 2 hours, or until tender.

4. Remove the lamb, discard the twine, and place on a platter in a warm place, or cover with aluminum foil. Skim the juices in the pan and place on the range. Add the rest of the wine and deglaze the food particles over high heat; then mash the cooked carrots and onions. Add the meat stock, adjust the seasonings, then bring to a boil for 10 minutes, stirring constantly.

5. Strain the sauce and pour over the stuffed lamb, which has been garnished with blanched twigs of fresh tarragon, rosemary, or parsley.

Bonus Ideas: Stuffed Breast of Lamb is also featured in *la cuisine bourgeoise*. To prepare **Poitrine d'Agneau Farcie** for six servings, have your butcher bone a 4-pound breast of lamb and remove the layer of fat under the skin. Sew all but one end to form a pouch, as in preparing **Cima ala Genovese.** Prepare the stuffing by blending 1 pound chopped lean pork or sausage meat, ½ pound chopped Canadian bacon, and 3 tablespoons minced parsley. Add 3 egg whites, 2 tablespoons corn oil, ½ pound raisins, 1 teaspoon coarse salt, 5 twists of a pepper mill and ⅛ teaspoon nutmeg. Mix the stuffing well, then stuff the meat, leaving room for expansion. Sew the open end and pierce each side of the pouch several times to allow steam to escape. Dip the meat in water, drain but do not pat dry. Brown in a very hot skillet on all sides. In a large casserole, sauté 2 tablespoons of wine, 2 chopped onions, and 1 mashed clove of garlic for 5 minutes. Place the browned meat on top of the onion mixture and roast in an oven at 375° F for about 1½ hours, or until fork tender.

You can garnish this dish with blanched fresh herbs, as with Stuffed Shoulder of Lamb, or you can garnish with **Épinards au Sec** (Steamed Spinach). Wash, but do not drain, 2 pounds of fresh spinach; steam over medium heat in a tightly covered pan with ½ teaspoon coarse salt, until the spinach is *al dente.* Mix the spinach with 4 tablespoons polyunsaturated margarine, ⅛ teaspoon fruit sugar or pure maple syrup, and a pinch of nutmeg. Heat through before serving in 6 mounds surrounding the roast and topped with 3 grilled cherry tomatoes on each mound.

One of the easiest and most economical lamb dishes the French make is one that you can prepare in half an hour. Instead of stuffing the meat, you roll it with herbs and enhance its flavor by garnishing with sautéed artichoke bottoms filled with cooked fresh peas. This is a delightful dish for entertaining.

NOISETTES D'AGNEAU AUX FONDS D'ARTICHAUT
(Lamb Noisettes with Artichoke Bottoms)

1 loin of lamb from the neck end, 6 ribs or more

1 *Bouquet Garni*
2 each carrots and celery stalks
1½ cups water
1 teaspoon coarse salt
5 twists of a pepper mill
¼ teaspoon each, dried rosemary and
   thyme
1 can artichoke bottoms or 8 large
   mushroom caps
3 tablespoons polyunsaturated margarine
4 tablespoons cooked fresh or frozen peas
2 tablespoons Maderia or sherry
1 bunch of water-cress
YIELD: Four to six servings

1. Have your butcher remove the skin and excess fat from the loin of lamb, and separate the meat from the rib and base bones (or try this yourself with a sharp knife). Place the bones in a saucepan with the *Bouquet Garni,* the carrots and celery, and 1½ cups of water; simmer over medium heat for at least 1 hour. Drain, discard the bones, the *Bouquet Garni,* and the vegetables, but reserve the stock. This can be prepared well in advance.

2. Sprinkle the inner side of the boned meat with the salt, pepper, and herbs; roll up tightly into a long cylinder and tie with kitchen twine at 1½-inch intervals. Cut through the meat between the twine, preparing 6 or more 1½-inch *noisettes.*

3. Wash and drain the artichoke bottoms and pat dry. If using mushroom caps, gently rub with a damp cloth. Sauté with a third of the margarine and set aside in a warm place. Heat the cooked peas with a dab of margarine.

4. Sauté the *noisettes* with the balance of the margarine over medium heat for about 5 minutes on each side. Transfer to a warm platter, place an artichoke bottom or mushroom cap on each *noisette,* and fill with the peas.

5. Prepare the sauce by adding ¾ cup of the lamb stock and the Maderia to the pan juices; bring to a boil and stir for 3 minutes. Season and stir in 2 tablespoons of margarine. To serve, garnish the center of the platter with **Carrots Vichy** or **Glazed Carrots,** arrange the *noisettes* around the carrots, follow with a rim of watercress sprigs. Serve the hot sauce separately.

Bonus Ideas: *Glazed Carrots* are made by cooking 1 pound of baby carrots or larger ones cut into 2-inch lengths *au sec* until they are *al dente.* Simmer the cooked carrots with 2 tablespoons margarine, 1½ tablespoons honey or pure maple syrup, and ½ teaspoon cinnamon or ground ginger until the carrots are glazed all over.

If you have reserved 3 to 4 pounds of boned shoulder of lamb, you can easily prepare another favorite, *Glazed Shoulder of Lamb.*

AGNEAU GLACÉ*
(Glazed Shoulder of Lamb)

3½ pounds shoulder of lamb, boned,
   rolled, and tied
1 6-ounce can frozen orange juice
   concentrate
4 tablespoons lemon juice
6 tablespoons polyunsaturated margarine
½ teaspoon coarse salt
½ cup minced celery
1 tablespoon dried mint
YIELD: Six to eight servings

1. Roast the rolled and tied lamb in a

casserole in an oven at 350° F for about 45 minutes. Combine the thawed orange concentrate with the lemon juice, margarine, and salt; simmer over low heat for 5 minutes.

2. Brush the lamb with the juice mixture every 15 minutes, continuing to roast until lamb is fork tender (about 1½ hours in all). Place the meat on a warm platter, or wrap in aluminum foil if not serving immediately.

3. Place the casserole on the range. Add the celery to the pan juices and simmer over medium heat for 5 minutes. Stir in the mint before serving the hot sauce with the lamb.

Bonus Ideas: Either a microwave oven or a pressure cooker can considerably cut down the cooking time for Glazed Shoulder of Lamb. If using a microwave oven, place the juice mixture in a glass measuring cup and cook uncovered for 1 minute. Place an inverted ovenproof saucer in the oven and rest a baking dish containing the lamb on the saucer. Baste the meat with the hot juice mixture and roast, uncovered, for 10 minutes. Turn the roast, baste again, and cook for 5 minutes. Baste and roast for an additional 15 minutes, basting at least 3 more times. Wrap the lamb in aluminum foil. Insert a meat thermometer; it should read about 155° F when the meat is medium rare, and after standing 30 minutes, will rise to about 170° F. Add the celery to the cooking juices in the baking dish, heat for 2 minutes, then stir in the mint. Serve the sauce with the lamb.

If using a pressure cooker, dip the rolled lamb in cold water, drain, but do not pat dry. Remove the trivet from the cooker and brown the meat on all sides over very high heat. Lift out the lamb; add the juice mixture; replace the trivet and the meat. When the valve is engaged, cook at 15-pound pressure for 12 minutes per pound of meat. Reduce the pressure with cold water, remove the lamb to a warm place, or wrap in aluminum foil until ready to serve. Add the celery to the pan juices and cook over medium heat for 5 minutes. Stir in the mint leaves before serving the hot sauce with the lamb.

HARICOTS VERTS
(French Green Beans)

Although frozen green beans may be used in this recipe, tender, young, whole green beans are preferred. If older and larger beans are used, they should be cut into 1½-inch lengths. *Haricots blancs,* or wax beans, can be used interchangeably or in combination with green beans in these recipes. If possible, use the tender dwarf variety that are a specialty in France and can be grown in your garden.

1½ pounds green beans
½ teaspoon coarse salt
3 tablespoons polyunsaturated margarine
4 twists of a pepper mill
YIELD: Four to six servings

1. Trim off the tips of the beans, wash and drain, but do not pat dry. Cook *au sec* in a tightly covered pan with the salt for about 10 minutes until *al dente,* shuffling the pot occasionally.

2. Drain in a colander, adding cold water to stop the cooking process. Pat dry with paper toweling and set aside.

3. Just before serving, melt the margarine in a skillet and toss the green beans in the pan over medium heat, until they are entirely coated. Serve on a warm platter sprinkled with black pepper.

Bonus Ideas: Instead of the black pepper, sprinkle the coated green beans with 1½ tablespoons of fresh *fines herbs* for **Haricots Verts aux Fines Herbes.** You can prepare your own *fines herbes* with equal parts of fresh or dried parsley, chervil, tarragon, and chives. The combination can be varied to taste with such aromatic herbs as basil, thyme, celery, and fennel seed. When dried herbs are used instead of fresh, always use only half the quantity called for.

A heartier version is **Haricots Verts à la Provençale** (French Green Beans with Tomatoes). After cooking the beans, sauté one small chopped onion with 2 tablespoons of broth or white wine until the onions are translucent. Add 1 cup fresh or canned Italian-style plum tomatoes, 1 mashed garlic clove, ½ teaspoon salt, and 4 twists of a pepper mill. Simmer over medium heat for 15 minutes, or until the sauce has the consistency of a purée. Add the cooked beans and simmer over low heat for 10 minutes. Garnish with chopped parsley before serving.

These heartier versions, including **Salade Liègeoise** (Belgian Green Bean and Potato Salad), can be served with hot or cold meat entrées and are often prepared as luncheon dishes. After cooking the beans, boil 3 large potatoes in their skins. Cool, peel, and slice the potatoes. Prepare a salad bowl with the cooked beans rimmed with the sliced potatoes; sprinkle with ¼ cup each of minced onion and parsley, 1 teaspoon salt, and 5 twists of a pepper mill. Sauté ¼ cup diced Canadian bacon with 1 tablespoon margarine until crisp; then add to the bean combination. Before serving, sprinkle with ¼ cup of wine or rice vinegar and toss.

Another well-known variation is **Sauce Ravigote,** which involves the addition of 1 teaspoon each of fresh parsley, chervil, tarragon, and chives; ¼ cup minced onion; and 1 tablespoon of minced unsalted capers to **Sauce Vinaigrette.**

SALADE DE TOMATES
(Brittany Tomato Salad)

The tomato, especially popular in southern France, is enjoyed in many variations: sliced, stuffed with seafood and/or other ingredients, or in salads.

When served uncooked in France, tomatoes are usually peeled, as explained below. This is done simply by placing them in a large heat-proof container and covering them with boiling water for about 30 seconds. The drained tomatoes can then be easily peeled and the stem sections trimmed away.

4 large, firm tomatoes
½ cup *Sauce Vinaigrette*
1 teaspoon minced onion (optional)
2 tablespoons chopped chives or parsley
YIELD: Six servings

1. After covering the tomatoes with boiling water for 30 seconds in a large heat-proof container, peel and discard the stem sections. Cut the tomatoes crosswise into ¼-inch slices and arrange them, slightly overlapping, in a deep serving platter.

2. Sprinkle with optional onion and the chives or parsley before pouring the **Sauce Vinaigrette** evenly over the slices. Chill in the refrigerator, occasionally basting with the dressing before serving.

Bonus Ideas: An attractive variation is **Tomates Accordéon** (Accordion Tomatoes). For this, slice the tomatoes up to but not through the stem end; then open the slices accordion fashion. Insert thin slices of cucumber, green sweet pepper, or *fromage blanc,* as in preparing **Insalata Caprese.** Add a tablespoon of **Slimming Mayonnaise,** which is made as follows:

SLIMMING MAYONNAISE

2 egg whites, hard boiled
2 egg whites, uncooked
2 tablespoons olive or corn oil
1 cup plain yogurt or part-skim ricotta cheese
1 teaspoon dry mustard
1 teaspoon lemon juice
1 teaspoon diced scallions or ½ teaspoon grated onion
⅛ teaspoon dried basil
1 tablespoon minced parsley
Coarse salt and pepper to taste
⅛ teaspoon Tabasco or cayenne
YIELD: One-and-one-third cups

1. The eggs, oil, and blender bowl must be at room temperature, about 70° F. If not, warm the oil and eggs gently and rinse the utensils with warm water; then dry thoroughly.

2. Finely mash or rice the hard-boiled egg whites; mix with the raw egg whites and olive oil. Place in a blender with the yogurt and beat for 30 seconds. Add the balance of the ingredients except the Tabasco and blend for an additional 30 seconds.

3. Adjust the seasonings to taste, adding additional small quantities of lemon juice as necessary before adding the Tabasco. Chill in the refrigerator or briefly in the freezer before serving. Store unused portions in the refrigerator up to a week for future use.

Bonus Ideas: Try this mayonnaise with **Tomates Farcies au Crabe** (Tomatoes with Crab Stuffing). Remove the skins of 4 firm tomatoes by covering briefly with boiling water. Cut off the top third of each tomato and reserve for capping later. Spoon out the flesh; dice and combine with 1 peeled, seeded, and diced cucumber and 1 chopped green sweet pepper. Mince 1 cup of frozen or canned crabmeat and blend with the vegetable mixture and mayonnaise. Stuff the tomatoes; cover with the reserved tomato caps; garnish with strips of green pepper or sprigs of watercress or parsley.

For **Tomatoes Stuffed with Mussels,** add 1 tablespoon of tomato paste or ketchup to the mayonnaise; prepare the tomatoes as for Tomatoes with Crab Stuffing, but reserve the flesh for other purposes. Chop 3 hard-boiled egg whites and blend with 1 cup of cooked or canned mussels, 1 tablespoon chopped parsley, and the mayonnaise. Stuff the tomatoes and chill. Serve on crisp lettuce.

SALADE NIÇOISE
(Salad, Nice-style)

½ **pound green beans, cooked** *au sec*
    Sauce Ravigote
1 **heart of lettuce**
1 **7-ounce can tuna fish**
8 **anchovy filets**
1 **small onion, thinly sliced**
2 **large firm tomatoes, skinned and**
    quartered
1 **green pepper, seeded and cut into strips**
3 **hard-boiled egg whites, cut into strips**
12 **pitted black or green stuffed olives**
1 **mashed clove of garlic (optional)**
YIELD: Four servings

    1. Cook the green beans *au sec,* as in preparing **Haricots Verts.** Place half of the Sauce Ravigote into a shallow salad bowl and toss the lettuce until well coated.

    2. Arrange the flaked tuna fish and the anchovy filets on top of the lettuce and bean mixture. Garnish the center with sliced onion, pepper strips, and olives; garnish the periphery by alternating quarters of tomatoes and strips of cooked egg white.

    3. Sprinkle with the **Sauce Ravigote** to which the optional garlic has been added; chill and serve.

    Bonus Ideas: Sauce Vinaigrette may also be used for this hearty salad. Other popular variations add 3 large cooked and peeled potatoes that have been sliced or diced into small cubes. Peeled and finely chopped cucumber, Belgian endive, or watercress may be added to or substituted for the other ingredients.

SORBET AU CASSIS*
(Cassis Sherbet)

The *sorbet,* or sherbet ice, has traveled virtually around the world for centuries. Originally attributed to the Chinese, sherbet is associated chiefly with the Arabs, who reportedly used mountain snow as an ingredient. The Arabs taught the Italians to make sherbet, and they, in turn, brought it to France via Catherine de Medici.

    Serving sherbet between the courses of a formal meal is a pleasant way of refreshing the palate, and as a dessert is an excellent final touch to almost any menu. It is both simple to prepare and easily varied. When wine or liqueurs are used in a sherbet, the same ingredient should be used to top the frozen dessert.

    Since the freezer compartments of many home refrigerators may not be adequate to thoroughly freeze sherbets, and since the use of wines and liqueurs can deter the freezing process, 2 teaspoons of unflavored gelatin dissolved in ¼ cup of water are included in many of the following recipes, as an optional ingredient.

⅓ **cup fruit sugar, or combination of fruit**
    sugar, honey, and pure maple syrup
1½ **tablespoons lemon juice or lime**
    juice
10 **tablespoons crème de cassis**
2 **teaspoons gelatin dissolved in ¼ cup**
    water (optional)
1 **pound frozen raspberries or blackberries**
2 **egg whites, stiffly beaten**
YIELD: Six to eight servings

1. Thoroughly mix, preferably in an electric blender, the sugar, the lemon juice, and all but 2 tablespoons of the cassis. Add the optional dissolved gelatin and half the berries; blend for 15 seconds. Add the balance of the berries and blend again. Fold in the beaten egg whites, pour the berry mixture into a shallow metal pan or ice tray, and freeze until almost firm.

2. Remove from the freezer and beat for 1 minute in a mixing bowl until smooth. Return the sherbet to the ice tray or pour into a decorative mold and freeze for at least 2 hours.

3. Before serving, unmold onto a chilled platter. If using metal trays, unmold and spoon into individual chilled parfait, stemmed wine or champagne glasses. Before serving, sprinkle the reserved 2 tablespoons of cassis over the sherbet.

Bonus Ideas: Fruits have a wonderful affinity for sherbet desserts, and have the further advantage that their shells can serve as natural molds. Oranges, lemons, tangerines, and cantaloupes work especially well. Using a sharp knife, remove a small portion of the stem end of the fruit, preferably using the sawtooth technique. This is accomplished by inserting the tip of the knife at a 45° angle. Continue moving the knife up and down at 45° angles, making V cuts around the circumference of the fruit. Reserve the cap, being sure it can be identified later to match the base from which it has been cut. Fill the base with the sherbet, fruits, and/or liqueur of your choice. Replace the cap and wrap each filled fruit individually with aluminum foil. Freeze for at least 2 hours and allow ½ hour or more for thawing at room temperature before serving. Garnish the cap with an appropriate leaf. With proper timing, these fruit molds can be used to enhance your table decoration while thawing, and will be ready to eat at the end of the meal. Meringue shells are also effective containers for sherbet and fruit combinations.

SORBET À L'ORANGE*
(French Orange Sherbet)

3 large oranges
½ cup fruit or date sugar
¾ cup water
2 teaspoons gelatin dissolved in ¼ cup water (optional)
2 tablespoons Curaçao, Cointreau, or Grand Marnier
2 egg whites, stiffly beaten
2 tablespoons lemon juice
YIELD: Six to eight servings

1. Peel the oranges; remove any seeds, and purée the pulp and rinds through a food mill or in an electric blender. Stir the sugar into the water and boil for about 5 minutes.

2. Combine the orange purée and the syrup in a mixing bowl; allow to cool completely. Stir in the optional dissolved gelatin and the liqueur; then fold in the beaten egg whites and lemon juice. Pour into a shallow metal pan or ice tray and freeze until almost firm.

3. Remove from the freezer and beat for 1 minute in a mixing bowl until smooth. Return the sherbet to the metal pan or a decorative mold and freeze for at least 2 hours. Before serving, unmold onto a chilled platter or into individual chilled glass stemware, and sprinkle with additional liqueur used in the recipe.

Bonus Ideas: If you substitute ½ pound of very ripe, pitted apricots for the oranges, you can make **Sorbet à l'Abricot*** (Apricot Sherbet), which does not require the addition of any liqueur. You can also use 1 pound of fresh or frozen raspberries for **Sorbet aux Framboises***, or 1 pound of strawberries and 2 tablespoons of kirsch or kümmel (eliminating the lemon juice) for **Sorbet aux Fraises***. Try experimenting with such interesting and exotic fruits as melon, papaya, and kiwi.

A personal favorite is **Sorbet au Citron*** (Lemon Sherbet), which I serve in a number of mold variations, circled by fresh or frozen fruits in colorful combinations and sprinkled with Cointreau or white rum.

CAFÉ FILTRE
(French Filtered Coffee)

In France, as in Italy, coffee never appears at the table until the end of the meal and is served in demitasse cups. A stronger version, combined with hot milk *(Cafe au Lait),* together with a roll or croissant is the popular national breakfast. Although most French restaurants serve Italian-style espresso, which is made in espresso machines, *Cafe Filtre* is still the traditional way to end a meal in French homes.

Ideally, French roast coffee should be ground in a coffee mill immediately before using. A French *filtre,* which can be purchased in specialty shops, is essentially a drip pot with a compartment on top for the ground coffee. Boiling water is poured over the coffee to slowly drip through to the glass pot below. However, you can use any filtered coffee maker satisfactorily, provided you use freshly ground French roasted beans.

2 tablespoons French roast coffee
1 cup freshly boiled water
YIELD: One demitasse cup

1. Grind the coffee and place in the upper compartment of a *filtre* or over the filter of a similar drip pot mechanism. Pour enough hot water to moisten the coffee, thereby releasing its flavor.

2. After 1 minute, pour in slightly more than half the boiling water and let it seep through before adding the balance. When the coffee has completely seeped through, serve immediately.

Bonus Ideas: French coffee does not lend itself to reheating, nor does passing the coffee through the filter more than once improve its strength.

To prepare **Café au Lait,** use 4 tablespoons of coffee per cup of boiling water combined with a cup of hot milk, or serve the hot milk separately, to be added to the coffee at the table. Remember, however, that this is a breakfast beverage and is never served with or at the end of meals.

MENU

Tarte à l'Oignon
Sole Véronique
Salade Lentille
Pomme en Charlotte

French Onion Tart
Filet of Sole with Grapes
Lentil Salad
Apple Charlotte

TARTE À L'OIGNON*
(French Onion Tart)

This appetizer or luncheon main dish is related to quiche and **Pissaladière**: each utilizes a pastry or pie crust and is filled with vegetables and/or cheese and often with heartier ingredients like seafood. There are innumerable variations, depending on the filling. I usually prepare several onion tarts at the same time, reserving some in the freezer for future meals.

Onion Mixture:

2 tablespoons white wine or dry vermouth
1½ pounds onions, coarsely chopped
1 clove garlic, mashed
1 bay leaf

Mushroom Purée (1 cup):

3 tablespoons polyunsaturated margarine
2 tablespoons minced shallots or scallions
8 medium fresh mushrooms or ½ cup
    dried mushrooms, soaked
2 tablespoons polyunsaturated oil
1 tablespoon nonfat dry milk
⅛ teaspoon minced garlic (optional)
2 tablespoons cornstarch or potato flour
¾ teaspoon coarse salt
4 twists of a pepper mill
1 teaspoon Bovril or other meat extract
2 tablespoons olive or corn oil
½ cup low-fat cottage or ricotta cheese
½ teaspoon grated nutmeg
2 tablespoons grated *fromage blanc* or
    Parmesan cheese
1 9-inch Wheatless Pie Crust (page 37) or
    frozen pie shell
1 egg white, beaten
¼ cup dry beans
Cookware spray
YIELD: Six to eight servings

1. Apply cookware spray to a skillet,
add the wine, and sauté the onions and garlic until translucent. Cover and cook over low heat for 10 minutes; add the bay leaf and continue cooking for an additional 30 minutes.

2. Meanwhile, prepare the Mushroom Purée: in a separate pan, melt the margarine and sauté the shallots and mushrooms over low heat for 10 minutes. Purée through a food mill or in an electric blender; then add the oil, dry milk, and optional garlic. Blend thoroughly and set aside.

3. Remove and discard the bay leaf from the onion mixture; add the cornstarch, seasonings, and meat extract. Blend thoroughly, cover, and simmer for 5 minutes. Remove from the heat and set aside to cool slightly.

4. Blend the onion mixture with the reserved Mushroom Purée, olive oil, cheese, and nutmeg. (If a smoother consistency is desired, slightly purée the onion mixture.) Adjust the seasonings as necessary.

5. Line a quiche dish or pie pan with the pie shell and brush lightly with beaten egg white. Prick crust. Cover the crust with waxed paper and layer with dry beans. Bake in an oven at 350° F for 5 minutes; remove the beans, which can be reserved for future use, and bake an additional 3 minutes. Spread the filling into the pie shell and sprinkle evenly with the grated cheese. Bake for 20 minutes at 400° F; then reduce the temperature to 350° F and bake an additional 20 minutes, or until nicely browned. Serve hot.

Bonus Ideas: Some versions of this dish call for ¼ cup of diced Canadian bacon when sautéeing the onions and garlic. Others call for a mixture of leeks and onions, or leeks alone, to prepare **Tarte aux Poireaux***. You can also use many other vegetables, such as asparagus, broccoli, zucchini, or cauliflower. The quiche is an equally versatile cousin to the *tarte*. At your option, the filling can be covered with a second pie shell.

The most popular variation of the quiche is **Quiche Lorraine***. The partially baked pastry shell is layered with ¼ pound Canadian bacon that has been cut into 1-inch strips, sautéed *au sec,* then covered with a purée made by combining ¾ cups each of sour cream and part-skim ricotta, 3 egg whites and 3 tablespoons corn oil, with coarse salt, pepper, and nutmeg to taste. Bake in the upper part of an oven at 400° F for about 30 minutes, or until the quiche is puffed and golden brown. Serve in wedges, either hot or at room temperature.

Quiche can be prepared with more substantial fillings as an entrée for your luncheon, dinner, or supper menu. To prepare **Quiche aux Fruits de Mer*** (Seafood Quiche), sauté *au sec* ¼ pound shelled shrimp, crab, or lobster meat with the onions and optional garlic called for in the basic recipe. Add 1 tablespoon tomato paste or ketchup to the cottage cheese mixture before combining with the seafood and filling the partially baked pastry shell. Sprinkle with grated cheese and bake in the upper part of an oven at 400° F for about 30 minutes.

PISSALADIÈRE PROVENÇALE*
(Provençal Tart)

Pissaladière—often referred to as the French pizza—is usually made with a thick shell of French Bread Dough. A double thickness of **Wheatless Pie Crust** may also be used, however.

2 tablespoons olive or corn oil
1 double-thickness Wheatless Pie Crust (page 37), French Bread Dough (page 159), or frozen pie shell
¼ cup dry beans
2 tablespoons white wine or dry vermouth
4 onions, thinly sliced
1 clove garlic, mashed
4 large tomatoes, sliced, or 2 pounds Italian-style canned plum tomatoes
2 tablespoons tomato paste
4 twists of a pepper mill
¼ teaspoon each, dried basil, thyme, and coarse salt
¼ cup grated Parmesan cheese or *fromage blanc*
12 anchovy filets, drained
12 pitted black olives
Cookware spray
YIELD: Six to eight servings

1. Brush a baking sheet or pie plate with some of the oil. Roll the dough into a 12-inch round and overlap the outer rim so that the shell is thicker at the edge than in the center. Prebake covered with waxed paper and dry beans in an oven at 350° F for 5 minutes. Remove the paper and beans and bake an additional 10 minutes until golden. Set aside to cool.

2. Apply cookware spray to a skillet, add the wine, and sauté the onions and garlic until the onions are translucent. Discard the garlic and add the tomatoes, tomato paste, herbs, and seasonings. Stir well, cover, and cook over medium heat for 10 minutes. Uncover and reduce over

high heat for about 5 minutes more. Set aside.

3. Sprinkle half the grated cheese into the pastry shell and fill with the onion and tomato mixture. Split the anchovies lengthwise and halve the olives. Crisscross the anchovies over the surface in a lattice pattern and fill each square with an olive half. Brush with the balance of the oil and put back in an oven preheated to 400° F for about 20 minutes, until the shell is browned. Set aside for at least 10 minutes before cutting and serving.

SPANOKOPITTA*
(Greek Spinach Pie)

Another variation—this one featuring spinach enhanced with herbs and onions—is Greek Spinach Pie *(Spanakopitta)*. Traditionally, this dish is made with sheets of *phyllo* pastry, which you can buy (with feta cheese) at Greek grocery stores or in specialty shops; alternatively, you can top with a second pie crust.

2 pounds fresh or 3 packages frozen whole leaf spinach
½ cup each, chopped parsley and dill
1 bunch scallions, chopped
1 tablespoon chopped fresh mint or 1 teaspoon dried
1 teaspoon coarse salt
2 tablespoons white wine or dry vermouth
1 pound onions, coarsely chopped
1 cup olive or corn oil
½ pound feta, low-fat cottage, or ricotta cheese
6 twists of a pepper mill
½ teaspoon grated nutmeg

⅓ cup grated Parmesan cheese
2 egg whites, lightly beaten
1 single Wheatless Pie Crust (page 37), or a double shell if *phyllo* is not used
4 layers *phyllo* dough, preferably the eggless version (optional)
Cookware spray
YIELD: Six to eight servings

1. Wash the spinach, removing any coarse stems; drain well. If frozen spinach is used, thaw and drain thoroughly. Mix in a bowl with the parsley, scallions, dill, mint, salt; set aside for 15 minutes.

2. Apply cookware spray to a skillet or brush with some of the oil. Add the wine and sauté the onions until translucent. Stir in ¾ cup of the oil, cover, and simmer for 5 minutes. Set aside.

3. Cut the spinach as for a salad, draining off any water. Mash the feta cheese with a fork; add to the spinach with the pepper and nutmeg and mix thoroughly. Purée the onion and oil mixture through a food mill or in an electric blender and combine with the spinach mixture. Blend thoroughly; then add the grated Parmesan cheese and foamy egg whites and mix well.

4. Heat the balance of the oil. Line a 9-inch pan or quiche dish with a single pie shell and fill with the spinach mixture. If using frozen *phyllo,* defrost 2 hours ahead of time, keeping it covered to prevent drying. Layer the surface with 1 sheet of *phyllo* at a time, brushing with the heated oil before applying the next layer. Roll and tuck the layers of *phyllo* around the inside edge of the pan, and brush the top and edges with the remaining oil. A second pie shell can be used instead of the *phyllo* topping and brushed with the heated oil.

5. Bake in an oven preheated to 350° F for about 1 hour or until golden brown and crisp. Remove from oven to set about 15 minutes before cutting and serving.

Bonus Ideas: Although the pastry shells are traditionally used for pies, they are not absolutely necessary: natural shells can be made with spinach, Swiss chard, cabbage, or the large leaves of other edible vegetables.

The leaves can be cooked *au sec* or blanched with **Bouquet Garni** for several minutes, until tender but still crisp. Discard the *Bouquet Garni*. Drain and dry the leaves on paper toweling or with a dry cloth. Line a pie plate or baking dish with enough leaves to completely cover the bottom, overlapping them sufficiently to cover the filling of your choice. Sprinkle the filling with bread crumbs or wheat germ; then cover the surface with the overlapping leaves. Garnish with some of the ingredients of the filling or with other colorful edibles before baking in the oven set at 350° F and serving hot.

FRENCH BREAD DOUGH*

When French bread is made commercially, the ovens are equipped with a device that releases steam into the oven during the baking process, producing a crisp but moist loaf of bread. I have found that inserting a cool trivet or other metal object into a pan of boiling water, placing the pan on the lowest shelf of your oven,

will produce a burst of steam with similar results. I use an antique hand iron for this purpose, which works admirably, and I usually provide the burst of steam after the first 5 minutes of baking. For moister bread, some pastry chefs recommend additional bursts of steam at 5-minute intervals. For coarser textured bread, try using boiling potato water in the scalded milk mixture.

This versatile bread dough also can be used to prepare a **Pissaladière** or *grissini* (bread sticks).

¼ cup scalded skim milk
½ cup boiling water or potato water (water in which potatoes have been boiled)
1 teaspoon dry or a half (⅔-ounce) package compressed yeast
1 tablespoon melted polyunsaturated margarine
2½ teaspoons honey or pure maple syrup, or 1¼ teaspoons fruit sugar
1 cup white rye flour
1 cup rice flour, cornstarch or potato flour
4 teaspoons baking powder
1 teaspoon coarse salt
1 tablespoon each, coarse salt and sesame or caraway seeds (for bread sticks only)
1 egg white, lightly beaten
1 teaspoon cornmeal (for French bread only)
YIELD: One loaf of bread, one *Pissaladière* shell, or three dozen *grissini*

1. Scald the milk, preferably in a double boiler over boiling water, until it begins to form tiny bubbles around the edge of the pan. Add the boiling water and remove from the heat. When the temperature of the milk mixture is about 110° F, sprinkle the surface with the dry yeast so that it dissolves. If using compressed yeast, dissolve it in 2 tablespoons of lukewarm water (83° F) and let it rest for 10 minutes before adding it to the milk mixture, which must be cooled to lukewarm (83° F).

2. Add the margarine and half the honey to the lukewarm milk and yeast mixture. Sift the combined flours, baking powder and salt 6 times into a large mixing bowl. Add the balance of the honey and make a well in the center of the ingredients. Stir in the milk and yeast mixture, forming a soft dough, but do not knead.

3. Cover the dough with a damp cloth and let it rise in a warm place for about 2 hours, or until it has doubled in bulk. Punch down the dough and roll out as follows:

4. For a *Pissaladière* crust, roll into a 12-inch shell; fold in the edges so that the rim of the shell is thicker than the center. Place on a lightly oiled baking sheet and let the dough rise again in a warm place for about 1 hour, or until almost doubled in bulk.

5. If preparing bread sticks, roll into an 8-inch oblong and cut into 2-inch strips. Roll the strips into 8-inch long sticks and let them rise until almost doubled in bulk on a lightly oiled baking sheet. Brush the sticks with a glaze made by combining the egg white with 1 tablespoon of cold water, and sprinkle with 1 tablespoon each of coarse salt and sesame or caraway seeds before baking in an oven at 400° F for 15 minutes.

6. To prepare French bread, roll the dough on a lightly floured board toward you into an oblong loaf. Fold over the ex-treme edges toward the center and taper the ends slightly. With a sharp knife or scissors, make three ¼-inch-deep diagonal slits across the top. Set in a warm place to rise again for about 1 hour, or until almost doubled in bulk.

7. Place the loaf on a baking sheet that has been greased with margarine and sprinkled with cornmeal, and put into the top part of an oven preheated to 400° F. Also place a pan with ½ inch of boiling water into the bottom of the oven. After 5 minutes of baking, place a cool metal object into the pan of water, closing the oven door immediately to avoid loss of the burst of steam. Continue baking 10 minutes longer; then reduce the heat to 350° F and bake for about 25 minutes. Brush the loaf with a glaze of egg whites and 1 tablespoon cold water and bake an additional 5 minutes until golden brown, or until the loaf sounds hollow when tapped. Cool before serving.

SOLE VÉRONIQUE
(Filet of Sole with Grapes)

Sauce Véronique has perplexed me for many years. Although I understand it to be a sauce made with white grapes and served with fish or poultry, few restaurants serving dishes *à la Véronique* seem to prepare the sauce with any consistency. Even when *Véronique* dishes are delicious, they vary greatly from restaurant to restaurant. Surprisingly, *Larousse Gastronomique* does not even mention this sauce, nor do many culinary encyclopedias and comprehensive cookbooks; one would imagine that they would at least mention its existence.

One reference claims that the sauce was invented by a chef at the Ritz at Place Vendôme in Paris. Since this sauce was not included in any of the major codifications of *haute cuisine* dishes, I have come to the conclusion that any sauce combined with grapes is technically *Veronique* and most likely is adapted from *la cuisine bouregeoise.*

6 filets of sole or flounder
1 tablespoon lemon juice
3 tablespoons polyunsaturated margarine

Court Bouillon:
3 large mushrooms, sliced
1 cup white wine or dry vermouth
½ teaspoon lemon juice
½ teaspoon coarse salt
¼ cup dry sherry
¾ cup water
6 twists of a pepper mill
1 bay leaf

Sauce Mornay:
⅓ cup cornstarch or potato flour
⅛ teaspoon cayenne
¾ cup skim milk
1 cup fresh or canned seedless grapes
⅓ cup part-skim ricotta, sour cream, or yogurt
YIELD: Six servings

1. Wash the filets in a mixture of water and the tablespoon of lemon juice; drain and dry well. Brush a baking dish with some of the margarine and arrange the filets lengthwise, skinned sides down.

2. Prepare the *Court Bouillon* by sautéeing the mushrooms with 2 tablespoons of the white wine, the lemon juice, and salt. After 3 minutes, add the balance of the white wine, the sherry, water, pepper, and bay leaf; bring to a boil.

3. Ladle the hot bouillon over the filets and cover loosely with aluminum foil. Poach in an oven preheated to 350° F for 15 minutes. With a slotted spoon, transfer the filets to a warm serving platter. Strain and reserve the stock.

4. To prepare the *Sauce Mornay,* melt the balance of the margarine in a saucepan and remove from the heat. Using a wooden spoon, stir in the cornstarch and the cayenne pepper; stir to the consistency of paste. Gradually add the milk and the reserved stock, stirring constantly, until the sauce is thick and smooth after several minutes of cooking over medium heat. Add the grapes and ricotta and cook for 3 minutes, stirring constantly.

5. Pour the sauce and grapes over the filets, and brown quickly under a hot broiler immediately before serving.

Bonus Ideas: Although I find it unnecessary, the French often skin the grapes by pouring boiling water over them briefly, then removing the skins.

According to Madame Vaillant of Le Biarritz restaurant, a **Sauce Hollandaise,** instead of the Mornay, is often used in preparing this dish. You can prepare it after poaching the filets, using the strained stock; or you can use chicken stock.

SAUCE HOLLANDAISE
(Slimming Hollandaise Sauce)

1 teaspoon melted polyunsaturated margarine
2 teaspoons cornstarch, potato flour, or arrowroot

½ cup stock or consommé
2 egg whites at room temperature
2 tablespoons polyunsaturated oil
⅛ teaspoon each, coarse salt, white
     pepper, and cayenne pepper
1 teaspoon lemon juice
YIELD: One cup

1. Blend the margarine and cornstarch in a *bain-marie* or double boiler. Add the stock and simmer over medium heat for 5 minutes, stirring constantly until the mixture thickens.

2. Beat the egg whites with the oil for about a minute, and blend in some of the thickened cornstarch mixture before gradually stirring into the balance of the cornstarch mixture. Add the salt and the white and cayenne peppers. Simmer over low heat for about 2 minutes, stirring constantly. Remove from the heat, and blend in the lemon juice.

Bonus Ideas: The above recipe can be used for preparing **Sauce Béarnaise** by substituting a **Bouquet de Vinaigrette** for the lemon juice after removing the sauce from the heat.

BOUQUET DE VINAIGRETTE
(*Vinaigrette* Essence)

¼ cup tarragon or other wine vinegar
¼ cup white wine or dry vermouth
1 tablespoon minced shallots or scallions,
     or 1 teaspoon grated onion

2 tablespoons minced fresh tarragon or 1
     tablespoon dried
½ teaspoon minced fresh parsley, or ¼
     teaspoon dried
⅛ teaspoon grated nutmeg
YIELD: Two tablespoons of concentrate

1. Place all the ingredients into a saucepan, stir, and bring to a boil. Reduce the heat to medium and simmer for 15 minutes, or until the mixture is reduced to about 2 tablespoons of concentrate.

2. To prepare 1 cup **Sauce Béarnaise,** add the concentrate, instead of the lemon juice, after the sauce has been removed from the heat (see previous recipe). You may also wish to add 1 teaspoon of meat glaze.

Bonus Ideas: If 2½ tablespoons of purchased meat glaze, rather than a teaspoon are added to 1 cup of **Sauce Béarnaise,** you have prepared **Choron Sauce** (Béarnaise and Tomato Sauce), which is an excellent accompaniment to grilled meat dishes.

Instead of cooking the grapes with the fish in preparing **Sole Véronique,** you may wish to prepare **Garnish Véronique** separately, adding it after the filets have been poached in step 3. Melt 1 tablespoon polyunsaturated margarine in a saucepan; add 1 cup of seedless grapes, 1 tablespoon Cognac, and 1 teaspoon minced parsley; heat through over low heat. Arrange the grapes over the filets before spooning the sauce over them.

Garnish *Véronique* can be used with **Perdrix Véronique** (Partridge or Cornish Hens with Grapes). Squab or quail can also be made in the same manner.

PERDRIX VÉRONIQUE*
(Partridge or Cornish Hens with Grapes)

**4 young partridges or Cornish game hens,
  oven ready**
1 teaspoon coarse salt
½ teaspoon ground pepper
**1 cup fresh or canned seedless white
  grapes**
4 tablespoons polyunsaturated margarine
2 tablespoons lemon juice
1 cup *Garnish Véronique*
4 sprigs of tarragon or parsley
YIELD: Four to eight servings

  1. Sprinkle the insides of the birds with salt and pepper; insert 4 grapes and 1 tablespoon of margarine into the cavity of each.
  2. Arrange the birds in a casserole and brush all sides thoroughly with the lemon juice. Place in an oven at 450° F and brown on all sides. Reduce the temperature to 400° F; turn the birds breasts down, cover the casserole, and bake for 20 minutes, or until tender. Remove to a warm platter.
  3. Press the remaining grapes through a sieve or food mill and add to the juices in the casserole. Prepare the *Garnish Véronique* in a separate saucepan; spoon the garnish around the bird and pour over them the sauce from the casserole. Garnish further with blanched fresh tarragon, parsley, or fresh bay leaves.

Bonus Ideas: Poulet Véronique (Chicken Breasts with Grapes) is simply made by sautéeing 4 chicken breasts in a skillet with 2 tablespoons of polyunsaturated margarine until they lose their pink color. Add 1 chopped onion and 2 cups of chicken stock or consommé; simmer for 30 minutes, covered. Transfer the chicken to a warm platter, reserving the pan juices. In a saucepan, melt 2 tablespoons of margarine and gradually stir in ¼ cup cornstarch and ¾ cup of reserved pan juices. Bring to a boil for 1 minute, stirring constantly. Remove from the heat and blend in 1¼ cups white wine, coarse salt and pepper to taste, ¾ cup sour cream, and 1 cup white seedless grapes. Blend well and heat through without permitting to boil. Spread the sauce over the chicken breasts and add **Garnish Véronique**.

  Filets of Sole with **Sauce Mornay** (Filets de Sole Mornay) will serve six, using 6 ½-pound filets and 1 cup *Sauce Mornay*. Prepare the filets and poach in **Court Bouillon,** as for **Sole Véronique.** Transfer the filets to a heat-proof platter brushed with margarine; then reduce the *Court Bouillon* over high heat to half its original volume. Combine with the *Sauce Mornay* and spread over the fish. Sprinkle with ¼ cup grated Gruyère or Cheddar cheese and brown briefly under the broiler.

  Filets de Sole aux Bananes (Filets of Sole with Bananas) is another delightful version, using fruit with the fish. To serve six, first prepare curried rice by sautéing over moderate heat 1 cup of rice in 3½ tablespoons of polyunsaturated oil for 3 minutes, stirring constantly with a wooden spoon. Add 2 cups of boiling bouillon or water seasoned with ½ teaspoon coarse salt and 1½ tablespoons of curry powder. When the liquid returns to a boil, reduce the heat to low and simmer covered for 20 minutes. Remove from the heat and do not stir until ready for use. Lightly coat the filets with cornstarch and sauté them in a skillet over low heat with ⅓ cup of polyunsaturated margarine. Transfer the filets to a warm place. Cut each of 4 bananas lengthwise into 3 strips and sauté in the skillet, adding additional margarine as necessary. Spoon the cooked rice onto a warm serving platter, arrange the filets over the rice, and top each filet with banana strips.

SALADE LENTILLE*
(Lentil Salad)

Although lentils have been a part of virtually every culture since biblical times, lentil dishes had been relegated to the humble and the poor. With time, however, many imaginative dishes using these dried legumes have found their way into the menus of elegant restaurants—and onto the tables of true gastronomers throughout the world.

An excellent accoutrement to many entrées, this salad can also be served in smaller quantities as an appetizer.

1 pound dried lentils
1½ teaspoon coarse salt
2 onions, peeled and spiked with 2 cloves
2 whole carrots, peeled
1 clove garlic, mashed

Bouquet Garni:
2 celery stalks
5 peppercorns
2 sprigs parsley
¼ teaspoon each, dried thyme and basil
1 bay leaf

1 teaspoon Dijon or English mustard
½ cup olive or corn oil
3 ounces Canadian bacon, diced
2 tablespoons white wine or dry vermouth
3 tablespoons chopped parsley
Cookware spray
YIELD: Six to eight servings

1. Reconstitute the dried lentils by soaking overnight, or cover 2 cups of dried lentils with 6 cups of cold water and boil for about 5 minutes. Remove from the heat, tightly cover, and let stand for at least 1 hour.

2. Add the salt, the spiked onions, carrots, garlic and *Bouquet Garni;* bring to a boil, then simmer over medium heat for about 45 minutes, or until lentils are tender but not too soft.

3. Discard the vegetables, garlic, and *Bouquet Garni;* simmer lentils over low heat for 5 or more minutes, stirring constantly, to permit the excess water to evaporate.

4. Mix the mustard with the olive oil and blend the mixture into the lentils. Apply cookware spray to a skillet and sauté the diced bacon with the wine for about 5 minutes over medium heat. Add the bacon to the lentils, sprinkle with the parsley, and serve hot.

Bonus Ideas: Once the dried lentils are reconstituted, you can cook them in a pressure cooker at 15-pound pressure for 20 minutes. If using a microwave oven, cook for 25 minutes, stirring occasionally; let stand 5 minutes before draining and completing the recipe.

Many Europeans drain the lentils after they have been reconstituted and continue the recipe with the addition of fresh water and whatever ingredients are called for. However, I agree with the excellent Indian cooks who insist that lentils should always be cooked in the water in which they have been soaked or boiled. One of the basic dishes of Indian cookery that bears this out is *dal*, which can be made with red, green, or black lentils or yellow split peas.

To prepare **Moong Dal*** (Curried Lentils) for six servings, reconstitute 1½ cups of green lentils in 3 cups of water. Skim the surface and bring to a boil with 1¼ teaspoons salt and ¼ teaspoon ground turmeric. Reduce the heat and simmer for an hour, or until lentils are tender but not too soft. Apply cookware spray to a skillet and sauté with 2 tablespoons of wine or broth, 2 sliced onions, 2 bay leaves, 2 chilies, 1¼ teaspoons grated ginger, and ⅛ teaspoon cumin seeds. After 3 minutes, when the onions are translucent, add 3 tablespoons chopped coriander or parsley, ¼ teaspoon each of ground cardamom and honey, 3 tablespoons of presoaked raisins (soak 20 minutes in warm water), and ¼ cup shredded coconut. Pour the onion mixture over the lentils and simmer over low heat for 10 minutes.

POMME EN CHARLOTTE*
(Apple Charlotte)

Like many provincial desserts, Apple Charlotte can be enhanced by using Italian Sponge Cake instead of the traditional strips and rounds of bread. In either version, it is an enticing dessert, whether served hot or chilled.

3 tablespoons polyunsaturated margarine
5 medium cooking apples
2 layers Italian Sponge Cake *(Pan di Spagna),* or ½ loaf sliced French bread
¼ pound polyunsaturated margarine and ½ cup corn oil (optional)
2 tablespoons lemon juice
¼ teaspoon ground cinnamon
½ cup Apricot and Pineapple Sauce (page 166)
YIELD: Six servings

1. Use 1 tablespoon of the margarine to grease a 3-pint Charlotte mold. Peel, core, and slice the apples and set aside.

2. Cut the cake into fingers ¾ inch by 3 inches long. Completely line the bottom of the mold; arrange the balance of the fingers around the inside. If using sliced bread, remove the crusts and cut enough 2-inch squares to cover the bottom of the mold; cut the balance into ¾-inch fingers. Heat the margarine and optional oil in a skillet to 375° F (on the range or in an oven). Brown the pieces of bread until golden; drain and line the mold.

3. Melt 2 tablespoons of the margarine in a large pan; add the apples, lemon juice, and cinnamon, and stew over medium heat, tightly covered, until the apples are soft and translucent. Stir in the Apricot and Pineapple Sauce and cook until dissolved.

4. Fill half the mold with the apple mixture and cover with additional cake or fried bread; then repeat until the mold is filled and topped with a layer of cake or bread. Place into a pan of water up to two thirds the height of the mold, and bake in an oven at 375° F for 15 minutes. Cool

slightly; then unmold onto a serving platter. Serve hot or chilled.

Bonus Ideas: *Apricot and Pineapple Sauce** that is kept under refrigeration can be used as a jam. It is prepared in a heavy-based pan by combining 1 cup dried apricots that have been presoaked overnight in cold water, 2½ cups canned pineapple, ¾ cup water, and ½ cup honey or pure maple syrup. Bring to a boil, slightly cool, and spoon into jars; cover and refrigerate.

MENU

Coupes d'Oeufs Farcis au Caviare
Couilibiac de Saumon
Carottes Vichy
Mousse au Carob

Eggcups Filled with Caviar
Salmon in Brioche
Carrots Vichy
Carob Mousse

COUPES D'OEUFS FARCIS AU CAVIARE*
(Eggcups Filled with Caviar)

The French have used caviar (also spelled *kavia* or *caviat*) for centuries, often with the accompaniment of eggs in some form. Influenced most notably by Persia, Greece, and Russia, the French have developed a number of interesting ways of serving caviar as an hors d'oeuvre. This particular appetizer is a conversation piece, since it always appears to be a labor of love—in spite of how easily it can be made.

I have a collection of colorful eggcups, which I use for this recipe. Small ramekins or actual eggshells can also be used; and natural molds, such as scooped-out lemon or lime shells, will provide attractive containers for your "caviar in a cup."

1 4-ounce bar of low-fat cream cheese
4 ounces whipped low-fat cottage or part-skim ricotta cheese
1 tablespoon plain yogurt or sour cream
½ teaspoon lemon juice
2 tablespoons minced fresh onions or 1 tablespoon dried
1 teaspoon minced fresh chives or chopped parsley, or ½ teaspoon dried
1 ounce (28 grams) of black or red caviar, or fish roe
YIELD: Six servings

1. Combine and mix until well blended all the ingredients except the caviar and chives. Fill each eggcup or container of your choice to about two thirds full with the cheese mixture. With a small fork, burrow out a pocket and flute the edges of the mixture, which should rise to about ¼ inch above the rim of the cup used.

2. Spoon into the pocket about ¾ teaspoon of the caviar and sprinkle the fluted edges with the minced chives. If using a ramekin, garnish the cheese mixture with suitable colorful edibles, to contrast with the red or black caviar; you may use thin slices of a red radish or black olive, or chopped chives or parsley. Refrigerate before serving at room temperature.

Bonus Ideas: Many chefs, notably Michel Guérard and Jacques Manière, serve caviar appetizers in an eggshell with its own cap. About a third of the eggshell is cut from one end with a serrated knife (which takes a little practice) and reserved to be used later as a cap to the caviar filling. Remove and reserve the contents of the egg; rinse both pieces of the shell in warm water, storing in the refrigerator as necessary until ready to use. Pat the shells dry before filling with the cheese mixture and caviar. Top the mount of caviar with the reserved cap.

If using lemon or lime shells, cut off about a third from one end in a sawtooth pattern. This is done by inserting the tip of a sharp knife at a 45° angle. Move the knife up, then down, making V cuts and repeating until you have a sawtooth circle and can remove the cap. Scoop out the pulp, rinse, and refrigerate until ready to use, being sure to identify each cap to properly match the shell from which it has been cut. Before serving, pat the shells dry, fill with the cheese mixture and caviar, and top with the cap.

Less expensive lumpfish caviar can be used in the above recipe, but should be chilled before using and drained well, since the juices can run and spoil the appearance of the garnish. When using caviar, never serve it in a silver container or with a silver spoon; use ceramic or wooden utensils instead. For those who may be concerned with excess salt in red caviar, drain it first in a fine sieve and wash with a very gentle stream of slightly warm water, being careful not to bruise the tiny eggs. When the salt has drained off, the caviar is ready for use.

COUILIBIAC DE SAUMON*
(Salmon in Brioche)

There is little question that *Couilibiac*—originally a Russian specialty called *kouili blaka*—can be the *pièce de résistance* of one of your festive buffets. The Russian version is a kind of salmon pie using a hearty pastry. In its French adaptation (a specialty of both *haute cuisine* and *la cuisine bouregeoise),* brioche takes the place of the pastry. You may use either a brioche or bread dough for the crust, depending upon your approach.

Although fresh salmon is preferable, canned salmon can be used most satisfactorily—especially if you buy the squat 3-inch cans containing center sections of the sturgeon, as opposed to the taller cans, which usually contain meat from the tail end. Sockeye, King and Chinook are the better known varieties you may consider for this dish.

Although rarely included in contemporary recipes, it is traditional to place a layer of coarsely chopped *veziga,* the spinal marrow of the sturgeon, in the center of *Couilibiac de Saumon. Veziga* is available in the United States in frozen form from sources listed at the end of this book. Once thawed, it is simmered in lightly salted water for about 2 hours until it is translucent, then chopped coarsely. Once cooked, it should not be refrozen. The dried version, more often available abroad, is soaked in cold water for several hours to swell and then rinsed, drained, and simmered in lightly salted water for 4 hours. It is then drained and chopped coarsely before using.

2 ounces *veziga* (optional)
double recipe Slimming Brioche Dough
    (page 171)
1½ pounds fresh or canned salmon filets
½ pound filet of sole (optional)
4 tablespoons melted polyunsaturated
    margarine
½ pound mushrooms, sliced
6 shallots or 1 onion, minced
½ tablespoon each, chopped parsley and
    chives
4 tablespoons Madeira or sherry
1 teaspoon coarse salt
6 twists of a pepper mill
1 cup cooked rice or buckwheat
1 egg white and 1 tablespoon
    polyunsaturated oil, lightly beaten
    (optional)
2 hard-boiled egg whites cut into strips
2 egg whites, lightly beaten
¼ cup wheat germ or bread crumbs
    (optional)
½ teaspoon paprika
YIELD: Six to eight servings

1. Reconstitute the frozen or dried *veziga*, as indicated above, chop coarsely, and set aside. Prepare a double recipe of Slimming Brioche Dough. After kneading, set aside to rise.

2. Cut the salmon filets and optional sole into small strips or pieces and sauté with the melted margarine for 2 minutes until the pieces become firm; remove and set aside.

3. Sauté the mushrooms and shallots for about 3 minutes; then add the parsley, chives, Madeira, all the seasonings except the paprika, and the salmon strips. Simmer for about 3 minutes and set aside. If using buckwheat, blend with the optional lightly beaten egg white and oil and cook in a skillet over medium heat until the kernels separate.

4. Roll out two thirds of the dough into an oblong about ½ inch thick. Roll out the balance of the dough into a thinner oblong and set aside. Place the thicker oblong on a lightly greased baking sheet; spread the center with layers of rice or buckwheat, the fish-mushroom mixture, strips of hard-boiled egg whites, a layer of chopped *veziga*, a final layer of rice or buckwheat. Dot the rice with margarine; cover with the thinner layer of dough.

5. Moisten the edges of the bottom layer with water and fold the lower edges over those of the upper layer. Tuck in as necessary so that the dough completely seals the filling. Brush with lightly beaten egg whites, sprinkle with the optional wheat germ and then the paprika. Cut a slit in the top to permit steam to escape during baking. Set aside to rise in a warm place for about 30 minutes.

6. Bake in an oven at 400° F for 30 minutes, or until browned and cooked through. Let stand for 5 minutes before transferring the *Couilibiac* to a hot serving platter. Slice and serve at the table with **Sauce Hollandaise**, **Sauce Mornay**, hot fish stock, clam juice, or **Lemon Butter**, which is made by combining ¾ cup of melted polyunsaturated margarine with the juice of 3 lemons.

Bonus Ideas: *Couilibiac* also can be made with meat, as we shall see in the section on American-International cuisine.

Another version popular with many three-star French restaurants is *Le Couilibiac de Saumon Colette*, presumably named after the famous French writer.

COUILIBIAC DE SAUMON COLETTE*
(Salmon Pie Colette)

6 filets of salmon, about 1½ pounds
1½ tablespoons cornstarch or potato flour
⅓ pound fresh or canned lobster meat, diced
½ cup *Sauce Mornay* (page 161)
½ tablespoon each, minced chives, parsley, and tarragon
Dash Worcestershire sauce
⅓ cup rice
1 cup fish stock or clam juice
1 *Bouquet Garni* (page 164)
½ teaspoon each, coarse salt and white pepper
2 hard-boiled egg whites, minced
¼ cup chopped chives
1 tablespoon polyunsaturated margarine
1 Slimming Brioche Dough (page 171) recipe
1 egg white, lightly beaten

Sauce Colette (1 cup):
2 tablespoons melted margarine
1 cup part-skim ricotta or plain yogurt
3 tablespoons lemon juice
½ teaspoon coarse salt
¼ teaspoon each, dried parsley, chives, and tarragon
⅛ teaspoon each, cayenne pepper and Worcestershire sauce
YIELD: Six servings

1. Sprinkle the salmon filets with the cornstarch and top each one with equal parts of a mixture made by combining the diced lobster, *Sauce Mornay,* the minced chives, parsley, tarragon, and a dash of Worcestershire sauce. Roll into *paupiettes,* or in the shape of large corks; set aside.

2. Place the rice in the fish stock or clam juice; add the *Bouquet Garni* and the seasonings and bring to a boil. Cover; simmer over low heat for 20 minutes, or until the rice is tender. Combine the drained rice with the minced egg whites and the chopped chives.

3. Grease the bottom of a deep earthenware casserole with margarine and layer with half the rice mixture; add a layer of the *paupiettes,* arranged to simplify slicing the pie later; then add the balance of the rice mixture.

4. Roll out the brioche dough and cover the casserole, being sure that the shell adheres to the inside edge of the casserole. Brush lightly with the egg white. Make a hole in the center of the shell and insert a pie funnel, or make one by rolling a small square of aluminum foil around a pencil. Set the casserole in a warm place for about 30 minutes to allow the brioche dough to rise. Bake in an oven at 375° F for about 30 minutes.

5. Prepare the *Sauce Colette* by combining the melted margarine with the ricotta and heating through over low heat. Stir in the lemon juice, seasonings, and herbs; set aside to be served separately in a sauceboat. Alternatively, you may prepare **Sauce Raifort** (French Horseradish Sauce) by combining 4 tablespoons freshly grated horseradish, 1 teaspoon lemon juice, ½ teaspoon salt and 4 twists of a pepper mill. Fold the mixture into ½ cup of sour cream, part-skim ricotta, or yogurt.

6. To serve, slice the pie between the *paupiettes,* not through them. Serve hot with the *Sauce Colette,* French Horseradish Sauce, or Lemon Butter.

Bonus Ideas: To facilitate cutting the pie between the *paupiettes,* I prepare 6 ½-inch strips of extra brioche dough and place them in a swirling pattern over the shell. This is not only decorative but helps to identify the *paupiettes* below the crust. I also roll an extra thin strip of dough into a rosette, brush it with egg white and bake it with the pie. This is later used to cover the hole made for the funnel during baking.

SAUMON MAYONNAISE ANETH
(Salmon with Dill Mayonnaise)

This is a dramatic cold party dish and an ideal center piece for a special buffet. It is equally delicious whether fresh salmon or salmon-trout is used.

1 whole 5-pound salmon, cleaned

Court Bouillon for Salmon:
2 lemons, sliced
1 teaspoon coarse salt
1 teaspoon fresh dill or ½ teaspoon dried
8 peppercorns
2 shallots, minced, or 1 teaspoon grated onion
1 large bay leaf
1⅓ cups white wine or dry vermouth

Dill Mayonnaise (2 cups):
1⅓ cups Slimming Mayonnaise (page 152)
¼ cup sour cream or part-skim ricotta
1 teaspoon unflavored gelatin (optional)
1 tablespoon lemon juice
¼ teaspoon each, coarse salt, white pepper, cayenne pepper, and dry mustard
1 cup cooked fresh, frozen, or canned shrimp
1 tablespoon fresh dill, minced

1 head lettuce
1 cucumber, thinly sliced
6 each, hard-boiled egg whites and firm tomatoes, sliced
2 ounces red caviar
1 bunch watercress
6 scallions
YIELD: Ten to twelve servings

1. Wash the salmon and pat dry. Place all of the ingredients for the *Court Bouillon,* except the wine, into a large casserole. Add the whole salmon, pour in the wine, and bring to a boil. Cover and simmer over low heat for 45 minutes, or until the fish flakes; set aside to cool.

2. Gently take the fish from the casserole and carefully remove its skin without damaging the flesh. Strain and reserve ¼ cup of the *Court Bouillon.*

3. Prepare the Dill Mayonnaise by mixing the Slimming Mayonnaise and sour cream in a bowl, stirring in the reserved bouillon, and adding the optional gelatin, the lemon juice, seasonings. Blend thoroughly into a smooth sauce; then fold in the shrimp and dill and refrigerate for at least 30 minutes.

4. When the salmon is completely cooled, line the bottom of a large oval or fish platter with a bed of lettuce leaves and place the salmon in the center of the dish. Coat the salmon evenly with the chilled Dill Mayonnaise. Garnish the platter with alternate rows of slightly overlapping slices of cucumber and egg whites, placing mounds of red caviar on each slice of egg white, and slightly overlapping tomato slices. Garnish with sprigs of watercress or several scallion brushes before serving.

Bonus Ideas: A simpler family version is **Mayonnaise de Poisson** (Fish with Dill

Mayonnaise), which can be prepared with 1 pound of canned salmon, cooked white-fleshed fish, or shellfish. To serve four, place lettuce on a platter and arrange the cooked fish on the lettuce in a decorative pattern. Coat evenly with Dill Mayonnaise and garnish with 9 anchovy filets that have been previously soaked in milk for 15 minutes and drained. Arrange the anchovies on top of the mayonnaise coating in a lattice pattern; place a caper or a half-stuffed olive in each square of the lattice and garnish the rest of the platter with any of the garnish suggestions for Salmon with Dill Mayonnaise.

The French also use smoked salmon in preparing **Canapés au Saumon Fumé.** Toast or sauté squares of bread with polyunsaturated margarine or oil; then spread with a thin layer of margarine blended with curry or mustard powder to taste and ⅛ teaspoon lemon juice. Cover with thin slices of smoked salmon, strips of gherkins and hard-boiled egg whites, with or without caviar mounds. Glaze the entire canapé with **Aspic,** and keep chilled until ready to serve.

Salmon rolls —prepared by rolling up smoked salmon slices and filling them with a mixture of low-fat cream cheese or **Slimming Mayonnaise** blended with a little mixed vegetable salad—are simple to make and very effective.

SLIMMING BRIOCHE DOUGH*

2 cups each, cornstarch and white rye or rice flour

8 teaspoons baking powder
½ teaspoon coarse salt
⅔ cup skim milk
2 teaspoons dry or 1 package compressed yeast
¾ cup chilled polyunsaturated margarine
¾ tablespoon fruit sugar, pure maple syrup, or honey
4 egg whites, lightly beaten
4 tablespoons polyunsaturated oil

Pastry Glaze:
1 egg white, lightly beaten
1 tablespoon skim milk
¼ teaspoon honey
YIELD: Two 9-inch shells, 2 loaves, or 30 brioches

1. Sift together 6 times the combined cornstarch and flour, baking powder, and salt. Scald the milk, then cool to 110° F if using dry yeast, or to 85° F if using compressed yeast. Cream the chilled margarine and blend gradually with ½ cup of warm milk and the fruit sugar. Sprinkle the dry or crumbled compressed yeast into the balance of warm milk and stir until dissolved. Combine the yeast and creamed margarine mixtures; then add the beaten egg whites, oil, and the flour combination. Beat for 10 minutes, or use a dough hook on an electric mixer, or the metal blade of a food processor, until the ball of dough forms.

2. Place the dough in a greased bowl; cover and set aside in a warm place for 2 hours, or until it has doubled in bulk. Punch down the dough, knead it several times, then set aside in a warm place to rise again until it has almost doubled in bulk, about 1 hour. If preparing **Couilibiac** or pie, roll out according to the instructions in the recipe.

3. If preparing a brioche loaf, after punching down and kneading the dough, shape into 2 loaves and place in greased 5-cup loaf pans. Cover and let rise in a warm place until almost doubled in bulk, about 1 hour. Brush with a **Pastry Glaze** made with a lightly beaten egg white, 1 tablespoon skim milk and ¼ teaspoon of honey. Bake in an oven at 400° F for about 30 minutes.

4. If preparing brioches, after punching down and kneading the dough, place in a greased bowl and chill in the refrigerator for 1 hour. Using 2 tablespoons of the dough, form a ball and place in the traditional flared and fluted brioche tin or muffin tin. Make 3 crisscross slashes on the surface and a small center gash. Using 1 tablespoon of the dough, form a pear-shaped oval and insert the pointed end into the center gash. Repeat this procedure for each brioche, and set them aside in a warm place for 30 minutes, or until they rise to almost double in bulk. Brush with the above Pastry Glaze and bake in an oven at 450° F for about 10 minutes, or until the oval top is puffed and nicely browned. Serve hot, or cool on a rack and reheat immediately before serving.

SALMON IN PASTRY WITH HERB SAUCE*

Salmon is, of course, a specialty in those regions surrounding the waters in which the fish abound. One such place is the River Wye, near the ancient city of Bath in England; and this dish is a specialty of the charmingly Bohemian The Hole in the Wall restaurant in Bath, during the summer, when salmon are plentiful.

2 thick filets of fresh salmon, about 2½ pounds
½ teaspoon coarse salt
6 twists of a pepper mill
1 Wheatless Pie Crust (page 37), or Slimming Brioche Dough (page 171)
4 pieces preserved ginger
½ cup polyunsaturated margarine
1 tablespoon golden raisins
1 tablespoon chopped blanched almonds (optional)

Herb Sauce:
2 shallots, minced, or 1 teaspoon grated onion
⅓ teaspoon each, chervil, thyme, and tarragon
1 teaspoon chopped parsley
4 tablespoons polyunsaturated margarine
1 tablespoon cornstarch or potato flour
1½ cups part-skim ricotta or sour cream
1 teaspoon Dijon mustard
¾ teaspoon coarse salt
5 twists of a pepper mill
2 egg whites
2 tablespoons corn oil
1 teaspoon lemon juice
YIELD: Eight servings

1. Season the salmon filets with the salt and pepper, and set aside while you roll out the pastry into a single thin shell, large enough to wrap around the 2 filets and filling. Place one of the salmon filets in the center of the pastry shell.

2. Drain and chop the preserved ginger and combine with the margarine, raisins, and almonds. Spread half the mixture over the filet; cover with the second filet, pinching the edges together; then spread the balance of the mixture over the top filet.

3. Wrap the pastry over the salmon and filling, completely enclosing and sealing it. Make several slashes on top to permit steam to escape and decorate with designs made from unused pastry. Brush with **Pastry Glaze,** place on a baking sheet, and bake in an oven at 400° F for 40 minutes.

4. Meanwhile, prepare the herb sauce by sautéing the shallots, herbs, and parsley in the margarine for 5 minutes. Stir in the cornstarch; blend over low heat, then stir in the ricotta. Cook for about 10 minutes over moderate heat, stirring until completely smooth. Add the mustard and seasonings. Lightly beat the egg whites and oil and blend with 2 tablespoons of the hot sauce. Beat the egg mixture into the sauce and stir over low heat until thickened. Sprinkle with lemon juice and serve separately in a sauceboat with the salmon in pastry, which has been transferred to a hot platter.

CAROTTES VICHY
(Carrots Vichy)

The French prepare these delicate carrots with Vichy or sparkling water. Boiling tap water can be used, but preferably with about ¼ teaspoon of baking soda (bicarbonate of soda), which closely approximates the sparkling water.

4 cups scraped, thinly sliced carrots
2 cups Vichy or sparkling water
4 tablespoons polyunsaturated margarine
2 tablespoons fruit sugar, pure maple syrup, or honey
2 teaspoons lemon juice
¼ teaspoon coarse salt
⅛ teaspoon white pepper
2 tablespoons minced chives or parsley
YIELD: Six to eight servings

1. Place the sliced carrots in a saucepan with the Vichy water, margarine, fruit sugar, lemon juice, salt, and pepper. Cover tightly and simmer over medium heat for 15 minutes, or until the carrots are almost tender.

2. Remove the cover and continue cooking for about 10 minutes, until the carrots are tender and sizzling in the thickened margarine mixture. Transfer the carrots to a warm serving dish and pour the sauce over them. Sprinkle with the chives and freshly ground pepper.

Bonus Ideas: I like to add ½ bay leaf for extra flavor, while the carrots are simmering. A close cousin to this dish is **Carottes à la Beaujeu** (Glazed Carrots and Onions). Trim carrots into 4 cups of ovals about the same size as each of the 2 dozen small white onions you will add to this recipe. Place in a saucepan with 4 cups of Vichy water, 1 tablespoon each of salt and honey, 6 tablespoons of polyunsaturated margarine, 1 mashed clove of garlic, and a **Bouquet Garni.** Cover and simmer for 30 minutes, or until the carrots are almost tender. Remove the cover and continue cooking (about 15 minutes) until the carrots are glazed. Discard the garlic and *Bouquet Garni* and sprinkle with chopped parsley before serving.

Carottes Véronique (Carrots with Grapes) is another variation you may wish to try. To serve six, place in a saucepan 2 cups of chicken stock or consommé, 1 cup white wine or dry vermouth, 3 tablespoons of polyunsaturated margarine, ¼ teaspoon each of salt, dried basil, and thyme, and 5 twists of a pepper mill. Bring to a boil over medium heat, add 4 cups of carrots cut into strips julienne-style, and cook until *al dente* (for about 10 minutes). Add 1 cup of seedless white grapes and cook for several minutes until they are heated through. Transfer the carrots and grapes to a warm serving dish and reduce the cooking liquid over high heat to about ⅓ cup. Add ½ teaspoon lemon juice and pour the sauce over the carrots and grapes before serving.

MOUSSE AU CAROB*
(Carob Mousse)

For dessert lovers, a velvety smooth chocolate mousse can be the crowning glory to a fine meal. Carob powder, which has been used for centuries, is the principal ingredient of this slimming version. As noted previously **(Italian Carob Bread)**, toasting the powder enhances its chocolate-like flavor. A note of caution, however: never heat carob powder beyond 325° F, at which point it is liable to burn.

Carob Mousse is easy to prepare, but should be made several hours in advance of serving since it must chill for at least 4 hours to properly set.

½ cup carob powder
Grated zest of 1 orange, or 1 teaspoon
    dried orange peel
3 tablespoons rum, Grand Marnier, or
    Cognac

1 tablespoon polyunsaturated margarine
4 tablespoons honey or pure maple syrup
⅛ teaspoon coarse salt
2 teaspoons unflavored gelatin (optional)
8 egg whites, beaten until peaked
2 drops vanilla or crème de menthe
    (optional)
¼ cup chopped pistachio nuts or toasted
    almonds
YIELD: Six servings

1. Thinly layer the carob powder in a pie tin and toast in an oven at 300° F for 3 minutes; smooth out any lumps with a spoon.

2. Combine the carob powder and grated orange zest and place in the top of a double boiler (or *bain-marie)* with the rum, margarine, honey, salt, and optional gelatin. Stir over simmering water until the ingredients are dissolved and smooth in consistency. Remove the upper pan and set aside to cool to room temperature.

3. Beat the egg whites with the optional vanilla or cremè de menthe until stiffened into peaks, but not too dry. Fold a third of the egg whites into the carob mixture; then quickly fold in the balance.

4. Spoon the mousse into custard cups, ramekins, or stemmed glasses, and garnish with sprinkles of chopped nuts or toasted almonds. Refrigerate for 4 hours, or until set, before serving.

Bonus Ideas: Instead of vanilla extract, it is preferable to use the scrapings of ¼ inch of vanilla bean. Instead of garnishing with nuts, **Candied Fruits** may be used.

Carob Mousse Normandy* is a noteworthy variation. Prepare the Carob Mousse, adding ⅓ cup of blanched almonds during the simmering. Line a 5-cup Charlotte mold snugly with a circle of white paper. Line the inside walls of the mold with fingers of **Italian Sponge Cake**. Fill the mold with the mousse, cover with plastic wrap, and place in the refrigerator or freezer to set. Unmold onto a chilled serving platter and garnish with chopped nuts or Candied Fruits. About 2 feet of satin ribbon is traditionally tied around the middle of the mousse to hold the sponge cake fingers in place.

The Italians favor **Vanilla Mousse*** (*Mousse Dolce di Vaniglia*). You can prepare it in the same manner as Carob Mousse, replacing the carob powder with 2 teaspoons of vanilla extract, or preferably the scrapings from a 2-inch length of vanilla bean. Vanilla Mousse can also be used for **Vanilla Mousse Normandy**, prepared in the identical manner as the Normandy recipe above.

MENU

Pâté de Campagne
Poularde à la Moutarde
Fenouil Braisé
Beignets d'Ananas

French Rustic Pâté
Roast Chicken with Mustard
Braised Fennel
Pineapple Fritters

PÂTÉ DE CAMPAGNE*
(French Rustic Pâté)

This pâté, a traditional appetizer, is the pride of French home cooking. It improves when set aside overnight, wrapped in foil and refrigerated, allowing the flavors to blend.

Since pâté freezes well, you may wish to make more than one recipe to reserve for future use as an appetizer, luncheon, or supper dish. It lends itself to infinite variations, permitting a creative cook to develop a personalized *pâté maison*.

1 pound lean veal
½ pound each, lean beef and pork
½ pound beef, pork, or chicken liver
½ cup Madeira or sherry
½ cup dried mushrooms
2 teaspoons coarse salt
6 twists of a pepper mill
⅛ teaspoon each, allspice, mace, and thyme
1 bay leaf, crumbled
1 teaspoon minced garlic

Panade:
6 tablespoons water
2 tablespoons polyunsaturated oil
4 tablespoons cornstarch or potato flour
2 teaspoons unflavored gelatin (optional)
½ cup evaporated skim milk
2 slices gluten or white bread, crusts removed

¼ cup Cognac or brandy
3 egg whites
¾ pound boiled ham or Canadian bacon, sliced ¼-inch thick
2 tablespoons chopped parsley
YIELD: Two quarts

1. Trim membranes and excess fat from the meat and liver, and cut into ½-inch cubes. Place the cubed meat in a ceramic or glass bowl with the Madeira, dried mushrooms, all the seasonings, and

the minced garlic to marinate for several hours, preferably overnight.

2. Prepare the *Panade* in a saucepan by heating the water and oil; remove from the heat and blend in the cornstarch and optional gelatin. Add the skim milk and bring to a boil over medium heat, stirring constantly. Dice or cube the bread, add to the *Panade,* and chill in the refrigerator or freezer.

3. Add the Cognac to the marinated meats, mixing thoroughly with a wooden spoon. Lightly beat the egg whites, add to the meat mixture, then blend in the *Panade.*

4. Fill an electric blender two thirds full with the mixture and coarsely blend. Repeat with the balance of the mixture. Cut the slice of ham or bacon into 1-inch strips. Layer the bottom of a 2-quart loaf pan with half the ham strips. Fill the mold, pressing the mixture to avoid any air pockets. Form the surface into a slight mound and top with the balance of the ham strips. Cover the top with a double thickness of aluminum foil and place the mold in a roasting pan half filled with hot water. Bake in an oven at 325° F for 1½ hours, or until the loaf shrinks and pulls away from the sides of the pan. Remove from the oven and cool to room temperature.

5. Cover a brick or other heavy weight with aluminum foil, place on the cooked loaf, and refrigerate overnight. Place a platter on top of the mold; invert and unmold the cooked loaf onto the platter. Spoon its own juices over the pâté before sprinkling with chopped parsley. Serve whole and slice at the table.

Bonus Ideas: Crusty bread and *cornichons,* small, tart gherkins, are traditional accompaniments to pâté. Slice the gherkins lengthwise up to the stem and serve several, decoratively flared out, with each slice of pâté.

You may wish to serve the pâté with chopped **Aspic,** in addition to its natural jelly, as a garnish. To prepare 2½ cups, combine 4 cups chicken stock, 4 teaspoons unflavored gelatin, ¼ cup tomato juice or 1 tablespoon tomato paste, ¼ cup dry white wine, and 3 egg whites beaten to soft peaks. Whisk over low heat until the mixture boils. Set aside for 10 minutes; then strain through several layers of cheesecloth. Flavor with 1 tablespoon Madeira or Cognac, place in a mold, and chill until set. **Aspic for Fish** is made by substituting strained fish stock or **Court Bouillon** for the chicken broth.

Quick Aspic can be made by adding 1 teaspoon of Madeira, sherry, or Cognac to a can of chicken, beef, or turtle consommé that already contains gelatin; or you may add ½ teaspoon gelatin. Chill, chop into cubes, and serve as garnish.

Pâté en croute* is a glamorous version, with the loaf enclosed in a glazed pastry crust. Line the loaf pan with **Wheatless Pie Crust,** being careful that the crust is not torn. Cover the pâté loaf with a second pastry shell, sealing the edges of each shell. Make a hole in the center of the top to permit steam to escape. With extra strips of dough, make rosettes by rolling ½-inch-wide strips of pastry into the form of a flower; decorate the edges with some of these and arrange others on top. Reserve one rosette to cover the steam vent later. Brush with **Pastry Glaze.** Place a funnel in the hole (or make one by rolling a 2-inch square of aluminum foil around a pencil) to prevent the liquid from overflowing into the pastry during baking. Place pâté in an oven at 350° F along with the extra rosette, and bake for 2 hours. Reserve the extra rosette. Cool, then chill in the refrigerator for several hours. Meanwhile, prepare the Aspic, and when partially set, pour as much as the loaf can contain through the hole in the chilled pie. Cover with aluminum foil and refrigerate overnight. Unmold, top side up, onto a platter and cover the steam vent with the reserved rosette.

TERRINE DE CANARD*
(Terrine of Duck)

The French are very fond of game terrines —a type of pâté named after the design of the containers they are made in, which feature animal heads on their covers. Typical game terrines include *lapin* (rabbit), *faisan* (pheasant), and *canard* (duck). Of course any suitable oven-proof 4-quart container will do for this recipe.

1 5-pound duck
½ pound each, lean veal and pork
½ cup each, Cognac and Madeira, or
    Cognac and sherry
1 *Bouquet Garni* (page 164)
1 cup diced carrots

1 teaspoon each, rosemary and marjoram
2 tablespoons coarse salt
10 twists of a pepper mill or 8 green
    peppercorns
½ pound beef, pork, or chicken liver
1 cup minced onions
2 cloves garlic, minced
4 egg whites
2¾ pounds ham or Canadian bacon, sliced
    ¼ inch thick
2 tablespoons polyunsaturated margarine
2 black truffles, diced, or 6 black olives,
    pitted and sliced
1½ cup (or more) Aspic (page 176), or
    canned consommé with gelatin
Cookware spray
YIELD: Four quarts

1. Remove the fat from the cavity and wrap the duck in aluminum foil; place on a rack in a roasting pan and bake in an oven at 400° F for about 20 minutes. Remove from the oven and discard the skin and remaining fat. Bone the duck, reserving the boned breast intact. Use the carcass to prepare a broth for **Aspic** (substituting the duck broth for the chicken broth in that recipe).

2. Cut the duck meat, except the breast, and the veal and pork into 1-inch cubes reserving the duck liver. Place the cubes and the whole breast in a ceramic or glass bowl with the Cognac, Madeira, **Bouquet Garni,** carrots, and seasonings; marinate covered in the refrigerator overnight, or preferably for 2 days, tossing occasionally.

3. Drain; reserve the marinade, discarding the **Bouquet Garni** and carrots; set the marinated meat aside. Apply cookware spray to a skillet, cube the liver, and sauté the onions, garlic, and liver with 3 tablespoons of the marinade for several minutes, or until the liver cubes are pink and the onions are translucent.

4. Prepare the forcemeat by grinding the marinated meat, except the breast, and the liver mixture in a meat grinder; or coarsely grind, using some marinade, in an electric blender or food processor. Transfer to a mixing bowl; blend the meat mixture with the lightly beaten egg whites and enough marinade to produce a smooth, but firm consistency.

5. Brown a small bowl of the forcemeat in margarine; taste it and adjust the seasonings as necessary. Cut the ham slices into 1-inch strips lengthwise; layer the bottom of a 4-quart terrine with a third of the strips. Fill the terrine with half the forcemeat; brush the breasts with margarine and arrange them on top of the mixture. Arrange another third of the ham strips and the liver around the breasts and sprinkle with diced truffles or olives and some of their juice. Fill the terrine with the balance of the forcemeat, pressing down to avoid air pockets, and form the surface into a slight mound, a little above the top of the terrine.

6. Cover with the remaining strips of ham. Insert a layer of aluminum foil between the terrine and its lid, or use a paste of flour and water along the rim to ensure a tight seal. If using an uncovered mold, cover with a double thickness of aluminum foil and tie the foil tightly in place around the sides of the mold.

7. Place in a roasting pan half filled with hot water and bake in an oven at 350° F for 2½ hours, or until an inserted skewer comes out clean and hot to the touch. Cook gradually to room temperature, with a wrapped brick or weight pressing down on the uncovered terrine. When cooled sufficiently, pour off the fatty liquid into a measuring cup and refill the terrine with the same measure of slightly set Aspic, which has been made with the duck broth. Return the wrapped weight to the top of the terrine, and refrigerate overnight, or preferably for 2 days, before serving at room temperature with crusty bread and *cornichons.*

Bonus Ideas: A turkey breast plus 2 pounds of turkey meat can be used instead of the duck to prepare **Terrine de Dindon***, using the turkey carcass to prepare the broth for the aspic. If 2 pounds of pounded veal scallops are used with 2 pounds of sliced chicken, you can prepare a 2-quart loaf of **Terrine de Veau Loire***. Line the bottom of the mold with strips of ham or Canadian bacon, cover with a layer of pounded scallops, and sprinkle with a portion of a mixture made with 2 minced onions and ¾ cup of chopped parsley seasoned with 1 teaspoon each of thyme and freshly ground pepper and ⅛ teaspoon each of crumbled bay leaf and nutmeg. Cover with a layer of sliced chicken sprinkled with more of the seasoning; then repeat the layers beginning and ending with the strips of ham. Pour in 1 cup of white wine or sherry and refrigerate for several hours or overnight. Cover with aluminum foil and bake in an oven at 325° F for 2 hours. Proceed with the rest of the instructions for **Terrine de Canard.**

POULARDE À LA MOUTARDE
(Roast Chicken with Mustard)

I first savored this moist and tantalizing chicken in Belgium, which many culinary experts consider in some ways a greater stronghold of fine *cuisine bourgeoise* than present-day France.

Chickens are popular and plentiful in France, and are cooked in many imaginative ways, none more distinctively tasty than this one. A larger chicken, usually a roaster, is used for this recipe, as for most French dishes featuring roasted chicken or chicken done on a rôtisserie.

1 3-pound roasting chicken
2 tablespoons coarse salt
2 tablespoons Dijon mustard
¼ cup olive, corn, or peanut oil
Sprigs of watercress
YIELD: Four or more servings

1. Discard all excess fat from the cavity of the chicken, rub all surfaces and the cavity with salt, and truss for roasting. Brush the mustard generously over all surfaces of the chicken, then sprinkle the olive oil on all sides.

2. Place the chicken wing side down on a rack in a roasting pan, and place in the center of an oven at 400° F. Roast for 10 minutes, basting occasionally, then repeat after rotating the chicken to its other side. Reduce the temperature to 375° F and roast each side for an additional 25 minutes. Turn the chicken breast side up and brown for 10 minutes.

3. Remove the trussing twine and transfer the chicken to a warm platter.

Carve beforehand or at the table, as you prefer. Garnish with watercress.

Bonus Ideas: A variation is **Chicken Roasted with Herb Butter** (*Poularde Rôti au Beurre*). Instead of the mustard and oil, coat all surfaces and the cavity of the chicken with 4 tablespoons of melted margarine blended with ¼ teaspoon each of dried thyme, tarragon, and parsley. Roast as for *Poularde à la Moutarde,* basting regularly. While the chicken is roasting, simmer the giblets, a sliced onion, and a sliced carrot, with water to cover seasoned with ¼ teaspoon coarse salt and 4 twists of a pepper mill. After the chicken is cooked, strain this stock into the roasting pan and deglaze over high heat until it is reduced to slightly more than a cup. Serve as gravy with the roasted chicken.

A simple variation (and a favorite of mine) is **Poularde Rôti Provençal.** Prepare the chicken as for Chicken Roasted with Herb Butter, then garnish with 3 sweet red roasted peppers and black and green pitted olives.

POULARDE PAYSANNE EN COCOTTE*
(Rustic Chicken Casserole)

In the French provinces, chicken cooked en cocotte, or as a casserole, is a popular tradition.

1 3-pound chicken

1 teaspoon lemon juice
1 teaspoon coarse salt
8 twists of a pepper mill
2 tablespoons polyunsaturated margarine
2 slices Canadian bacon, cut into 1-inch
strips
1 dozen small white onions
3 each, carrots and medium-size white
turnips, quartered
1 cup chicken stock or consommé
½ cup white wine or dry vermouth
1 tablespoon cornstarch, arrowroot, or
potato starch
Sprigs of watercress
Cookware spray
YIELD: Six servings

1. Truss the chicken and dip into cold water; drain but do not pat dry. Sprinkle the cavity with the lemon juice and rub the skin with half the salt and pepper. Apply cookware spray to a large skillet and brown the moist chicken on all sides over high heat.

2. Preheat the oven to 400° F. Brush a large casserole with margarine, transfer the chicken breast side up to the casserole, and cover the breast with strips of Canadian bacon. Arrange the vegetables around the chicken; then add the chicken stock and the balance of the seasonings.

3. Cover and bake for 30 minutes; reduce the temperature to 325° F and continue roasting for 1½ hours, or until the chicken is tender. Transfer the chicken and vegetables to a warm platter; add the wine to the casserole and deglaze over high heat for 3 minutes. Blend the cornstarch with 2 tablespoons of water, stir into the casserole; cook 3 minutes more.

4. Untruss the chicken, carve into serving pieces, and serve either in the casserole or on a warm platter with the vegetables and gravy, using the strips of Canadian bacon and watercress for garnish.

Bonus Ideas: An economical and inventive variation is **Poulet Paysanne** (Rustic Boiled Chicken), made with a 4-pound fowl or older hen to serve six. Wrap the fowl in aluminum foil and bake in an oven at 400° F for 15 minutes. Remove and discard the skin and pockets of fat. Place the chicken in a large pot, with water to cover; add a **Bouquet Garni,** a carrot, onion spiked with 2 cloves, and 6 peppercorns. Bring to a boil, then simmer covered for 1 hour. Drain and cut the chicken into serving pieces; strain and reserve the broth. Sauté the chicken parts in a skillet with 2 tablespoons polyunsaturated margarine for 10 minutes on each side; set aside. Place in the skillet and sauté for 10 minutes 12 button mushrooms, a sliced carrot and onion, 1 mashed clove of garlic, and 2 slices of Canadian bacon cut into strips. Stir in 2 tablespoons cornstarch, ¾ cup white or red wine, 1 teaspoon tomato paste or ketchup, and 2 cups of the reserved chicken broth. Bring to a boil, add the reserved chicken parts, and simmer covered for 1 hour or until tender. Meanwhile, in a saucepan, place a carrot, onion, and turnip, all thinly sliced, and 1 cup of the reserved broth and simmer for 20 minutes. Transfer the chicken to a warm platter, garnish with the vegetables, and pour over the gravy, which has been reduced over high heat until thickened.

WATERZOOI OF CHICKEN*
(Flemish Chicken Casserole)

Waterzooi, the most popular of the Flemish dishes in Belgium, is a cross between a stew and a soup. It is served in deep plates.

1 4-pound roasting chicken
3 tablespoons polyunsaturated margarine
⅛ teaspoon each, dried thyme, parsley, and nutmeg
2 each, carrots, leeks, and celery stalks, sliced
3 cups chicken or veal stock
2 tablespoons wheat germ or toasted bread crumbs
3 egg whites
3 tablespoons polyunsaturated oil
1 teaspoon lemon juice
1 teaspoon coarse salt
6 twists of a pepper mill
2 tablespoons chopped parsley
YIELD: Four to six servings

1. Discard all excess fat from the cavity of the chicken; wrap the chicken in aluminum foil and bake in an oven at 400° F for 15 minutes. Remove and discard the skin and remaining fat. Disjoint the chicken into serving pieces and sprinkle with the herbs.

2. In a heavy casserole, heat the margarine and arrange a layer of carrots, leeks, and celery. Cover and cook for 5 minutes over low heat, until the vegetables are soft. Cover with a layer of the chicken pieces and pour in the stock, covering the chicken. Bring to a boil, then simmer covered for about an hour, or until tender. Remove the chicken and vegetables, bone the chicken, discard the bones, and set the chicken aside in a warm place.

3. Strain the broth and return it to the casserole; then stir in the wheat germ, lightly beaten egg whites, and oil, and heat until the sauce is slightly thickened. Blend in the lemon juice and seasonings, then return the chicken pieces to the casserole. Garnish with chopped parsley and serve hot in soup plates, accompanied by French bread, pumpernickel, or boiled potatoes.

Bonus Ideas: *Waterzooi* is equally good when prepared with rabbit **(Waterzooi of Rabbit*).** It can also be made with white-fleshed fish **(Waterzooi of Fish*)** poached in white wine **Court Bouillon.**

FENOUIL BRAISÉ
(Braised Fennel)

Fennel is extremely popular in France, where it is served both raw and cooked in a number of delightful ways. Because of its popularity among Italians living in the United States, it is often known here as *finocchio.*

Fennel has a strong anise flavor that is even more distinctive when the vegetable is eaten raw. A popular story I first heard in Italy, and later in France, is about a man who brought home several bottles of inferior wine. When his wife tasted the wine, she immediately assumed that the vendor had first offered her husband a stalk of *finocchio,* which is notorious for deadening one's taste buds and hence one's ability to evaluate the quality of wines. If serving wine with your meal, therefore, avoid serving raw fennel until the end of the meal, and be sure to follow it with a strong cup of **Café Filtre** or **Caffé Espresso**. When quartered and served sprinkled with olive oil and lemon juice, with seasonings to taste, fennel can be a refreshing salad.

9 medium-size fennel bulbs
2 teaspoons coarse salt
4 tablespoons polyunsaturated margarine
¼ pound Canadian bacon, diced
2 each, carrots and onions, minced
6 twists of a pepper mill
1 cup chicken stock or bouillon
2 tablespoons olive or corn oil
1 teaspoon each, fresh dill, parsley, and
    thyme or ½ teaspoon each, dried
YIELD: Four to eight servings

1. Remove the tough outer leaves and cut off the green shoots and the tough bottom stems from the fennel bulbs. Cut in half lengthwise; blanch in boiling water with half the salt for 3 minutes. Drain thoroughly.
2. Heat the margarine in a casserole; add the diced bacon and vegetables. Cover with a layer of fennel; then add the pepper, chicken stock, and oil. Cover and simmer over low heat for 30 minutes, or until tender.
3. Transfer to a warm serving dish and pour over the cooking juices. Serve hot, sprinkled with the herb mixture.

Bonus Ideas: Fenouil à la Moutarde (Braised Fennel with Mustard) is initially prepared in the same manner. When the fennel bulbs are tender, transfer them to a warm ovenproof serving dish. Prepare a mustard sauce by straining the cooking juices and combining with chicken stock to measure 1 cup. In a saucepan, combine 1 tablespoon of melted polyunsaturated margarine, 1 tablespoon cornstarch, 1 tablespoon dry mustard, 1 teaspoon coarse salt, 6 twists of a pepper mill, and the cup of combined stock and juices. Bring to a boil over low heat, stirring constantly. Add 1 teaspoon fresh dill and 1 tablespoon skim evaporated milk. Spoon the sauce over the fennel, sprinkle with 3 tablespoons Parmesan cheese, and brown briefly under the broiler.

The French also braise other vegetables: Belgian endive *(witloof),* celery *(celeris),* leeks *(poireaux),* and the more exotic and distinctively flavored *cardons,* or cardoons, which (like the artichoke) is a member of the thistle family.

Endives Braisées (to serve four) is made by placing a layer of 12 Belgian endives in a skillet with 2 tablespoons of melted polyunsaturated margarine. Add ½ cup of water, 1 teaspoon lemon juice, and 1 teaspoon coarse salt. Bring to a boil and simmer covered over low heat for 15 minutes. Add ¼ pound diced Canadian bacon and ½ cup of chicken stock or bouillon. Simmer for 30 minutes; then transfer the endives to a serving dish. Reduce the cooking liquid over high heat until slightly thickened, stir in 2 tablespoons of margarine, and pour the sauce over the endives. Serve hot.

Poireaux Gratinés à la Béchamel (Leeks *au Gratin*) to serve four are made simply by boiling the white part only of 12 leeks in water to cover for 15 minutes, or until tender. Grease an ovenproof serving dish with margarine, insert the leeks in a single layer, and coat with 2 cups of **Sauce Béchamel.** Sprinkle with 3 tablespoons grated Gruyère or Parmesan cheese, dot with margarine, and sprinkle with ¼ cup of wheat germ or bread crumbs. Place under the broiler for 3 minutes, then serve hot. **Celery au Gratin** is made in the identical way.

CARDONS À LA MOELLE
(Cardoons with Beef Marrow)

The *pièce de résistance* of the vegetable family, *cardoons,* have a distinctive flavor not unlike that of salsify (oyster root) or the artichoke. In the United States, cardoons can be found in talian markets, where they are called *cardi.* Only the inner ribs of the large celery-like vegetable should be used in a recipe. To serve six, you will need 2 4-foot bunches of the silvery green thistle plant.

2 4-foot bunches of cardoons or 2 pounds off their inner stalks

Acidulated Water:
4 quarts water
3 tablespoons vinegar or lemon juice
1 lemon

Court Bouillon Blanc:
2 quarts boiling water
4 tablespoons lemon juice
2 tablespoons cornstarch, potato flour, or arrowroot
1 onion spiked with 2 cloves

6 tablespoons polyunsaturated margarine
1 tablespoon cornstarch

4 cups beef bouillon
1½ teaspoons coarse salt
⅛ teaspoon white pepper
¼ cup grated Gruyère or Parmesan cheese
Marrow of 1 large beef bone
YIELD: Six servings

1. Remove and discard the tough outer stalks of the cardoons, reserving the tender inner stalks. Beginning from the bottom of each stalk, cut into 3-inch sections, discarding the upper leafy end. Peel and discard all threads and rub with lemon juice before placing in acidulated water.

2. Prepare the *Court Bouillon Blanc* by combining all ingredients and bringing to a boil, stirring constantly. Drain the cardoons, place in the bouillon, and boil for about 10 minutes. Drain and rinse in cold water to remove the bitterness. Simmer, covered, in boiling acidulated water for about 2 hours until tender.

3. Meanwhile, heat the margarine in a saucepan over low heat, add 1 tablespoon cornstarch, and blend into a **roux blond.** Pour in the bouillon and cook for 20 minutes, stirring occasionally. Season with salt and pepper.

4. Drain the cardoon pieces, mix into the sauce, and arrange on an ovenproof serving dish. Remove the marrow from the bone with the point of a knife and poach the marrow in salted water for 10 minutes. Drain and cut into thin rounds. Top each cardoon with slices of marrow, sprinkle with grated cheese, and bake in an oven at 375° F for 30 minutes. Serve very hot.

Bonus Ideas: The French frequently use marrow as a garnish for braised vegetables; rounds of marrow are often added, for example, to braised celery or endives.

The Italians, also very fond of cardoons (*cardi*), do not cook the vegetable for such long periods. **Cardoons Florentine** to serve six are made with 2 pounds of the inner stalks, which are threaded and cut into 3-inch lengths and soaked in acidulated water. After draining, they are cooked for 1 hour in fresh acidulated water and 1 teaspoon salt. Meanwhile, a thinly sliced onion is sautéed with 2 tablespoons margarine. The drained cardoons are then added with 1 teaspoon salt and ¾ cup of the reserved acidulated broth and simmered over low heat for 25 minutes. They are then drained and served hot, sprinkled with grated Parmesan cheese.

Cardi Siciliani (Cardoons, Sicilian Style) are prepared in the same manner initially. After the cardoons are cooked and drained, they are dipped into lightly beaten egg whites and coated with a mixture of wheat germ or bread crumbs blended with grated Parmesan cheese. Olive or corn oil in a baking dish is heated in an oven at 400° F until the oil is 375° F (when a cube of bread dipped into the oil turns golden brown). Brown the coated cardoons on both sides, drain and pat dry on paper toweling, and serve hot with lemon wedges.

BEIGNETS D'ANANAS
(Pineapple Fritters)

Chef Adelio Pagani of the Grand Hotel in Rome insists that beer is the secret ingredient of these wonderfully light and airy fritters—a trick of the trade I first learned years ago from Chef Albert Stockli at the Stonehenge Inn in Ridgefield, Connecticut.

1 fresh pineapple
1 cup dark rum
½ cup apricot jam or Apricot and
    Pineapple Sauce (page 166)

2 cups Beignet Dough:
½ cup each, cornstarch and white rye flour.
2 teaspoons baking powder
½ teaspoon coarse salt
1 tablespoon melted polyunsaturated
    margarine
⅓ cup beer
¾ cup lukewarm water
1 egg white, beaten to peaks
1 tablespoon Cognac or brandy

½ cup olive, corn, or peanut oil
2 tablespoons Vanilla Fruit Sugar (page
    119)
YIELD: Six servings

1. Peel the pineapple, cut into 12 slices, and marinate for several hours in the rum. Drain, spread half the slices with the apricot jam, and cover each with a second slice of pineapple.

2. Prepare the *beignet* dough by sifting the cornstarch and flour, baking powder, and salt 6 times; separately mix the balance of ingredients for the dough except the egg whites and Cognac, then combine with the flour mixture. Beat with a wooden spoon into a smooth consistency and refrigerate for 2 hours, or preferably overnight. Immediately before using, fold in the beaten egg whites and Cognac.

3. Pour the oil into a baking dish, place in an oven at 400° F, and heat until the oil is 375° F. Test with a cube of bread, which will turn golden brown when the oil is ready. Dip the pineapple sand-

wiches a few at a time in the batter, then place in the hot oil, and fry until they are golden on both sides. Drain on paper toweling.

4. Sprinkle with the Vanilla Fruit Sugar and serve with the balance of the jam or sauce on the side.

Bonus Ideas: You may wish to try *beignets* using other fruits. To make six servings of **Beignets de Pommes** (Apple Fritters), you will need 9 tart green apples. Peel, core, and cut the apples into wedges; marinate overnight with ½ cup pure maple syrup and 3 tablespoons of rum or your favorite liqueur. Drain on paper toweling and pat dry. Dip into the batter, brown on all sides in oil at 375° F, and drain again on paper toweling. Serve with **Vanilla Fruit Sugar,** or sprinkle with the fruit sugar and return to the oven for 5 minutes, until the fritters are glazed.

Beignets d'Abricots (Apricot Fritters) are made with 1 dozen very ripe apricots, peeled, pitted, and cut in half. Marinate overnight in rum or liqueur, drain, and pat dry before dipping into the batter and proceeding with the basic *beignet* recipe.

Beignets Suprêmes are filled with a soufflé of **Candied Fruits.** To serve six, marinate 6 tablespoons of finely chopped Candied Fruits in 3 tablespoons rum. In a mixing bowl, blend 2 egg whites, 1 tablespoon polyunsaturated oil, and ⅛ teaspoon salt. Sift together 6 times 1½ tablespoons each of cornstarch and white rye flour and a pinch of baking powder. Blend the flour mixture, with 2 tablespoons fruit sugar and combine with the egg mixture. Beat thoroughly with a wire whisk, then add ½ cup skim evaporated milk and 1 teaspoon unflavored gelatin.

Pour the mixture into a saucepan and heat over low heat until thickened. Remove from heat and add the Candied Fruits and rum marinade. Pour the mixture into a pie plate and chill thoroughly. Dip small balls of the mixture into the batter and proceed with the basic *beignet* recipe.

JAR NGAAR CHU
(Chinese Candied Banana Fritters)

The fritter has been part of the repertoire of Chinese cuisine for centuries. These banana fritters can be served either as a dessert or savory, and will be fun for those who participate in the ceremony of completing the recipe at the table.

¾ cup each, cornstarch and white rye flour
3 teaspoons baking powder
⅛ teaspoon salt
2 egg whites, lightly beaten
¾ cup water
⅓ cup honey or pure maple syrup
⅓ cup peanut or corn oil
6 medium ripe bananas
Peanut oil for frying
6 bowls of iced water
YIELD: Six servings

1. Sift the cornstarch and flour, baking powder, and salt 6 times into a mixing bowl. Make a well in the center of the mixture; add the egg whites and water and mix into a smooth batter. Set aside for 15 minutes.

2. Meanwhile, combine the honey and oil in a saucepan and stir constantly over low heat until thickened. Peel the bananas; cut lengthwise and then into quarters; dip them into the batter and coat well.

3. Brush a serving dish with peanut oil to prevent the cooked fritters from sticking. Place the peanut oil in a baking dish and heat in an oven at 400° F until the oil is 375° F (when a cube of bread dropped into the oil turns golden brown); then brown several of the fritters at a time until golden on all sides. Drain on paper toweling. Stir the fritters into the hot syrup and transfer to the serving dish; repeat the process with the balance of the fritters.

4. Serve immediately at the table with individual bowls of iced water. Using chopsticks or a fork, each diner will dip the fritters one at a time into the cold water to harden the syrup coating, which, to everyone's delight, will crystallize in the form of tiny bubbles.

Bonus Ideas: Chinese Candied Apple Fritters can be made in the identical manner using 3 crisp apples, peeled, cored, and cut into eights.

• • •

It is time to take our leave of France and travel to the land that rightly boasts the oldest continuing culture and one of the world's finest cuisines: China, the source and inspiration of many of the Western culinary ideas we have explored thus far. This part of our tour will be of special interest to the slimming gourmet, since Chinese cuisine has been called the most healthful cookery in the world. We shall see how it is currently practiced in China, the Far East—particularly in Hong Kong and Taiwan—and distinctive Chinese restaurants in New York City.

CHINA

*"Cantonese cuisine is the
best food in China. I hope
we have it in heaven!"
—Monsignor John
Romaniello, the "Noodle
Priest," who arrived in
China in 1928 and
stayed thirty years*

THE CUISINE IN PERSPECTIVE

China has the oldest continuing culture of any nation in the world and a cuisine that had already become an art during the great classical age of the Chou Dynasty, more than a century before the birth of Christ. Almost from its beginning, Chinese cuisine was profoundly influenced by the scholars and philosophers who were so important in founding and developing Chinese culture. Writers and scholars such as Confucius, Su Tung Po, and Lao-tze used their great prestige with the populace to influence the development of cookery as an art and to establish a protocol for the proper preparation, serving, and enjoyment of fine food.

However, it was the legendary Emperor Fu Hsi who almost two dozen centuries before Christ taught the populace how to improve the basic concepts of hunting, fishing and cooking of food. Although China is one of the largest countries in the world, covering more than 3.5 million square miles, more than half of it is mountainous or unsuited to cultivation. The climates of its various regions run the gamut from the arctic temperatures of Mongolia in the north to the semitropical temperatures of Yunnan, Fukien, and Canton in the south. With this in mind, Emperor Fu Hsi encouraged the populace to cultivate as much of the land as possible and to expand its food supply by hunting and fishing.

About 500 B.C., the philosophies of Confucianism and Taoism became the prime motivating forces in the development of the cuisine. Kung Fu-tse, whom we know as Confucius, established an ethical system based on personal virtue, justice, and a responsibility and devotion to the family group. In his *Analectics,* he also set forth rules for the preparation and serving of good food, which he called the "first happiness." Confucius cautioned the populace not to eat any ingredient that was discolored, had a bad odor, or was out of season. He encouraged a sense of balance and harmony; whenever meats were used as ingrediients, for example, they could not overpower the rice included in the same meal. He also emphasized the aesthetic aspects of cooking and eating: a proper dish, he said, should appeal to the eye as well as to the palate.

While Confucius emphasized the culinary and aesthetic aspects of food, Taoism, founded by Lao-tze, stressed primarily its nutritional and medicinal qualities, especially its effect on longevity through harmony with nature. Taoists were encouraged to explore the products of nature in order to discover their lifegiving elements, particularly the value of roots, fungi, herbs, and marine vegetation. While Confucianism placed a more material emphasis on the flavor, texture, and eye appeal of food, Taoists were concerned that the nutrients found in vegetables not be destroyed by overcooking; Lao-tze, indeed, encouraged the consumption of raw, or at least very briefly cooked, plants and vegetables.

The counterbalance of these two major philosophies became the basis of Chinese cuisine as an art and its eventual refinement into one of the world's great cuisines. Through necessity, then, and at the behest of its philosophers, the Chinese people began exploring all forms of edible ingredients—a search that provided a variety in their cookery unmatched before or since by any other of the world's cuisines. It is reported that there have been more than 50,000 recipes in the Chinese repertoire. Ingredients from the land and sea—lotus roots, lily buds, birds' nests, sea cucumbers, shark fins, and many other seemingly exotic items—were adopted. Many of these ingredients, including perishable items from the sea such as squid, clams, mussels, and shrimp, were air-dried and thus made available for long periods of time.

Other factors important to the growth of Chinese cuisine were the development of chopsticks as eating utensils and the scarcity and high cost of fuel in ancient China. Chopsticks were already in use in about 2000 B.C., while it was not until the 15th century after Christ that Westerners developed utensils like the fork and stopped eating food with their hands. (It amazes me that after two decades in China Marco Polo failed to bring back to the Western world the concept of using the wok or chopsticks.) Because of the use of chopsticks, all meats and other ingredients in Chinese cookery are necessarily chopped into small bite-size pieces that can be managed by the chopsticks. And because of the scarcity of fuel and the admonitions of both Confucianists and Taoists that food not be overcooked, ingredients were, and still are, cooked for very short periods of time (with the exception of some dishes that call for stewing or braising). Techniques of stir-frying *(chow)* and steaming *(jing)* were developed, using the marvelously versatile wok, the steamer, and the brazier. Even today, the majority of Chinese homemakers use these same utensils, and with a single burner, or rarely with more than two burners, prepare family meals of four or more courses and even banquets of ten to twelve courses.

The Chinese awareness of and dedication to fine food, as an integral part of the Confucian tenet of devotion to the family, have continued through the centuries, influencing the cuisines of not only neighboring countries but of others around the world. High culinary standards were maintained by the close family ties inherent in Chinese culture and passed on from one generation to another.

In the People's Republic of China, however, Mao Tse-tung's revolutionary Communist Party had for the past several decades made a point of minimizing the traditionally strong family relationships; it was reported that husbands, wives, children, and relatives rarely had opportunities to be together. This, of course, negatively affected the traditional family training of the young, resulting in the minimization of the techniques and much of the glory of Chinese cuisine.

This past year the liberalizing policies of Vice-Premier Teng Hsiao-p'ing have made great strides toward improving the economy of China and the production of steel, petroleum, and other raw materials. For the first time in decades, the People's Republic is welcoming experts and tourists from the West and permitting its students to study abroad, particularly in the United States. Various international hotel chains have announced new hotel projects throughout China; fast-food operators like McDonald's have plans for expanding into China; and Coca-Cola reportedly will soon be available throughout the vast country.

Presumably, these Western innovations are intended to serve the increase of foreign tourists to China; however, it seems inevitable that the billions of Chinese also will become a huge consumer market for these products and services. The Communist government also announced that it was negotiating with a Japanese firm to provide the Chinese populace with packages of processed vegetables and other ingredients to expedite the hastier cooking of meals. As one government official put it candidly, "The less time our people take to cook their meals, the more time they will have to work in the factories." The face of the revolution may have changed, but it still continues in China.

During this period, the traditions of cookery have been maintained by those who left China for Taiwan, Hong Kong, Bangkok, Malaysia, Singapore, and the numerous other Chinese communities all over the world.

The People's Republic of China has been consciously altering the standards of the cuisine of the country. It has officially codified the many thousands of Chinese recipes, with an intention to reduce the variety and number that it encourages to be used in contemporary China. Whereas many culinary experts believe that there were more than 10,000 basic recipes in the active repertoires of Chinese cooks—50,000, including variations with alternate ingredients—the current government is trying to reduce the number to less than 2,000 throughout the entire vast country, notwithstanding its varying climate, availability of ingredients, and geographic limitations.

One reason for this is that during the

recent decades, when China closed itself off from the Western world and its imports, a smaller range of ingredients was available for the huge population. As Master Cook Chiun Bao of the prestigious Bei-yuan (North Garden) restaurant told us during our tour of Canton, the government had issued instructions that chickens, ducks, and geese in abundant supply and seasonally bountiful vegetables were to be favored in preparing daily meals.

In addition to its being virtually impossible for the elders to train their children in the nuances of Chinese cookery, most of the experienced chefs are limited in their opportunity to train younger gifted cooks. Since the government assigns the personnel who serve in public kitchens, regardless of their capability, desire, or aptitude, much of the subtlety and creativeness of fine Chinese cuisine are being lost.

As is well known, there are distinctive schools of Chinese cookery, corresponding to the major regions of China. These are the Cantonese cuisine of southern Canton; the Mandarin cuisine of Peking and its neighbors to the north; the southern inland cookery of Szechuan and Yunnan; Shanghai cuisine, from the central region of China; and the cuisines of Fukien and Hunan, across the Formosa Strait from Taiwan. Let's explore the distinguishing features of these regional schools.

CANTON:

Canton, or Kwong Chau, has long been famous for its excellent cuisine, considered by many to be the country's finest. The Chinese have a saying: if you want to eat well, you must eat in Kwong Chow.

Since the mid-1800s, when Chinese immigrants began arriving in the United States, chiefly from Canton, Americans have been accustomed primarily to Cantonese cooking, which has not, however, necessarily been up to the high standards practiced in Kwong Chau. For this style is considered the most diversified and subtle, using oil, soy sauce, and herbs sparingly. Since Canton is a harbor city, seafood is plentiful and an important ingredient in many dishes. A major factor in explaining the diversity of Cantonese cooking is that at the time of the overthrow of the Ming Dynasty in the mid-1600s, the imperial chefs escaped to Canton, bringing with them their recipes and expertise. Besides seafood, Cantonese cooking is noted for its dumplings, its shark's fin, winter melon, and bird's nest soups, its **Roast Pork** and roast duck, and such distinctive sauces as black bean garlic sauce and **Lobster Sauce.**

Of all the regional schools, Cantonese cooking is the most compatible with slimming cuisine. Chicken stock is used to a greater extent than oils; the seasonings are predominantly light soy sauce, ginger root, and wine; and the basic cooking processes are quick stir-frying or steaming. It is a style of cookery that retains the flavors and textures of the basic ingredients, rather than overpowering them in sauces.

PEKING AND THE NORTH:

Before the fall of the Ming Dynasty in the 17th century, Peking was the gourmet capital of China, attracting the finest chefs to the Imperial Palace, where fine food was prepared and served with an elegance unknown to any other culture before or since. The cuisine of Peking was influenced by those of Shantung and Mongolia, the nomadic tribes of which roasted meats or simmered them using the hot pot; other specialties were barbecued lamb and poultry, especially ducks. These techniques were introduced to the Imperial Palace, resulting in, for instance, the now famous specialty of Peking duck.

Northern cooking uses garlic and scallions, bamboo shoots, and chinese cabbage, among other ingredients. Because the north is a grain center, noodles and steamed buns are common—particularly the **Spring Roll.** Soybean paste and egg whites are blended with other ingredients in the preparation of the slightly more seasoned but still delicate specialties of the region.

It should be pointed out that a major accomplishment of the People's Republic of China is the flood control programs that have enriched the cultivated areas near Shantung and Honan, increasing the production of meats, fresh vegetables, fruits, and nuts.

SZECHUAN AND YUNNAN:

The hot pepper *(fagara)* indigenous to Szechuan characterizes the hot and spicy dishes of these two regions, with those of Yunnan being appreciably hotter. The climate, not unlike that of Mexico, where spicy foods are common, is subtropical, and there are long, uncomfortable summers.

Szechuan cuisine utilizes fat, "cloud" or "tree ear" fungi, hot chili-pepper oil, bamboo shoots, and nuts as popular ingredients. Specialties include hot and sour soup, deep-fried chicken wrapped in paper, and sweet and sour crispy fish. Szechuan duck and other meats are often twice-cooked, a special technique that begins by steaming, then deep-frying, resulting in a crisp texture unique to Chinese cookery.

While family meals are hot and spicy, banquet dishes are surprisingly bland. This is probably a result of the fact that the northerners who migrated to this area brought with them the subtler dishes from the court in Peking, and these are still the dishes predominantly served at formal banquets.

SHANGHAI AND THE CENTRAL COAST:

Rice and vegetables, the chief produce of this region, are used extensively in its cooking. Generally, meats, fish, and vegetables are steamed, maintaining natural flavors. But another favorite cooking process is the red-simmering of meats with soy sauce, which provides the distinctive color of these dishes. Vegetables are so bountiful they are often cooked without the addition of meats or seafood. However, the Shanghai school tends to sweeten dishes with liberal amounts of unrefined sugar, and their sweet and sour dishes are prepared with rice wine vinegar.

Specialties of this school include the pork meatballs called **Lion's Head,** sweet and sour pork, **Roast Pork Strips,** and innumerable vegetable dishes, many of which imitate meat dishes—**Chinese Mock Pressed Duck** or **Goose,** or **Vegetarian Mock Ham.**

FUKIEN AND HUNAN:

Fukien, across the Formosa Strait from Taiwan, naturally specializes in the abundant fish and seafood from the sea and its rivers. This region is also famous for its clear soups, which are often served several times during a meal. Unlike other Chinese soups, Fukienese broth is simmered for very long periods of time, and raw chicken bones are added for about 10 minutes before the soup is strained and served.

Inasmuch as the finest soy sauce in China is produced here, red-simmering of meats and poultry is a popular cooking technique. **Stuffed Dumplings** are made with *yen pi,* which is produced by pounding chopped lean meat with a blend of flours until it can be rolled out into a thin and transparent doughlike skin with a distinctive flavor. Specialties of the region include **Red-Simmered Pork, Spring Rolls,** giant shrimp, and, of course, the famous clear soups.

We will begin our third tour. This time we will consider present-day Chinese cuisine as it is practiced particularly in Hong Kong, Taiwan, China, and some of the best Chinese restaurants in New York City.

A COOK'S TOUR OF CHINA

Our first stop is the British Crown Colony of Hong Kong, traditionally, the stepping-stone to China. Although its 4.5 million people are predominantly Chinese, Hong Kong's other tongues, including English, help us to absorb the fascination of the Orient with a minimum of culture shock.

At first, Hong Kong resembles any modern city: there are skyscrapers, elegant hotels and restaurants, abundant taxis, double-decker buses; and an efficient tunnel as well as ferry service connecting the Kowloon side of the city situated on the mainland with the Hong Kong side, which is technically but rarely called the City of Victoria. A major port, Hong Kong's harbor is always crowded with huge luxury liners, cruise and cargo ships, and naval vessels.

Shortly, however, one becomes aware of the uniquely Chinese character of this bustling commercial center. Along the western waterfront on the Hong Kong side in the densely populated street market in West Point, you become aware of the high-pitched Cantonese dialect, vendors offering an incredible range of items for sale, and massive crowds of shoppers and sightseers. On the mainland side, there is the Jade Market on Canton Road: spirited bargaining, fortunetellers, the village bazaar; and a night market for clothing and appliances on Temple Street—all demand our attention.

However, Saigon Street will hold the greatest fascination for any cook. It offers the largest variety of edibles that we have ever seen in one place: live ducks and chickens, live "rice" birds (whose nests are used for soup because of the birds' cleanliness and exclusive diet of rice), pigs, frogs and eels, live snakes. It is virtually an endless list. Butchers' stalls display cuts of meat, hanging ducks, fresh-caught fish, and a wide variety of other seafood and edibles from the sea. Exploring further, we find countless stalls with incredible displays of dried foods and condiments. Contributing to the bustle are the ubiquitous decorative pushcarts, their vendors selling *dem sem,* Chinese snacks that include the popular **Cantonese Steamed Filled Dumplings.**

And one must mention the equally

ubiquitous junks and sampans. The *Tanka,* or boat people of Hong Kong, nomads from Fukien, have lived on their bobbing junks for centuries, so closely jammed together one hardly realizes that these people live permanently afloat. They have their own distinctive customs and festivals.

The Cantonese language and Cantonese food predominate in Hong Kong because of its close proximity to Kwong Chau (Canton) on the mainland. The Chinese, who represent about 98 percent of Hong Kong's population, began migrating from Canton almost ten centuries ago, and are called the *Punti,* or land people. The *Hakka,* who arrived much later, are considered the "guests" of the *Punti.*

People always seem to be eating, or concerned with food, in Hong Kong. *Dem sem* vendors are virtually everywhere, and inexpensive food is bountiful in the many diversified restaurants. While the more well-known restaurants are predominantly Cantonese, additional influences are reflected in the many other Chinese schools of cuisine represented, as well as the cuisines of Malaysia and Indonesia; particularly popular are curried rice, noodles, and fish cakes—specialties of neighboring Singapore.

Lunch in Hong Kong is a light meal at midday, dinner being the main meal; dining begins in most restaurants about 6:30 P.M. and usually lasts for several hours, while at home people eat earlier. Workers eat where they work, in accordance with *gon shi sik:* the concept that "Chinese workers eat the company."

Before exploring Taiwan, another stronghold maintaining the traditions of fine Chinese cuisine, and then proceeding to China, let's visit with Monsignor John Romaniello, who has lived in China, Taiwan, and Hong Kong for close to 50 years. Father John first arrived in China in 1928 as prefect of the Roman Catholic Maryknoll Fathers. He remained with his parish during the 1938 invasion of Shanghai by the Japanese, and after Pearl Harbor in 1941 was assigned to the famous Flying Tigers. Subsequently, Father John became internationally known as the "Noodle Priest," devoting all his energies to converting donations of flour into noodles, which he distributed to the hordes of hungry refugees fleeing from China.

According to Father John, there are no important differences among the Chinese people of the People's Republic, Hong Kong, or Taiwan. Especially in the preparation and serving of food, there is an identical basic sense of decorum and etiquette, as well as a desire to share food with family, relatives, and friends.

Father John explains that the uniformity of Chinese etiquette is related to the universality of the written language. The calligraphy is always the same, though the characters may be voiced differently, in accordance with local dialect. For example, the Chinese calligraphic symbol for the word "day" can be described as a square with a dash in its center. It is always written in the same way; however, in Cantonese it is pronounced *yat,* while in Mandarin it is *yi.* Even *egg foo young* is pronounced in such regional variations as *yung dun, foo yong, foo yung,* and *fu yong.*

During our forthcoming tour, it will become strikingly apparent that although the Chinese can read their standard calligraphy, generally they cannot understand one another's regional dialects. Neither those in Taiwan who speak Fukienese and those in Hong Kong who speak Cantonese can understand each other. Shanghai friends explain that they cannot understand the Peking Opera. In each Chinese community, Mandarin is the official language taught in school, but the regional dialects prevail. In Hong Kong and Taiwan, the local television programs are spoken in Mandarin accompanied by calligraphic subtitles for the convenience of the vast audiences who speak only the local dialects.

In old China, Father John relates, everyone knew about cooking, even the very poor, who had their own sense of dignity and personal discipline. "They made an advantage of poverty, which they interpreted as a necessary frugality rather than a moral breakdown. There was never a skid row with defeated human beings; rather poverty among the Chinese led to frugality and the concept that everything edible is to be used in cooking, but always in small quantities." The family was drawn together by this poverty, and a major reason that many dishes are shared at the family table is that originally it was considered a more economical method of feeding large families.

Father John recalls a meeting with Lin Yutang, who like most Chinese scholars had a profound interest in the art of cooking. On a ship some years ago, Lin Yutang noticed that a large steak that had not been touched by a diner was being taken away to be thrown out. Reacting to this waste, he said sadly, "That steak could have flavored several meals for an average Chinese family." In many homes, meat is eaten once a week or perhaps once a month, and is always served with great appreciation.

As noted previously, the Chinese use virtually everything edible as an ingredient, including the sea cucumber or sea slug, birds' nests, lotus and other roots, and marine vegetation, particularly seaweed. Father John considers this an extension of the sense of frugality; it is also consistent with the teachings of the Taoists, who advocated the search for life-giving elements in all the produce of land and sea.

Father John tells us that everyone in China knows how to cook because the Chinese love to eat. "They love to talk about food, which they seem to be doing all the time." And everyone in China seems to know the expression, *"Fei lo-hai foot lo!"* which means, "A fat man is a rich man." Even among the poor, the most important place in the world is in the kitchen, which is generally a simple affair with a single burner, a single wok, steamer baskets, and modest storage and work areas. "Having seen so many of these minute kitchens and how they cook," says Father John, "I am constantly amazed that with so little to work with, they can come up with the greatest food." Perhaps this is because of the role of the wife, who in a Chinese family is the undisputed boss of the home and the sole cook in the kitchen. She will prepare the food, place several dishes on the table for her family to begin eating, then join them when the final dish is cooked. Each member of the family will dip into the communal dishes presented at the table; there are at least three or four different dishes, plus rice and tea, even for an average rural family. Generally, the family in old China would eat twice a day: at 9:00 A.M. there would be soup, rice, and a vegetable such as broccoli flavored with tomatoes or bits of meat or poultry; and at 5:00 P.M., the main meal of the day.

As we will learn later, during our tour of Kwangtung province, the current lifestyle has changed. The Chinese now eat breakfast at about 7:00 A.M., and all of our meals in China would prove to be lunches promptly at noon and dinners at 6:00 P.M. Also, this proved to be the strict schedule of Chinese friends in Singapore, Macao, Hong Kong, and Taiwan. A perfect indication of this is when I met Chinese friends in Tapei for a 1:00 P.M. appointment, assuming we would lunch together, only to learn that the punctual Chinese had already eaten.

In large cities, however, the dishes and routine vary. In China, breakfast is usually some variety of **Congee,** which is rice gruel flavored with onion, other vegetables, and occasionally meat or fish. In the north, steamed bread is served for breakfast, or *say beng*—dough rapidly fried on a griddle, then salted and rolled into a crumpet. However, this traditional Chinese breakfast is often considered too heavy by many Chinese. As Father John recalls, "When eating away from home, they order *dem sem* in restaurants or buy the dumplings from the ubiquitous vendors, who are also much in evidence in rural areas."

Although *dem sem* and other types of food carts will be highly visible during our tours of Hong Kong and Taiwan, they will not be in current day Canton. Lee Cheng-

ling, our excellent guide during our tour of China, tells us: "Noodle and *dem sem* carts on the streets of Canton were understandable twenty years ago when the population was under 1 million. But now the population of the city of Canton is 3 million, and it's much too crowded to permit street vendors except on certain streets set aside for this purpose."

"The Chinese have a feeling for people and one another," Father John likes to say. "Even a so-called Chinese coolie dresses the way he does because of the nature of his work. When he is off from work, he wears clean clothes with dignity, which is inherent in the philosophy and teachings of Confucius."

If the wife is the key person in the kitchen, the kitchen is the unquestioned family center of the Chinese home. Evidence of this is the charming festival held each year for the god of the kitchen hearth, Jau Wang Yeh, who on his feast day returns to heaven. The family, on this day, honors him by refraining from cleaning and cooking, having prepared ahead in anticipation of his feast. (I am told that the Chinese honor the kitchen god because they don't want him to relate to the other gods all the gossip and tales he is bound to have heard around the stove.)

We should not be too surprised to learn during our tour of China that the Communist government does not honor the traditional gods of the past; hence, most young people we met did not know the name or the customs associated with the kitchen god. In Singapore, Hong Kong, and Taiwan, however, we will be equally surprised to learn most young people have converted to Buddhism or

Catholicism and that they, too, do not honor the kitchen god, although their parents and grandparents still do.

Father John considers friendship among the Chinese the greatest he has ever known. "It is reflected in the way they play chess together and in the many banquets held on special occasions. Among family celebrations, weddings are major events. *Moon Yit,* a festival for a baby's first month, is most important, as are the celebrations of the key birthdays of the elderly, especially the 61st, 71st, and 81st birthdays. (The Chinese consider a newborn babe already one year old.) Other festivals include the August Moon and New Year's Eve, which is really a spring festival, since it falls in February and represents the end of winter and the beginning of spring. Banquets are also held on the occasion of funerals.

These banquets range from the most elaborate and expensive affairs among the wealthy, impressive but more moderate affairs among average families, and touching communal meals among the very poor. "Among the very poor," Father John explains, "a group of twenty or thirty poor people will band together and make contributions of chickens and other ingredients, and share in the cooking, serving, and enjoyment of a festive banquet together."

At all Chinese banquets, including those in the People's Republic of China today, the Chinese begin the meal with a toast and continue making toasts throughout the fifteen or eighteen courses customary at formal banquets. In an average family, the banquet is limited to about ten dishes, and the first toast is always made to the *t'ai-t'ai,* or the wife, of the family.

Even in wealthier families, which might have a cook, the toast is made to the wife, who is credited with the supervision of the meal. It is a subtle way of complimenting the actual cook as well. For banquets in average homes, the wife does all the cooking, often assisted by a woman relative, who helps out with the more complicated preparations of ingredients. In old China, a family-style banquet involving outside guests was usually arranged so that the women sat at one table and the host and male guests at another. More generally today, everyone sits at one huge table.

The Confucian concept of love for one's self and family is reflected in the generosity and strong expressions of friendship during a banquet. "The host," we are told by Father John, "will pick out the choicest pieces of food in each dish and present them to his guests. There is a feeling of deep communion among the host, his family, and other guests that is extremely warm and always memorable."

Father John, as we indicated, is widely known for his efforts to aid the refugees from China during the war years. He is the originator of the program called "Millions of Noodles for Millions of Refugees." *Newsweek* magazine wrote of him: "An extroverted crusader from New Rochelle, New York, John Romaniello virtually lives and breathes noodles. He shamelessly solicits contributions for his refugee program from every visiting American he can reach. 'For centuries,' John Romaniello says, 'my Italian forebears enjoyed spaghetti, the secret brought from China by Marco Polo. Now I'm returning noodles to the Chinese refugees at the rate of five million pounds a year.' "

In Hong Kong and Taiwan, as Father

John explains, you can buy noodles already cooked on street corners, very much like hot dogs in the States." They are served with slivers of pork. "In fact, noodles have a wholesome meaning of dignity," he says. "You should have seen how the Chinese in old China would take a piece of dough and work and stretch it as long as they could to make the noodles. Symbolically, the longer it is the greater is its contribution to a stronger and longer life." As an expression of this symbolism, noodles are served at all feasts as the last dish.

Father John never really learned to cook. "But I certainly learned to share the Chinese love and enthusiasm for fine food," he says, "and I guess to talk about it all the time, too, the way the Chinese do." He does have one possibly understandable prejudice, however: his preference for the food of Canton. "Cantonese food is the best food in China," he says. "I hope we have it in heaven!"

A short airplane flight from Hong Kong brings us to Taipei, capital of Taiwan and another stronghold of traditional Chinese cuisine. Again we find a combination of modern buildings and distinctive Buddhist and Taoist temples and pagodas. The Japanese invaded this key island during World War II; however, the impact of foreigners was not new to Taiwan, the first major one being Portuguese. It was Portuguese sailors who gave the island its original name, Formosa (meaning beautiful), in the 1500s. The Dutch arrived a hundred years later, soon to be followed by the Spanish. Not long after, refugees from the Manchu invasion of Peking came to the island, led by Chen Cheng-kung, who is still considered a national hero. The island be-

came a Japanese possession in 1895 and was a military base until 1945, when it became Chiang Kai-shek's provisional seat of government. It is now the Republic of China, opposed to the Communist government on the mainland, and is led by the son of the former premier, Chiang Ching-kuo, who is credited with its current prosperity.

Understandably, the people of Taiwan still reflect the initial disappointment and shock they expressed when the United States recognized the People's Republic of China last year, but their mode of life is still substantially as it has been for the past two decades, confident that the Americans will eventually recognize that they are superior to and more trustworthy than the Communists across the Strait of Formosa.

Considering these varying ethnic influences, it is not surprising to find that the cuisine of Taiwan is both excellent and diversified. In addition to the Chinese, we find Japanese, Korean, and other ethnic cuisines, all utilizing the tremendous variety of ingredients grown in this subtropical climate. The immigrants mentioned above have been augmented by Chinese refugees from the People's Republic, including some of China's foremost chefs representing each of the dominant schools of Chinese cuisine. Another factor is that in Taiwan, unlike China, each *tai see foo* (master cook) has been able to train younger apprentices in his specialties, thus carrying on tradition and maintaining standards of excellence.

Some experts take issue with that estimate of Taiwan's cuisine, claiming that all this has been accomplished to a lesser degree in Taiwan than in Hong Kong. Robert M. Arnold, who was born in Hong Kong, and at the time of our visit was food and beverage manager of the Hong Kong Hilton, like Father John, believes that the finest Chinese food is the Cantonese and that the best exponents of it are to be found in Hong Kong. On the other hand, James A. Smith, former executive chef and author of *Chinese Culinary Heritage* (Hilton Press) as well as general manager of the Taipei Hilton, insists that the Hunanese cuisine is the more extraordinary and the most traditional of Chinese regional cooking. "The master cooks in China are not as outstanding as they were many years ago," says Terry Ko, assistant food and beverage manager at the Taipei Hilton. "While the master cooks in Hong Kong are superior to those in Canton, the highest level is to be found in Taiwan, where the superior standards of traditional Chinese cuisine—both in concepts and methods of preparation—are religiously followed by the excellent master cooks, who over the years came down from the mainland. Rudolf Mack, former executive chef and now food and beverage manager of the Taipei Hilton, is confident that its kitchen, under the aegis of Master Cook Wong Dong Shen provides the finest Hunanese cuisine to be found in Taiwan as well as the entire Far East.

Both advocates of the superiority of the cuisine in either Hong Kong or Taiwan over that to be found in China itself agree that this is due to the far smaller range of ingredients to be found on the mainland as well as to the government's attempts to influence the preparation of food and the staffing of the kitchens. There is wide acceptance of the fact that the standards of quality and performance have been lowered drastically. Even Master Cook Chiun Bao, of the North Garden restaurant in Canton, told us that more than 30 percent of the staff assigned by the government to work in his kitchen were not suitable, and he was obliged to reassign them to function as waiters or dishwashers.

The partisan discussions concerning the superiority of Hong Kong or Taiwan cuisine are extended as well to the United States, where Yvonne Wong, co-owner of the Ultimate Lotus restaurant in New York and originally from Hong Kong, believes that her hometown has the greater number of superior master chefs. She says that chefs who leave China and arrive in Hong Kong tend to remain there, eager for the chance to take on apprentices. On the other hand, Peter Lee of New York's Flower Drum restaurant thinks that the newly arrived chefs in Taiwan are more consistently maintaining the traditions and standards of Chinese regional cuisines.

Another influence on the cuisine of Taiwan has been Buddhism, which is particularly strong on the island, as exemplified by its many Buddhist temples. Buddhists, of course, eschew using animals for food unless it is absolutely necessary; the result in Taiwan (as in other parts of China, especially Shanghai) has been an emphasis on vegetarianism.

As Yvonne Wong points out, vegetarianism first developed as a specialized cuisine for the monks themselves; later, pilgrims who came to visit the temples became fascinated with vegetarianism. The monks, proud of their creativity, prepared dishes such as **Mock Pressed Duck** and **Mock Goose,** which not only have the appearance of meat dishes but taste like them. The test of a good chef is how closely he can prepare a dish that resembles, say, ham or chicken, both in appearance and in taste. The main ingredient used to accomplish this is bean curd, in a wide variety of forms.

It is interesting to see how the partisanship we have noted between the Hong Kong and Taiwanese approaches to Chinese cuisine, and even developments like Chinese vegetarianism, have been transplanted to the United States. The *tai see foo* at the Ultimate Lotus, Master Cook Kao, for example, went to Taiwan after fleeing from the mainland and became the owner of a restaurant in Taipei specializing in Buddhist-inspired vegetarian dishes. As a result, the Ultimate Lotus now features vegetarian specialties; but at the same time, since the Szechuan and Mandarin cuisines are practiced widely in Taiwan, which provides most of the chefs and cooks at the restaurant, those two cuisines are the mainstay of the Ultimate Lotus.

Incidentally, the current popularity of Szechuan cuisine in the United States was originally initiated by an entrepreneur, Joseph Chen, who a decade ago originated the many Lotus restaurants in New York. Since his background was in the Mandarin and Szechuan schools, the kitchen staffs he recruited came principally from Taiwan.

Although Peter Lee of the Flower Drum restaurant draws his kitchen staff from both Hong Kong and Taiwan, he is concerned mainly with the adaptability of each applicant. "I believe," he told me in an interview, "that mainland and Taiwan cooks cannot adapt immediately to the Flower Drum's repertoire of dishes without additional training and focusing of their talents to blend with those of our master chef and management." Like most Chinese chefs, those at the Flower Drum and the Ultimate Lotus know traditional recipes by heart. But it is the role of the master chef to be to be responsible for uniformity of technique. Peter Lee speaks of the "smoothing" of personnel and says that the biggest problem of all Chinese restaurants is being sure that a new cook will cooperate with the established kitchen system.

With this brief survey of Hong Kong and Taiwan, let's turn to China itself. Since our visit coincided with Red China's invasion of Vietnam on February 20, 1979, our tour is limited to Kwangtung province in southern China and begins with a short half-hour airplane flight from Hong Kong to the city of Canton. From the airport we proceed by bus through the crowded streets to the Tung Fang Hotel, which, because of its proximity to the Trade Fair Building, which attracts foreign visitors each spring and fall, is particularly familiar with servicing the needs of Western visitors.

Although we are among the first group of Western tourists permitted to visit China, the People's Republic had for some time invited professionals in areas of particular expertise to visit China before us. One of these is George Lang, cookbook author, restaurant consultant, and owner of two restaurants in New York City. Writing in *The New York Times* (May 1, 1977), after what he describes as a mediocre banquet at the still highly rated Tung Fang Hotel, Lang quipped, "It seemed to me that a funny thing had happened in China on the way to the revolution—they had lost a sense of the art of dining." After a number of meals at this hotel, we were to find that the dishes were less than outstanding, and did not compare favorably with the quality and the preparation of other meals we were soon to savor from the kitchens of the Overseas Chinese Hotel in Fauhon, the Lou Kan commune in the countryside northeast of Canton—and especially that of the North Garden restaurant in Canton. In fact, only the dishes at the latter restaurant even approached the standards we had come to expect in Chinese cuisine as prepared in Hong Kong, Taiwan, Bangkok, Singapore, and the United States. The menus were generally far more limited in China, with fish and seafood a surprising rarity, and the emphasis was on poultry and the seasonally abundant Chinese kale, which is far more delicate than our tough American version of this vegetable. In the Lou Kan Orchard Commune, where the food surpassed that of the Tung Fang Hotel, we found that Chinese kale was an ingredient in five of the eight dishes served at the same meal. However, since it appeared each time as one of other harmonious ingredients, one was less aware of the repetition. We later learned that in Peking, because of the limited ingredients available, entire ten-course Chinese banquets are prepared with each of the dishes featuring duck, which is one of the items that are both bountiful and encouraged by government protocol. Probably for similar reasons, even the quality of high-level gov-

ernment banquets has declined. Peter Lee notes that the banquets the Chinese gave in honor of President Nixon in 1972 and President Ford a few years later had neither the "subtle composition" nor the number of dishes that comparable banquets had in pre-Communist days. (The Presidents were treated to eight different dishes each, as against the fifteen considered traditional.)

On the basis of our firsthand experiences, we found that we, too, shared the far from optimistic reactions of George Lang and other observers concerning the survival of the traditions and culture of old China. Lang stresses that under the Communist regime former concerns with aesthetics and gastronomy are looked upon with deep suspicion. Peter Lee points to the sad evidence that the family and its culinary skills "are getting lost." Indeed, from every side we hear that in recent decades the family is no longer the strong unit it had been traditionally, its members no longer able to be close together. However, among the liberating innovations Vice-Premier Teng Hsiao-p'ing is reported to have made recently are those toward the correction of this situation. As Lee Chen-ling, our guide in China, told us, the government has "listened" to the many posters (China's traditional method of advising the government of the man-in-the-street's views on important issues) that mysteriously appear on the walls of high traffic areas in such large cities as Peking, Shanghai, and Canton.

We must bear in mind that Lee is an official guide of the China International Travel Services; however, he is among the fortunate Chinese who live with their family. Lee lives in an apartment in Canton comprising three bedrooms, a sitting room, a bathroom and kitchen which are shared with two other families. The family includes Lee, his grandmother, his parents and older brother who work away from home, and a younger sister in the second grade of elementary school. Grandmother is in charge of shopping and cooking, aided by Lee's younger sister and occasionally by Lee when he arrives home early. The shared kitchen comprises three stations, one of which is used by each family, these stations in turn comprise two burners and preparation counters lining a six-foot wall. One burner is used for boiling water (in China, as in Taiwan and much of the Far East, water must be boiled or distilled before using) and one burner for general cooking by wok or steamer. The facilities for each family are not unlike those we found in kitchens in Hong Kong and Taiwan, where each family had an individual kitchen as part of the apartment complex. Here the two burners were gas jets, whereas in the city of Canton coal is used.

Judging from the kitchens we saw in the Orchard Commune at Lou Kan (and, admittedly, these were in model homes with facilities superior to average homes in the countryside), the individual kitchens are six to eight feet square with more space for storage, preparation, and serving of food. Here, shredded wood is used for fuel, and the kitchen adjoins the sitting room, thereby becoming a more central part of family life.

Based on our own observation, and various reports from knowledgeable sources, the indication is that not only in the homes but in the formerly memorable restaurants of China and in the communes, the emphasis is on revolutionary change rather than excellence of cuisine. As we have noted, it is the government that assigns personnel to public restaurants and commune facilities; apart from that, the government's interest in cuisine is limited to promoting the use of ingredients found in abundant supply in China and controlling the use of fuel in all facilities, public as well as private. Suffice it to say that George Lang's reaction to the meals he had and the restaurant operations he saw was, "I have seen the future and it needs more seasoning."

The 800-room Tung Fang Hotel was almost fully booked during our visit (with Japanese and American tourists, and even a Hollywood film crew headed by Steve Allen and Jayne Meadows, who have been negotiating with the Peking government to produce films in China); hence, the dining rooms were crowded and the kitchen staff much too busy to permit us to visit the kitchen. George Lang, however, did see the kitchen during his earlier visit which he described in the same *Times* article as "huge and airy, with windows to the outside." He saw large stone-topped tables, chopping blocks, pastry boards, ranges, steamers, woks, and "a built-into-the-wall, very primitive, tiled refrigerator with exposed coils" apparently built by the hotel workmen themselves. The room had, he said, "a lived-in, good feeling. It must be a pleasant place to prepare food, compared with the basement kitchens where I used to work." The same description could apply to the kitchen we visited in depth at the Overseas Chinese Hotel in

Fauhon. With our helpful guide Lee, we toured every aspect of the kitchen operation with Master Cook Li Chen. It was about 1:15 P.M., and most of the diners in both the upstairs and downstairs dining rooms had been served, but there was still sufficient activity in the kitchen for us to evaluate the method of operation. The kitchen is planned and equipped in what we might call the "Mandarin pattern," an organizational scheme developed centuries ago by the master cooks of Peking. (Of course, the equipment we saw in similar kitchens in Hong Kong, Taiwan, Singapore, Bangkok—and especially in the Flower Drum and the Ultimate Lotus restaurants in New York City was far more modern and efficient, reflecting the latest technological improvements not readily available in China during the last several decades of self-imposed isolation.)

Essentially, this pattern is suited to the fundamental techniques common to all Chinese schools of cuisine, which call for the preparation and chopping of all ingredients in advance—to be ready for relatively short periods of cooking in a wok. As James Smith was to tell us in Taiwan, based on his extensive background as executive chef in numerous international kitchens throughout the world, "The major difference between the 'French pattern' and the 'Mandarin pattern' is that the Chinese kitchen uses only raw materials, whereas the French kitchens have precooked, already prepared ingredients and sauces." In the Chinese kitchen, there is the master cook, or chief cook, as he is often called, and a number of assistant cooks, depending upon the capacity of the restaurant, who are solely responsible for the actual cooking of each dish. But the prime backup member of the staff, and probably the most important assistant to the master cook, is the special assistant cook or *drow mahr,* which literally means "to grab with your hands." It is his task to be sure that the proper ingredients for every dish to be served are ready and immediately available for the chef and cooks in the quantities and the specific order that they will be required during the fast-cooking process for each dish. The *drow mahr* can be considered equivalent to the *sous-chef* in French restaurants. (In connection with the variations of Chinese pronunciation discussed previously, Peter Lee, originally from Peking, pronounces it *drow mahr;* while in Hong Kong, I was given the pronunciation *dwai ma;* and in Taiwan both *jua ma* ("to grab the ingredients") and *pai tsai* ("lining up the food").

In any case, it is the *drow mahr* who supervises the preparation, cutting, and marinating of all raw ingredients by other members of the kitchen staff, then arranges that adequate supplies are available in a series of trays immediately behind or near the range where the cooking is done. When an order is given, the *drow mahr,* knowing each recipe as well as the cooks themselves, rapidly provides the cooks with ingredients in the specific order and quantities required. Obviously this requires considerable expertise and teamwork on the part of the *drow mahr,* the master cook, and the other cooks.

In the kitchen of the Overseas Chinese Hotel in China, as well as in the other Chinese kitchens we visited in Singapore, Hong Kong, Taiwan, and Bangkok, the waiters bring in the specific orders to the *drow mahr,* who then prepares an individual tray for the particular dish involved.

The tray is identified with a hinged clothespin with the table number inscribed on it. The *drow mahr* assembles all the ingredients for each dish ordered, as we discussed, then passes them to the cook who proceeds to draw on the necessary oils, broth, and sauces near his cooking station to complete the cooking of the dish. The tray is then returned to the waiter, with the identifying clothespin marker, to be served to the waiting diners.

This Mandarin pattern is rather consistent with traditional Chinese restaurants in all countries, with an important variation in Singapore, where, as a result of the large Muslim population there and in nearby Malaysia, the kitchen is divided into the traditional Chinese pattern as well as a separate area for the Muslim cooks with their distinctive black velvet hats. In this section, the cooks for religious considerations utilize their own special ingredients, pots, and pans—not unlike those required in an orthodox kosher kitchen in the West. Perhaps the operation of the Mandarin pattern can best be described by a tour of Chinese restaurant kitchens in the United States, where the traditional concepts have been refined and augmented with the most up-to-date kitchen equipment.

Let's begin by joining Peter Lee for a tour of the kitchen at the Flower Drum restaurant, close to the United Nations in New York City. The restaurant seats about 200 persons and generally has two seatings for luncheon and in the evening; it can serve up to 400 meals either at luncheon or dinner. Unlike French restaurants, which have two shifts of kitchen staff, most Chinese restaurants, serving from noon to about 11:00 P.M., utilize a

single staff for their entire operation. This is possible because ingredients and sauces can be prepared well in advance (ready in the series of trays set up by the *drow mahr*), the range fired, and all necessary equipment in place for the preparation of dishes in a matter of minutes.

The schedule for the Flower Drum begins at 10:30 A.M., when the *drow mahr,* his meat and vegetable assistants, and the appetizer chef arrive. By 11:45, the two assistant cooks and the master cook are at their stations, and, interestingly, the entire staff is ready to serve luncheon only fifteen minutes later, when the diners begin to arrive at noon. The Mandarin pattern works most effectively in meeting the special requirements of preparing Chinese food professionally for large numbers of diners, and results in the amazingly short waiting periods between the placing of an order and the serving of the food.

The main focus of the kitchen at the Flower Drum is the range and auxiliary cooking areas. There are three cooking stations for the master cook and his assistants, each of whom has a family-size wok, for the preparation of two- or three-portion dishes, and a larger, professional-size wok, with a capacity for preparing five or six portions of any dish. The several woks are necessary because one of the principles of using a wok is not to overcrowd it with ingredients, which would lower the intensity of the heat necessary for stir-frying. The larger woks avoid the necessity of cooking portions of a dish in more than one operation, as would be required with a family-size wok.

Besides the two different woks, each firmly resting on a flameproof collar to hold it steady, each cook's station has a container for the oil required for stir-frying; the oil is strained and reused, unless it has been used with strongly flavored ingredients, which would negatively affect future dishes. The last item in each station on the range is a swinging water line used for quickly washing the wok after each use. A simmering pot of consommé is also available to all three chefs, and concentrated sauces, located immediately behind each station, are generally blended with consommé to be used in cooking as necessary.

In the center of the long kitchen, running parallel to the range, is a counter with several dozen trays, each about 10 by 15 inches, containing the prepared and properly cut ingredients that the *drow mahr* has arranged for almost immediate use.

Peter Lee tells us that all of his cooks and the *drow mahr* know all of the recipes in his repertoire by heart. As an order is called in, the *drow mahr* quickly assembles a dish with the necessary ingredients in the order and quantities required, while the cook prepares the wok and considers which of the concentrated sauces he will use. The dish of ingredients is then passed to the cook, who rapidly carries out the stir-frying and transfers the finished product to a serving dish in minutes.

A series of trays on the preparation counter contain meat and fish ingredients, already cut and marinated. Another set of trays contain vegetables, including such items as scallions, peppers, orange peel, dried lily buds, straw mushrooms, water chestnuts, snow peas, and bean sprouts. When necessary, these trays are refilled by the backup kitchen staff on orders from

the *drow mahr*. Peter Lee says that with these backup ingredients, the cooks can prepare quickly more than fifty dishes on the menu.

During our visit, the appetizer man, who is also responsible for steaming rice, is preparing the dough for **Spring Rolls,** a specialty of the Flower Drum. Peter Lee explains: "The dough is made with flour and water, then placed in the refrigerator overnight. Now, he is placing a large ball of the refrigerated dough into a plastic bowl, which is inserted into a larger bowl layered with ice cubes; it [the dough] must be chilled until used." We watch the appetizer man adeptly take a sizable clump of the chilled dough and rub it into a hot skillet, leaving a thin residue of dough on the inside of the pan. When cooked, it is gently removed, looking very much like a crêpe. These skins are reserved for the final preparation of the **Spring Rolls.**

One member of the kitchen staff is cutting vegetables, another is shredding pork, a third is marinating large quantities of shrimp. "The main feature of authentic Chinese cuisine is that all fish, seafood, and meats are marinated before cooking," Peter Lee explains. "Usually egg whites, cornstarch, and wine or sherry are used to marinate ingredients, which are then covered and refrigerated for at least 20 minutes until the marinade settles and the ingredients have the necessary protective coating."

We notice that the staff assistant marinating the shrimp seasons them with coarse salt and white pepper, then pours in unbeaten egg whites and wine, and tosses them gingerly by hand. Following this, he sprinkles cornstarch over the mixture in several relays, always tossing until the shrimp are thoroughly coated. The final ingredient added is peanut oil, and the tossing in the marinade continues until the glossy shine produced by the oil has disappeared. "When the shrimp have lost their gloss," Peter Lee explains, "you know the marinating is done. Now we cover and refrigerate the shrimp for 15 to 20 minutes until the marinade is properly settled; they are then stir-fried with very little oil—just enough to 'wet' the wok—a technique that results in very crisp shrimp."

We asked Peter Lee whether MSG (monosodium glutamate) is used by master Chinese chefs. "Hardly," he replied. "Good chefs use natural juices and sauces. Frankly, I think using MSG is amateurish. It is never used on fresh ingredients; if commercially bought eggrolls are used, MSG may be necessary to restore their flavor after refrigeration. Personally, I prefer the natural flavors. I remember my grandfather speaking to me about MSG when I was about ten in Peking many years ago. It was called "essence of taste" in Chinese. He cautioned me never to use it; and if I must, then to be sure to use very, very little. I rather think MSG is of Japanese rather than Chinese origin."

I also asked whether condiments were set at the table in China. "No, in China neither sugar nor pepper is ever presented at the table, except when serving Szechuan duck, which is dipped into a special pepper sauce. Soy sauce, plum sauce, and mustard sauce are never used at the table, as is customary in Western Chinese restaurants; however dipping sauces, like duck sauce, are used when appropriate."

One is amazed at how smoothly and efficiently the master cook, *drow mahr,* and assistant cooks work together. "You must realize," Peter Lee explains, "that all of the cooks have been trained in accordance with the custom of old China. They begin their trade at about fifteen years of age, after completing normal schooling. The system calls for working in a restaurant as a dishwasher and kowtowing to the master cook for about five years. This is followed by several years' training in cutting ingredients as an assistant to the *drow mahr,* and years of experience as assistant cook. All in all, it takes between twenty and thirty years of hard work and experience in professional kitchens. Both our master cook, Shoh Chow Sheng, and our *drow mahr,* Shih Check Wong, have had this kind of extensive training. These two have administrative responsibilities in the kitchen in addition to their other functions. The master chef is essentially responsible for maintaining uniformity of technique among the cooks and the administration of the kitchen and staff; he is also responsible for the ordering of ingredients, in close consultation with the *drow mahr.* "

A special person in Chinese kitchens, especially in China, is the experienced and creative "decorator," who is responsible for preparing stunning garnishes for the presentation of important dishes. In his *Times* article, cited earlier, George Lang describes a banquet he attended in the famous Friendship Restaurant in Canton: "The luncheon began with a cold plate, one of the most elaborate I have ever seen —especially the carved vegetables, which were pure ivory-lace workmanship. Each table of ten had one of these plates, surrounded with many small dishes. Estimating the time spent on the carvings, which after all were only the garnish for the first course, each plate must have been a full day's work for a specially trained decorator."

Apparently George Lang was not able to see how deftly and quickly these intricate "ivory-lace" vegetable cuttings are prepared. We were fortunate to witness this intriguing operation being performed in China, where long white turnips were used, and in Taiwan, where carrots were used to produce delicate **Chinese Vegetable Nets** to garnish dishes for banquets. With skill and knowledge of the particular techniques involved, each vegetable can be cut into a lacelike net in a matter of ten minutes. At the Taipei Hilton, a chef demonstrated this technique during one of the finest and most spectacular Chinese banquets I have ever attended. He used a long carrot (which in Taiwan can be at least four inches in diameter and easier to handle for this purpose) previously soaked in salted water, using two ounces of salt for each pint of water to make it more pliable. In the United States, daikon (a large Japanese radish) is more readily available with diameters of sufficient thickness. A four-inch length is trimmed so that all four sides are parallel, and pierced with a chopstick through its center.

To be sure to make uniform slices about ⅛-inch thick, begin by cutting side 1 until the knife meets the chopstick, then turn twice and cut side 3 in the same manner. Rotate the vegetable to side 2, cut down to the chopstick, rotate and cut side 4. Proceed in this manner making uniformly thin cuts down to the chopstick on sides 1, 3, 2 and 4, until the entire length of the vegetable is cut.

Trim each of the corners until the carrot is tubular in shape. Cut the carrot as if peeling it lengthwise, into a thin sheet until only ¾- to 1-inch of the vegetable cylinder is left.

Remove the chopstick and cut every other slice into separate circles. Gently pull apart the strands to form the inticate net effect. It is a spectacular technique to witness, and with a bit of practice rather simple to do in a matter of minutes. Also, the vegetable net can be reused to garnish future dishes. Press the strands close together, rewind the cylinder, and store under refrigeration up to ten days. Bring to room temperature before unwinding the strands and forming the net for reuse.

At the Flower Drum, the *drow mahr* can be seen artistically utilizing the time available between the main cooking periods to decorate the platters that accompany the hot pot specialty of the restaurant. It is fascinating to watch him use the basic ingredient for each dish (chicken breast, marinated shrimp, or lamb) to create a symbolic design suggesting the animal involved. For example, strips of chicken are arranged to form the body, wings, and tail of a chicken; bits of carrot make the crown, and an eye is made with a slice of maraschino cherry with a single green pea in the center. Carrot pieces are intricately carved into the shape of chicken feet, other strips delineating the feathers and tail. Strips of lamb are formed into the shape of a lamb's head; shrimp are grouped into one huge shrimp, with carrot strips for the delicate tentacles. Watching him work, and noting the admiration of everyone in the kitchen, one senses the great delight the Chinese have in presenting their dishes with as much appeal to the eye as to the palate.

This is particularly the case with special dishes served at Chinese banquets. Here the ingredients are generally arranged into a collage representing the phoenix, the dragon, or other shapes that have special meaning to the Chinese, most often symbolizing good fortune and long life and other virtues honored throughout the many centuries of their culture. In the North Garden restaurant in Canton, our first course was a "seven-color rainbow" of cold appetizers in the shape of a huge queen bee. The body was a loaf of braised beef, the wings circular slices of the beef stuffed with an orange carrot purée dotted with black olive bits and surrounded with delicate grated orange carrot and white cabbage (which were also used to shape the head with capers as eyes), and the tail was two flowing collages of thin slices of preserved duck eggs. The final touch was a fresh purple flower suggesting the quest of the bee. Other special dishes are decorated to illustrate old proverbs of the Chinese, such as the delicate two fish presented on a platter as if swimming toward a carved dragon made of vegetables we savored at a banquet at the Sesame Hotel in the countryside outside Taipei. As Master cook Cham Pui explained, "The two fish are swimming against the current into the dragon's door. We are the fish, and if we are able to get past the doors guarded by the dragons, we will have great success in our lives!"

Another kitchen in the Mandarin pattern is that of the Ultimate Lotus restaurant, under Master Cook Yuan Hung Kao, respectfully referred to as Chef Kao.

There are four assistant cooks, including the *dwai ma* (as he is called here) and rice and barbecue specialists.

Unlike Western restaurants, Chinese restaurants in the United States serve the kitchen and the dining room staffs at 3:00 P.M., after, rather than before, the diners' luncheon period. Again, the kitchen staff eats in the kitchen, the waiters and captains in a secluded part of the main dining room. Says Chef Kao: "This is the toughest assignment of all. The staff and help are the greatest critics I have to face, since they really know good food!"

Yvonne Wong and Ming Wang, the owners of the Ultimate Lotus, maintain the highest standards of Mandarin and Szechuan cuisine, their other specialties including Chinese vegetarian cuisine, as we mentioned previously. In fact, this is one of the rare restaurants in the United States that serve an entirely vegetarian banquet. Master Cook Mr. Kao, former owner and chef of the only vegetarian restaurant in Taipei, was also chef to President Yen Chai-kan of Taiwan. An indication of his skillful and imaginative approach to Chinese vegetarian cuisine is the Buddhist specialty **Lohan Jai.**

On the other hand, the Flower Drum restaurant offers the cuisines of Canton, Szechuan, Peking, Hunan, and Shanghai, and has the tradition of preparing a new menu for each of the four seasons of the year. The emphasis is on fine food presented at its peak of freshness and natural flavor, which is not unlike the policy of the Four Seasons restaurant in New York, whose executive chef and owners we will be visiting with on our tour of the United States. A traditional Chinese dish at the Flower Drum associated with spring is **Peony Blossom with Broccoli.**

But what of the importance of women, vis-à-vis that of men, in Chinese cuisine? Peter Lee shares the widely held opinion among culinary experts that the greatness of any ethnic cuisine is maintained and encouraged by the men of the particular society that produced it, although the women do the actual cooking. In India it is the men who are known for fine cooking, and it is not unusual for a father to hand down recipes and techniques to the son of the family. In old China, as we have seen, cooking began to reach the heights of refinement when philosophers and scholars became articulate about the importance of food creatively prepared and served. "This is becoming evident here in the United States among scholars," Peter Lee likes to point out. "In the old days in China, the scholars directed the professional cooks and created new recipes and approaches. The average man took on a similar role in the home, while the ladies did the actual cooking. The man knew the basics and aesthetics of cooking, but it was the woman who learned the nuances and details of preparation. The woman is the chef of the house. She must purchase the best ingredients, learn the techniques of cooking and seasoning, and be responsible for the preparation of festive meals." Peter Lee emphasizes that in China the wife, mother, or daughters do the cooking. However, only one person is in charge of the kitchen, usually the senior lady of the family.

Jim Hon, the former bartender at the Ultimate Lotus, recalls his youth in Hong Kong (his family was originally from Shanghai): "My sister would help my mother in the kitchen, preparing and cutting the ingredients for both family and banquet meals. As soon as my mother was ready to start cooking, everyone sat down at the table and would start eating the first dishes served. My mother continued cooking until the last dish was prepared; then she would join the family at the table and partake of the meal."

Danny Kaye, the renowned actor-comedian (who happened to be staying at the outstanding Peninsula Hotel during our visit to Hong Kong), has developed an enviable reputation for his Chinese cooking, which he began after tasting fine Chinese cuisine in Shanghai in the 1930s. His carefully planned Chinese meals, cooked on a professional range especially built to his specifications, have been acclaimed by numerous famous friends and visitors—including heads of state and such outstanding French chefs as Paul Bocuse, Roger Vergé, and Jean Troisgros. True to the tradition of Chinese cooks, Danny Kaye never sits with his guests during the meal. He prepares all of his dishes, moreover, with the assistance of only Ming Lo Chin, who more or less functions as his *drow mahr.*

Jokingly, in my discussions with Peter Lee, I referred to his not joining his guests during the meal as the "Danny Kaye syndrome." (The actor has eaten at the Flower Drum a number of times, particularly when he was working with UNICEF at the United Nations.) "It is understandable that he can't join the guests," Mr. Lee reminded me, "because he is cooking in the kitchen. These meals are virtually banquets, and as in the case of a housewife cooking for a banquet in China, he must greet the guests, but then disappear into the kitchen. A housewife will appear for the first toast to the *t'ai-t'ai* in appreciation of the meal, and only if she has a cousin or someone helping her in the kitchen will she come out occasionally to see how the meal is progressing. If it is a special meal for relatives, she will come out of the kitchen more often. However, if there are special guests, she stays in the kitchen until she is finished with all the cooking; then she joins the others and begins eating from the covered dishes that are still on the table."

Since there is often only one burner for the wok and the steamers, dishes utilizing different cooking processes must be planned ahead. Usually, steamer dishes are prepared first since they take longer; red-simmered dishes are often simmered for hours, well beforehand. (There is generally one red-simmered dish for each family banquet.) As we mentioned previously, although the large cities generally have coal for fuel, in the country wood-burning stoves are used. The steamer is used for appetizers or steamed fish, which are then removed from the wok and put aside to stay warm. The water in the wok is removed (and reserved for other use) so that the cook can proceed with the sautéing or stir-frying required for the balance of the meal.

In Hong Kong and Taiwan, most apartments have gas stoves with two burners, one used for the boiling of water or the preparation of rice, the second for the wok. Although in the People's Republic a single heating source is not uncommon, housewives are able to prepare family banquets involving ten to twelve different dishes to serve up to ten diners with these limited facilities—and the aid of an assistant such as a cousin or close friend. Larger banquets for more than ten diners are considered too difficult with the use of a single heating unit.

According to Peter Lee, a banquet in China and Hong Kong traditionally begins with assorted cold cuts, including such items as meat, Chinese sausage, chicken, abalone, and jellyfish skins, accompanied by rice wine. The host or senior member of the family will offer a toast to the wife, who comes out of the kitchen briefly at this point. The plate of appetizers is arranged decoratively and symbolically in the shape of a phoenix, the mythological bird with an imposing crown, or in the shape of a dragon. The appetizer is followed by a light soup, such as winter melon or shark's fin. A number of smaller dishes follow, such as deep-fried shrimp, squab, stir-fried fish with dried tiger lily pods, or paper-wrapped chicken. After these come the bigger dishes such as Peking duck, **Lion's Head,** red-simmered rabbit, or steamed sweet and pungent fish. Another soup may be served after the big dish to prepare the palate for the balance of the meal, and toasts continue throughout the length of the entire banquet.

In the North Garden restaurant in Canton we were served *Pirin,* a grape wine liqueur, and Moutai, a white liqueur made from sorghum, during our banquet, in Taipei, Shao Shing, with a taste very much like dry sherry (Westerners are cautioned against consuming too much *Pai Ka'rh,* a liqueur which has a high alcoholic content); and at our banquet at the Sesame Hotel in Taiwan, imported Scotch was featured.

Generally each is served in small glasses, the size of a liqueur glass without a stem. The host and other guests make general toasts to the cook, then to one another with invitations to *yam sing* (Cantonese) and *gam bay* (Fukienese), which are roughly equivalent to our own "bottoms up." As the banquet progresses, the toasts between any two individuals around the large table are made as playful challenges testing the capacity of each of the diners. Although the impression is one of a great deal of drinking during the several hours of toasting during a banquet, I noted in Taiwan that at the end of the evening less than a pint of alcoholic beverages had been consumed at the standard banquet table of twelve diners. Nonalcoholic drinkers toast with a brilliant orange soda which is popular among the Chinese throughout China and the rest of the Far East. When I expressed curiosity as to why orange rather than any other flavored soda, Clement Chan, a business assiciate who was born in Canton, explained that the color orange symbolizes good fortune to the Chinese. "That's also why we Chinese offer fresh oranges to our guests during the festivities of our New Year. It's our way of wishing our friends and relatives good fortune for the new year." For a people so obviously dedicated to the enjoyment of fine cuisine, it is surprising that most Chinese are very heavy smokers and continuously smoke between servings of the many dishes throughout a formal banquet. When I mentioned this to Jeffrey Cheung, another business assotiate, during a banquet in Taiwan, he said, "We Chinese invite our guests to the hospitality of smoking cigarettes. The Japanese, however, do not!"

Ordinarily, soup is served at the end of a family meal, but a banquet is virtually several meals consumed at the same time; therefore, except for a possible sweet soup intended for dessert, the soups are served in the middle of a banquet meal, after the appetizer and a main dish. Peter Lee also points out that each of the banquet dishes traditionally represents a major cooking process, including the mandatory red-simmered, deep-fried, stir-fried, and steamed dishes, and those which combine several processes. Generally, there are three main types of sweets that are served at the end of a banquet: honey dishes, such as **Candied Banana Fritters** or **Honey Apples;** fresh fruit; or sweet soups, such as sweet fermented rice soup or walnut soup.

Although rice is served with the meal for family dining at home, rice or noodles are never served until the end of the meal during banquets or at meals when the Chinese are entertaining. According to Robert Arnold, who was born in Hong Kong, "this would be an insult to guests. It's like saying among the Chinese that one is too poor to serve sufficient dishes to satisfy his guests." James Smith in Taiwan, however, does not believe serving rice at formal meals is an insult. Rather, he thinks that rice is just not appropriate with the special dishes served at banquets such as Peking duck. "At home," he adds, "rice is always served and used to cut down the strong taste of the dishes, permitting the blending of flavors to suit the individual tastes of the various members of the family." Robert Arnold also points out that in restaurants, chopsticks and a spoon are provided for each setting. "A spoon or community chopsticks should be used to transfer the food from the platter to each diner's bowl," he adds. "Never use chopsticks that have touched your mouth to serve others." Having lived in Hong Kong most of his life, he points out that the Chinese there eat out and entertain several times a week, and always eat out on Sunday (which the Italians, whose attitude to fine dining is not unlike that of the Chinese, tend to do as well). As Ming Wang, who is an architect as well as co-owner of the Ultimate Lotus, told me recently, "There is an old Chinese saying that when the Chinese have money, the first thing they will spend it on is food. When there is more money, he will spend it on new clothing; but the last thing he will spend his money for is to provide better housing." (Herein lies a prime difference in the attitude of the Italians, who traditionally fuse the appreciation of fine food and the comfort of their homes as the first priority.)

To sum up, here are the important things to remember in preparing the Chinese menus and recipes offered in the next section: Chinese family dining calls for a soup and at least four different dishes, depending upon the number of persons served; usually one entrée is served for each person. Rice and tea are served with each meal, and soups are served at the end of the meal, except as noted previously during banquets. The Chinese do not have desserts at family meals, preferring savories (as snacks with tea) during the day. For the purposes of our Chinese menus that follow, we are providing sweet dishes that will serve as desserts in American homes.

Generally, our new cuisine recipes will yield about six servings, as entrées served Western style. If serving Chinese style, with all diners sharing a number of smaller entrées, you may reduce the ingredients by half. Customarily, to serve six persons, twelve to fourteen portions of the total number of entrées, plus rice and an optional dessert, are standard. A convenient rule is that one entrée and one cup of rice (½ cup uncooked) should either be added or eliminated for every two persons varying from our standard menus for six servings. You may wish to serve beer, tea, or dry white wine with your Chinese meals, and possibly red wine with the hearty red-simmered dishes.

I suggest that you do not attempt to emulate Danny Kaye, preparing banquet-like meals for a large number of guests, until you have the advantage of his experience and special equipment. Remember that even experienced Chinese cooks find the banquet meal too complicated for the home kitchen and prefer to enjoy these festive meals in restaurants, which are better equipped to prepare them.

Although Chinese cooks do not as a rule join their guests until all cooking chores have been completed, this practice is neither necessary nor always desirable in Western-style entertaining. With well-equipped kitchens, covered serving dishes, and heating units for buffet serving, many dishes can be prepared *hung shao,* or stewed in advance. Ingredients can be prepared beforehand, refrigerated in plastic bags, and arranged in the sequence required for cooking; but they must be brought to room temperature about an hour before using. If varying any of the menus, try to avoid presenting more than one stir-fried dish, which requires last-minute cooking immediately before serving. Also, family-size woks should not be

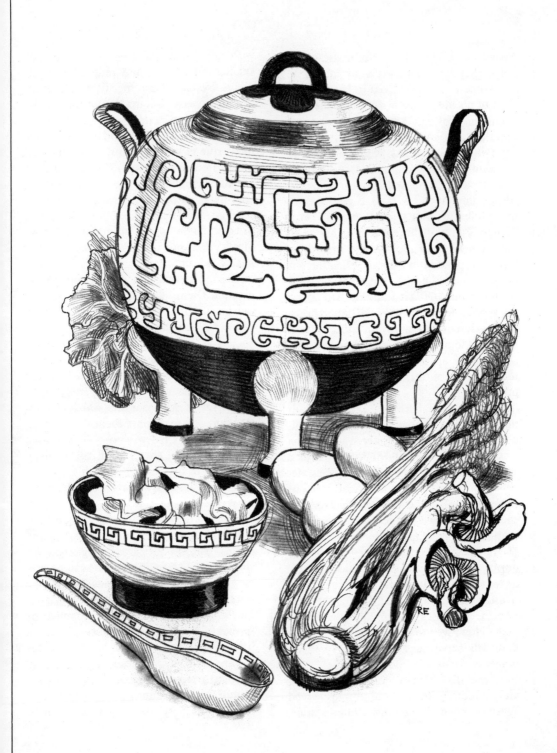

overloaded with ingredients; overloading will reduce the 400° F of heat necessary for stir-frying, with the result that your final dish will not be properly cooked. As a general rule, one pound of meat, fish, or seafood is a good limit to keep in mind.

Neither is it necessary to serve in community bowls in the center of the table, each diner drawing from the bowls with chopsticks, Chinese style. Most of my Chinese friends and I serve in the usual Western manner, with individual table settings, but preferably with chopsticks instead of forks and knives. Entrées, however, are served in covered platters; individual bowls are used to serve rice and soup. For dinners with a large number of dishes, I have found it preferable to serve buffet style, encouraging my guests to help themselves to the combinations of entrées they prefer.

Lastly, it is not necessary to prepare an all-Chinese menu, and certainly not until you have mastered the various cooking processes of Chinese cuisine. Personally, I prefer to blend one or more Chinese dishes with specialties from other ethnic cuisines. It is important, however, to do so judiciously, keeping in mind the Chinese tradition that the dishes served must harmonize with each other. The Chinese notion of *yin* and *yang* calls for the balancing of pleasantly contrasting ingredients and dishes in terms of flavor, texture, and colorful presentation, suggesting the contrast of parts yet the harmony of the whole. Once you relax and enjoy the pleasant challenge of creating imaginative menus of your own, balancing the dishes you present, you might find it fun to prepare a completely Chinese slimming menu.

MENU

Suan La Tong
Pai Fan
Ch'ao Hsia Jen
Ning Mung Gai
Sih Tzu Tou
Tsao Tsu Nien Kao
Cha

Hot and Sour Soup
Chinese Boiled Rice
Stir-Fried Shrimp with Peas
Cantonese Lemon Chicken
Imperial Lion's Head Casserole
Chinese Red Date Cake
Chinese Tea

SUAN LA TONG*
(Hot and Sour Soup)

Basically, there are three varieties of Chinese soup: light soups, which are quickly made to accompany family dinners; hearty, long simmering soups, which are served as main courses at luncheon meals; and sweet soups, which are enjoyed as snacks or served as desserts at formal meals. Of course, with the tremendously wide classic Chinese repertoire, these categories are subdivided into many variations.

A popular light soup common to every school of Chinese cuisine is the Hot and Sour Soup often called pungent and sour. Each region has its own version, and probably all are variations of an original Szechuan soup. Our slimming version is reasonably but not overpoweringly hot; its pungency can be varied according to taste, and suggestions for doing so can be found in the Bonus Ideas below. A marvelous soup to whet one's appetite for the meal that follows, it is easily prepared and always effective. It is also economical—often made with leftover pork or chicken.

⅓ cup each, dried Chinese mushrooms, tree ears, and dried tiger lily buds
2 tablespoons cornstarch mixed with ⅓ cup water
1 tablespoon light soy sauce
½ teaspoon white pepper or ¾ teaspoon Szechuan hot bean paste
5 cups fresh or canned chicken broth
½ cup 1-inch strips uncooked lean pork, chicken breast, or combination of both
½ cup shredded bamboo shoots
2 water chestnuts, diced (optional)
3 tablespoons rice or cider vinegar
2 4-inch pads of fresh bean curd, cut into slivers
2 egg whites, lightly beaten
2 teaspoons hot sesame oil
2 tablespoons chopped scallions or minced fresh coriander
YIELD: Six to eight servings

1. Rinse the dried mushrooms, tree ears, and tiger lilies; place in a mixing bowl and cover with warm water to soak for about 20 minutes. Drain, reserving the liquid.

2. Cut off and discard the mushroom stems and tough parts of the tree ears; cut the mushroom caps and tree ears into thin slivers. If the tiger lilies are more than 2 inches long, cut them in half, then tear into shreds. Mix the cornstarch solution with the soy sauce and pepper and set aside.

3. Bring the chicken stock to a boil; add the meat and all the vegetables; boil for 1 minute before adding the cornstarch mixture; stir until the soup thickens. Stir in the vinegar; then add the bean curd and cook only until the soup returns to a boil. Remove from heat, cool slightly, then stir in the egg whites; transfer to a soup tureen or individual covered soup bowls. Stir in the hot sesame oil and garnish with the scallions or minced coriander. Serve immediately.

Bonus Ideas: Some versions of this soup call for briefly stir-frying the meat with 2 tablespoons of chicken broth or a tablespoon of polyunsaturated oil. Then soy sauce and the vegetables are added and stir-fried over high heat for 1 minute. Chicken stock is poured over the stir-fried mixture before proceeding with the balance of the recipe. You may use lemon juice instead of vinegar, Tabasco instead of pepper or hot sesame oil. Many Chinese cooks add ¼ teaspoon of honey (or fruit sugar) and ½ teaspoon of coarse salt; I find that the soy sauce is sufficiently salty, making the addition of salt unnecessary.

In the Peking region, the vinegar and pepper are often omitted in preparing **Imperial Mandarin Soup***. The Peking version also substitutes strips of ham for the pork or chicken (or Canadian bacon can be used).

If using leftovers such as cooked meat, poultry, or shrimp, these ingredients, slivered, are added after the egg has been stirred into the soup; then the entire mixture is heated through.

Pungent Soup with Crab*, to serve six, is made with ¾ cup of fresh or frozen crabmeat that is stir-fried with polyunsaturated oil and 1 teaspoon each of coarse salt and chopped fresh ginger for 2 minutes, then for 5 minutes longer after 2 sliced tomatoes have been added. Add the chicken stock and simmer for 15 minutes, before continuing with the balance of the basic recipe.

TIEN SUAN SHA
(Sweet and Sour Shrimp with Pineapple)

The concept of using contrasting yet harmonious flavors is also expressed in sweet and sour (as opposed to hot and sour) dishes. Also called sweet and pungent, these can be made with meat, seafood, and a variety of vegetables, as in the Bonus Ideas below; some of these dishes are not unlike European dishes like **Italian Sweet and Sour Onions.**

6 rings canned pineapple, drained
2 dozen jumbo shrimp

Marinade:
1 tablespoon rice wine or dry sherry
¼ teaspoon each, grated ginger and coarse salt
¾ teaspoon light soy sauce
⅛ teaspoon sesame oil, or dash of Tabasco

2 egg whites, lightly beaten
5 tablespoons water chestnut flour or cornstarch
2 tablespoons peanut or corn oil, or consommé
1 garlic clove, mashed
¾ cup rice or cider vinegar
⅓ cup honey or pure maple syrup
1 teaspoon light soy sauce
1 teaspoon sesame oil

2½ teaspoons ketchup
1 tablespoon cornstarch mixed with 2 tablespoons water
3 tablespoons flaked almonds
YIELD: Five to six servings

1. Cut the pineapple rings in half and set aside. Remove the shrimp from the shells, leaving the tails intact; rinse, drain, and pat dry. Mix the shrimp thoroughly in the Marinade until completely coated; then let stand covered in the refrigerator for about 30 minutes.

2. Prepare a batter by combining the egg whites and water chestnut flour. Holding each marinated shrimp by its tail, dip into the batter, thoroughly coating the shrimp except for the tail. In a wok or skillet over medium heat, heat half the peanut oil to about 350° F. Stir-fry the shrimp several at a time for several minutes until golden brown. Drain and set aside, continuing with the balance of the shrimp.

3. Heat the remaining peanut oil in the wok, adding a tablespoon if necessary, and lightly brown the garlic over medium heat. Using a slotted spoon, discard the garlic, then add the vinegar and honey, thinning with a little water as necessary; heat until thoroughly blended. Add the soy sauce, sesame oil, and ketchup, and bring to a boil. Add the cornstarch mixture and stir until thickened. Place the pineapple rings into the sauce and heat through.

4. Arrange the pineapple on a platter, then the shrimp; sprinkle with the almonds, and pour the sauce over all.

Bonus Ideas: Sweet and Sour Pineapple Fish may be prepared using 2 pounds of the filets of any white-fleshed fish instead of shrimp. Cut the fish into 2-inch pieces; marinate and coat with the batter as called for in the above recipe. The pineapple, however, should be cut into chunks rather than half rings. When the fish are stir-fried until golden brown, drain and pat dry; heat the pineapple pieces in the sauce and sprinkle with flaked almonds.

Any of the following vegetables can be prepared in a similar manner, to serve six, using the same combination of condiments: 1 pound asparagus cut into 1½-inch lengths (**Sweet and Sour Asparagus**); 1 peeled eggplant cut into 1½-inch pieces (**Sweet and Sour Eggplant**); 1 pound zucchini, peeled and cut into 1-inch pieces (**Sweet and Sour Zucchini**); 1 pound red cabbage, shredded (**Sweet and Sour Cabbage**); or 1 pound celery, shredded (**Sweet and Sour Celery**). Whichever vegetable you use, stir-fry with 2 tablespoons polyunsaturated oil for 3 to 5 minutes; then add the standard condiments for the sauce, which are 1 tablespoon light soy sauce, 3 tablespoons each of vinegar and honey, and coarse salt to taste. Optionally, you may add 1 tablespoon sherry and a dash of Tabasco. Add 1 tablespoon cornstarch mixed with 2 tablespoons water and cook for 1 minute until thickened. Serve hot.

PAI FAN
(Chinese Boiled Rice)

Except in northern China, where wheat products are used, the vast majority of Chinese eat rice with their daily meals. Rice is the symbol of long life and fertility. The Western custom of throwing rice on a bridal couple originated in China and is evidence of the almost sacred attributes of this most fundamental of Chinese foods.

Either long-, short-, or round-grained rice may be used, but most Chinese cooks prefer the long-grained Carolina or Texas Patna rice, both readily available. The Japanese prefer round-grained rice, which results in a softer texture and utilizes more water. Some experts prefer using a combination of both types, which results in a dish with both the fluffiness of long-grained and the flavor of round-grained rice.

Rice may be either boiled or steamed. Most Chinese prefer it boiled, since steamed rice takes longer to prepare, although it has the advantage that it cannot burn.

One-half cup of raw rice, which will double in bulk when cooked, is used to serve each diner. I recommend using long-grained rice, washing it thoroughly, then letting it soak for about 30 minutes in cold water before boiling. Generally, 1¼ cups of water are required for each cup of rice. Many Chinese cover the raw rice with water to the height of the first joint of their index finger when the fingertip is placed on the surface of the rice: in other words, they cover and add an extra ¾ to 1 inch of water.

Since boiled rice can burn, once it has come to a boil, the balance of cooking must be done on low heat, and the cover must not be removed, permitting any steam to escape, until the rice is completely cooked. Copper-based pots are not recommended because of their greater conductivity of heat; an aluminum pot is preferable. The same pot should be used whenever preparing boiled rice, so that you can be consistent in the amount of water and the level of heat that provide the best results for you.

3 cups long-grained Carolina or Patna rice
3¾ cups water
YIELD: Six servings

1. Place the raw rice in a fine sieve and wash several times under running water, stirring the rice with a wooden spoon or chopsticks or rubbing it between the palms of your hands until water runs clear.
2. Place the washed rice in a pot with the required water. Cover and set aside to soak at least 30 minutes, or preferably overnight. Do not drain.
3. Tightly cover the pot and bring to a boil over high heat. Uncover and cook over medium heat for 2 minutes, stirring the rice gently; then replace the cover. Reduce the heat to low and simmer for about 15 minutes, or no longer than 20 minutes, without removing the cover and permitting steam to escape until ready to serve.
4. Remove the pot from the heat and let it stand for 15 minutes. Fluff the rice with chopsticks or a fork immediately before serving in covered bowls.

Bonus Ideas: Steamed Rice *(Cheng Fan)* will require 1½ cups of water for each cup of rice. After washing and letting the rice soak in the required water for 30 minutes, cook in boiling water for 3 minutes. Drain and place in a tightly covered heat-proof bowl on a rack in a steamer. Place enough water in the steamer to reach to ¾ of the height of the bowl. Tightly cover the steamer; bring to a boil and steam for 30 minutes. Remove the bowl of rice and let it stand for 10 minutes, without removing the cover. Fluff and serve in covered bowls.

Baked Rice **Kao Fan** will require 1½ cups of water for each cup of rice. After washing and letting the rice soak for 30 minutes, place the rice and soaking water in a tightly covered casserole and bake for 20 minutes in an oven preheated to 350° F. Reduce the temperature to 200° F and bake for 10 minutes longer; fluff the rice with chopsticks or a fork and serve immediately. Baked rice can be kept warm for an hour or more by placing the covered pot on a heat-proof pad over very low heat. Boiled or steamed rice can be kept warm over simmering water.

The crusts of cooked rice at the bottom of the pot can be reserved in the refrigerator for future use. They can be fried in oil and used as garnishes for soup and other stir-fried dishes; stir-fried and cooled for crunchy snacks; or converted to a *congee* by simmering the crusts in water and combining with leftover meats, poultry, or seafood. **Chicken Congee** to serve six is made by bringing to a boil 3½ cups each of chicken stock and water; add 5 cups of cooked rice or 3 cups of rice crusts, and 2 cups of raw or leftover chicken; cook until the mixture returns to a boil. Add 1¼ cups of fresh or leftover vegetables; cook for an additional 3 minutes and serve hot.

CH'AO HSIA JEN*
(Stir-Fried Shrimp with Peas)

Of all the seafood available to the Chinese, none is more popular than shrimp. Jumbo, miniature, and dried shrimp are all utilized with great imagination. It is only recently that Western cuisines, notably the French, have overcome the taboo of combining fish and seafood with meat; the Chinese have done so for centuries. Shrimp are also used as an alternate to other ingredients, such as lobster in **Lobster Cantonese** and **Shrimp with Lobster Sauce,** which is so-called regardless of the fact that no lobster is used in the recipe.

This is one of the most popular dishes utilizing shrimp in Chinese cuisine; it also has many interesting variations you may wish to try.

1 pound small fresh or frozen shrimp, about 3 dozen

1 pound fresh, or 1 cup frozen, peas; or 1 cup diced snow peas

Coating:
½ teaspoon coarse salt and ¼ teaspoon white pepper
2 teaspoons rice wine or dry sherry
1 egg white
2 teaspoons cornstarch
1 tablespoon peanut oil

1½ tablespoons polyunsaturated oil or consommé
2 slices fresh ginger
1 scallion cut into 2-inch lengths
YIELD: Six servings

1. Shell, devein, and wash the shrimp; drain and pat dry. Split each shrimp lengthwise; then cut in half diagonally. If using fresh peas, blanch in boiling water or steam them *au sec* for about 7 minutes until *al dente;* rinse in cool water and set

aside. If using frozen peas, thoroughly thaw and drain.

2. Place the shrimp in a large mixing bowl and sprinkle with salt and pepper. Add the wine and egg white; toss well while adding the cornstarch, until the shrimp are completely coated. Add the peanut oil and continue tossing until the coated shrimp have lost their oily glaze. Cover with plastic wrap and refrigerate for at least 20 minutes, or preferably 1 hour.

3. Swirl a small amount of oil or consommé in a wok or skillet, using only enough to coat it. Over medium heat, cook the ginger and scallions for 30 seconds; then discard them. Add the shrimp and stir-fry over high heat for 2 minutes, or until they turn pink. Add the peas and heat through (about 1 minute); then transfer immediately to a warm platter and serve.

Bonus Ideas: If you use 1 pound of washed and cleaned frogs' legs (in the Orient, they are called meadow chicken), preparing them in the identical manner, you will have **Frogs' Legs with Peas***. Equally popular is **Chow Har Ding** (Stir-Fried Shrimp with Vegetables), which, because of the addition of vegetables, will serve six using only ¾ pound of small shrimp. Prepare and coat the shrimp as for *Ch'ao Hsia Jen.* Stir-fry until pink, then set aside in a warm place. Soak 5 dried black mushrooms in warm water for 15 minutes; remove the stems; dice the mushroom caps and 1 cup Chinese cabbage. Prepare for stir-frying by cutting into bite-size pieces ⅓ cup each bamboo shoots and button mushrooms, and 1 dozen each snow peas and water chestnuts. Stir-fry all the vegetables, except the snow peas, in 2 tablespoons of polyunsaturated oil that has been heated for 30 seconds with 1 mashed clove of garlic, which is then discarded. Stir-fry for 1 minute; add ½ cup of chicken stock or consommé, cover and cook for 2 minutes. Add the diced snow peas and cooked shrimp pieces and heat through for 30 seconds. Add 2 teaspoons cornstarch mixed with 2 teaspoons of water and stir until the sauce thickens. Remove from the heat and serve immediately. If you stir in 2 or more tablespoons of walnut meats at the very last moment of cooking, you will have prepared **Stir-Fried Shrimp with Walnuts.**

The Chinese have expressive and often symbolic names for many of their favorite dishes. One of these is **Phoenix-Tailed Shrimp in Clouds.** To serve six, shell and marinate 18 jumbo shrimp, as in preparing **Sweet and Sour Shrimp with Pineapple.** Heat 3 tablespoons polyunsaturated oil over medium heat; when hot, quickly toss in and stir-fry 2½ cups of rice vermicelli, cut into 4-inch lengths. Cook for several minutes but do not brown. Drain the vermicelli and arrange as a cloudlike bed on a warm platter. Clean the wok and add only enough oil to lightly coat it. Coat the shrimp, but not the tails, in the same batter used for cooking Sweet and Sour Shrimp with Pineapple. Stir-fry for 2 minutes; drain and arrange the shrimp on the vermicelli in a star-burst, with their tails facing the rim of the platter. Garnish the rim of the platter with 1 dozen washed and trimmed fresh spinach leaves and serve with **Chinese Shrimp Dip.** The dip is made simply by blending 2 teaspoons red wine vinegar with 4 tablespoons light soy sauce, 1 teaspoon of shredded fresh ginger, and ½ teaspoon sesame oil.

WOR TEEP HAR
(Butterfly Shrimp)

One of the most popular ways to prepare jumbo shrimp is this striking and delicious dish cooked with slices of ham and bacon.

2 dozen jumbo shrimp
4 egg whites, lightly beaten
6 tablespoons water chestnut flour or cornstarch
12 slices Canadian bacon, cut into strips the size of the shrimp
2 medium onions

Shrimp Sauce:
⅛ teaspoon white pepper
½ cup ketchup
5 tablespoons Worcestershire sauce or ¼ teaspoon Tabasco
1 tablespoon honey or pure maple syrup
½ cup water
2 tablespoons cornstarch mixed with 2 tablespoons water
1 teaspoon light soy sauce
5 tablespoons polyunsaturated oil or consommé
½ cup rice wine or dry sherry
½ teaspoon coarse salt
1 clove garlic, minced

YIELD: Four to six servings

1. Remove the shell but not the tail of each shrimp; devein if desired; wash and pat dry. With a sharp knife, cut the undersides of the shrimp no more than three quarters through to the back, and flatten with the side of the knife.

2. Brush the cut sides of the shrimp with egg white. Blend the balance of the egg white with the flour into a pasty consistency. Brush one side of each bacon strip with the flour mixture. Stick the brushed sides of the bacon to the brushed sides of the shrimp, pressing until they are bound together.

3. Cut the onions in half; then slice into semicircular rings. Combine the ingredients for the shrimp sauce. Mix the dissolved cornstarch with the soy sauce, and set both mixtures aside.

4. Using 4 tablespoons of oil, fry the shrimp in a wok or skillet over medium heat with the bacon side of the shrimp facing down. After 2 minutes, carefully turn the shrimp and cook the other side for 3 minutes. Add the sherry, cover, and cook for an additional minute. Remove the shrimp and drain on paper towels.

5. Stir-fry the onion rings for 2 minutes. Remove with a slotted spoon and layer the onions on a warm serving dish. Add the balance of the oil, the salt, and the garlic; when the oil is very hot, add the **Shrimp Sauce** and bring to a boil. Pour in the cornstarch mixture and stir until the sauce is thickened. Arrange shrimp over the onions and garnish the edges of the platter with washed and trimmed fresh lettuce leaves. The sauce may be either poured over the shrimp or served separately as a dip. For a **Pungent Shrimp Sauce,** substitute 2 tablespoons curry powder for the ketchup.

Bonus Ideas: Dried shrimp, like dried mussels, oysters, scallops, and fish, can be purchased in Chinese markets and will keep indefinitely when properly stored in tight, moisture-free containers. To prepare Dried Shrimp with Cabbage **Jing Go Bai Tsai** to serve six, wash and soak 2 dozen dried shrimp in water or preferably dry sherry for about 15 minutes, reserving the soaking liquid; drain and pat dry. In a wok or skillet, heat 3 tablespoons polyunsaturated oil or consommé, and stir-fry for a few seconds 2 scallions, cut into 2-inch lengths, and 2 shredded slices of fresh ginger. Add the shrimp and stir-fry for 30 seconds. Add 6 cups of shredded Chinese cabbage and stir-fry for an additional ½ minute. Pour in 5 tablespoons of the reserved soaking liquid, 1 teaspoon honey, and 1 teaspoon coarse salt; continue stir-frying for 5 minutes before serving hot.

For Szechuan Dried Shrimp with Cabbage **(Har Tsao Bai Tsai-Ching),** parboil 2 pounds of shredded Chinese cabbage for 1 minute and drain. Soak 15 dried shrimp for 15 minutes in 3 teaspoons dry sherry and drain, reserving the sherry. Heat 3 tablespoons of polyunsaturated oil or consommé, and stir-fry the drained shrimp for 30 seconds; then add half the sherry and cook for an additional 30 seconds. Stir in the cabbage, then the balance of the sherry, ¾ teaspoon honey, and 3 teaspoons light soy sauce; stir-fry until the liquid evaporates. Garnish with 1½ tablespoons chopped scallions and blend in 1 teaspoon sesame oil immediately before serving.

CHOW LUNG HAR*
(Lobster Cantonese)

1 2-pound live lobster
¼ pound lean pork, minced or coarsely
    ground

Lobster Sauce:
½ cup chicken stock or consommé
1 tablespoon cornstarch mixed with 1
    tablespoon water
1 tablespoon light soy sauce
½ teaspoon each, coarse salt, and honey
    or pure maple syrup
3 egg whites, lightly beaten with 2
    tablespoons polyunsaturated oil

3 tablespoons polyunsaturated oil or
    consommé
2 slices fresh ginger, shredded
1 clove garlic, minced
¼ pound lean pork, minced or coarsely
    ground
3 scallions, cut into 2-inch lengths
2 tablespoons dry sherry or rice wine
2 tablespoons chopped parsley or
    coriander (optional)
YIELD: Six servings

1. Either have your seafood supplier prepare a live lobster for you, or you can chop the lobster in half lengthwise, remove and discard the food sac and antennae, and chop each half, including the shell, into 2-inch sections. Chop each claw in half.

2. Combine the ingredients for the **Lobster Sauce,** except the egg white and oil mixture, and set aside. Heat the 3 tablespoons of oil or consommé in a wok or skillet; then stir-fry the ginger and garlic until the garlic browns. Add the pork and stir-fry for 2 minutes; then add the scallions and finally the lobster pieces; stir-fry for 2 minutes. Add the sherry, cover and cook for an additional minute.

3. Uncover and stir in the Lobster Sauce, cooking over medium heat until the sauce thickens. Turn off the heat, add the egg white and oil mixture, and cover the pan until the egg whites are slightly firm. Transfer to a warm platter and garnish with the optional chopped parsley or coriander.

Bonus Ideas: Shrimp with Lobster Sauce, using 1¼ pounds medium shrimp, does not utilize lobster as an ingredient—an example of the Chinese ingenuity for preparing numerous variations of basic traditional dishes; in this case, of **Lobster Cantonese*.** For six servings, substitute shrimp for the lobster in the above recipe. Six crabs, shelled and quartered, with the claws cracked and the feet discarded, can also be used instead of lobster to prepare **Crabs with Lobster Sauce*.**

NING MUNG GAI*
(Cantonese Lemon Chicken)

This popular Chinese dish, one of a series referred to in China as *vot gai,* or velvety-smooth chicken, may be served hot or cold, as an appetizer or as a main dish.

The recipes for Velvet Chicken, the preliminary step in preparing Lemon Chicken, vary among the different Chinese schools of cuisine. Some cook the chicken

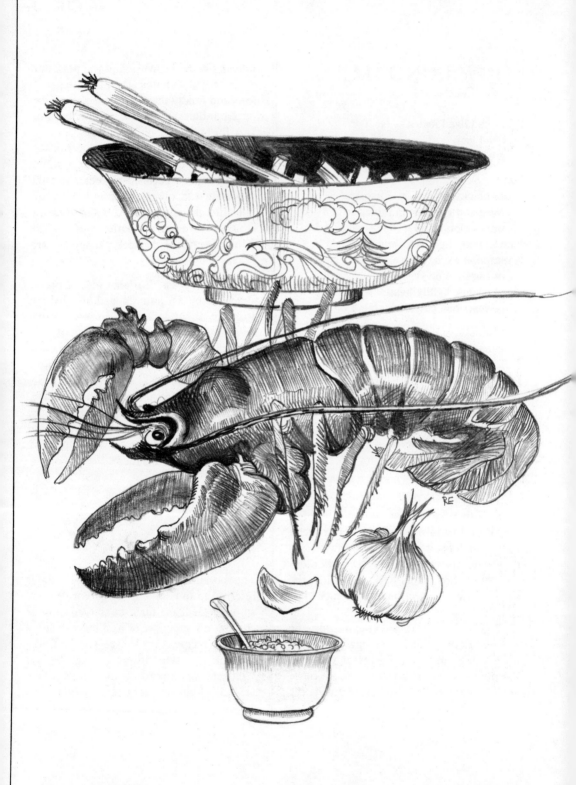

for long periods of time; others marinate it in a mixture of soy sauce, egg white, and cornstarch before boiling; some versions call for cooking the chicken whole, while others recommend deboning and cutting into pieces or cubes.

My favorite method for preparing Velvet Chicken involves one of the most imaginative cooking processes in Chinese cuisine, obviously created to utilize as little fuel as possible. The secret is placing one or two metal spoons in the cavity of the chicken to act as heat conductors, thus hastening the cooking process. The whole chicken, spoons inside, is placed with condiments in a tightly covered pot that has been filled with water to cover. After the water has been brought to a boil, the heat is immediately turned off. The pot is not opened for about 4 hours, until the chicken has cooked and cooled. You will find this technique results in one of the most delicately smooth chicken dishes you have ever tasted.

Velvet Chicken can be enjoyed as a dish in itself and can be used in any of the tantalizing *vot gai* variations. Bear in mind that a 2-pound chicken will yield 2 cups of cooked meat.

Velvet Chicken:
1 large or 2 smaller chickens—about 5 pounds in all
½ lemon
1 slice ginger, shredded
3 scallions, cut into 2-inch lengths
6 dried Chinese mushrooms
2 fresh hot red peppers, cut into strips (optional)

Lemon Sauce:
½ lemon, thinly sliced
1 teaspoon dried mandarin orange peel or dried lemon peel
1 teaspoon minced garlic
1 teaspoon light soy sauce
1 teaspoon coarse salt
¾ tablespoon honey or pure maple syrup
¼ teaspoon ground cinnamon
3 tablespoons polyunsaturated oil or consommé
2 tablespoons cornstarch mixed with 2 tablespoons water
1 teaspoon lemon extract (optional)
3 tablespoons sliced roasted almonds (optional)
YIELD: Six to eight servings

1. Rub the cavity of the chicken with the lemon; then insert two metal spoons well into it, securing them in place. Using kitchen twine, make a harness that will support the weight of the chicken; this should have a "handle" or loop at one end, to facilitate removing the chicken after cooking.

2. Fill a large pot about two thirds full with fresh water; add the ginger and scallions and bring to a boil. Lower the chicken with its harness into the boiling water, adding hot water, if necessary, to cover it. Bring the water back to a boil and tightly cover the pot, using wet paper toweling between the rim of the pot and its cover, if necessary, for proper sealing. Turn off the heat and do not uncover the pot until the chicken cools (about 4 hours).

3. Soak the mushrooms in warm water for 30 minutes and combine the ingredients for the Lemon Sauce.

4. With the aid of the harness, remove the chicken, reserving the broth. Remove the harness and the metal spoons. Using a sharp knife, carefully detach the chicken breast, cut into bite-size pieces, and set aside. Chop the legs, thighs, and wings (with their bones) into bite-size pieces and set aside.

5. Drain the mushrooms, squeeze out the excess moisture, and discard the tough stems. Heat the oil in a wok or skillet over high heat and stir-fry the mushrooms for 30 seconds; add the optional pepper strips, then add 1 cup of the reserved chicken broth and bring to a boil. Thoroughly mix, then add the Lemon Sauce and chicken; heat through over medium heat for about 30 seconds. Transfer the chicken to a serving platter. Stir the cornstarch mixture into the sauce and simmer until it thickens. Add the optional lemon extract if a stronger lemon flavor is desired. Pour the sauce over the chicken and serve hot, or let it cool to room temperature if a cold dish is preferred. If desired, sprinkle 3 tablespoons of sliced roasted almonds over the dish.

Bonus Ideas: Tsui Chi* (Drunken Chicken) is a popular cold entrée or hors d'oeuvre. To serve six to eight, prepare a 5-pound chicken as called for in Velvet Chicken, reserving the broth for future use. Cut the chicken into 8 serving pieces and sprinkle on all sides with 1 tablespoon of coarse salt. Arrange the pieces in layers in a deep ceramic or glass bowl; then add 3 cups of Chinese rice wine or dry sherry and enough of the reserved broth to cover the chicken pieces; cover the bowl with

plastic wrap or aluminum foil. Marinate in the refrigerator for at least one day, preferably for three days, turning the pieces occasionally. Before serving, cut the chicken into bite-size pieces, transfer to a serving platter, and pour over one third of the marinade, or ½ cup of chicken consommé mixed with rice wine or sherry. Serve at room temperature.

An example of how one chicken can be used imaginatively—and economically—to provide three varied and delicious dishes is **Many-Splendored Chicken,** which uses the wings for one dish, the boned meat for another, and the balance for broth. Prepare a 3-pound chicken as called for in Velvet Chicken; remove the breast and other pieces of boned meat; reserve broth.

With the boned meat, prepare **Paper-Wrapped Chicken*.** To serve four, slice the meat into 1½-inch squares and marinate for 30 minutes in a mixture of 1½ tablespoons each of dry sherry and light soy sauce, 1 chopped scallion, 1 shredded slice of fresh ginger, and 1½ tablespoons cornstarch dissolved in 2 tablespoons of water. Coat the chicken pieces evenly. Cut waxed paper or aluminum foil into 4-inch squares; wrap each piece of chicken in a square of paper, being sure to tuck in the ends of the paper firmly. Heat enough peanut oil for deep-frying in a wok or skillet to 375° F. Deep-fry each chicken packet for 5 minutes, or until cooked. Drain, serve still wrapped, to be opened at the table by each diner. Before deep-frying the chicken, you may wish to stir-fry ½ pound of thinly sliced mushrooms for 2 minutes in 1 tablespoon of oil; serve the mushrooms with the chicken.

For **Red-Simmered Chicken Wings***, as appetizers for six, cut each of 1 pound of chicken wings into two sections. Place in a pan with water to cover and simmer covered for 45 minutes, or until tender. Drain and cool, reserving the cooking liquid. Gently slip out the bones from each section. Using ¼ pound of lean ham or Canadian bacon cut into slivers, stuff the slivers into each cavity of the wing sections. Reduce the cooking liquid to slightly more than 1 cup and season with ½ teaspoon salt. Bring to a boil, add 2 tablespoons each of soy sauce and dry sherry, and thicken with 1½ tablespoons of cornstarch dissolved in 3 tablespoons of water; stir until the sauce is thickened. Heat the chicken wings through in the sauce and serve on a hot platter.

Velvet Chicken can also be the basis of interesting soups, including **Velvet Chicken Cucumber Soup***. You will need 1 cup cooked velvet chicken, 2 peeled cucumbers cut into ¼-inch cubes, and 2 cups of the reserved (or canned) chicken broth. Bring the broth to a boil, add the cucumbers, and simmer for 3 minutes over medium heat. Turn off the heat; add the chicken and let stand, covered, until heated through in about 2 minutes. Serve hot.

SIH TZU TOU*
(Imperial Lion's Head Casserole)

This is one of the important dishes at formal Chinese banquets. Consisting essentially of ground pork, shaped into huge meatballs, and cabbage, its imaginative name is derived from the imposing balls of pork, each of which suggests the head of a lion, and the surrounding cabbage, representing the lion's mane. Traditionally, the meat should be the size of baseballs, each of which will serve two. Lion's Heads are occasionally made smaller, serving one person, but traditionalists consider that this minimizes the impressiveness of the dish.

6 dried Chinese mushrooms
1¼ pounds lean pork, finely minced or
    coarsely ground
¼ pound polyunsaturated margarine,
    softened
2 each, scallions and fresh ginger slices,
    minced
6 water chestnuts, minced
2 egg whites, lightly beaten
2 tablespoons cornstarch dissolved in 3
    tablespoons water
1 tablespoon dry sherry or rice wine
2 tablespoons light soy sauce
½ teaspoon fruit sugar, honey, or pure
    maple syrup
½ teaspoon coarse salt
2 twists of a pepper mill
4 tablespoons peanut or corn oil
2 pounds cabbage leaves (preferably
    Chinese cabbage) or mustard greens,
    trimmed
1 cup meat or chicken stock, fresh or
    canned
YIELD: Six to eight servings

1. Soak the mushrooms in warm water for 15 minutes; drain, squeeze, discard the tough stems, and mince. In a mixing bowl, combine the meat with the margarine, the minced mushrooms, scallions, ginger, and water chestnuts.

2. Combine the egg whites, cornstarch mixture, sherry, soy sauce, fruit sugar, and

seasonings. Using a wooden spoon, gently blend the egg white mixture with the meat mixture. With moist hands, form the combined mixture into 4 to 6 large balls, about 4 inches in diameter.

3. Heat the oil in a wok or skillet and fry the meatballs for 5 minutes, or until golden on all sides. Remove, drain, and set aside. Stir-fry the cabbage leaves for 3 minutes, or until slightly softened.

4. Diagonally slice the cabbage leaves into 3-inch strips and line the bottom and sides of a 4-quart heat-proof casserole with half the strips. Pour the pan juices over the cabbage strips; then arrange the meatballs on the bottom layer. Heat the meat stock. Place the balance of the cabbage strips over the meatballs, tucking in the strips to completely enclose the meatballs between the two layers. Pour in the meat stock.

5. Cover and simmer over low heat for about 1½ hours, or cover and bake in an oven at 300° F for 2 hours, or until done. Serve in the casserole or transfer to a deep platter, arranging the meatballs over the cabbage. Pour the pan juices over the meatballs and serve.

Bonus Ideas: You may wish to blend 1 tablespoon cornstarch dissolved in 2 tablespoons of meat stock to thicken the pan juices before pouring over the meatballs and serving. Sprinkle a little sesame oil on the dish before serving.

Red-simmering and long-simmering dishes, such as this one, can be cooked in a microwave oven or pressure cooker in less time. If using a microwave oven, arrange the cabbage and meatballs in a glass or ceramic casserole and cover with waxed paper. Bake for 8 minutes, turn, and bake

an additional 8 minutes; then let the dish stand for 10 minutes before serving. If using a pressure cooker, you will require 2 cups of meat stock; cook for 20 minutes at 15-pound pressure after the valve is engaged. If using a clay pot, presoak the pot for 15 minutes in cold water, arrange the cabbage and meatballs as called for in the recipe, and place the covered pot in an oven set at 450° F, not preheated. Cook for 1 hour, or until done. The meatballs may be frozen either before or after frying; when ready to use, thaw thoroughly and proceed with balance of recipe.

In Shanghai, **Seafood Lion's Head*** is a popular variation, and since the meatballs are braised rather than simmered, the dish can be prepared in less time. Using 1 pound of minced pork and ¼ pound each of minced shrimp and shredded crabmeat, prepare the meatballs with the other ingredients called for in the basic recipe for Imperial Lion's Head Casserole. Fry the meatballs until golden, about 5 minutes, and set aside. Add 2 tablespoons of polyunsaturated oil to a wok or skillet and sauté the cabbage for 2 minutes; then add the stock and meatballs. Cover and braise over medium heat for 30 minutes. When the liquid has been almost completely absorbed, arrange the meatballs on a bed of cabbage in a deep platter and serve.

TSAO TSU NIEN KAO*
(Chinese Red Date Cake)

This cake is a favorite throughout China and specialty during the New Year festivities. Chinese red dates, except for their color, resemble prunes and taste like prunes, but with a more memorable combination of sweetness and pungency. Prized for their distinctive taste and fragrance, red dates are often used as sweetening agents in *congees,* soups, puddings, and moon cakes.

Called *hoong tsou* (jujubes), dried red dates are obtainable in Chinese shops, and when kept in moisture-free containers, will last for months, even years. Before using, they must be soaked and their pits and thick skins discarded.

Red Date Cake can be frozen and reheated in a microwave oven or in a steamer. It is cooked by steaming, and it is important to note that glutinous rice flour is used so that the cake will remain soft; regular rice flour has a tendency to harden when steamed. If you have any difficulty obtaining glutinous rice flour in Chinese shops, Japanese sweet rice flour has the right glutinous qualities for this dish, which has been compared to English plum pudding.

½ pound Chinese red dates (jujubes)
¼ cup polyunsaturated margarine
1 tablespoon honey or pure maple syrup
1 teaspoon vanilla (optional)
½ pound Chinese or Japanese glutinous rice flour
YIELD: Twelve to sixteen individual cakes

1. Wash the dates, cover with water, and bring to a boil. Reduce heat and simmer for 1 hour, or until the dates are tender; remove and discard the pits and tough outer skins. Reserving the cooking water, drain; purée the dates through a food mill, sieve, or in an electric blender.
2. Mix the date paste, margarine, honey, and optional vanilla in a bowl; add the rice flour and knead the mixture into a pliable but thick dough, moistening with some of the cooking water if necessary.
3. Sprinkle some rice flour on your hands and roll the dough into a long cylinder, ¾ inch in diameter. Cut into ½-inch slices, flattening each round slightly, or cut into interesting shapes with assorted cookie cutters.
4. Cut sheets of waxed paper into 2-inch squares and place 1 round on each square. Arrange the cakes on the trays of a steamer over boiling water and steam, tightly covered for no more than 10 minutes until cooked, which is when an inserted toothpick comes out clean. Serve hot.

Bonus Ideas: This recipe is also prepared as a large cake, the dough having been placed in an 8-inch cake pan, either greased or lined with waxed paper. This requires about 30 minutes of steaming, so be sure to put plenty of boiling water in the steamer and add boiling water as necessary. Remove the cake carefully and allow to cool before cutting as desired; it can also be garnished with plain or toasted almonds. Four ounces of canned Chinese red bean paste is sometimes added before kneading the dough.

Koreans prepare their own version of **Rice with Jujubes***. To serve six or eight, cook ½ pound red dates as for Chinese Red Date Cake. Discard the pits and tough outer skins and cut into small pieces. Add to 4 cups of rice in a large pot with 6 cups of water. Bring to a boil, cover tightly, and cook over low heat for about 30 minutes. Remove from heat, but do not uncover for 10 minutes before serving.

Red Date Wontons*, an excellent dessert, are prepared with ½ pound Chinese red dates that have been cooked, skinned, and pitted as in the above recipe. Combine with ½ cup of minced walnuts, 2 teaspoons of grated mandarin orange peel or dried orange peel, and 1 teaspoon orange juice. With wet hands, knead the mixture, shaping cylinders 1 inch long and ⅓ inch in diameter. Cut 1 pound ready-made egg-roll wrappers (available in Oriental stores) into 2-inch squares. Place 1 roll of filling diagonally across the lower corner of each wrapper and roll up; with a wet finger, moisten the end of the wrapper to seal the roll, and twist the ends to completely enclose the filling. Deep-fry in 2 cups of peanut or corn oil for 3 to 5 minutes until golden brown and crisp. Drain on paper toweling and cool. Sprinkle with fruit sugar or brush with honey immediately before serving.

Wontons*, often referred to as the Chinese ravioli, consist of thin dough wrapped around a meat filling. **Wonton Soup*** is made simply by boiling *Wontons* in broth and serving as an appetizer or luncheon entrée. *Wontons* are filled with minced meat, seafood, and vegetables. For six servings, combine and blend 1 teaspoon light soy sauce with ½ pound ground pork, chicken, or beef; ¼ pound minced shrimp, crabmeat, or fish fillet; ½ cup of minced water chestnuts, celery, or Chinese cabbage; 2 minced scallions, and ½ teaspoon coarse salt. Let the mixture stand for 30 minutes. Using *Wonton* wrappers, place ¾ teaspoon of filling in the center of each square wrapper, positioned with one point toward you. Fold the point facing you over to the opposite point, forming a triangle. Seal by brushing with lightly beaten egg white. Fold the point to your left over the mound of filling and brush the top with egg white. Brush the point to your right with egg white, then fold it to slightly overlap the edge previously folded. Pinch the two moistened edges to seal, if necessary. In addition to boiling in soup, *Wontons* can be steamed or deep-fried and served as snacks.

CHA
(Chinese Tea)

Always served with meals in China and unquestionable the national beverage, tea is associated with quiet contemplation and appreciation of the beauty of nature. Some culinary experts believe it originally was taken as an aid to digestion and an antidote to oily dishes, especially those of Manchuria and Mongolia.

The Chinese have a variety of teas for different occasions and purposes: Green teas, served throughout the day, are considered the finest of the various types; Dragon's Well, or *Lung Ching,* is particularly popular. Since it is now possible to purchase teas from China, I recommend Goldfish brand green tea, which is served in contemporary Peking at banquets.

Keemun is an excellent black tea served with meals. Most restaurants serve *Oolong,* which is a semifermented black tea that is generally served with the main family meal in China.

Jasmine tea *(Mook Lay Faar)* is favored by many Chinese between meals and at banquets. Delicate and aromatic, this is a combination of either *Keemun* or *Oolong* tea and jasmine buds.

There are numerous other special teas, including some that are so richly flavored they are served as liqueurs; one such is *Wun Mo* (Cloud Mist Tea); another is Goddess of Mercy tea. Whichever tea you prefer, it should be properly prepared to bring out its distinctive flavor.

2 tablespoons black, green, or jasmine tea leaves
6 cups freshly boiled water
YIELD: Six servings

1. Pour some boiling water into a (preferably squat) china or glass teapot, in order to scald the inside. Drain, then place the tea leaves in the pot.
2. Bring the 6 cups of water to a rolling boil; remove from the heat and pour into the teapot. For best results, the water must not overboil. The leaves will rise to the surface, then settle at the bottom of the pot.
3. Cover the pot and let the tea steep for 3 to 5 minutes. Serve hot.

Bonus Ideas: Since Dragon's Well *(Lung Ching)* green tea is stronger than Chinese black teas, use 2 teaspoons of tea leaves to 6 cups of water. Boiling water may be added to any tea that has been brewed too strongly.

MENU

Hai Yoke Foo Yung Don
Pai Fan
Lohan Jai
Tsen Yu

Guy Lon Ngow
Ba Bao Fan
Cha

Crabmeat Soufflé *Foo Yung*
Chinese Boiled Rice
Buddhist Vegetarian Casserole
Steamed Sea Bass
Peony Blossom Beef with Broccoli
Eight-Precious Pudding
Tea

HAI YOKE FOO YUNG DON
(Crabmeat Soufflé *Foo Yung*)

Unfortunately egg *Foo yung* has not fared very well in Chinese restaurants in this country because it rarely compares to the versatile soufflés that are made properly in Chinese homes. These can be a welcome addition to any meal.

Foo yung is derived from some of the oldest traditions in China and can be easily and quickly prepared plain, using egg whites only, or in combination with meat, poultry, seafood, or ham. It is served with gravy, and/or on a bed of stir-fried mustard greens or spinach leaves, or on a nest of rice vermicelli.

A visually stunning variation is the Shantung specialty **Mount T'ai Shan Foo Yung**; the souffle is presented in a mound representing that sacred mountain peak, with fluffy rice vermicelli suggesting clouds surrounding its summit (the recipe for this dish is included in the Bonus Ideas below).

1 cup shredded crabmeat
1 tablespoon dry sherry or rice wine
1 cup fresh or canned bean sprouts
3 tablespoons polyunsaturated oil
1 slice fresh ginger root, minced
2 tablespoons chopped scallions
⅛ teaspoon honey or pure maple syrup
6 egg whites
½ teaspoon coarse salt
2 tablespoons cornstarch dissolved in ½
   cup skim milk
2 tablespoons minced Canadian bacon
¼ teaspoon light soy sauce
¼ cup chicken stock or clam juice
⅛ teaspoon sesame oil
YIELD: Six servings

1. Combine the crabmeat with the sherry; set aside and let stand for 15 minutes. Parboil the bean sprouts for 2 minutes; drain and keep warm in a covered bowl.

2. Heat 1 tablespoon of the oil in a skillet and briefly sauté or stir-fry the ginger and scallions; add the honey, then the crabmeat and sherry mixture. Mix well and heat through. Remove and set aside.

3. Beat the egg whites with the salt until the whites form moist peaks; then fold in the cornstarch and milk mixture. Fold in the crabmeat and sherry mixture, blending well.

4. Heat the balance of the oil in a skillet over medium heat until it is almost smoking. Add the minced Canadian bacon and crabmeat and egg mixture and cook quickly until the mixture thickens, stirring constantly. Add the soy sauce; then gradually add the stock as necessary for a thick but fluffy consistency. Remove from heat and transfer to a warm platter; serve the soufflé at once, surrounded by the bean sprouts and sprinkled with sesame oil. If serving on a bed of mustard greens or spinach leaves, trim off the hard veins, cut into 3-inch diagonal shreds, and stir-fry until slightly softened. Drain and transfer to a warm platter before placing the soufflé on top.

Bonus Ideas: You can add 5 minced water chestnuts or Chinese black mushrooms, or ½ cup shredded bamboo shoots to the crabmeat mixture for additional texture and flavor.

One-half pound shrimp, shelled and cut into small pieces, can be substituted for the crabmeat for six servings of **Shrimp Soufflé** *(Foo Yung Har)*. However, don't blend the shrimp with the egg white mixture; instead, stir-fry the shrimp in hot oil for 2 minutes, add the egg mixture; blend and cook over low heat until thick.

To prepare the attractive **Mount T'ai Shan Foo Yung***, shell 1 dozen medium shrimp and cut in half lengthwise before marinating for 15 minutes in the sherry mixture used for Crabmeat Soufflé. Add the 1 cup of parboiled bean sprouts and 4 tablespoons shredded Canadian bacon to the basic *foo yung* mixture, blending all the ingredients well. Brush the inside of a 1½-quart Charlotte mold with oil or margarine and pour in the mixture. (The sloping sides of this mold are important to the proper rising of the soufflé, thus forming the symbolic mountain peak.) Place a rack in a steamer and add water sufficient to reach up to two thirds the height of the mold. Heat until boiling, and do not place the mold into the steamer until the water boils. Remove from the heat, insert the charlotte mold, cover, and steam for 30 minutes over high heat.

Prepare the rice vermicelli by heating oil in a wok until the point of smoking; then quickly add the vermicelli, tossing until they burst into fluffiness; remove immediately and drain on paper toweling. Prepare **Foo Yung Sauce** by blending in a saucepan 1¼ cups chicken stock, 1 tablespoon cornstarch dissolved in 2 tablespoons of stock, 1 tablespoon of light soy sauce, ⅛ teaspoon each of sesame oil, coarse salt, and ground pepper. Over medium heat, bring to a boil, stirring constantly. Simmer over low heat until thickened; set aside and heat briefly when ready for use.

When cooked, remove the *foo yung* from the steamer and let it set for 15 minutes before brushing with 1 teaspoon of oil or margarine. Place in an oven at 400° F or under the broiler until the *foo yung* is golden brown. On a warm platter, arrange the cloudlike vermicelli around the "mountain peak" and serve with the sauce separate.

LOHAN JAI
(Buddhist Vegetarian Casserole)

According to Mr. Kao of the Ultimate Lotus restaurant in New York City, *Lohan Jai* was created as an offering to Buddha by Ming Dynasty monks more than 500 years ago as part of their vow to refrain from using meat in their food. The monks also created a number of "mock" dishes, using nonmeat ingredients only, that cleverly maintained the appearance, taste, and texture of traditional nonvegetarian specialties. Among them are **Mock Duck,** **Mock Chicken, and Mock Ham.** Mock dishes, however, are not necessarily vegetarian: in Szechuan, where fresh fish is not readily available, they ingeniously prepare **Szechuan Mock Fish** using pork as an ingredient.

All of the ingredients for this recipe are available in Chinese markets and shops.

½ cup each, sliced carrots, snow pea pods, baby corn, and Chinese cabbage or mustard greens
¼ cup each, canned or dried sliced lotus root, whole straw mushrooms, Chinese black mushrooms, and dried red dates (jujubes)
¼ cup each, hair seaweed and water chestnuts
¼ cup potato starch (optional)
¾ cup bean-sprout or other stock
¼ cup peanut or corn oil
½ teaspoon salt
1 tablespoon cornstarch
YIELD: Six servings

1. Prepare all ingredients for stir-frying by slicing the carrots, greens, lotus root, and black mushrooms; all ingredients should be about 1-inch bite-size pieces. Parboil the carrots for 2 minutes, and blanch the balance of the vegetables by pouring boiling water over them and draining immediately. Individually soak dried ingredients—black mushrooms, lotus slices, jujubes, and hair seaweed—in warm water to cover for about 20 minutes. Reserve mushroom soaking water, drain the mushrooms, and remove stems before slicing them.

2. If making fresh **Bean-Sprout Stock,** use a proportion of 1 cup bean sprouts to

3 cups water, season with 1 tablespoon light soy sauce, and simmer for 30 minutes. Strain and discard the bean sprouts, reserving the stock. **Emergency Chinese Stock** can be prepared in the same manner without the bean sprouts as a base for various soups.

3. Heat the oil in a wok or large skillet over medium heat until very hot. Stir-fry all the ingredients except the cornstarch and salt for 3 minutes until *al dente*. Add ¾ cup of the bean-sprout broth and ¼ cup of the reserved mushroom water; then add the salt and sprinkle the cornstarch over the vegetables. Stir and simmer for 2 to 5 minutes, depending on the crispness desired. Serve hot.

Mr. Kao says that traditionally this dish is made with at least 10 superior ingredients, including whichever fresh vegetables are seasonally available, which makes it very versatile, indeed.

SU HO TWEI*
(Vegetarian Mock Ham)

Mock Ham and **Mock Chicken** *(Su Chi)* are excellent main course dishes or can be served as appetizers; both are made in the same manner, with only a minor variation of 1 or 2 ingredients. Fresh or dried soybean milk sheets, the chief ingredient, come in various sizes and shapes. This is Mr. Kao's traditional recipe.

1 pound triangular 12- by 3-inch dried soybean milk sheets
8 quarts warm water
2 tablespoons baking soda
1 cup light or ¾ cup dark soy sauce

¼ cup dry sherry or rice wine
1 tablespoon honey, pure maple syrup, or fruit sugar
1 tablespoon peanut or corn oil
1 egg white (optional)
YIELD: Six main course or twelve appetizer servings

1. Place the soybean milk sheets in a large pot with half the warm water and bring to a boil over medium heat. Add the baking soda and stir the sheets until soft (about 5 minutes). Then drain them in a colander and rinse thoroughly with warm water to remove most of the baking soda solution; drain again.

2. Place the sheets back in the pot with the remaining 4 quarts of warm water; boil for 20 minutes, or until the sheets are very soft. Drain and rinse again with warm water.

3. Return to the pot with the soy sauce, wine, and honey; bring to a boil and cook over medium heat until the sauce is reduced to half its original volume. Remove the soybean sheets with a slotted spoon, reserving the sauce; divide the soybean sheets into two equal portions.

4. Prepare either muslin or layers of cheesecloth as you would for 2 large sausage rolls. Sew or tie the cloth into long narrow bags (4½ by 10 inches) and brush with the optional egg white, if necessary, to avoid unraveling. Place each bag in a pan and fill with 1 portion of sheets. Using twine, tie the top of the bag securely; then loop the twine around the length of the bag, tying it tightly around the diameter every quarter inch as in a sausage roll. Repeat with second bag and stack of sheets.

5. Place the 2 rolls into the pan with the reserved sauce and any that has drained while tying, and bring to a boil. Add the tablespoon of oil and turn the rolls in the mixture until coated evenly. Cook over high heat, turning the rolls occasionally, until all of the liquid has been absorbed into the rolls. Cool completely, then chill in the refrigerator. When ready to serve, remove the cloth casing and twine and serve thinly sliced.

6. If preparing **Chinese Mock Chicken** *(Su Chi)*, substitute 2 teaspoons of coarse salt for the soy sauce and honey (included to give color to the Mock Ham) and serve warm or chilled with a dip made of 1 tablespoon sesame oil and 3 tablespoons soy sauce.

Bonus Ideas: As appetizers for twelve, **Mock Ham** or **Mock Chicken** can be served, sliced Chinese style, with a number of other appetizers on 1 large platter. Try serving with crisp and crunchy vegetables like **Celery and Carrot Salad:** place ½ cup each of shredded celery and carrots and 2 slices of shredded ginger root in ice water with 2 tablespoons of coarse salt. Let stand for 30 minutes; then drain and serve, tossed with 2 tablespoons light soy sauce and sprinkled with six drops of sesame oil.

Other salad possibilties are julienned string beans or snow peas, both tossed in soy sauce and sprinkled with sesame oil. Canned pickled cabbage, seaweed poached in warm water, and stir-fried vermicelli or agar-agar noodles are also popular appetizers. Nonvegetarian items include **Drunken Chicken,** marinated abalone, pig ear strips, and **Red-Simmered Beef.**

SU YA*
(Chinese Mock Pressed Duck)

Another Mr. Kao vegetarian specialty.

10 dried soybean milk sheets, half-moon shaped, 10- by 14-inch size

Filling:
½ cup each, dried black mushrooms and shredded bamboo shoots
1 cup peanut or corn oil
1 tablespoon light soy sauce
¼ teaspoon honey, pure maple syrup, or fruit sugar

Sauce:
1 cup concentrated vegetable or soybean stock
2 tablespoons dark or 2½ tablespoons light soy sauce, mixed with 1 teaspoon coarse salt
1 teaspoon honey, pure maple syrup, or fruit sugar
YIELD: Six to eight main course or twelve appetizer servings

1. Dampen a cloth and place the brittle soybean milk sheets between its folds for 15 minutes, or until pliable.

2. Prepare the Filling. Soak the mushrooms in warm water for 20 minutes; squeeze dry, remove any hard stems, and slice into shreds. Reserve the water. Heat 2 tablespoons of the oil in a wok until very hot and stir-fry the bamboo shoots and mushrooms for 2 minutes. Add the soy sauce, honey, and ½ cup of reserved mushroom water, and cook over medium heat for 10 minutes, or until the liquid has virtually evaporated. Remove and set aside.

3. Divide the filling into 10 equal portions, and the sheets into 2 groups of 5 sheets each. Spread 1 portion in the middle of each soybean sheet, which has the curved side facing away from you. Make an envelope by folding the left side of the half-moon to the center, then folding over the right side, slightly overlapping it, and folding the top of the sheet down to form a rectangular envelope. Set aside.

4. To prepare 2 mock pressed ducks, you will proceed very much as in the famous Chinese box puzzle, which contains a number of varying sizes of small boxes inside. Spread the second portion of filling on a second soybean sheet; then place the first rectangular envelope, folded side down, on top of the filling. Fold up the second sheet as before—but this time with the first envelope inside the second envelope.

5. Repeat the process until you have folded the fifth sheet, containing the fifth portion of filling, over the fourth envelope, which already has 3 filled envelopes inside. Repeat with the balance of sheets and portions of filling. Set aside the 2 large envelopes, each filled with 4 filled envelopes. These are your mock pressed ducks.

6. Heat the oil in a wok or skillet; when about 375° F, deep-fry each mock pressed duck, 1 at a time, for about 3 minutes on each side until lightly browned. Drain the ducks on paper towels and set aside.

7. Pour the oil out of the wok; combine the stock, soy sauce, and honey in the wok and bring to a boil. Reduce to low heat, add the ducks to the sauce, and simmer for 15 minutes, basting the ducks often with the sauce. When cooked, there

should be very little sauce left in the pan. Cool, then chill the ducks. When ready to serve, slice each duck diagonally into 1½- by 2-inch strips. Serve with rice and crunchy vegetables, such as snow peas or bean sprouts with diced water chestnuts. The slices can also be served as part of a Chinese appetizer platter.

Bonus Ideas: To prepare **Mock Goose** *(Su Ngeh),* proceed with the above recipe for Mock Pressed Duck through step 5, at which point you have prepared the 2 large filled envelopes. Instead of frying, place the envelopes on the upper tier of a steamer and sprinkle with 1 teaspoon of coarse salt. On the lower tier, place a bowl containing a mixture of ½ cup black oolong tea and 3 tablespoons of raw rice; steam over boiling water for 5 minutes in your homemade Chinese smoking oven. Remove the tea and rice mixture from the lower tier and continue steaming the goose packets over boiling water for 20 minutes. Drain, pat dry, then proceed with deep-frying as in step 6 of the Mock Duck recipe, and continue with the balance of that recipe.

SU YU
(Szechuan Mock Fish)

As we have said, not all mock dishes are vegetarian. This mock fish recipe is made with pork.

¾ pound lean pork, thinly shredded
2 teaspoons rice wine or dry sherry
1 tablespoon light soy sauce
1 tablespoon cornstarch dissolved in water
¼ cup peanut or corn oil

Szechuan Brown Sauce:
2 tablespoons canned brown bean sauce
½ teaspoon crushed Szechuan peppercorns
1 tablespoon vinegar
½ teaspoon honey, pure maple syrup, or fruit sugar
1 teaspoon finely minced fresh ginger
4 drops of sesame oil
½ teaspoon cornstarch dissolved in 2 tablespoons water
YIELD: Six to eight servings

1. Mix the pork with the wine, soy sauce, and cornstarch, blending thoroughly. Cover and place in the refrigerator to marinate for at least 2 hours.

2. Drain the meat and deep-fry for 2 minutes, or until browned. Drain on paper toweling.

3. Combine the ingredients for the **Szechuan Brown Sauce** except the cornstarch mixture, and transfer to a hot wok or skillet. Add the pork and heat through over medium heat for several minutes. Add the cornstarch mixture and stir until the sauce is thickened. Serve hot.

Bonus Ideas: Mock Bird's Nest is a favored Chinese garnish for any soufflé-like or *Foo yung* dish, such as **Crabmeat Soufflé.** Simply fry 2 cups of rice vermicelli or transparent noodles in hot oil until lightly brown. Arrange the noodles on a platter in the shape of a nest and cover with the *foo yung* of your choice.

TSEN YU
(Steamed Sea Bass)

White-fleshed fish, whole or sliced, is often steamed with aromatic vegetables, herbs, and spices—a process that results in memorable, quickly cooked dishes. In France, *la nouvelle cuisine* has adopted this traditional Chinese technique, as have other ethnic cuisines around the world.

When served Chinese style, not in individual portions but on a single platter, the fish is shared by all the diners at the table, each diner picking off the meat with chopsticks. I prefer to lift off and discard the skin, then remove the meat from the bones on both sides of the fish and serve it separate with an appropriate sauce.

Seafood, particularly lobster, lends itself to the steaming technique. Using the wide range of aromatics necessary for steaming fish and other items is a fine art that you will want to master.

2 tablespoons fermented black beans
1 whole 3-pound sea bass, tile fish, or other firm-fleshed fish, cleaned and gills removed, but not scaled
1 teaspoon coarse salt
1 clove garlic, minced
3 slices fresh ginger, shredded
2 scallions, chopped
1 tablespoon dry sherry or rice wine
2 tablespoons light soy sauce
2 tablespoons peanut oil
¼ teaspoon sesame oil
6 Scallion Brushes (see Bonus Ideas)
YIELD: Six to eight servings

1. Soak the fermented beans in warm water for about 20 minutes; then drain and set aside. With a sharp knife, make crisscross slashes about 1½ inches apart on both sides of the fish. Sprinkle the slits with salt, combine the garlic, beans, ginger, and chopped scallions, and mash together into a paste.

2. Insert the bean paste mixture into the slits of the fish on both sides before placing the fish into a heat-proof dish large enough to accommodate it and its cooking juices.

3. Sprinkle the fish with the sherry and soy sauce; place the dish with the fish into a steamer. Cover and bring the water in the steamer to a boil. Reduce to medium heat and steam for 30 minutes, or until the fish is flaky.

4. Remove the platter with the fish and set aside. Heat the combined oils until almost smoking; then pour over the fish and serve garnished with the Scallion Brushes.

Bonus Ideas: Instead of the combined oils, you can sprinkle ½ teaspoon of Pernod over the fish during the last 2 minutes of steaming. The above recipe is wonderfully aromatic, and can be further enhanced by placing 2 stalks of celery, 2 scallions, and 1 carrot on the dish before placing the fish over them during steaming.

Scallion Brushes are made by trimming the roots and the green ends of the scallions, leaving about 2½ inches of the firm white root. Make 4 crisscross cuts on both ends about ¾ inch deep and place in ice water until the fringed ends curl to form brushes.

One of the most popular and effective ingredients as an aromatic for steaming fish is fresh seaweed or dried laver (edible seaweed), sold in Oriental markets in sheets. Two pounds of fresh wet seaweed or 10 sheets of the dried laver are soaked in warm water for 15 minutes, and half is placed on a heat-proof platter under the fish. The fish is covered with the balance of the seaweed; then it is steamed over boiling water for 8 to 10 minutes, until flaky but not overcooked. Discard the seaweed, skin and bone the fish, and serve with an appropriate sauce. Jacques Manière, one of the first famous French chefs to adapt this technique, told me he uses fresh parsley whenever seaweed is not available.

GUY LON NGOW
(Peony Blossom Beef with Broccoli)

A spring speciality at New York's Flower Drum restaurant, which serves traditional seasonal dishes.

For economic reasons, the Chinese use pork far more often than beef. Whenever beef is used, therefore, it is treated as a most special, if not precious, ingredient. It is never overcooked and, except when beef is being stewed, it is usually the last ingredient of a dish to be cooked. It may also be seared or browned first, then set aside for last-minute cooking. The Chinese learned centuries ago that beef (and other meats) should be cut *across* the fibers, which assures that it will be tender when cooked; also, stock is never added to beef during cooking, since it has a tendency to toughen the meat.

Since the leanest beef is preferred for family dishes, flank and skirt steak are popular in Chinese communities. More expensive cuts, such as sirloin and filet mignon, are used only in festive or special dishes—for instance, **Chinese Steak Cubes** *(Dik Kau).*

2½ tablespoons honey or pure maple
   syrup
2 tablespoons dry sherry or rice wine
1 teaspoon coarse salt

2½ quarts water
½ cup dry sherry (optional)
3 tablespoons chopped fresh parsley or
   coriander
YIELD: Eight to twelve servings

1. Trim the meat of membranes and excess fat, but do not slice. Using a large, heavy saucepan, simmer the meat in the spice Marinade over medium heat for 15 minutes, turning occasionally.

2. Add the water and bring to a boil; lower the heat and simmer for about 3 hours until the meat is tender and the sauce has reduced to about 1 cup. Remove and discard the cheesecloth containing the spices or star anise.

3. Transfer the meat to a platter; cool, then cover with plastic wrap and refrigerate. Strain the sauce into a bowl, add the optional sherry, and refrigerate until it has jelled. Cut the cold beef into ¼-inch slices and arrange on a platter with cubes of the jelled sauce. Serve as an appetizer or main course garnished with chopped parsley.

Bonus Ideas: If you prefer to serve this dish hot, cut the meat into 1½-inch cubes before marinating; then proceed with the balance of the recipe. It can also be prepared with excellent results in a microwave oven, slow-cooking crock pot, clay pot, or pressure cooker, using the cooking time recommended for braising 3 pounds of meat.

Not all Chinese beef dishes use the more economical cuts of meat. **Chinese Steak Cubes** (*Dik Kau*)* calls for the finest cuts of beefsteak—shell, club, sirloin, even filet. It is one of the rare Chinese dishes with a greater proportion of meat than vegetables. For four to eight servings, trim the fat from 2 pounds of steak that has been at room temperature for an hour; bone and cut into 1½-inch cubes. For rare meat, place the cubes in a freezer for 30 minutes before cooking. Marinate the cubes for 15 minutes in 2 tablespoons each of light soy sauce, peanut oil, and gin or vodka; ½ teaspoon honey or pure maple syrup, and ⅛ teaspoon each coarse salt and ground white pepper. Mince 2 onions and stir-fry in a wok in 1½ tablespoons peanut oil until translucent. Add the steak cubes and stir until the cubes are seared in about 2 minutes. Then pour in the marinade. Remove the steak and juices and set aside. Add a tablespoon of oil, and when very hot, stir-fry ¾ pound fresh or 6 soaked and squeezed dried black mushrooms, ¼ pound snow peas, ½ cup thinly sliced bamboo shoots or celery, and ¼ cup diced water chestnuts for 2 minutes. Turn up the heat, add the steak cubes, and toss in the vegetable mixture until cooked to taste. Remove from heat and serve immediately.

BA BAO FAN*
(Eight Precious Pudding)

Although the Chinese prefer sweet soups at the end of a meal, here is one of their traditional desserts.

The classic recipe calls for numerous dried or preserved fruits and for roots and nuts that may not be readily available

even in Chinese markets. As substitutes, fresh, dried, or preserved fruits, such as apricots, raisins, and apples, can be combined with a variety of blanched nuts. **Candied Fruit** may also be used. But to be consistent with the name of the pudding, use a mixture of at least 8 items.

2 cups long grain, glutinous rice
4 cups water
6 tablespoons polyunsaturated margarine
1½ cups assorted fresh or preserved fruits combined with nuts
3 tablespoons honey, pure maple syrup, or fruit sugar
1 cup canned red bean or chestnut paste

Sauce:
1½ cups water
1 tablespoon cornstarch
5 tablespoons of honey, pure maple syrup, or fruit sugar
1 teaspoon almond extract
YIELD: Eight servings

1. Wash the rice well to remove excess starch; drain, place in a pot with the water, and bring to a boil. Cover and boil for 5 minutes; then reduce heat and simmer for 15 minutes, or until dry and fluffy. Set aside to cool slightly.

2. Brush the inside of a 7-inch heat-proof 2-quart bowl with 2 tablespoons of the margarine and arrange the fruits and nuts in a decorative circular or flower pattern on the bottom of the bowl.

3. Mix 4 tablespoons of the margarine and 3 tablespoons of honey into the rice and blend thoroughly. Place half the rice mixture into the bowl, being careful not to disturb the pattern of fruit and nuts.

4. Press the rice down gently. Place a layer of red bean paste on the rice, covering the center, but extending only to 1

inch of the sides of the bowl. Cover this with the balance of the rice mixture, leaving 1 inch from the top for expansion. Cover the bowl with aluminum foil and set in a steamer over boiling water for about 45 minutes.

5. Place a flat serving plate over the pudding and quickly invert, unmolding it on the plate; the pudding will now have the decorative surface on top. In a saucepan, combine the water, cornstarch, and honey; bring to a boil, stirring until thickened; then stir in the almond extract. Serve the pudding, hot or chilled, with the sauce.

Bonus Ideas: I prefer to freeze extra quantities of this pudding for future use. The frozen pudding does not need to be thawed before steaming, but you may have to allow an extra 10 to 15 minutes to cook the frozen pudding.

Rice and nuts are also combined in an interesting dessert soup often served at formal banquets, **Walnut Soup***, which can be made to serve six to eight by using 1 quart of the starchy water reserved from steaming rice. Boil 2 cups of walnut meats in this water and simmer for about 10 minutes, or until the walnuts are soft. Add 2 tablespoons of honey or pure maple syrup, or to taste, and serve hot.

For **Walnut Date Soup***, in addition to the ingredients for Walnut Soup, you will need ¼ pound of dried Chinese red dates (jujubes) that have been first soaked for several hours, then simmered in 1 quart of starch water for 2 hours. This will produce ¾ cup of date pulp, which is added to 1¼ cups of cooked walnuts and puréed in an electric blender with 2 cups of the reserved cooking water. The mixture is then brought to a boil with 2 cups of starch water, honey is added, and the soup thickened with ½ tablespoon of cornstarch dissolved in 1 tablespoon of water. Serve very hot.

MENU

Shau Mai
Pai Fan
Chao Shek Loh
Hoong Shao Nui Seh To
Cha Shiu
Li Tsoo Tan Kao
Cha

Cantonese Steamed Pork Dumplings
Chinese Boiled Rice
Snails Cantonese Style
Red-Simmered Tongue
Cantonese Roast Pork Strips
Peking Dust
Tea

SHAU MAI*
(Cantonese Steamed Pork Dumplings)

These steamed dumplings or buns, among the most popular Chinese savories or snacks, called *dem sem,* can be made with a variety of fillings. Served with tea, they can be a meal in themselves.

Usually, either sweet or spicy meats or vegetable mixtures are used as fillings, a traditional red dot of food coloring placed on the sweet dumplings to differentiate them from the others. Wonton wrappers, commercially available in Chinese shops, can be used for a number of *dem sem,* which can also be fried or boiled.

50 homemade or purchased wonton wrappers

Pastry Dough:
1 cup each, cornstarch and white rye flour
2 teaspoons baking powder
1 teaspoon salt
2 egg whites, lightly beaten
4 tablespoons water
1 teaspoon cornstarch

1 pound Chinese cabbage, spinach, or celery, diced

½ pound lean pork, minced or coarsely ground
3 water chestnuts, minced
¼ cup minced bamboo shoots
1 tablespoon each, light soy sauce and sesame oil
1 tablespoon dry sherry or rice wine
1 teaspoon coarse salt
⅛ teaspoon each, white pepper and honey or pure maple syrup
1 egg white, lightly beaten
YIELD: Six to eight servings

1. If preparing homemade wontons, sift the flours, baking powder, and salt 6 times into a mixing bowl. Make a well in the center of the mixture; add the egg whites and half the water, and mix until well blended. Add extra water gradually as necessary to hold the mixture together. Knead until smooth, cover with a damp cloth, and refrigerate for 1 hour.

2. Dust a hard surface with the cornstarch and roll out half the dough as thin as possible, about ¹⁄₁₆ inch in thickness. Cut into 3-inch squares and cover with a damp cloth until ready to fill. Repeat with the balance of pastry dough.

3. Remove the hard stalks from the cabbage; wash, drain, then dice. Place the

diced vegetable in a cloth and squeeze out as much moisture as possible.

4. In a bowl, combine the cabbage with the pork and the balance of the ingredients except the egg white, and blend thoroughly. Cup 1 wonton in the palm of 1 hand and fill the center with 1 tablespoon of the filling. Close your hand so that the sides of the wonton wrapper will meet and pinch together. Tap the dumpling on a hard surface to flatten its bottom. Repeat this process with the balance of wonton wrappers and filling.

5. Place each *dem sem* on a 2-inch square of waxed paper or aluminum foil and transfer to a steamer rack. Steam over boiling water for about 30 minutes. Serve hot—plain, with duck sauce, or with soy sauce flavored with vinegar to taste.

Bonus Ideas: Since egg rolls and wontons are made in the same manner, I usually roll out the dough and cut into 6-inch squares, which is the desired size for egg rolls. When I want to use them for wontons, I cut each larger square into quarters, making the 3-inch squares required for wontons.

If you wish to store wontons, flour them well, stack together, wrap in aluminum foil, and refrigerate or freeze until required. If brittle after thawing, cover with a damp cloth until they are pliable.

Any combination of beef, chicken, pork, fish, or seafood may be used for filling. Lettuce, scallions, or leeks may also be substituted for Chinese cabbage.

Walnuts and peanuts are often used for their flavor and crunchy texture in many dishes; many may be surprised that the Chinese also use peanut butter, in **Sweet Shanghai Wontons***. Five teaspoons of sesame seeds are heated and shuffled, without scorching, in a frying pan until they turn golden. The seeds are then blended with ¾ cup of peanut butter and ⅓ cup of honey or pure maple syrup into a paste. Using 50 wontons, fill the center of each with 1 scant teaspoon of filling. Fold, moisten, and pinch together the edges. Deep-fry in peanut oil that has reached 375° F for 2 minutes until golden. Drain on absorbent paper and serve.

CHWIN GUIN*
(Spring Rolls)

In the Chinese calendar, the first day of spring follows the Chinese New Year; and the Spring Roll, served with tea, is the traditional snack for family, friends, and guests.

12 homemade or purchased Spring Roll skins, 6 inches square (see wonton dough, page 248)
2 large dried black mushrooms
2 cups bean sprouts
½ cup shredded Chinese cabbage or spinach
½ cup shredded bamboo shoots
2 tablespoons light soy sauce
1 tablespoon dry sherry or rice wine
½ teaspoon coarse salt
⅛ teaspoon white pepper
2 tablespoons polyunsaturated oil
2 scallions, minced
¼ pound pork, chicken, or ham, or in combination
¼ cup minced raw shrimp
1 beaten egg white mixed with 1 tablespoon water
Polyunsaturated oil for frying
YIELD: Six servings

1. If preparing homemade Spring Roll skins, follow directions for homemade wontons in the recipe for **Cantonese Steamed Pork Dumplings.** Roll out the dough into 6-inch squares and set aside. Soak the mushrooms in warm water and drain the bean sprouts. Discard the stems, squeeze the mushrooms, and slice, combining with the cabbage, bean sprouts, and bamboo shoots. In a separate bowl, combine the soy sauce, sherry, salt, and pepper, and set both mixtures aside.

2. Heat the oil in a wok or skillet, then stir-fry the scallions until translucent. Add the pork or meat combination and cook over high heat for 4 minutes; then add the minced shrimp and stir-fry for 3 minutes longer. Stir in the reserved cabbage and soy sauce mixtures; stir-fry for 2 minutes, then remove from the heat.

3. Place 1 tablespoon of the filling in the middle of each Spring Roll skin. Fold the edge nearest to you over the filling; fold both sides over the filling, then roll up, sealing the remaining edge with some of the egg and water mixture. Prepare the balance of the Spring Rolls in the same manner. Heat the oil until it has reached 375° F, then deep-fry the Spring Rolls for about 5 minutes, or until golden brown. Drain on paper toweling and serve hot with duck sauce, mustard, or soy sauce flavored with vinegar.

Bonus Ideas: In Hong Kong, **Egg Rolls*** are prepared with the same filling as used in Spring Rolls; however, instead of the skins, thin pancakes are utilized as wrappers. These are prepared by beating 12 egg whites, 6 tablespoons polyunsaturated margarine or oil, and ¾ cups of white rye flour and cornstarch, 3½ teaspoons baking powder and ¾ teaspoon salt that have been sifted together 5 times. Pour enough of the smooth batter for a small pancake into a heavy-based pan or griddle; cook each pancake on one side only. The pancakes are filled, rolled, and deep-fried in the same manner as Spring Rolls.

HO GEE
SHIAO TUNG BAO*
(Steamed Bao with Turkey)

Chinese pastry used for stuffing and steaming is called *fun kuo*. With a variety of savory fillings, it becomes steamed *bao*.

Fun Kuo Dough:
1½ cups skim milk or water
2 teaspoons dry yeast (optional)
1½ cups cornstarch or potato flour
½ cup tapioca flour
1 tablespoon peanut or 1 teaspoon sesame oil

12 dried or ¼ pound shelled raw shrimp, minced
2 tablespoons dry sherry (optional)

6 dried black mushrooms
2 tablespoons peanut or corn oil
1 scallion, chopped
1 cup chopped turkey or chicken breast
1 cup chopped cabbage, celery, or spinach
¼ teaspoon coarse salt
⅛ teaspoon ground white pepper
2 teaspoons cornstarch
YIELD: Six servings

1. To prepare the dough, bring the skim milk to a boil. If using the yeast, dissolve in warm water. Sift the combined flours 3 times into a mixing bowl and add the milk combined with the optional yeast mixture. Mix until a soft dough is formed; add the oil and knead until smooth. Cover with a damp cloth and set aside in a warm place to rise for 1 hour. If yeast is not used, cover and set aside for 30 minutes.

2. Soak the shrimp in the sherry for 15 minutes; drain and mince the shrimp, discarding the liquid. Soak the mushrooms in warm water for 15 minutes; drain and reserve the liquid. Remove the hard stems and mince the mushrooms.

3. Heat 2 tablespoons of oil in a wok or skillet and stir-fry the scallion, mushrooms, turkey, and shrimp for 30 seconds. Add the shopped cabbage and stir-fry for 2 minutes longer. Add the seasonings and the cornstarch, mixed with ¼ cup of the reserved mushroom water; stir until the sauce thickens. Remove from the heat.

4. When the dough is ready, roll out half of it on a lightly oiled, hard surface into a 2-inch-wide long roll. Cut the roll into 12 ½-inch-wide slices, and flatten each slice to a width of 4 inches with the lightly oiled blade of a knife. Repeat with balance of the dough.

5. Place 1 scant tablespoon of the cooked filling into the center of each round of dough and wrap by gathering up the edges or folding into a half-moon shape. Place each *bao* on a 2-inch square of waxed paper and steam over boiling water for 15 minutes. Serve hot.

Bonus Ideas: Although traditional recipes call for stir-frying the ingredients for the filling, I don't find this necessary, since they will cook during the steaming process. After mixing the ingredients well, I set the mixture aside for 30 minutes to let the flavors blend, then proceed with the recipe.

Baos can be made with a variety of fillings to suit your taste and fancy; ½ pound of crabmeat or 1 cup of ground pork are popular ingredients. Half a cup of bamboo shoots can be substituted for the celery, cabbage, or spinach; and 2 chopped carrots, 2 tablespoons Chinese pickled lettuce, or 2 tablespoons of peanut butter are all ingredients you may wish to try.

Fillings can be sweetened with 1½ teaspoons of honey or pure maple syrup, especially when 3 cups of minced roast pork is the meat ingredient. To distinguish sweetened steamed dumplings, the Chinese dip a chopstick in red food coloring and make a dot on top of each sweet *bao*.

CHAO SHEK LOH*
(Snails Cantonese Style)

Although we are more familiar with terrestrial snails, the Chinese consider the smaller periwinkles (sea snails) a particular delicacy. And when eating snails, it is no breach of manners for the Chinese to make slurping sounds. This is particularly true in the case of periwinkles, which the Chinese prefer to eat by puckering their lips and quickly and noisily drawing the meat into their mouths. Of course, Westerners can eat these snails with a toothpick or snail fork—but when sharing snails with Chinese friends, this is an admission of defeat.

To provide the necessary suction for

drawing out the snail meat in the Chinese manner, however, it is necessary to puncture the tail end of the snail; this can be done with a hammer and a heavy duty nail.

3 pounds periwinkles
3 tablespoons peanut or corn oil
½ teaspoon sesame oil
3 each, ginger root slices, shredded, and garlic cloves, minced
6 scallions, chopped
½ teaspoon Tabasco or hot pepper sauce
1 tablespoon cornstarch mixed with 2 tablespoons chicken stock
1 tablespoon fermented black beans, soaked
2½ tablespoons light soy sauce
2 tablespoons bean sauce (hoisin jheung) (see Hard-to-Get Ingredients)
1¼ cups chicken stock or consommé
3 tablespoons dry sherry or rice wine
YIELD: Six to eight servings

1. Wash and soak the snails thoroughly in running cold water until the water remains clear. Periwinkle sea snails do not jut their heads out as do terrestrial snails, so only discard those that have an odor. If serving Chinese style, puncture a hole in the tail end of each snail, then rinse again in fresh water. Drain the snails and set aside.

2. Heat the combined oils in a wok or large skilllet and stir-fry the ginger, garlic, and scallions for 1 minute; add the Tabasco sauce. Place the snails in the sauce mixture and mix well until coated.

3. Add the balance of the ingredients except the sherry; cover and simmer over medium heat for about 5 minutes. Add the sherry and blend well. Simmer, covered,

for 1 minute before serving with boiled or steamed rice.

Bonus Ideas: One or two chili peppers can be used instead of the Tabasco sauce. Instead of the garlic sauce, try the periwinkles with **Chinese Red Seafood Sauce***. For six servings, combine ⅓ cup of ketchup, *hoisin* sauce, 1 teaspoon honey or pure maple syrup, 1 cup fish stock or clam juice, 1 tablespoon of cornstarch in 2 tablespoons of water, and ¼ teaspoon Tabasco or hot pepper sauce. This sauce is also appropriate for clams and oysters.

Terrestrial snails can be used either fresh or canned to prepare **Shanghai Snails with Spicy Sauce***. To serve six, prepare 3 dozen fresh or canned snails as in **Snails Bourguignonne.** Stir-fry with a spicy sauce made by first stir-frying 1 tablespoon each of shredded ginger and chopped scallions, then adding 2½ tablespoons each of light soy sauce and *hoisin* sauce and ¼ teaspoon of Tabasco sauce. Stuff this mixture into the shells, sprinkle with chopped parsley or coriander leaves, and steam for about 10 minutes until cooked. The stuffed snails are served hot in China as an appetizer with drinks.

HUNG-SHAO NUI SEH TO*
(Red-Simmered Tongue)

Red-simmering *(Hung-shao)* is an ancient Chinese braising or stewing process that takes its name from the reddish-brown color produced by the soy sauce in which the food is cooked. Most poultry and meat, including game, lend themselves admirably to this method, and red-simmered dishes are considered mandatory for any Chinese banquet.

Some of the sauce can be reserved as a starter for **Chinese Master Sauce***, which can be a perpetual sauce; among some Chinese, it is passed down from generation to generation. Sauce from any red-simmered dish can be used as a starter, but the reserved Master Sauce must be used regularly or brought to a boil weekly, and replenished with additional ingredients. If you have the patience to watch over a perpetual sauce, this is one of the simplest to maintain and is a richer sauce each time it is used.

Because of the considerable time required for red-cooking dishes, they are rarely prepared in restaurants except for formal banquets; even in Chinese homes they are prepared ahead of time. However, they are easily done at home since they require little attention during the cooking process and are suited to various cooking equipment—microwave oven, pressure cooker, slow cooking crock pot, or roman clay pot; they may also be cooked in an oven or on top of the range. Red-simmered meat should be parboiled first to seal in its juices.

1 5-pound fresh beef tongue

Red Simmering Sauce:
½ cup soy sauce, preferably a blend of
  light and dark
2 cups water
2 star anise
4 tablespoons dry sherry
1 teaspoon sesame oil
1 tablespoon each, honey and wine vinegar

8 Scallion Brushes (page 243)
YIELD: Six to eight servings

1. In a Dutch oven or large pan, bring to a boil enough water to cover the beef tongue. Add the meat and boil for 10 minutes; discarding the cooking water, drain and rinse the tongue in cold water.

2. Trim the tongue as necessary; place back in the Dutch oven with the ingredients for the sauce. Cover and simmer for 3 hours, or until tender, adding boiling water as necessary. Adjust the sauce with salt or honey to taste as necessary. Slice and serve garnished with Scallion Brushes.

Bonus Ideas: The reserved sauce should be refrigerated. If used as a starter for **Chinese Master Sauce,** it is important to reuse the sauce weekly with other meats or poultry, or bring it to a boil at least once each week. When the sauce has been used several times, enrich it with ¼ cup each of dry sherry and soy sauce, 2 shredded slices of ginger, ½ teaspoon of honey, and ⅛ teaspoon of salt.

The red-cooking technique can be used with a 5-pound capon, chicken, duck or half of a turkey as in **Hung-Shao Hoa Chi.** Dip the poultry in boiling water to toughen its skin; rinse in cold water and drain. Place in a Dutch oven with the sauce; cover and cook for 3 hours over low heat until tender. Adjust the honey, sherry, and salt to taste before cutting into serving pieces and garnishing with **Scallion Brushes.**

Red Savory Chicken or other poultry can be prepared in less time if cut into serving pieces and stir-fried first in a wok. Cut the chicken and stir-fry in a wok with 2 tablespoons of peanut oil, or dip in cold water and sear while still moist until the pieces are golden brown. Add 1 teaspoon each of minced garlic, ginger, and scallions, and stir-fry with the chicken for 2 minutes.

Add the sauce and toss the chicken until entirely covered, then add 1½ cups of broth or water. Bring to a boil; then cover and simmer over low heat for 45 minutes or until tender. If necessary, thicken with 1 tablespoon of cornstarch mixed with 2 tablespoons of water.

To prepare **Red Savory Chicken with Vegetables,** during the last 15 minutes of cooking, vegetables can also be added; onions, chopped celery, cabbage, string beans, bamboo shoots, water chestnuts, and/or whole dried presoaked mushrooms.

Red-Simmered Beef, Pork and **Lamb** are made in the same manner, with 3 pounds of lean meat suitable for braising that is first parboiled, rinsed in cold water, placed in a Dutch oven with the sauce, then covered and simmered for about 3 hours or until tender.

CHA SHIU*
(Cantonese Roast Pork Strips)

Wherever there is a Chinese community you will find shops that have a prominently displayed barbecue unit with strips of roast pork hanging on hooks. Pork is the most popular meat among Chinese, and no method of preparation is more popular than barbecuing.

Although preparing Roast Pork Strips at home requires some ingenuity, the results will be worth your while. *Cha Shiu* can be refrigerated or frozen for future use, so I recommend you make additional quantities to reserve for future meals; this dish can also be prepared in an oven, over a charcoal grill, or hibachi.

2 pounds boneless pork butt or fresh ham

Pork Marinade:
5 tablespoons light soy sauce
1½ tablespoons honey, pure maple syrup, or fruit sugar
1 tablespoon hoisin sauce (see Hard-to-Get Ingredients)
1 tablespoon oyster sauce (optional)
1 tablespoon each, minced fresh ginger and scallions
2 drops red food coloring (optional)
2 tablespoons peanut or sesame oil
3 sprigs of fresh parsley or coriander
YIELD: Six to eight servings

1. Have your butcher cut the meat (along the grain), dividing it lengthwise into 4 strips. Place the strips in a ceramic or glass bowl with the Marinade and mix until the meat is well coated. Cover and refrigerate for at least 3 hours, or overnight, turning the meat occasionally.

2. Using 4 S hooks (which are available in hardware stores), or improvising hooks with heavy wire, impale each piece of meat about ½ inch from one end. Preheat oven to 450° F and place a roasting pan with a thin layer of water at the bottom of your oven to catch the meat drippings. Hook the meat strips on the uppermost oven rack. Roast for 25 minutes. Glaze by brushing the pieces with peanut or sesame oil, and roast 5 minutes more until done.

3. Slice the pork against the grain, and arrange the slices on a warm platter garnished with parsley sprigs. Serve with the dripping juices or the heated marinade, or with plum sauce, Chinese hot pepper, or mustard.

Bonus Ideas: Honey can be used to glaze the pork strip during the last 5 minutes of roasting. If you wish to prepare your own Chinese-style **Mustard Dip,** moisten 3 tablespoons of mustard powder with enough dry vermouth or rice wine for the desired consistency. If freezing, tightly wrap the roast pork in aluminum foil; when ready for use, reheat in an oven without unwrapping or thawing.

Roast pork can be minced for use in *baos,* or sliced for sandwiches. For snacks or appetizers, commercially prepared frozen party rolls can be steamed for about 15 minutes and used to prepare sandwiches with the sliced roast pork.

A personal favorite is **Aburage with Roast Pork***. Deep-fried bean curd (available as *dow foo pok* in Chinese shops or as *aburage* in Japanese stores) is cut into 12 2-inch squares for six servings. Make crisscross cuts part way through the bean curd to form a pouch. Stuff each pouch with a portion of roast pork filling made by combining ¾ pound of minced roast pork, 2 minced scallions, and ¼ teaspoon honey or pure maple syrup. Steam covered over boiling water for about 10 minutes and serve hot.

LIT TSOO TAN KAO
(Peking Dust)

One of the rare Chinese desserts, traditionally served after soup at the end of formal banquets. This slimming version uses frozen yogurt in place of the heavy whipped cream that customarily is used. Chinese candied fruits are included in some Chinese recipes.

2 pounds chestnuts or 3 8-ounce cans of chestnut purée
1½ cups water
⅓ cup honey, pure maple syrup, or fruit sugar
3 teaspoonfuls Candied Fruits (optional; page 91)
1 quart frozen Vanilla Yogurt (page 307)
½ cup honey or pure maple syrup
2 teaspoons light corn syrup
YIELD: Six to eight servings

1. If using canned chestnut purée, proceed to step 2. If not, make crisscross slashes in each chestnut, bring chestnuts to a boil with water to cover, and cook for 20 minutes. Drain and shell the chestnuts, then blanch with boiling water; the chestnuts should be sufficiently tender to purée. If not, cook boiling water until tender. Purée the chestnuts through a food mill or in an electric blender into a smooth consistency.

2. Blend the purée with the honey and arrange the mixture in the center of each of 6 round dessert dishes. Using a melon scoop, place 5 small balls of the frozen yogurt around the rim of each dish and 1 ball on top of the purée mixture. Place a piece of candied fruit on each yogurt ball.

3. Boil the honey and corn syrup mixture until it registers 300° F on a candy thermometer. Using a thin-pronged hors d'oeuvre fork, spin long threads by pulling quickly from the mixture. Arrange the golden strawlike threads over each dish and serve slightly chilled.

Bonus Ideas: Instead of candied fruit, 1 cup of glazed shelled pecans or walnuts can be used. Bring a pint of water to a boil with the nutmeats; then drain off the water. Add ⅓ cup of honey, pure maple syrup, or fruit sugar, and evenly coat the nuts. Spread the coated nuts on wax paper or a lightly oiled platter to dry for 30 minutes. Deep-fry the nuts in hot oil (375° F) until they are entirely glazed. With a slotted spoon, transfer the glazed nuts to a lightly oiled platter until ready for use.

• • •

And now, let's explore the menus and recipes of the most diversified cuisine in the world—our own! The final leg of our tour takes us back to the United States, which, thanks to the many ethnic groups that make up its vast population, affords a truly distinctive international cuisine.

UNITED STATES

THE CUISINE IN PERSPECTIVE

"Americans have the most catholic tastes of any people in the world."
—George Lang, cookbook author and restaurant consultant

America, the land of promise, has truly become the melting pot of the world, and each of us has two heritages: the common heritage of the American past and the individual heritage of the ethnic center from which our forefathers originally came. First came the English Puritans, who settled in New England in the early seventeenth century; they were bolstered by settlers from Holland, as the Colonies spread north and south along the Atlantic Coast. Even before we acquired the southern and midwestern parts of our country through the Louisiana Purchase, the Spanish and the French had imparted strong ethnic influences, as did their black slaves. After the American Revolution, other Europeans began to migrate to our shores in ever increasing numbers, moving farther and farther west, until finally the great gold rush of the mid-1800s attracted the Chinese, Japanese, and Mexicans, who became settlers.

The story of American cuisine, however, begins in the early colonies of New England and Virginia. Most of the women who came to settle in New England were young brides who had been taught cooking skills by their English mothers. At first, out of necessity, their approach to food was in terms of basic sustenance, since most of their energy had to be given to the building of homes and the cultivation of land. Fortunately, they were able to rely on the abundant foods they found in the New World. Many of these foods had been unknown to them in their former homeland. Among the new foods were sweet potatoes, pumpkins, squash, native beans, and maize (corn). Here also were wild game, turkeys, and an almost unbelievable abundance of fish and seafood, including huge oysters, clams, and lobsters.

Initially, the severe winters were the greatest threat to survival. The Puritan wives soon learned to protect their families by maintaining larders of salted, corned, and smoked meats, salted cod, and dried vegetables, roots, and herbs. The Colonial diet changed with the seasons. During the winter, meals depended on provisions from the larder; but corned or dried dishes gave way to fresh vegetables, fish, and fruits when the warmer weather arrived.

Once homes were built and the land cultivated, the Puritans began to learn from the Indians how to plant (and cook) corn and other native crops, such as beans, peas, pumpkins, melons, sweet potatoes, and cranberries. The Indians also taught them how to tap maple trees. Ships routinely returned from England with cows to provide fresh milk for the children, and soon all the milk that was not consumed was churned and pressed into cheeses that could be stored for long periods. The variety of ingredients inreased, but still the Puritanical sense of frugality remained. Nothing was wasted, and even the residue from cheese-making was fed to the hogs. Breads and other dishes like baked beans were baked in the same oven to conserve as much heat as possible. With time, the more refined English cookery they had learned at home was adapted by the Puritan women to the native ingredients available to them—especially corn: pancakes and griddle cakes were made with cornmeal. The Puritans also produced thick, wholesome chowders and a variety of pies. Many of the innovations developed by the Puritans are still traditions of New England cuisine, including the clambake, boiled dinners, lobsters boiled in seaweed and served with butter sauce, and Thanksgiving turkey.

Thesettlements in Virginia, on the other hand, benefited from the more temperate southern climate. Here, in addition to an abundance of seafood from the coastal waters, the early settlers found venison, turkey, and wild geese, as well as native vegetables, such as the Jerusalem artichoke, broccoli, and watercress. With the cultivation of tobacco, the Colonies became prosperous, and slaves from Africa were brought over to help run the large plantations. At first, hogs were raised; and cured ham, spare ribs, and chitterlings became staples.

Here, too, the settlers learned to cultivate and cook corn, which with time developed into such traditional dishes as hominy grits, cornbread, biscuits, and fritters. As the Colonies spread even farther south, the English were bolstered by the Scotch, the Irish, and the French—all of whom influenced the new Colonial cuisine. While the Portuguese were arriving in Providence and Cape Cod, settlers from the early French colony of Acadia in Nova Scotia migrated to southern Louisiana and intermingled with the Spanish and the native Choctaw Indians of the area. The Indians taught the settlers to cultivate and use their native roots and herbs, notably sassafras, which the African slaves, who did the cooking called filé. In their skillful hand, filé became an important ingredient of the distinctive Southern **Gumbo.**

These early ethnic influences came from either of two extremes: from the very low-class, back-of-the-stove, strong-flavored cookery of the working class; and the refined cookery of the wealthy aristocracy. A perfect example of the latter was the multitalented Thomas Jefferson, who introduced extraordinary dinners and fine imported wines to the White House. But even before he became President, he was fascinated with the idea of refining American cuisine. Influenced during his travels abroad and by his French chef, Jefferson introduced many culinary concepts and new ingredients to his compatriots.

It was not until the Industrial Revolution that a substantial middle class came into being in our country, and America began to become a true melting pot. Immigrants from virtually every ethnic group flooded into the country, and a crossover of ethnic influences became evident in our cuisine.

As John Mass expresses it in his book *The Gingerbread Age* (Rinehart & Company, Inc.), "For better or for worse, the period between 1840 and 1880 made America what it is today. The Civil War was such a traumatic event that it has somewhat overshadowed the many other dramatic developments of this era of our consciousness. At the outset, America was a largely agricultural country on the outer fringes of Western Civilization—at the close, the United States was one of the great industrial powers of the world. The population tripled from 17 to 50 million. Twelve states were admitted to the Union. In 1840 most travelers and goods still moved on coach, wagon and canalboat; there were only 2,800 miles of railroad track against 95,000 miles forty years later. The technological advances of this era are unmatched. The telegraph, the ocean steamer, modern machine tools, farm machinery, petroleum, photography, the sewing machine, the telephone, electric lighting, all were invented and introduced during those forty years. The social changes were even more decisive—from this era date our present two-party system, direct popular elections, our public school system, all our graduate schools, most scientific and professional societies, the first large corporations, mass immigration."

Thiswas the period during which the Midwest attracted German, Scandinavian, and Polish immigrants; California attracted the Chinese, Japanese, and Mexicans; and the Italian, Irish, Jewish, Romanian, and immigrants from other ethnic centers settled all through our expanding new country. Each brought with him favorite dishes and cooking concepts which were shared with new compatriots. Italian lasagna, German wursts and sauerkraut, Romanian pastrami, Irish corned beef and cabbage, and Scandinavian cheeses, among other dishes, soon became staples of the new American cuisine. Our hard-working middle class, bolstered by immigrants from all over the globe, had come into being. The intermingling of ethnic influences now became dramatically apparent in the development of an American/International cuisine.

We discussed these influences with Paul Kovi, co-owner with Tom Margittai of The Four Seasons restaurant in New York City, both of whom we will be meeting during our American tour. "From the turn of the century," Paul Kovi told me, "up to the 1930s, or perhaps with the discovery of the can opener, the United

States probably had the finest home cooking in the world. Those who came to America from a village or little town in Europe, China, and so many other places, came usually because they could not find their own niche at home. Nevertheless, the immigrant was a little more adventurous than the rest of the people in his community. In all probability, whatever his specialty, he had more initiative; and he wanted a great deal more from life when he came to the United States. He brought with him his know-how and that initiative, and when he arrived here, new opportunities began to open up for him. He began to prosper, and one of the very first expressions of well-being was that he wanted to eat better. Now, he and his wife decided that they were going to cook better, and eat better, than they were able to back home. First of all, he had different and usually better ingredients now available to him. Items that he didn't know even existed back home, such as grapefruits, limes, or whatever, were now his to incorporate into his own concept of cooking. Second, the only influence on him in his old country had been neighbors with the same nationality and traditions as his. Here he was surrounded by Swedish immigrants, Italians, Greeks, Poles, Hungarians—you name it! He was influenced by many ethnic groups, by a large variety and availability of ingredients, and the fact that he had more money than previously to spend for cooking. There just was no such situation where he had come from. Just think that in a small town half the size of Chattanooga, a country fair offered 150 different entries of strawberry marmalade; there simply was no such thing in Europe or wherever he came

from. But here, because of the various ethnic influences on his own cooking, we constantly find a tremendous number of varieties of every kind of specialty dish at all of the fairs in the different states and regions of this country."

We are now fifty states, including the most recent additions of Alaska and Hawaii, and still the intermingling of ethnic influences on our cuisine keeps going on. The Indians and early Russian settlers were major influences on the Alaskan pioneers who built their cuisine around the abundant game and seafood available. Salmon, herring, and king crab are staples, as are moose, elk, reindeer, and wild ducks—and, of course, their famous sourdough breads.

Hawaii, in its own way, is also a melting pot. The native Polynesians have been joined by Americans and Puerto Ricans, as well as by large populations of Japanese, Koreans, Chinese, and Filipinos—all of whom have influenced Hawaiian cuisine. In turn, this cuisine has influenced our own in the use of pineapples, coconuts, avocados, and macadamia nuts—and, above all, has introduced us to the outstanding specialty of Hawaiian cuisine: the luau, in which a whole pig and chickens are cooked in underground ovens lined with banana leaves.

In addition to the abundant new foods, the early settlers to America discovered grapes, fruits, and vegetables from which they made wine, and grains for making beer and whiskey. The Vikings who first visited our Eastern shores were so impressed with the grapes they found that they named our land Vineland; however, the early English settlers discovered that these grapes produced poor wine.

1 pound lean beef, preferably London broil
   or flank steak
½ pound fresh broccoli florets with 2-inch
   stems
2 egg whites

Beef Marinade:
2 egg whites, lightly beaten
2 tablespoons cornstarch
¼ teaspoon ground white pepper
1 clove garlic, mashed
1 teaspoon dry sherry or rice wine
¼ teaspoon honey or pure maple syrup
   (optional)

1 onion cut into 1-inch slices
2 red sweet peppers cut into 1-inch strips
2 scallions, finely chopped
2 tablespoons each, light soy sauce and
   oyster sauce
2 slices fresh ginger root
2 tablespoons dry sherry or rice wine
2 tablespoons chicken stock or consommé
2 tablespoons finely diced cooked ham or
   Canadian bacon
YIELD: Four to six servings

1. Trim the beef of excess fat, and with a sharp knife lightly score both sides with crisscross slashes. Cut into 1-inch cubes. Boil the broccoli florets for 10 minutes; drain and set aside. Poach the egg whites and set aside in a warm place.

2. Combine the ingredients for the beef Marinade and toss the beef cubes in the mixture until completely coated. Cover and let stand for 15 minutes.

3. Heat the oil in a wok or skillet until almost smoking and sear the beef, stir-frying constantly, for 30 seconds; then add the onions and pepper and stir-fry for 3 minutes. Remove, drain, and set the meat mixture aside.

4. Heat the wok again, adding 1 tablespoon of oil if necessary; then stir-fry the scallions for 30 seconds. Add the balance of the ingredients except the broccoli, poached egg white, and diced ham; continue stir-frying for 30 seconds. Return the meat mixture to the wok and stir-fry for 2 minutes. Serve immediately in the center of a warm platter, garnishing with the broccoli around the border, and top with the egg whites and diced ham.

Bonus Ideas: Many of your favorite vegetables can be combined with beef in a similar manner: Chinese cabbage, cauliflower, mustard greens, and asparagus tips, for example.

NG HEUNG NGAU YUK*
(Five Fragrances Spiced Beef)

Here is a dish that is not stir-fried but stewed—with the distinctive **Chinese Five Fragrances Spices,** a combination of star anise, fennel, anise pepper, cloves, and cinnamon. If necessary, the flavor can be approximated by using equal portions of anise seeds, fresh ginger, fennel, cloves and/or cinnamon, or allspice alone. Since it is a very strong currylike addition to any dish, very little is used.

3 pounds boneless chuck roast, whole, or
   shins of beef

Marinade:
1 tablespoon Five Fragrances spices, or 6
   star anise, tied in cheesecloth
6 tablespoons light soy sauce

Dandelions, elderberries, and other ingredients were discovered to produce more satisfactory wines. Although there were no apples indigenous to our land, the Puritans had the foresight to bring apple seeds with them. In fact, the first native New Englander, born aboard the *Mayflower* in the harbor, was to grow up to plant apple seeds. John Chapman, as legend has it, ventured out beyond the Alleghenies introducing the first apples and cider. Among the early settlers, cider became the country drink and was also used to make vinegars, including tarragon, mint, garlic, and dill vinegars.

Some beer was made in rural kitchens from various roots and plants, but it was more than a century before beer became a popular beverage with meals. Whiskey, however, and rum (made in New England from imported molasses) were in production before the end of the seventeenth century. Rum was initially the more popular in the American colonies, and first efforts at distilling whiskey by the Dutch took place in 1660 on what is now Staten Island in New York Harbor. However, it wasn't until 1789, the year President Washington was inaugurated, that a Baptist minister, the Reverend Elijah Craig, set up the first bourbon stills in Georgetown, Virginia (now part of Kentucky). The corn mash was stored in oak barrels that had been charred to remove any trace of their original contents, such as flour, dried fish, or salt pork. Bourbon gets its flavor and distinctive amber color from the charcoaled oak of the barrels. Reverend Craig sold his whiskey before it had had a chance to mellow and age, and so bourbon was born—and with it an American tradition. Eventually rye was substituted for corn, to produce rye whiskeys; and corn whiskey was made from a predominantly corn base and aged in barrels for two years.

The story of wine in America is a dramatic one. It began in 1769, when a Franciscan priest, Junipero Serra, planted the first wine grapes at the San Diego mission in California to meet the needs of his church. Soon, these efforts had expanded to the famous twenty-one missions of the Spanish Franciscan friars, and wine-making flourished until the Mexican government confiscated the mission properties in the 1840s. Fortunately, two decades earlier, the American John Chapman (this John Chapman was probably named after the legendary Johnny Appleseed) had settled in California and had planted his vines at the *pueblo* of Los Angeles, an act that was to be followed a few years later by Louis Vignes, from the Bordeaux region of France, who was the first to plant vines of the classic European grape varieties. Vignes developed a reputation for producing the best wine and brandy in California, and encouraged other Frenchmen to join in wine growing. During the gold rush in '49, Agoston Haraszty, the father of modern California viticulture, arrived on the scene form Hungary via Wisconsin. He introduced and planted more than 100,000 choice foreign vines from France, Italy, The Netherlands, Prussia, Bavaria, Spain, Switzerland, and England.

About twenty years later, a worldwide calamity occurred in the form of an epidemic of root lice that virtually devastated the vineyards of Europe as well as those in California. The embryonic growth of fine grapes in California was almost permanently destroyed by blight. When it was discovered that the rootstock of an inferior grape vine, indigenous to the eastern and central regions of the country, was not susceptible to the root louse, both California and European vineyards imported the resistant rootstock and successfully grafted it to the classic vines, which are still the source of some of the finest wines available.

Today, the California wine industry provides wine for three-quarters of our population of wine users. Yet wine growing in America is still a relatively young industry, and it has only been a decade since the concept of designating vintages was established. Many international experts, however, consider many of our American wines to be the equals of French and Italian wines. In fact, some of our wines are already available as imports in Europe, and leading French wine producers, like Moët, have already acquired vineyards in California—as did some of their compatriots a century and half ago.

Considerably behind in the volume of production and still second to California in other ways is the Finger Lakes district of New York State, which is noted for its sparkling "champagne" wines made from grapes grown on vines that were transplanted from the Champagne country of France. Here again, when years ago a blight destroyed the original French vines, French wine makers were able to obtain cuttings from New York State to transplant back to their original homeland.

Other states, like Ohio, have a growing number of wineries, and some experts believe that Oregon is a potential major wine producer of the future. Obviously the growth of production is an indication of the ever increasing consumption of wine by Americans for use at the table and in cooking. Our superior wines, like American cookery, have been influenced strongly by many ethnic traditions; they have become a fitting complement to the American specialties that constitute one of the outstanding cuisines of the world.

A COOK'S TOUR OF THE UNITED STATES

Selecting an American city for the final stage of our tour might at first seem difficult: Boston, New Orleans, or even Williamsburg, Virginia—the birthplace of some of the cuisine of our Colonial past—are obvious candidates. But today the specialties of those regions are only a few of the many that can be called truly American; for the cookery of the United States, like American society itself, is almost unbelievably complex. It is both dynamic and ever changing, reflecting the multinational ethnic influences of the American population.

We have accordingly arrived at the one city that is fully representative of the contemporary culinary scene in the United States: New York—that melting pot *par excellence,* the mammoth capital of the worlds of finance, art, and entertainment, the gastronomic center of the country and indeed of the world. On the streets of New York, you will meet people of every conceivable national and racial origin. You will mingle with Puerto Ricans, Blacks, Jews, Poles, Italians; with recent immigrants from Hong Kong and India; with expensively dressed businessmen and with the distressingly poor.

Here also you will find every conceivable type of restaurant: for the rich, such elegant and expensive establishments as Lutèce, La Caravelle, and La Côte Basque; for the not-so-rich, numerous coffee shops, tiny Hispanic restaurants, and other eating places. In Chinatown (one of the country's largest), literally hundreds of bustliing (and inexpensive) restaurants feature specialties of every region of China. Adjacent to Chinatown, New York's Little Italy offers Neapolitan, Northern Italian, and Sicilian cuisines. And the city has many other ethnic sections: a German quarter on and around Eighty-sixth Street in Manhattan, Indian communities in midtown and on Long Island; Slavic and Jewish districts throughout the city; and numerous Hispanic communities—all offering typical ethnic restaurants. More and more, these ethnic restaurants are spreading throughout the city and its suburbs, and are no longer solely dependent for patronage on customers from the ethnic community.

New York is also the center of food research and worldwide restaurant operations; it is a huge laboratory in which new culinary ideas are conceived and tested. To gain an insight into the dynamics of the food industry on today's grand scale, we will visit the fabulous complex of restaurants called Windows on the World atop the World Trade Center. We will also explore the crosscurrents of today's thinking on culinary developments: we will talk to the owners and chefs of the now classic Four Seasons restaurant; we will meet with excellent cooks and authorities on re-

gional cuisines; and we will ask questions of noted writers, food consultants, and other experts.

Many knowledgeable people believe that the Four Seasons restaurant may have originated what is now known as *nouvelle cuisine*—years before it became the trademark of Paul Bocuse and his *bande à Bocuse*. Interestingly, it was in the kitchens of The Four Seasons that Bocuse himself, the Troisgros brothers, and Alain Chapel, among others, first cooked in America, with the encouragement of Tom Margittai and Paul Kovi, the co-owners of this distinctive center of gastronomic delight.

We asked Messrs. Margittai and Kovi about their experience with the new cuisine. Paul Kovi said, "I think the term *nouvelle cuisine* was born here at The Four Seasons. I recall that when Paul Bocuse came here the very first time with his agent Yanou Collart, they referred to Bocuse's approach as the '*grande cuisine française.*' They were sitting with me in the corner of the bar, and I said, 'You know, Yanou, the *grande cuisine française* may be a great name, but we already have *la grande cuisine* and *haute cuisine française*—so what's the difference? What you should do is find a name that says "new" cuisine.' And then instantly she began referring to Bocuse's dishes as '*nouvelle, nouvelle.*' 'You're absolutely right,' she said. 'It's got to be *la nouvelle cuisine.*'" (A year later, Yanou Collart disclaimed this story, saying *nouvelle cuisine* was the creation of the famous culinary team of Gault and Millan.)

Besides introducing the *nouvelle cuisine* chefs to America, The Four Seasons is responsible, some believe, for many of the innovations of the lighter cuisine. George Lang, the international food consultant and former director of The Four Seasons for Restaurant Associates, says, "Bocuse didn't bring a blessed thing to *nouvelle cuisine,* nor did any of the others, beyond what we were already doing at The Four Seasons." Charles Bell, executive vice-president for Hilton International, who is responsible for the creation and operation of all of the restaurants in the Hilton hotels in more than fifty foreign countries, goes even further. "A lot of the *nouvelle cuisine,*" he says, "really started in the United States in terms of the innovation of preparing basically simpler foods. I think we're being ripped off a little bit. The Four Seasons really did a lot of it many years ago before these concepts became popular in France."

Joseph Baum, formerly of Windows on the World, whom we will be meeting later during our tour of that restaurant, was for many years president of Restaurant Associates, which created The Four Seasons. Reflecting on the original menus he created with Executive Chef Albert Stockli when the restaurant first opened late in 1957, Joseph Baum told me, "In my opinion, the leaner feeling we strove for in our menus was the beginning of what I call 'my *minceur.*' In fact, if you look at the original menus, you'll still see many of these dishes on Tom's and Paul's menus—and I think they are doing a terrific job. You will find that a great many of the original dishes are still there after twenty years. Also, we were innovative in preparing our sauces by reduction, without any thickening agents." Barbara Kafka, the consultant who did much of the research

for the menus at Windows on the World, added, "You had already started then the business of garnishing food with food, rather than with artificial masking things that were put there purely for decorative effect." "Absolutely," Joseph Baum added. "There never was a buffet or an hors d'oeuvre that was decorated other than with vegetables and vegetable carving—which at that time was an innovation that we had introduced."

Sipping a cup of espresso with Tom Margittai, we discussed his and Paul Kovi's current approach to food at The Four Seasons. "We agreed," Tom said, "that probably the best and simplest cuisine was 'contemporary New York,' which reflects all ethnic groups in New York City and the best of the world's ethnic cuisines." In previous visits to The Four Seasons, I was aware of many innovative specialties and a lighter cuisine with apparent Chinese and Japanese influences. I pointed this out. "Of course," Tom responded. "Specifically, we were among the first to use the Japanese technique of shredding vegetables, and the Chinese technique of stir-frying. We place a great deal of emphasis on vegetable cookery. Vegetables have usually been treated in the past as a side dish, while we have tried to elevate them into something quite different. We don't overcook them, we don't blanch them, and we don't purée them, but we do combine vegetables in an exciting way." I wondered whether this might be a vegetarian approach. "No, not at all," Tom pointed out. "It's an approach to simple, fast, and healthy preparation of vegetables without sauces."

The idea of preparing vegetables quickly and simply reminded us of the Buddhist mock dishes of China and of vegetarianism in general. Tom reflected that the Chinese mock meat dishes are not unlike those served in kosher vegetarian restaurants in New York City's Lower East Side. He averred that Chinese cuisine is far more complex than French. He did not think there is a strong vegetarian tendency in France. Warming to his subject, Tom stressed, however, that vegetables always have been important in French cuisine. "They had the wonderful thing we called *'primeurs,'* the first things in season. Everybody was anxious to eat new asparagus during the asparagus season, new lettuce during the lettuce season, and so forth. We have the advantage here in America of having these new vegetables raining on us all the time. In France there may have been 10,000 items, but these were not easily accessible to 40 million Frenchmen—so mainly the French enjoyed the new vegetables when they specifically were in season. On that score, we Americans are quite spoiled."

I had read that when some of the noted French chefs, such as Paul Bocuse and Alain Chapel, first came to cook their specialties at The Four Seasons, they brought hundreds of pounds of fresh and special ingredients, because they assumed these ingredients were not available here. When Alain Chapel came on his second trip, however, the only thing he brought along was truffles, having learned of the availability of all the other ingredients he might need. Tom said it had been the same with the other chefs who had come to cook their specialties at The Four Sea-

sons. "Without blowing our own horn," he added, "we really pioneered the concept of bringing over the famous chefs. Bocuse cooked his first meal in America here, so did Troisgros, Le Nôtre, Chapel, Guérard—they all cooked their first meals here; and this was their first introduction to America. The press and the public picked it up, and there was a great deal of interest."

Having a second cup of espresso with Tom Margittai, we discussed the relatively limited menus featured by virtually all of the French chefs specializing in *la nouvelle cuisine.* Tom pointed out that when they came here, some would cook only one meal, some would cook for several days, others for a number of weeks—but always with limited menus. Even in their own restaurants in France, they have very restricted menus. This is a lot easier for them than it is here, with more diversified menus and a greater percentage of repeat customers. Having the same menu for several months gives them plenty of opportunity to perfect individual dishes. "But it isn't quite the same challenge as it is here," Tom reminded us.

At this point Paul Kovi joined our conversation. It was about 3:30 P.M. and a particularly good time for restaurateurs to relax between the pressure periods of luncheon and dinner. Paul is considered one of the outstanding experts on wines in America, and has a reputation as one of the pioneers and strongest advocates of American, especially Californian, wines. I knew that French wine growers are now buying vineyards in our country; that France is the greatest importer of Italian wines, which the French incorporate into their *vin ordinaire;* and I wondered whether our California wines would ever be imported by the French, along with Italian, German, and African wines, for the same purpose. I grasped the opportunity to question Paul Kovi on the subject. "It's simply a matter of expense and economics," he said, "and in the past few years, we are getting closer and closer economically. When the economics warrant it, I am convinced that our production of wines will compete with the production of other countries for importation by France." Paul added that the Europeans are beginning seriously to appreciate the quality of our California wines. "If our wines are put to a testing," he said, "the European specialist doesn't have to be hit over the head or go through an intellectual exercise. He will say it *is* a fine wine. There is no question about it."

Having been in Paris during the exciting fall season, when *Beaujolais nouveau* is the rage of that city, I wondered why we in America did not have a similar enthusiasm for our young wines. Paul thought that the excitement is not for the new wines as such, but rather is an expression of tradition, part of a ritual. He pointed out that in France there are hundreds of wine societies and hundreds of special holidays connected with food and wine. Here, these influences are just on the verge of development: "The wine societies, the food societies, the holidays, the country fairs—it's just starting. Why, it's only ten years ago that we came out with our first vintage wines. Before that, the wine producers would say that all vintages are great and steady, but we know that isn't so. The past two years there has been a

tremendous dryness in California, so every vintage is different. Still, we are very young in this regard."

I mentioned my preference for slightly cooling a red wine, especially in overheated restaurants and those that improperly store their wines over electric motors and refrigerator units. "Is it traditional snobbishness," I asked, "that accounts for the imperious reactions waiters have when I ask them to cool a red wine?" Paul Kovi reflected. "Snobbishness," he said, "is part of the whole nuance of wine. Actually, snobbishness is part of life: everyone is snobbish about food, about what they wear, their eating preferences, the places they go to—and about their wine. Regarding the temperatures of wine, Paul maintains that one should start with a cellar temperature of about 60° F. White wines are chilled from that temperature; red wines, cool to start with, should be brought up to room temperature slowly, which permits one to enjoy the bouquet of the wine. Room temperature for wines, of course, was set up before the days of central heating. It should definitely be in the 60s, and never higher than 68° F. As to chilling a red wine, Paul said, "Not chilling, perhaps, but cooling it to bring it down to the 60s—and letting it breathe properly. Too many restaurants store wines improperly in overheated spaces. It ruins the wine within two months!"

Since Paul Kovi had to leave for another appointment, I asked Tom Margittai to name the major influences on him and other restaurateurs in this country, especially with respect to the evolution of an American/International cuisine. He mentioned Claude C. Philippe of the Waldorf-

Astoria, a major factor, he said, in training great hotelmen. But Philippe, according to Tom, was not as important as Henri Soulé. "Soulé is the father, the creator of the great French restaurants in this country. However, I would say that the individual who most influenced restaurant cuisine in America, especially in terms of international and ethnic cuisines, is Joseph H. Baum of Restaurant Associates—without equivocation or any doubt." Restaurant Associates was formed by Abraham F. Wechsler, owner of the Rikers Coffee-Shop chain in New York, to develop new concepts in restaurants. Jerry Brody was president. Joseph Baum joined Restaurant Associates in 1953 and, working closely with Brody, began putting together an impressive team of specialists, including Chef Albert Stockli, to create their first specialty restaurant, the Newarker at New Jersey's Newark Airport. "Jerry gave Joe Baum *carte blanche,*" Tom said, "and Joe proved himself to be a very, very thorough individual and a great innovator. He is probably the most outstanding restaurant man in his field in our era, including Soulé. Joe Baum changed the whole tenor and concept of Restaurant Associates, and the Newarker was the first restaurant in this new concept. This was followed by the Hawaiian Room in the Hotel Lexington, the first Polynesian restaurant in New York City. There followed the Forum, The Four Seasons, the Brasserie, Tower Suite, Charley O's, Charlie Brown's, the Trattoria, Zum Zum, and others.

Among the impressive number of restaurateurs who became part of Restaurant Associates and were certainly influenced by Joseph Baum were, besides Tom Margittai and Paul Kovi, George Lang, Alan Lewis, director of Windows on the World, and Stuart Levin, owner of Top of the Park. "No matter where you go," Tom continued, "you will find R.A. alumni from the Joe Baum days, anywhere in the world. I know you are particularly interested in the intermingling influences of ethnic cuisines. Certainly, Joe Baum introduced in a very serious vein, various ethnic cuisines of the world to America. For example, Alsatian cuisine in the Brasserie; Polynesian in the Hawaiian Room; Latin-American cuisines at La Fonda del Sol. He created an original restaurant and recipes in the Forum; and in The Four Seasons he created an original, successful, and contemporary New York restaurant that encompasses the excellence of all ethnic cuisines, provided that they are seasonal. In the Trattoria, he introduced good and modern Italian cuisine, not the garlic and oil variety we had known; Charley O's was Irish; Charlie Brown's Ale & Chop House was English; and now at Windows on the World, he is utilizing the best of all the world's cuisines." We will be meeting Mr. Baum—and Alan Lewis—at Windows on the World.

At this point, Executive Chef Joseph Seppi Renggli joined us. A Swiss who trained in his own country before working in Holland, Sweden, England, and the West Indies, Chef Renggli has worked in hotels, restaurants, and on ships. "At that time," Chef Renggli pointed out, "there wasn't much general interest in other ethnic cuisines. However, I did work in the Grand Hotel in Stockholm 25 years ago, and there we had many international visi-

tors who sought their own ethnic specialties. We had 80 cooks from between 25
and 30 different nations; so many more
things were possible and went on in that
kitchen than in a regular hotel restaurant
which was frequented only by the French
or the Swiss. Also, when I worked in the
West Indies, about 15 years ago, there
were many people from other countries, so
I had Italian specialties one night, English
on another, then Hungarian on the third,
and so on. These dishes always were the
first to go, and it is the same thing here at
The Four Seasons."

Executive Chef Renggli is a lean, ener-
getic man, which is more obvious when
one watches him moving about with quiet
authority in the vast and efficiently
planned kitchens of The Four Seasons.
His youthful appearance belies his extensive experience, and although he seems
younger than many members of his staff,
there is no question that this kitchen is his
domain. I asked whether he had been influenced by *la nouvelle* or other cuisines. "I
don't call my cooking by fancy names,"
the chef responded with a smile. "I give
the people what they like, and I find out
right after lunch if they did or not. As to
low-calorie or low-cholesterol dishes, I
just do it without calling it *nouvelle* or
whatever. I never believed in calling my
approach by any names."

I was especially curious about Chef
Renggli's experience with *la bande à
Bocuse* when the famous group of French
chefs began arriving to cook at The Four
Seasons. I wanted to know whether the
presence of these outstanding chefs might
have affected the standard routines and
preparation of the restaurant's own spe-

cialties, insofar as The Four Season's own
chef and staff were involved. "When the
French chefs arrive," Chef Renggli explained, "they would use my staff, and
there were no special problems. First of
all, the famous chefs don't do all the work
themselves, so we would do it for them.
For example, Bocuse has been here many
times. When he comes, he wants a certain
stock, and other basic things. He tells us a
day before what he will need, and we prepare these things for him because we have
the time to do it. Also, when Bocuse is
here, he doesn't actually perform as he
would in his own kitchen in Lyons. If
he were to perform that way, he would
need a staff of at least fifteen people. Here
he does it with two or three of our staff.
He may want leeks, or chicken bones, or a
stock of *poisson;* we will have it ready for
him, and then he puts it together. You
must realize that they have very limited
menus with not very many dishes. Most of
the things they need for their preparations, we already know how to prepare.
For example, when Chapel agreed to come
here I went to his restaurant first and actually worked with him. Then I knew immediately what he was going to do, what
ingredients and stocks he would want,
what meat, and so forth. Knowing them
and their needs before they get here makes
for a good rapprochement."

I had experienced so many instances
of returning to a restaurant to savor a specialty I had liked earlier, only to find a
new chef in the kitchen and the earlier
specialty a disaster. I asked Chef Renggli
whether a new chef didn't actually resent
or want to change the specialties of a former chef. "Of course," Chef Renggli re-

plied. "The new chef has to do away with the old specialties and as fast as possible, so he can establish his own specialties. The biggest mistake the management of a restaurant can make is to keep an old specialty on the menu when the original chef is gone. When we took over The Four Seasons, we got rid of all the old specialties because I didn't like to cook them, and my other chefs didn't. I had Tom's agreement to do so. You see, I don't believe one should cook something that one doesn't like, or force a cook to prepare anything he doesn't like. What I do is to make a menu which I can prepare with my cooks, never including any dishes with fancy or crazy things that I can't produce."

At 4:30 P.M., we toured The Four Seasons' kitchens, finding the evening shift busy with its preparations for the dinner service that would continue past midnight. Chef Renggli escorted us through the vast kitchen, describing the various functions of each major station. "Here we have our *saucier*," he pointed out. "And here are our butcher and oyster man. Concerning your question about how we order, it is not done at the end of the day, as is the case with many other restaurant kitchens. You see those phones at the various stations? The cooks call in continuously to our purchasing steward. Then the *sous-chefs* and I get together and decide on what we need, and orders are placed by the steward whenever necessary." We learned that the executive chef has twenty-six cooks, including seven in the pastry shop under the direction of Pastry Chef Bruno Comin. There are about twelve cooks on each of the two shifts at The Four Seasons, as well as ten or twelve

dishwashers and pot cleaners. Besides the chef, there is a night *sous-chef* and a morning *sous-chef.* The morning shift begins at 8:00 A.M. and ends at 4:00 P.M., when the evening shift begins, working on until midnight or 1:00 A.M. Executive Chef Renggli generally stays on until 11:00 P.M. to midnight every other night, alternating with Chef Christian Albin. The pastry shop, however, is closed only for two hours each day; functioning from 2:00 A.M. until midnight. During the luncheon and dinner periods, the main kitchen has on hand a cook from the pastry shop who prepares between 100 to 120 soufflés. Like the kitchen at Windows on the World, which we will be visiting later, this one is staffed in the French pattern; but the layout, design, and equipment are well beyond anything one can expect to find in France.

"We do not use a wok," Executive Chef Renggli explained, "but do our stir-frying in a sauté pan. Our vegetables are prepared in a very fast, pressurized steamer, and then we have a larger and even faster convector unit as well, so that all vegetables are prepared to order." The center of the main kitchen is dominated by a gas-fired range not unlike the one we saw at La Côte Basque, with a steaming and serving unit running parallel to it, which is consistent with the French pattern. Adjacent to the range is a sophisticated grilling section which the executive chef refers to as "my baby." The broiling unit, custom made, is his private domain: "Charcoal broiling is my thing." Chef Renggli indicated how he functions in the kitchen. There are two or three sauce cooks, a vegetable cook, and a frying cook at stations along the range. Positioned between them and the waiters, who come in with the orders, the chefs listen as the cooks put together the required dishes and later check that each completed dish meets with their standards. As we proceed through the kitchen, we notice luscious ducklings, live trout in a tank, and a series of huge stockpots. "We don't have the stockpots going night and day, as in many restaurants," Chef Renggli tells us. "We cook the bones for two or three hours, and that's it." They generally have four or five different stocks and cook them as they need them to last for two or three days. Nearby, we notice a Cleveland convector steamer, which the executive chef tells us is very fast; in it all the restaurant's fish is steamed; liver is also done *à la vapeur*. "Over here is a larger one, the Hobart, which is like a pressure cooker, and we can steam liver in one minute in that one."

As we proceed through the kitchen, the chef shows us the refrigerator with a series of trays on which ducklings are drying. Using no condiments of any kind, the eviscerated ducks are left in the refrigerator for seven days to permit the fat to run off and the skin to become firm with a varnished appearance. When ready to cook, the ducklings are dipped into a mixture of soy sauce, garlic, ginger, coriander, honey, and orange peel, then cooked in a low oven for about two hours over a pan of water with any kind of tea in it. "It's like a Chinese oven," Executive Chef Renggli likes to say, "or rather it's a Chinese and Swiss technique combined. The aroma is fantastic, and the skin is crisp. We serve the duckling with a pepper sauce, *à l'orange,* or with cherries or any

other fruit that is in season." Moving along, we notice a tray with interestingly coated large grapes. They are **Fried Grapes** to be served with quail, and as I learned, very easy to do. "We use white Malagas with their pits inside, rather than the seedless ones, which have no taste," said the chef.

On our tour, we notice a refrigerator on a lower level that is used for storage of frozen foods. "Believe it or not," Chef Renggli told us, "we do use some frozen foods, but never canned ones. Frozen spinach, for example, holds up better for creamed spinach, and the color is better, too. Fresh spinach just doesn't seem to work and still stay green during the luncheon period." Frozen shrimp are also used for shrimp cocktails, since customers didn't seem to care for fresh shrimp. Apparently, shrimp have to taste somewhat like iodine and be a little on the hard side. However, everything else in the kitchen is fresh, in keeping with the seasons. Tomatoes, for instance, are served almost every day when they are in season, and then may not be served again for the next seven months; apples are similarly served when in season. "Of course, it is preferable for a cook at home to use frozen vegetables," said the chef, "rather than a so-called fresh one which has passed its peak of quality. However, there are so many good things available in the markets that are fresh and at their peak. This is the first week of December, and you can find fennel, purple turnips, big yellow turnips, unbelievable carrots, two kinds of squash, and six or seven different greens."

On our way back to the main dining room, we chatted with Chef Albin, who is in charge of production and quality control in the kitchen. This includes all of the *à la carte* orders, parties—everything. "Obviously I don't prepare every dish," he tells us, "but I am in charge of supervising every dish before it goes out to be served. I receive the order, tell the other cooks what I want, then finally I check to see that each dish is finished right—garnished and presented as it should be. There is no problem keeping the food warm, since everything we prepare is *à la minute.* We cook it and serve it right away. About the hours, oh, well, I come in at 10:00 A.M. and am here to about 11:00 P.M. at night, every day except Sunday. It's an important and very good job. I enjoy it, and it's very nice, you know."

Enlightened by our conversations at The Four Seasons, we arrive at Windows on the World, the internationally acclaimed restaurant in the sky. High up on the 107th floor of the World Trade Center, the restaurant affords a magnificent view of New York Harbor, and, fittingly, it is the Statue of Liberty—that symbol of the multinational character of our land—that strikes our eye. Before touring the restaurant, we have been invited to chat with Joseph H. Baum, who was then responsible for the complex of restaurants at the center. As Jay Jacobs wrote in *Gourmet* magazine (January 1978), "Baum ... produces restaurants the way Michelangelo produced sculpture, moving from one big concept to another but rarely misguaging even the smallest details. To stretch an analogy that art lovers may already have found sacrilegious, Baum, like Michelangelo, tends to work on a heroic scale with monumental themes, setting himself the task of breathing life into materials that aren't inherently inviting to the touch."

We met with Joseph Baum in his offices on the floor below the restaurant, and were introduced to Barbara Kafka, who had done much of the research on the menus at Windows on the World, and Mike Whiteman, who has a similar function in the Market Bar & Dining Rooms and the other eating facilities on the lower level of the Trade Center. As president of Inhilco, Joseph Baum and his staff were responsible for feeding 25,000 people daily in the complex of 22 eating places in the World Trade Center.

Stimulated by our interest in ethnic influences on American cuisine, we launched the conversation by asking Mr. Baum about his own evident interest in the ethnic elements in our society—for virtually all the specialty restaurants he created for Restaurant Associates, with the possible exception of the Newarker, had ethnic themes. In answer, he told us something of his background. Born of a Jewish family that had been in the hotel business in upstate New York for 50 years (Kosher cooking and excellent Hungarian chefs), Mr. Baum later moved into a Polish neighborhood. ("All the grocery stores were ethnic," he said, "and that's where I learned Polish.") After a stint in the resort worlds of Florida and Virginia, he did operational analyses for the hotel and restaurant clients of an accounting firm, worked in theatrical and restaurant design, and managed the Monte Carlo restaurant in New York. There, he said, he "began to get the idea of national cuisines and learned such things as what made a good pastry shop, where the best music was, where to go for venison and **Polenta** late at night, and where all the ethnic neighborhoods were. I learned from all the people who worked in these places."

After working at the Cocoanut Grove on the West Coast, Mr. Baum again worked in Florida, this time for three years in Miami Beach and Boca Raton. Commenting on the romantic look of the restaurants of the period, he said: "We began to look at it and to see the incongruity, especially in Boca Raton, of the ambience—and to see the sterility of the food."

When he was asked by Jerry Brody to join Restaurant Associates, he began assembling a team of accomplished professionals, drawn from his earlier involvement in the field.

"I practiced my usual procedure of overkill," Joseph Baum told us with a smile, "by getting people who are far more professional and accomplished to be interested in the Newarker than anyone assumed to be possible. As a result, we had great chefs, great pastry people, first class service—and they all came out of my background. None of them had ever worked in the marshes of New Jersey, and the very incongruity of it and its unexpectedness made it popular. We began to see that we had to merchandise these individuals in interesting ways to keep the interest of the community. I would say that a great many of the diners we now serve here were from New Jersey and were former customers of the Newarker some twenty-five years ago. Well, they began to be interested in the fact that we had Albert Stockli, a great Swiss chef, who was an international cook, as the Swiss are. So with

Albert Stockli and others we began to enjoy ourselves in opening up thoughts concerned with interesting food. You can blame me for things like dreaming up sparklers for birthday cakes—for cakes spattered with carbon. We did things like three-clawed lobsters; we'd use pig's blood to thicken our *coq au vin*. We tried to use basic dishes and went back to find what made them interesting in the first place."

Barbara Kafka pointed out that Joseph Baum tried to be authentic in his approach to these basic dishes. "Yes," he agreed, "but I also found that there were many 'authentics.' " Maybe that was an excuse, he explained, but some of the things he did were successful and some were not. One of the former was Coconut Shrimp, which is their biggest seller today in the Hors d'Oeuvrerie. To be able to get pickled herring "that wasn't bottled," is another of Mr. Baum's "authentic things." He also sought to provide a variety of "recalls" for people, which gives them a certain security in a restaurant. So it was not merely a sense of trying to create a picture, as he put it; he and his staff were genuinely involved with the use of ethnic elements. "And restaurants," he added, "have to do with what's appropriate to the clientele and the backgrounds of their interest."

The Newarker was soon followed by the Hawaiian Room, The Four Seasons, the Brasserie, Trattoria, La Fonda del Sol, Zum Zum, and others, most of which had strong ethnic themes. Mr. Baum's motive in developing each of these places, he very honestly explained, was not a missionary one. It was not because of an academic interest that he decided to bring the world's cuisines to the World Trade Center. It was rather a case of focusing, of what was appropriate to the solution of a problem—and what was comfortable to do, based on his background and knowledge, along with the skills that were available to him. It was a question of how he could best make each new place fulfill his ideas involving a totality having to do with food, ambience, design, and the overall experience. "It had to do with the sum of the illusions that I thought were interesting; the idea of providing accessibility of feeling to people, for them to enjoy without a sense that they are being lectured to or educated. Pleasure is the overriding principle of whatever technique is used to achieve it."

Joseph Baum concedes that exhaustive research is a prime tool in his approach to creating outstanding specialty restaurants. This has included researching various cuisines as well as methods for organizing these findings so that they could be used in his restaurants to make these cuisines interesting to clientele. He believes that the method with which this research was conducted was an important factor in the success of each of the specialty restaurants. "My interest always was, and still is, to provide research as a total kind of thing. Zum Zum was a prime example of this. Mimi Sheraton, to a great measure, did an enormous amount of the research on Zum Zum. I could mention fifteen or twenty people of the caliber of Myra Waldo that I would send out to write me tomes on things like the background of chocolate in Latin America. You have to know things like that, and how can every one know it?" Baum had a researcher

work with him for two years on The Four Seasons, providing anthropological history of the seasons and how such knowledge could be applied to the kind of food that they were interested in making. "The benefit of these skills was given to many people. And everybody in the organization got the idea, contributed, and got involved. I'm trying to give you an overall idea of these things, so that you don't attribute too much to my personal interest. Yes, I have skills, talents, like everyone else; I look at things and make use of them, initiate them, or one thing makes me inspired to think of another. I'm sort of paranoid and compulsive, so we pay a lot of attention to details and to their cumulative effect. But behind all of that is an enjoyment of all food, a sensuality."

The one apparent exception to Mr. Baum's use of ethnic themes are Chinese and Japanese cuisines: thus far he has not attempted Chinese or Japanese restaurants. The reason for this, he said, is that he is unable to "identify" sufficiently with those cultures, to the extent necessary for the creation of ethnic restaurants, and that he has too much respect for the "nuance requirements" of such an identification. "It's like speaking French from childhood," he explained, "or learning to ride a bicycle—or more to the point, it's a question of whether or not I can tell a good joke in Chinese." All such nuances, he suggested, are "expressed into food."

We broached the subject of *nouvelle* and *minceur* cuisines and explored our theory of the decline of French and Chinese cuisines in recent years. Joseph Baum spoke of *nouvelle cuisine* as a marvelously ascetic rather than a sensual experience.

He thought it had some aspects of a refinement, in terms of the senses, but didn't think it would replace classic cuisine or provincial cooking, and believed there was room for both. He agreed that the Chinese revolution has had a detrimental effect on the cuisine of that country.

We discussed Alain Chapel's prognostication that because of the many critical changes in France, America would probably become the repository of the French tradition for classic cuisine. "I used to think that a French chef was God," Joseph Baum said as if he were thinking out loud. "I still think he's God, but I don't think he knows very much beyond his normal domain. I used to think that if a Frenchman said a wine was good or bad, he must know because he is French. Similarly, we used to think a chef in a great restaurant must know good wine, whether he ever drank a glass of wine or not, and whether he was ever more than twenty miles away from his restaurant all his life. Frenchmen are not very good social observers, nor do I consider them extraordinary sociologists, economists, or interpreters of world movements in cuisine or other events. There have been about twelve chefs in the *bande à Bocuse* traveling to the same conferences and to meet the same people. They have made observations, some correct and others self-humbling or self-serving. You see, I have a confusion about the strength of traditions. It's a lot like the case of the Japanese: when you overlay other civilizations, you wonder how well the populace will take it and express it." He reminded us of the spread of supermarkets and snack-food bars in France, and thought that the French are "subject to these attacks" and

that they, like the Japanese, are beginning to react to the problems of inner cities and to other problems of distribution, profiteering, and the like.

"I think two important things," Joseph Baum added. "Eating is a pleasure, and eating is getting more important. The quality of food, the reality of food, and the use of food as pleasure are again becoming more important. Not only because there is more leisure time and disposable income, but because there is a generation that has gone through a plastic phase, and is now conscious of quality. They are adventurous, and I don't believe there are any holds barred today for the availability or the acceptability of any cuisine in this country. There's much more interest in regional cuisine; there is much more sensuality, as far as products are concerned; there's an interest in all of these things. And when you go upstairs through our kitchens today, you will find Japanese, Indonesian, Scandinavian and English—not just dishes, but cooks from those countries cooking these dishes."

With Alan Lewis, director of Windows on the World, we proceeded on a tour of the various restaurants and the kitchens.

On our way to the kitchens, we asked Alan Lewis his opinion of *nouvelle cuisine*. "You know Albert Stockli was doing those dishes 20 years ago," Alan told us. "Really, there is nothing new that has been contributed." Barbara Kafka interjected, "Even Escoffier thought he was doing the same things. In his books he talks of nonbound sauces, *jus* sauces, about lightening the meal, about natural purées —he talks about all of these things." We then asked how the kitchens at Windows on the World might differ from the French pattern, and particularly from the kitchens of the *bande à Bocuse*. "When I first went to France," Alan offered, "and saw the number of people they had on staff, it was simply mind-boggling." Barbara Kafka pointed out that the great French chefs *never* have had to deal with the economics of cooking in America. In Guérard's kitchen or Bocuse's, for fifty people in the dining room for the whole night, there will be fifteen to twenty people in the kitchen; and most of their restaurants, she added, have very few items on the menus.

In answer to my question, Alan Lewis said that the French pattern used in their kitchen differs slightly from the pattern abroad. The *garde manger* here is divided by what they call the cold pantry, from which the waiters pick up finished cold dishes. It is similar to the *buffet* of most hotel kitchens, in which grapefruit, shrimp, or oysters are prepared, but not cold main dishes. He pointed out that not many cold main courses are served in France. The *garde manger* does the bulk preparation of the pâtés and the dressings, and they are moved elsewhere to be served. Having visited a number of basement restaurant kitchens, we wondered about the special problems of operating a kitchen in the sky, 107 floors above the ground. "We have our kitchen up here with only one exception, which was carefully planned, and that's the commissary on the lower levels of the building," Alan explained. "The commissary orders and receives merchandise for all of our operations, including the Market Bar & Dining Rooms, the Delicatessen, and so forth. They do no cooking, but they will clean my fish, peel my potatoes and onions, string carrots, and even peel and chop my

garlic. That's because, if they didn't we'd have to bring garbage up here and then bring it down again. Also we would have to bring up most raw materials in their original state, which would make for more garbage. So they peel my potatoes and send them up to us in plastic barrels. Regarding ordering, the chef and I will give them our requirements, and our separate purchasing department buys for us, but that's a story in itself."

As Alan walked us through the vast and impressively equipped kitchen, he pointed out that it was planned so that no table or station was more than 23 big steps from a kitchen door. There were more than 50 cooks and a staff of 560 working, he informed me, basically on 2 shifts, 7 days a week. He normally served 500 for lunch; around 700 for dinner; and between 300 to 800 per day in the banquet department. He pointed out the various stations: the butcher, who does all the necessary cutting of meat into portions; the *garde manger*, which includes the preparation of all hors d'oeuvres for private parties and buffets as well as the preparation of vegetables. In actuality, the preparation of meats and hors d'oeuvres as well as the preparation of salads, is part of the *garde manger* functions. We saw huge kettles that function continuously for the preparation of stocks and soups; then the vegetable station nearby. The vegetables are steamed briefly, then sautéed in butter. Near a second entrance door to the kitchen, we perused the *pâtisserie*, which is divided into two sections. On one side, the pastry is prepared and cooked in huge electric ovens; on the other side, whole desserts, soufflés, and hot appetizers are prepared in a convection oven with continuously moving heat. The nearby pantry is where the waiters pick up salads, cold first courses, clams, and oysters. We learned that since no gas is permitted in the building, this is an all-electric kitchen, with the exception of the charcoal broiler.

It was now about 3:00 P.M., and Alan pointed out that the kitchen brigade at that hour was the dinner crew; they were preparing sauces and getting set up for the dinner service. He led us to the huge range that has a hot table running parallel to it, with electric heating units above for holding food so that it doesn't get a chance to cool. "Let me explain how it works," Alan offered. "When the waiters come in with their orders, they give them to a steward who stands here at the end of the steam unit, to the right. The steward has the responsibility of passing the orders on, and we use the same person all through the meal period to call in the orders, so that the cooks can become attuned to one particular voice. He will order two of this, or three of that, and put the waiter's slip on this clipping device above the steam table. When the waiter comes back, he will say, 'Waiter number 6, table number 42,' and he will take the slip for table 42 and pick up the respective dishes for that table."

We learned that the steward is an experienced member of the staff, and that the chef or *sous-chef* will be standing nearby during the entire meal period to supervise each completed dish, checking its garnishing and making sure it measures up to the restaurant's standards. It is a similar system to the one we witnessed at The Four Seasons. "That's a part of the French pattern," Alan explained, "a concept that goes back to the French system, where the chef or *sous-chef* will pass on every order. In a small resturant where the owner is the chef, then he passes on each order."

At this point we met Executive Chef André René, who commented on the restaurant's highly trained and multinational staff. Since harmony among the kitchen brigade is so important, we wondered who is responsible for the selection of new personnel. "The executive chef has the final word," said Alan Lewis, "about all of the people who work in the kitchen. If I don't like someone or think he is not doing the right job, I will discuss it with André, but he hires the men. If I know of someone who is good that I think we can get, I don't hesitate to bring it to the chef's attention." Alan and the chef had not worked together previously, and we learned that André René had been at the St. Regis Hotel for three years before joining Windows on the World; he had been executive chef at the Plaza Hotel for twelve and a half years before becoming its production manager.

During our tour, we were impressed by the many different nationalities among the staff; and Alan Lewis said that this was completely conscious because of the various types of ethnic cuisines the restaurant handles. Chinese dishes are prepared by cooks from Taiwan and Hong Kong; Japanese dishes by the Japanese staff; an Indonesian dish will be prepared by an Indonesian. "Even when we do Scandinavian open sandwiches for lunch in the grill," said the chef, "they are prepared by a Scandinavian member of our staff. We also have Koreans, Vietnamese, French—

just about everybody. Chef René explained his method of preparing **Roasted Ducklings** with purées of three vegetables (whichever are in season). This afternoon he was using broccoli, turnips, and carrots. We also saw the creation of **Sole with Watercress Mousse in Aspic,** a popular appetizer on the menu. The executive chef noted our fascination with the preparation of **Steak Tartare** and the *garde manger* station. "We grind up the specially purchased meat to order," Chef René told us, "because we know it's going to be nice and fresh. We add salt and pepper, egg yolk, some onions, anchovies, and a dash of brandy—and mix it here, just before serving, unless there's a specific order for mixing it in the dining room. In all cases, we use top round, because it has more flavor to it."

At this point, Alan Lewis suggested that we go over to the other kitchen, so we took leave of the executive chef. This was the kitchen for the Hors d'Oeuvrerie, where after 3:00 P.M. each day the entire menu is made up of first courses. From lunch to 3:00 P.M., it is known as the Grill of the Club. Realizing that the restaurant has virtually continuous service, we wondered what kind of hours Alan Lewis kept. "Oh, 10:00 to 10:30 in the morning until about 11:00 to 11:30 at night, except for Sunday. The chef puts in about the same hours, which, of course, is a very long day." As we passed the Food Bar, we could see a Japanese chef preparing *sushi* and *sashimi,* which are served every afternoon. In the second kitchen, they had finished luncheon and were now getting ready for their other menu. "Here we have pork *satays,* chicken *yakitori,* and our Co-

conut Shrimp, which is a holdover from earlier R.A. days," Alan said as he led the way. "We have two Chinese chefs here, and today we are featuring spare ribs and steamed clams; we also do fried wontons, spring rolls, lemon chicken—and a lot of other enticing bits and pieces. There is a *sous-chef* here, too, who supervises the finished dishes at lunch. In the evening, the room manager is in charge of the kitchen, and he has a steward who calls in the orders and keeps things going in an orderly fashion." As we left the kitchens and our friends at Windows on the World, we couldn't help but marvel at the smooth efficiency everywhere around us and realize the tremendous task of satisfactorily serving 3,000 meals every day of the week, given Joseph Baum's requirements for food and ambience and for providing a "totality of experience" for the diners.

With these insights into the operations of two of New York's great restaurants, we must broaden the focus of our tour. For we are just as interested in the considerable skills of American homemakers as we are in the expertise of the professionals in the big kitchens; and we are equally curious about the regional cuisines of the country—especially as they have been influenced from abroad.

First—for an abrupt change of scene—we find ourselves in New Orleans, Louisiana, the home of Creole and Cajun cookery. Our guide is Paul Fitzwater, a fine cook in his own right, whom we met during our tour of France. A longtime resident of New Orleans, Paul tells us something of the background of Creole cookery, and it is immediately obvious that it is an outstanding example of how many ethnic influences can mold a distinctive regional cuisine.

Many culinary experts believe Creole cooking was based originally on French cuisine. Strongly influenced by Spanish, Portuguese, Italian, and New England cookeries, it was finally accented by the Black slaves: they contributed their uncanny knowledge of herbs, inherited from their ancestors in Africa. Creole cooking is such a strong culinary statement that few international specialties can maintain their traditional character in the hands of a Creole cook. Most of the fine restaurants in New Orleans, such as Antoine's, Arnaud's, and Galatoire's have excellent male Black chefs. "A restaurant owner told me," said Paul Fitzwater, "that you can give any traditional French or Italian recipe to a Creole cook, and he will prepare it superbly; but within two weeks it will have been converted into a Creole dish!"

Paul explained the distinctions between Cajun and Creole cooking. The Cajuns, we learned, use red wine only in all their sauces, whereas the more refined Creole cooking, especially in New Orleans, uses both white and red wines. Game, especially ducks, are popular in Cajun country; and the men, who love to hunt, are all good cooks. Some of the best recipes you can get in Louisiana are from the hunters. Creole cooking almost invariably begins with a dark **roux**. This is cooked for hours over low heat, preferably in a black cast-iron pot, with constant stirring, and is taken off the heat just when it's about to burn. Since it is used so often, the dark roux is generally made in large quantities and kept in jars for months. Surprisingly—since it is constantly hot in Louisiana—this roux is one of the few items that isn't refrigerated.

We learned that gumbos—stews thickened with okra or a combination of herbs and sassafras leaves called filé—and **Creole Jambalaya**—a derivation of the traditional Spanish *paella*—are perennial favorites in Creole cookery. Okra and filé are never used together as thickening agents in the same dish, the former being cooked with the other ingredients and the filé added during the last minutes of cooking. Oysters are generally used with other seafood or poultry in preparing **Creole Jambalaya** with uncooked rice, but clams are never used. "It is surprising that in an area with abundant seafood, like New Orleans," Paul Fitzwater commented, "clams are not considered edible, and it is difficult to buy them here. However, you can get almost everything you would ever want in our fabulous markets. We are really veal eaters, so there is plenty of good veal; poultry is abundant, and there's lots of game, including rabbit and squirrel, which are sold commercially in all meat markets; but beef is not very popular. Of course, seafood of all kinds—except clams—are superabundant; and we probably get more fresh items than other parts of the country because everyone has a maid, a relative, or a close friend who fishes—and all generously share their catch. I usually get ten pounds of shrimp at a time, through friends, shell them, then freeze them in water, which is the only way to do it if you expect them to taste like anything."

Family meals, we were told, include much baking, especially of breads. Casseroles, particularly those made with seafood, are very popular. Red beans and rice are referred to as "the national dish," and virtually every family prepares red beans and rice religiously every Monday; this item is always served with smoked sausage or pork chops. Since the seasons are so much alike, there are few specialties for special holidays. A family meal generally begins with a soup, followed by a fish course, then a main course; and all the dishes are generally placed on the table at the same time. "We have lots of greens in New Orleans," Paul said, "but no one seems to know how to make good salads; they're mostly made with iceberg lettuce. Homemade orange and strawberry wines are often served, because these fruits are grown right here and are superb, especially the strawberries, which have to be the best in the entire world. Then desserts follow, a pecan or apple pie, and cup after cup of coffee; it's really a ceremony with us."

The traditions of cuisine remain strong in Louisiana. The natives still cook as they always have, according to Paul Fitzwater, and outside food chains are not very successful. In New Orleans, they stick to their own food because they know they have the best food in the world. Says Paul: "They just don't cotton to anything too different."

For an insight into ethnic influences on the cooking of a Midwest family during the Depression of the 1930s we chatted with Betty Silverman, a cookbook writer now living in Ardsley, New York. She remembers a very big farm kitchen (with a wood-burning stove) that was both the family center and the dining room. The farm was in Conrad, Iowa, popula-

tion 630 people including Germans, Scandinavians, English, and some Czechoslovaks.

"Farm families were generally big families," Betty Silverman reflected, "because hired men were expensive. Also my father and the neighboring farmers would rent threshing equipment on a cooperative basis, and teams of seven would share the work on the respective farms. During these periods, there would be major luncheons at my house—really dinners, since we'd feed fourteen to eighteen hard-working men at one time. And the women would vie with one another as to who could prepare the most impressive and satisfying meal. There would be several types of meats, pies, and cakes, and plenty to eat."

Betty said that her mother really was a pioneer, in the sense that all of her cooking and schooling were learned by word of mouth, from her neighbors. Especially during the summer, when manual labor was an essential part of the farm life, there was good, hearty food. The midday meal was the big meal of the day, followed by a light supper. Since the men were working in the fields during the summer heat, there would be iced tea and cookies served at about 10:00 A.M. and 3:00 P.M., "which, I guess," said Betty, "was the beginning of the coffee break idea."

There were memorable meals, particularly on Thanksgiving and Christmas. "Mother always served goose or roast beef, very much in the British style. Also, I remember that during the Depression years, my father arranged to get oysters packed in ice—which was a real luxury in the Midwest. There would always be a

quart of oysters, and Mom would serve them with vinegar, salt, and pepper over soda crackers; and the balance of them were used for the stuffing of the goose for Christmas dinner. Another treat at Christmas was to find a fresh California orange in our stockings. We lived simply but well; and after a Sunday or holiday dinner, there would be sandwiches for a late supper. Since there weren't many opportunities for entertainment, we would go sledding and then return to make popcorn and fudge."

Not all of the cooks we will be meeting on our tour are necessarily native Americans. Cynthia List, for example, who now lives in Pelham, New York, was born in England, but grew up in Angola, West Africa, where her father was involved in the building of the railroad in what was then the Belgian Congo. There she was influenced by British, Belgian, and German people working on the railroad; and, of course, there was the very heavy Portuguese influence, since Angola was a colony of Portugal. She became familiar with *bacalhau,* or salt cod. Each of the foreign nationals working on the railroad taught their housekeepers to cook in their own national style. When someone important was visiting, they would often borrow the staff from another household for the occasion to prepare a Belgian, Dutch, German, or French meal. Later, she returned to England and with her husband and young family moved to Montreal, Canada. "At that time the food and culture were English/French rather than French/English, as it has since become, so the influence of French cuisine was not very strong. Nonetheless the children were very dissap-

pointed with the food and would eat only meat and potatoes. They did love hot dogs and hamburgers and many of the things I associated with food in New York. I do recall, though, that when my father visited us in Canada he was most impressed with the *bouillabaisse,* but my mother was overpowered by the quantity of the individual servings, much the same as she was when she came to the United States. Many Europeans complain about our tremendous portions, which are double what they expect. For example, when I return to England and have a ham sandwich, it's just a small piece of ham with some bread."

Doctor Dorothy Kunstadt came to American cooking via Poland, where she was born, and Australia, where she went to live with her mother when she was eleven years old. "It was an interesting opening to an Anglo-Saxon culture for me," Dorothy recalled. "Most of my friends were English immigrants, but there was an Italian ghetto, called Carlton, with ethnic shops and restaurants with marvelous almond cookies and other Italian delicacies. Also, my mother worked in a factory with Italian co-workers; she would bring in her own ethnic sandwiches, and they would bring in things like lasagna; and the women would exchange samplings of each other's food."

Dorothy found that the Australians were interested in plain food and ate meat such as sausages, chops, and kidneys for breakfast. Since lamb was the cheapest meat, there was abundant lamb stew, minced pie, and roast lamb with mint sauce—which was the English influence. Beef was also popular. "But the thing I remember most," she said, "was the wonderful fruit of the kind which wasn't known in Europe. I found pineapples, bananas, mangoes, pomegranates, passion fruit, plums, and cherries. Among the vegetables, I particularly remember pumpkin, squash, and lettuce, which were not common items in Europe. And, then, when I came to America, I found the variety of fruits and vegetables here even more unbelievable."

Dorothy Kunstadt collects recipes from her friends involving various ethnic influences. "However," she points out, "food has an intimate meaning, and my memory of the food at my mother's table always evokes a sense of the greatest appreciation. I remember a chicken soup with dill that my mother made, and I can smell the fabulous aroma to this day. In fact, some relatives from Poland always make it for me when they can, because they know how much I like it. We must remember that in Europe particularly, food was a part of being together. Not only on holidays, or with relatives or friends; it was the warmth of the home."

The warmth of associations with food is expressed in another way by Humphrey Evans III, who was born in the United States, but lived as a young boy in Delhi, India, in the 1950s. His fondest recollections center on Desusah, an elderly but ageless man from Goa, a district on the west coast of India colonized by the Portuguese. "In India, most of the servants, including the cook, were male," Humphrey explained, "since women don't have much of a role outside of the family. My mother taught Desusah French and European cooking, and he taught her Indian dishes like **Country Captain**. I loved to watch him at work and spent all of my time in the kitchen, if I could. Even during a party, I would sneak back into the kitchen with my plate of French food and exchange it for the Indian food he had prepared for himself. Then, every day, after Desusah discussed the menu for the day, I would go with him to shop in the markets, watch him select the best items, and help him brush the incessant flies away." Later, when he returned to the United States and went to college, Humphrey Evans learned to cook most of the Indian specialties and dishes that Desusah had taught his mother, and still prefers Indian dishes that he cooks himself to French and European cuisine.

Since she is a native-born American, Alice El-Tawil's Mideastern cooking, on the other hand, is influenced by her Russian mother and Egyptian mother-in-law. She is married to Baghat El-Tawil, who is currently with the United Nations, and they have homes both in the United States and in Cairo, Egypt. "I learned to cook from my mother," Alice told us, "but in terms of cooking Egyptian dishes, my Greek father's specialties were most helpful, since they are very close to Egyptian food. Two years after our marriage, we went to live in Cairo, and my husband's mother and relatives taught me Egyptian cuisine; I found it very easy to come by, because of its similarity to Greek food. Actually, I now lean to Turkish food, which is actually the grandfather of both cuisines."

We now meet a native American, Paula Galusha, who has been most influenced by Pennsylvania Dutch cuisine, although she actually grew up in western

Pennsylvania. Her father was born and brought up not very far from the Pennsylvania Dutch country, she told us, and his parents owned a number of grocery stores and knew a great deal about fresh produce. Later, after he had married, her father moved to western Pennsylvania, and she could remember driving regularly from home to the other side of Pennsylvania as a young girl to enjoy an authentic Pennsylvania Dutch dinner. Paula was impressed that the Pennsylvania Dutch grew their own produce and used virtually every part of it in their cooking. She was amazed to learn that they used saffron, and after it was brought over here, had begun to grow it and use it in certain of their chicken dishes. "Otherwise," she said, "their food includes a great deal of pickling, pickled cucumbers, pickled eggs and beets; and a great deal of canning and preserving of the things they grow. I found the apple butter most memorable, and I believe it was prepared with a lot of cinnamon, cloves, and allspice."

Paula's husband, Joseph Galusha, grew up in Oklahoma on a large farm. "When we would visit there," Paula remembered, "there would be three or four different kinds of pies and breads, and they would grill several different kinds of meats. This summer, when I was in Oklahoma for a family reunion, they had built a big pit in the ground and smoked a whole turkey and a side of beef all day; and I never had tasted anything like it. They served a great variety of vegetables, although they have a tendency to overcook them. Generally, appetizers and first courses are not served there; they simply place all of the food on the table at the same time." Paula is the food consultant for the *Pelham Sun,* and has written cookbooks and devised recipes for a number of products for advertising agencies. She finds that her friends and neighbors are very interested in cooking and different ethnic cuisines. In fact, she and her husband belonged to a gourmet club in the community, which involved each of six couples preparing a gourmet meal on an alternating basis. When it came to her turn, she prepared an entire Pennsylvania Dutch meal with great success. When I asked her if she had been influenced by the cooking in Oklahoma, she said, "Well, for New Year's, Joe has to have black-eyed peas because that's his family's good luck symbol; and I have to make sauerkraut and pork; that's my family's good luck dish!"

Betsy Klein, who now lives in Brooklyn Heights and works in the fashion industry in New York City, comes from a Quaker family and grew up on a dairy farm near Greensboro, North Carolina; her mother's family was Dutch, her father's, Irish. Their neighbors, however, were Moravian, a sect that did not intermingle with the Quakers; but there were many other neighbors of varying ethnic backgrounds. It was like the situation Betty Silverman mentioned: during the summer months, Betsy's mother would serve a huge lunch to fifteen or twenty workers, on an alternating basis with the wives of the workers involved. The women, in what appears to be a standard pattern, competed in outdoing each other in the preparation of these meals. During these harvest months, her mother would serve two or three kinds of meat, lots of vegetables, two or three pies and cakes, pickles, and other preserves. "One of the most memorable pies my mother made was **Cantaloupe Pie,**" Betty told us. "Mother is now over 70, and doesn't remember where she first learned to make it, but none of her neighbors made it. I serve it often here in New York, as I do a number of wonderful things I remember from the days on the Bingham farm. Mother loved to make pies; she made one with red sliced tomatoes and allspice; a sweet potato pie; and one with Concord grapes with the seeds left in. She also made a Concord grape pie with just the leftover hulls, which was more chewy and equally as delicious. She even made a vinegar pie."

Some additional favorites that Betsy Klein still makes include **Fried Okra Dipped in Cornmeal,** which is simply cut wheels of okra dredged in cornmeal and sautéed or fried. She also prepares a vegetable dish, similar to a spinach salad, using the tender leaves of a four-foot-high-weed (whose dark magenta berries are believed to be poisonous) called polk. She blanches the leaves in boiling water until tender, ignoring the acrid smell that results. Then she sautées four or five strips of bacon and adds green onions until they are golden. The drained greens are mixed in, garnished with crisp bacon, and served immediately.

When I asked Betsy whether her husband's family had provided any ethnic influences on her cooking, she replied, "Well, my husband's mother is Mexican, and his father is from an orthodox Jewish family from Chicago; they originally came from Hungary. And let me tell you, my Mexican mother-in-law is now the "Jewish" matriarch of the Klein family!"

Thus far, we have had abundant evidence of the numerous foreign influences on American cuisine. The traffic in influences, however, has not been only one way, for American culinary ideas have had, in turn, a powerful impact on the cuisines of other countries. Especially in recent years, American concepts have reached out to literally every corner of the globe.

Perhaps the most important element of American know-how that has influenced the restaurant scene abroad is our finely honed technique of hotel and restaurant management. To explore the ramifications of this influence, we will meet first with Charles Bell, executive vice-president of Hilton International, and later, with food and hotel consultant George Lang.

We met Charles Bell in his offices at New York's Waldorf Astoria and were promptly introduced to Anton Aigner, then director of food and beverage planning and development for Hilton International. These two experts provided us with an almost bewildering wealth of information on restaurant operations around the world. Essentially a management company, Hilton International was, at the time of our meeting, involved in the planning and operation of 71 hotels in 52 countries, and was projecting an additional 15 to 20 hotels in another 12 to 14 countries. The company provides hotel builders with guidance in architecture, mechanical and interior design, layouts for kitchens and laundries, and advice on the type and scope of other facilities; these include the size and number of rooms, the size of ballrooms, and the type and number of restaurants and bars. After studying the particular country involved and synchronizing this with their experience, they attempt to create a hotel which has all the latest conveniences and, hopefully, retains the local ethnic characteristics. "Now that is sometimes tricky to do with architecture," Mr. Bell explained, "so we try to achieve it through interior design and our approach to cuisine."

The Paris Hilton has a very American Western steak house which, at first, seems a little incongruous, as does a pizzeria in the Nile Hilton in Cairo, Egypt. Such incongruities result from sizing up "what's going to go" in a given market. In Paris, the chances of doing a French restaurant that would stand up against the bistros and the *Michelin*-starred restaurants are pretty slim. So "it was a pretty easy choice," Mr. Bell averred, "to hit them with something that was totally new; we were able to get fresh beef flown in from the States, despite De Gaulle, and the idea of getting them off of French food and on to baked potatoes, bourbon, Caesar salads, roast beef, and the chowders—well, it worked and was uniquely successful."

The same approach was used to create Sutter's restaurant in the Zurich Hilton, named after the famous Swiss general who was an emigrant to our country. It is to an extent a steak house, but its menu is larded with a few Swiss dishes as well. As for the pizzeria in Cairo, he told us that since no one else had one there, they decided to try it and it has turned into a very good business. James Smith, who started it in Cairo, is now at the Taipei Hilton, where there is a pizzeria with an enlarged menu of specialties since Italian food is popular there as well.

The Taverna Ta Nissia, on the other hand, is an authentic and excellent Greek restaurant at the Athens Hilton—far and away the most continously successful restaurant in the entire Hilton International chain. We wondered what approach had been used in determining the type of restaurant and food for that location. "We didn't have a helluva lot of options," Mr. Bell replied. "At that time, we couldn't import any of the products that we can now, so we couldn't do anything else except meet them on their own ground. Besides, all there was available was lamb, the beef was rather lousy, and there was no veal; so we thought we could take it on. There were a lot of good *tavernas,* but there weren't any with any sophistication, you know. It wasn't like Paris, where besides the bistros, there were also Lasserre, La Tour d'Argent and the Grand Véfour. Not in Athens. We felt that with air conditioning, nicer utensils, better uniforms, and the talent that we had, we could do something that would be very indigenous, yet do it better design-wise. We didn't want it to be so chichi that nobody would come in. Then we were able to prepare a lot of authentic dishes, adapt a few more Greek ones, and still throw in a few of the Continential specialties."

At the Milan Hilton, there was originally an authentic Trattoria da Pepe, which served excellent food but was not very different from the marvelous *trattorie* on virtually every street in Milan. The restaurant was redesigned into an elegant international room with an entirely new menu. Mr. Bell considers that they have now come up with a fairly interesting Italian restaurant called **Da Giuseppe,** which attracts more of the Milanese and even more of the tourists. "We have a very good chef in Giuseppe Ruga, and that makes a difference. You see, with all the decoration and the gimmicks, if the food is not good, you're still not going to be successful."

Hilton International supplies the chefs and arranges for the kitchen brigade in each of its hotels. Its management is total and includes the responsibility for running each hotel once it has opened. All of the plans, specifications, and equipment that go into a hotel, including the hiring and firing of the manager right on down is strictly their responsibility. Of particular importance, of course, is the hiring of chefs. First, the company determines a specific concept, then makes sure that the executive chef is aware of it and is capable of handling it. Most of the chefs historically have been Swiss or German, and that is the case in about 90% of the countries. "That has been a bit of a problem, since many chefs don't travel as much today as chefs did in the past. They can now get better pay where they started, and there aren't as many going into the field." Charles Bell interjected. "Not only that. There are also problems when you want to do local ethnic food and the foreign chef many times wants to homogenize it, as it were, into his own ethnic cuisine. I'd say that in some of the situations where you want to go heavily on local ethnic dishes, for example in Greece, we would put a Greek cook very much in charge of the local food production. The supervising chef, who has probably moved around from

country to country, would be in overall charge of the kitchen."

The Hilton organization also has a Food Research Center, which we will visit on our brief side tour in Montreal. Basically, the center tries to set up a library of standards for each hotel, so that if there are changes in the manager, the *sous-chef,* the food and beverage manager, or whomever, there still will be continuity. "I hate to use the word standardize," said Mr. Bell, "but we do want to have standards for each particular location. What is standard in the library for Athens won't be standard for Tokyo, or any other location. Also, we are trying to introduce a reasonable degree of flexibility for the guy who moves from one country to another. We're collecting the recipes for all of our dishes in each location, which we then send out to assist the chefs in other locations as well. This has the advantage of making the ethnic dishes of one country available to others. Also, one of the long-range objectives—and this is kind of a dangerous thing to say—is to have enough talent and materials so that we can truly survive the loss and gain of a particular key man. We don't want to be like the basketball team without a star center that starts losing all of the games."

The factors Mr. Bell and his associates must consider in thinking out the concept of a new hotel, and then in setting one up, vary radically from location to location. A hotel in Kuwait, for example, would more likely be planned for the businessman who travels there than for the vacationer so that its restaurant would offer American as well as Continental items. Marketing studies are always done well in advance of deciding on a particular concept; the organization has food and beverage people stationed in various regions of the world, and their opinions are solicited. There is also a synthesis of local opinion. All such factors are blended into the planning process.

In my travels I had attended a number of weddings of local residents in such hotels as the Athens and Cairo Hiltons, and I considered it a compliment that local people would hold their special functions at these hotels. Charles Bell considered this a very important point. The most successful hotels, in his view, are those that are successful with the community, especially when the local people use them for weddings and banquets, and come at least occasionally to eat in their restaurants, or recommend them to business associates and friends. When a hotel like the one in Istanbul, or the Nile Hilton in Cairo, is the hub of social activities for the city, that always guarantees that the hotel is going to be a success. Actually, the organization makes more money from the rooms than from the food, "but when one works," says Mr. Bell, "it helps the other to work."

We asked him what considerations might be given in Hilton restaurants to guests with special food requirements—kosher, low-calorie and low-cholesterol, or salt-free foods, for instance. They try to accommodate special cases; knowing that people are calorie conscious, they are "looking for something in between health foods and *minceur* cuisine, with lighter low-calorie foods that are also satisfying."

We left Charles Bell to continue our discussions with Toni Aigner, since we were curious to learn more about the Montreal research center. Particularly proud of the "Culinary Heritages" he had asked the executive chefs to prepare for each country with a hotel operated by Hilton International, he had several dozen from different countries, ranging in quality of presentation from a student-like thesis to a beautiful illustrated and printed finished book. "This one is from Taipei," Toni said, showing us a printed book with exquisite color photographs. "Of course they went overboard here. We didn't ask them to print a book. (It has since been published in Taiwan and is on sale to the public.) What we asked each location to give us was basically an introduction of what kinds of products are available, a concise history of the country and its customs, and then a presentation of the food, specialties, and the techniques of that particular ethnic cuisine."

During our discussion, Manfred Bertele, director of the Food Research Center, joined us. From him we learned that the center is located at the Queen Elizabeth in Montreal, precisely because it is their largest hotel (1,200 rooms, 20 restaurants and bars, and banquet facilities for up to 5,000 people; also it is the nearest Hilton International hotel to the company headquarters in New York). "These large facilities," he said, "make it possible to conduct practical research in a commercial environment, which is essential for the success of the projects done at the center." Toni showed us a number of 6- by 4-inch plastic-coated color positives, which are called "microfiches," a product of Kodak. Each microfiche can contain about ninety individual photographs, which are tabulated for easy viewing. "These can be mailed inexpensively," Toni told us, "and with ninety images to work with on each microfiche, we can supply our chefs step by step with the details of each project we are working on. We have them on ethnic specialties such as Italian, British, or Chinese food; or as here, we have concentrated on one food item, asparagus. You know that in a lot of countries there is an asparagus season, and we felt a lot of our hotels weren't doing their best in this area. Too often, the chefs would suddenly remember a couple of days before that the asparagus were coming in season, so they would do a poor job. Here, the idea is to present promotional ideas for special menus, followed by the recipes, in order to prepare the many variations, as well as color photographs of the finished dish. Some of this may strike you as rather basic, but we don't have star chefs in every location all over the world."

Manfred Bertele showed us a well-prepared magazine called *F & B Trends,* which is distributed to the Hilton International food and beverage staffs throughout the world. Every microfiche project is complemented by the current issue of the magazine. A third vehicle for communication with their people is a bulletin that provides additional information too urgent to wait for the next issue of the magazine or to accompany any microfiche.

A few days later we visited the Food Research Center in Montreal for a comprehensive tour with Manfred Bertele. An excellent photographer and a chef of long experience, he personally takes all of the color photographs required for the microfiche projects.

"As an example of how we work,"

Manfred told us, "Evelyn Thurlby, coordinator here at the center, and I are leaving for our hotel in Israel tomorrow for a project we will bring out on kosher foods. We have already involved some of our people in other locations with experience in this area, and determined that there is a general interest and need among our other locations for this expertise. We want all of our people to know what kosher really is and to be aware of the dietary laws. By the time the others arrive at the conference, Evelyn and I will have contacted a lot of experts on the subject and be ready with all of the information we will need. By the end of the year we will have a major article in *Trends* magazine covering the customs and the foods of Israel, to be accompanied by microfiches with the actual recipes. After the conference, we will set up meetings with the executive chefs of our hotels in Israel and select approximately fifteen appetizers, maybe ten to twenty main courses, and another half-dozen desserts. We will want the most acceptable items that come up during our meetings, including new dishes or new creations of interest to our clientele."

Hilton International has already done considerable kosher catering in its hotels in London, Paris, and New York, and now wants to involve other locations. At this point they cater up to 600 and 800 people at kosher banquets for bar mitzvahs, weddings, and Jewish holidays that are celebrated in its hotels.

Another thing the Hilton organization does, Manfred explained, is to send along with the recipes full information on the manufacturers of equipment they have tested that will help to better prepare these dishes. "We try to marry the two, the recipes and the equipment, since you must realize that in many of our locations in foreign countries, items we would normally take for granted just don't exist. Why don't you come with me to our test kitchen, and I'll show you two pieces of equipment we're testing right now." He led us through the basement corridors of the Queen Elizabeth Hotel to a surprisingly large and well-equipped kitchen that provided a professional range, deep-fryer, commercial convection oven, and large steamers. The reason for the commercial equipment is that they wanted, as he put it, a "hundred percent testing environment." "We don't want people in the field saying the recipes didn't work for us as they did for you in your fantastic kitchen." We examined a cylindrical smoke oven which was being tested, and a miniature steamer which could conveniently be used on a small serving table to prepare certain foods; both used electricity.

Then we witnessed some of the tests. Manfred removed two large filets of fresh salmon from the refrigerator. One had been marinating with a combination of smoking and celery salt; the other had not been treated. He filled a small skillet with a combination of oak, maple, and ash sawdust topped with four juniper berries, and placed it on the heated base of the cylindrical smoking unit. Then he placed four servings of the marinated filet of salmon on a rack above, closed the front door of the unit, and set it to smoke the fish for 20 minutes. The unit is commercially available for about $200 and can be used for smoking fish, breast of turkey, spare ribs, and so forth.

While the salmon was smoking, Manfred took a pail of fresh seaweed from the refrigerator and layered it on the rack of a miniature steamer. Then he placed four servings of the untreated, fresh salmon filets on top. Marvelously compact, this unit was lined with a thick layer of lead, and under the racks at the bottom of the unit was a tube pierced with little holes. When the unit is operating, the exact quantity of water that is necessary spurts out, on a continuous basis. Manfred had already prepared his Nikon camera and lighting equipment to be ready to photograph both versions of the cooked fish when they were ready. In two minutes, the miniature steamer had perfectly cooked the salmon, which was still firm but flaked to the touch of a fork. In twenty minutes, the smoked salmon was ready and had a wonderful aroma. Manfred quickly took a number of color photographs of each of the two versions of cooked salmon, then offered samplings of each for our appraisal. The steamed salmon was wonderfully delicate as it was, but we both agreed it could be enhanced with a horseradish or other appropriate sauce. The smoked salmon was excellent, a taste experience. "You see," Manfred explained, "these units give a chef the option to get completely different textures, using the very same ingredient."

Manfred Bertele gave us some additional insights into his operations. During the previous year alone, they had put more than 1,200 recipes on microfiche; in five or ten years, they would easily have more than 10,000 recipes. A cross-reference system permitted quick access to any recipe or even information on any single ingredient.

Other projects by the center include growing herbs with special equipment available from a Canadian manufacturer, experiments with *nouvelle cuisine* specialties, and a continuing project involving preprepared frozen foods.

As a specific example of the advantages of the microfiche system, Manfred cited the notorious problem of obtaining hot food in Greece: "When I first arrived in Athens, as executive chef, I spoke to the Greek chef about this. His first argument was that Greeks never get ulcers because the food is never served cold or very hot. Then he made the point that their stuffed tomatoes were superb because they were prepared ahead and permitted to set and let the flavors exchange with one another; and he was right. However, I had to insist that in our hotel the guests expected hot food, and I made sure they got it. You see, we now have the advantage with these basic recipes that they are always in the kitchen and can be referred to. When you get a new *sous-chef,* for example, you give him the set of basic recipes, and then in the beginning you have to be with him constantly and taste what he does. You must realize that as a professional he knows how to make things like a **Sauce Mornay,** but there are dozens of different ways it can be prepared: with cream, egg white, rice flour, or whatever. He has to know how you want him to prepare *Sauce Mornay* in this particular kitchen and for this particular executive chef. When the new man's first attempts are not quite right, you go back to the recipe, and check what he might be doing differently. Then he prepares the sauce several more times until he gets the hang of the way you want it. Now, when a kitchen has a lot of turnover, then you have to train the brigade

every three to six months. On the other hand, if you have key people with you for several years, of course they know exactly what you want."

Returning to New York City, we were fortunate on relatively short notice to meet with George Lang, a food consultant and the first restaurateur to visit Communist China and Cuba. He had been associated with Joe Baum and Jerry Brody at R.A., and then left to purchase a restaurant and set up his own consulting organization.

Taking advantage of George Lang's firsthand knowledge of China and Cuba, we asked him to what extent the revolutionary goverment had negatively affected their cuisine; and we tried out on him our theory that the *haute cuisine* of France is moribund. I mentioned Alain Chapel's prognostication that America will be the repository of the great French traditions of cookery; and I suggested that the Communist desire to minimize the family unit in China (which is also happening probably to a lesser extent in Cuba) was a predominant factor in the fall of both cuisines. "You are wrong," George Lang said. "It is much more a factor in Cuba. First of all, there has been a most serious kind of rationing for the past fifteen years. This is a country which lives on sugar and has a sugar quota, also serious meat and rice quotas. As an example: I kept asking them to take me to their open-air markets, which you expect to find in all tropical countries, but they just ignored me. Later, when I had become very close to them, they told me there was no such thing anymore. The reason, they told me, is that there are no ingredients to sell; and what little farmer's produce they have they sell to the supermarkets. So I went into one of the supermarkets and found a few fresh vegetables, but even those were subject to ration coupons. So when you start with that premise, you either rise above it and create flowers from poverty that will be extraordinary, or you sink with the situation. Remember, the cathedral of Chartres had only five colors of glass to work with, so suddenly they became geniuses as to how to apply and mix them. This is similar to what the Chinese did with their hokka cuisine, which is simple, peasant cooking, using innards and odds and ends in the most incredible way."

The decline of Cuban cuisine seemed all the more surprising, since it had generally been conceded to be the most sophisticated of the West Indian cuisines. "That's correct," George Lang said. "It was evident in their use of wines, for example, and their avoidance of hot spices and so forth. Today, they don't have a chance to excel because of other priorities, just as in China. When I went there to evaluate their cuisine, I understood that things like the word *freedom* do not mean much to a hungry man, it's such an abstract term. To feed 800 million people, even a daily bowl of rice is probably an extraordinary achievement, so one can't belittle what they are or are not doing. I am only saying, as a person who wants to maintain this incredible cuisine, today is not the time to go—unless you are famous and they give you one of their dozen top chefs who has nothing else to do but cook for you, which is a possibility." George Lang paused, then said thoughtfully: "By the way, in Hong Kong and in Taipei,

Chinese cuisine on its highest level is *not* in decline, so I'm afraid you're going to have to delete that part of your theory, because there, if you know what you want to eat, the cuisine is incredible."

I explained that this was precisely part of my theory, which applies to both China and Cuba. It is those refugees who have left who are maintaining the original high standards of their cuisine, as part of their sense of freedom and nostalgia for the land as they knew it. "Very good," George Lang retorted, "and I have to include Hungary as part of your theory. Hungary really was a cooking nation, not just by instinct but also by artful, planned skill. They still have great restaurants, but tourism has been so successful that no restaurant industry could cope with it, and certainly not a state-controlled one. That's why the chefs at my new Hungaria restaurant in the Citicorp Building, apropos of your theory, say that you probably get a better meal in my restaurant than anywhere in Hungary today, except if someone there invites you to his home and saves up his money for two months or so." When I extended the discussion to Italian cuisine, however, George Lang's complete agreement was not forthcoming. "Let me tell you, I adore Italian cooking," he said, "and have lived all over Italy. The problem really is that while the Italians did not bastardize their cuisine, and it's still on a high level, the range of dishes available and cooked is extremely small."

Remembering Cynthia List's comments that our American portions are too large, I wondered how George Lang handled the situation in restaurants that cater to both Europeans and Americans. "It's a very difficult thing to cope with," he told us. "The smallest portions to my knowledge, strangely, were served in Italy, and the largest portions are here in the United States. Now, I do get a clientele that says they are turned off by large portions here, saying they're distasteful, sickening, and "we cannot eat it without losing our appetite." Then, there are certain places where it is justified to create a cuisine that is bigger than life, with huge portions of bread, a tub of butter, a large bowl of salad. But it has to be a style and a whole point of view that is not accidental. I think that you should consider the fact that *human greed* is one of the most important elements of merchandising. Steak and Brew and all its variations were enormously successful for years, and the salad bar is still enormously successful. One of the reasons is the whole idea of being able to eat as much as you want, as much beer as you can drink, and so forth.

Thinking about the preparation of food as a love gesture, we asked George Lang for his views on the subject. "My mother was an extraordinary cook; my grandmother was a fantastic one, and I dedicated my *Cuisine of Hungary* cookbook to her. I remember that when I complimented my mother on her cooking, she would say, "Well, if you have all the best ingredients, enough time, and someone special to cook for, it's not too much of a trick to create a great dish'" We discussed some associations of love with food, and Confucius' tenet that "fine food is the first happiness." "It's certainly not true in England," he offered, "nor is it evident in the articles by Erica Jong and Gael Greene alluding to the combination of food and physical sensuality in the kitchen. Of course, we have to separate *love* from *lust,* which is quite different. They are talking about lust, not love. The love gesture is one thing, ranging from mother's milk for her offspring to an offering of a kind of gift or present in the form of food. These are the most memorable offerings in most of our lives."

With these comments, this last stage of our tour comes to an end. I hope it has provided us not only with a greater awareness of the scope and magnitude of the restaurant scene in the United States, but, more important, with a new understanding of the many ethnic influences, drawn from the world's distinctive cuisines, that have contributed so dramatically to the growth of our own. American cuisine today is truly international, and can rightfully claim to be one of the foremost cuisines of the world. Let's now turn to the menus and slimming recipes we have discovered during our excursions around the country.

MENUS AND RECIPES

MENU

Black Bean Soup
Alaskan Roast Duck
Cranberry and Apple Jelled Salad
Frozen Yogurt Baked Alaska

BLACK BEAN SOUP*

This is undoubtedly America's most famous soup—beloved to the extent that our United States Senators took time out from their duties to officially decree that it appear regularly on the menu of the U.S. Senate restaurant in Washington, D.C. It has become an international favorite as well: Paul Bocuse, who first tasted the soup in New Orleans, liked it so much that he often includes it on the menu of his restaurant in Lyons. Jean Troisgros first had it at The Coach House in New York City, where it is a specialty, and, likewise, brought it back with him to Europe.

It is traditional to serve this delightful soup with **Corn Bread Sticks,** and to flavor it at your option with either Madeira or sherry just before serving.

2 cups black beans
2 tablespoons white wine, dry vermouth,
    or consommé
3 medium onions, chopped
2 stalks of celery, sliced, or 1 cup sliced
    celery root
2 carrots, chopped
2 tablespoons potato flour or cornstarch
⅓ cup parsley, minced
1 pound smoked ham hock, or ½ pound
    Canadian bacon, diced (optional)
2 bay leaves
1 teaspoon coarse salt
⅛ ground pepper or cayenne
⅛ teaspoon dry mustard (optional)
½ cup Madeira or sherry
2 hard-cooked egg whites, minced
1 lemon, thinly sliced
YIELD: Six to eight servings

1. Soak the beans overnight in cold water to cover; rinse under warm water and drain. Transfer the beans to a heavy kettle with fresh water to cover.

2. In a skillet, using the white wine, sauté the onions, celery, and carrots until the onions are translucent. Stir in the potato flour and parsley, mix well, and cook for 2 minutes longer.

3. Add to the beans the vegetable mixture, the optional smoked ham hock, bay leaves, and seasonings. Bring to a boil, then simmer covered for 3 hours, or until the beans are soft, adding additional boiling water as necessary. If using Canadian bacon, add during the last half hour of simmering.

4. Remove the bay leaves and optional ham hock. Force the bean mixture through a sieve or food mill, or purée in a food processor or an electric blender. Return the purée to the kettle with the broth and Madeira, and blend to the consistency of a heavy cream, thinning it slightly with boiling water if necessary. Cook for about 5 minutes until heated through, then remove from the heat. Serve hot, garnished with the egg whites and lemon slices.

Bonus Ideas: Mexican Black Bean Soup is made by simmering the presoaked black beans with 1 teaspoon coarse salt and 1 mashed garlic clove until the beans are tender; the beans are then puréed and set aside. The puréed beans are flavored with either of 2 popular sauces: in western Mexico, 1 cup of tomato purée is sautéed with 1 teaspoon of onion juice and 3 tablespoons of corn oil until the mixture is almost dry. The bean purée and the bean broth are added to the tomato mixture

and simmered together until they have thickened to a creamy consistency. This version is served hot with grated cheese and toasted tortilla squares. A second version, more popular in Mexico City, blends the bean purée with a mixture of 1 minced onion puréed in ½ cup of corn oil that has been flavored by cooking until wilted ½ cup of sorrel leaves. Discard the sorrel, blend the onion mixture with bean purée, and thin to the right consistency with reserved bean broth.

Cuban Black Bean Soup (Cuba's national dish) is cooked as in preparing Mexican Black Bean Soup, but the beans are not puréed. A sauce is prepared with 2 tablespoons of corn oil, 2 teaspoons of minced garlic, ¼ cup diced green pepper, 1 teaspoon salt, 1 bay leaf, ½ cup chopped onion, and 1 tablespoon vinegar. When the sauce has been reduced and thickened, it is poured over the beans and flavored with freshly ground pepper.

BOSTON BAKED BEANS

A classic of American cuisine and still as popular as it ever was, this dish comes out of the earliest traditions of the Puritans who first landed on our shores.

4 cups dried pea or navy beans
¼ pound Canadian bacon
1 cup pure maple syrup or molasses
1 teaspoon each, coarse salt and dry mustard
¼ cup chopped onion
⅓ cup each, ketchup and cider vinegar

4 twists of a pepper mill
2 tablespoons Worcestershire sauce (optional)
YIELD: Ten to twelve servings

1. Soak the beans overnight with water to cover. Drain and cover again with about 2 quarts of water; simmer for about 1 hour, or until the skins burst when blown upon. Discard any beans with cracked skins and drain. Reserve the bean broth.

2. Using a large casserole, preferably a traditional deep earthenware pot, layer the bottom with half the Canadian bacon. Blend the maple syrup with the balance of the ingredients.

3. Fill the pot with alternate layers of the beans and portions of the maple syrup mixture, ending with a layer of beans, covered with the balance of the Canadian bacon. Add enough of the reserved bean broth (or boiling water) to cover the beans. Cover and bake in an oven at 250° F for about 6 hours, then bake uncovered for an additional hour to brown before serving.

Bonus Ideas: Vermont Baked Beans are made in a similar manner, always using 1 cup of pure maple syrup instead of the molasses, however, and adding 1 teaspoon of baking soda to the mixture.

Swedish Baked Beans have a stronger flavor. This dish is served regularly with smorgasbords, and calls for 2 cloves of crushed garlic, 1 cup each of ketchup and cider vinegar. The maple syrup mixture is thickened with 2 tablespoons cornstarch dissolved in 3 tablespoons of the reserved bean broth, then baked in the oven as above.

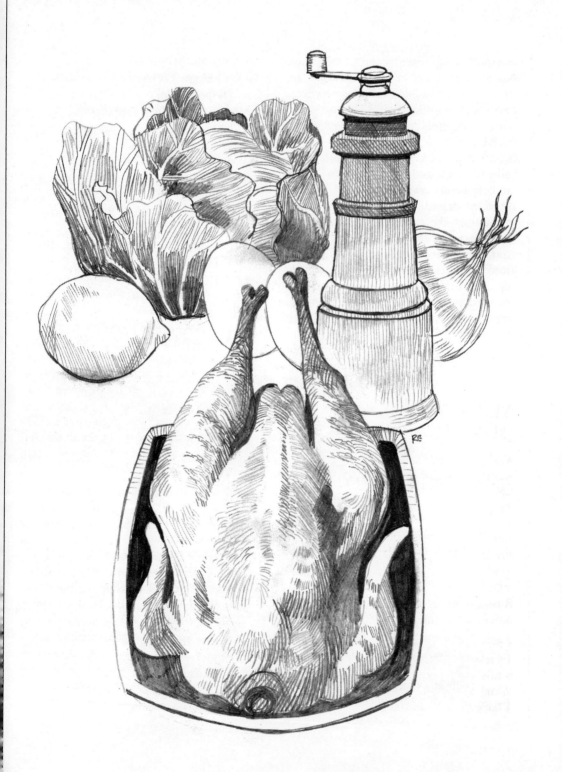

Another typically American legume that has become a traditional dish, often served in the South and Midwest on New Year's Day, is **Black-Eyed Peas,** often called field peas. To serve six, 1 pound of dried black-eyed peas is soaked overnight. Or, cover with 6 cups of water, bring to a boil and cook for 5 minutes, remove from the heat, cover, and let stand for 1 hour. Drain, cover with about 2 quarts of water, and simmer over low heat for 2 hours with 1½ teaspoons coarse salt, ¼ teaspoon of ground pepper or cayenne, and ¼ pound diced Canadian bacon. In the South, ¼ cup each of minced onion, celery, and green pepper are added. Add some of the reserved soaking water if necessary during simmering.

ALASKAN ROAST DUCK*

Wild duck is a favorite along southern borders and as far north as Alaska. Each region has developed its own technique for preparation, using ingredients for flavoring from the immediately available produce and influenced by surrounding ethnic groups. In Alaska, for example, the sportsman and housewife originally were influenced by Indian recipes, then by the Russians (from whom this territory was purchased in 1867).

1 5-pound duckling or wild duck
1½ teaspoons coarse salt
6 twists of a pepper mill
¼ cup polyunsaturated margarine
1 tablespoon lemon juice

Stuffing:
2 egg whites
1 tablespoon skim milk or water
2½ cups toasted bread crumbs or rolled oats
1 medium onion, minced
1 cup chopped red cabbage
½ teaspoon each, coarse salt and sage
¼ teaspoon ground pepper or cayenne
YIELD: Two servings per duck

1. If using wild duck, chill, then dry pluck and singe over a high flame. Draw and wash the duck, then pat dry. Season the inside and the surfaces of the duck with salt and pepper.

2. Melt the margarine, blend with the lemon juice, and set aside for basting. Lightly beat the egg whites with the skim milk and combine with the ingredients for the stuffing. Fill the cavity loosely with the stuffing.

3. Place the duck, uncovered and breast side up, in an oven about 500° F. Baste the duckling occasionally with the margarine mixture. Since wild duck is always leaner, it will require considerably more basting. When the meat is red, in about 25 minutes, the duck is rare and ready to serve. If you prefer the meat more well done, turn the breast side down and roast for 20 minutes longer. Serve cut into quarters with wild rice, or **Fried Hominy Grits, Polenta, Braised Celery, Purple Onions and Currant Marmalade** or **Sauce Abricot et Ananas.**

Bonus Ideas: When using wild duck, one is never quite sure how old and tough the bird may be. The tendons in the legs generally must be removed. If the duck is very old, you may well console yourself with preparing **Eskimo Duck Soup,** as they do in Alaska. Cut the plucked and cleaned duck into quarters and bring to a boil with water to cover, 1½ teaspoons coarse salt, 1 chopped onion and a **Bouquet Garni.** Simmer until the meat is tender; remove and cut the meat into ¾-inch cubes and set aside. Thicken the broth with 1½ tablespoons of cornstarch dissolved in 3 tablespoons of the broth and boil for 5 minutes longer. Return the cubed meat to the broth, heat through, and serve.

Throughout America, a number of interesting ingredients have found their way into stuffing for duck—no doubt as a result of their availability and the local ethnic influences. For example, wild rice, cornmeal, and oysters are used in the Creole cooking of new Orleans—except for the delicate teal duck and the celery-eating canvasback duck, which are served simply with melted polyunsaturated margarine flavored with lemon juice and/or minced parsley. In the Midwest, sauerkraut and apples are used; oranges and grapes in other regions; and aromatic vegetables and juniper berries in still others, to counteract the gamy taste of the wild birds.

There are also a number of ways of preparing the duck for cooking. Generally, these pertain to cultivated rather than wild ducks, since cultivated ones are inclined to have more fat under the skin. The variations are: simply piercing the skin with a fork before roasting, to release the fatty juices; boiling the duck first to release the fat; or one of the most intriguing processes I learned from Executive Chef Joseph Seppi Renggli of The Four Seasons restaurant in New York City:

FOUR SEASONS SMOKED DUCK*

1 5-pound duckling
½ lemon
½ cup light soy sauce
2 slices fresh ginger, shredded
1½ tablespoons honey or pure maple syrup
1 clove garlic, mashed
½ teaspoon fresh coriander, or ¼ teaspoon dried
½ teaspoon fresh grated orange peel, or ¼ teaspoon dried
2 tablespoons tea leaves, perferably black oolong
1 tablespoon raw rice
YIELD: Two to three servings per duck

1. Remove and discard any excess fat from the cavity and neck of the duckling, and place it breast side down on a large pan. Do not prick the skin. Season or rub with lemon. Refrigerate the duck for 7 days to permit the fat to run off and the skin to become firm. The degreased duckling will have a dry, crisp skin with a varnished appearance.

2. Combine the balance of the ingredients, except the tea and rice, and let the marinade stand for at least 30 minutes, permitting the flavors to blend.

3. Quickly dip the duckling into the marinade, or brush thoroughly, and place on a rack in the upper part of the oven. Add the tea and rice to a pan of water, and place on the lowest rack of the oven. Roast on low heat, at about 225° F for 2 hours in this Swedish variation of a Chinese smoke oven. Quarter the duckling

ing the winter, 1 cup each of broccoli, turnips, and carrots are sautéed separately in 2 tablespoons of consommé, 1 tablespoon of polyunsaturated margarine, ½ teaspoon coarse salt, and 3 twists of a pepper mill. When the vegetables are *al dente,* they are puréed separately, seasoned with salt and pepper to taste, and served as a colorful garnish to the roast duckling.

CRANBERRY AND APPLE JELLED SALAD

Wild cranberries and crab apples were among the foods the Puritans found upon settling in New England, and the Indians soon taught them how to tap trees for maple syrup. The crab apples were only edible after considerable cooking, but the Puritans had brought over apple seeds as part of their provisions, and these were soon planted to produce apples more suitable for cooking and making apple cider and vinegar. All of these ingredients soon found their way into many dishes that the Puritans adapted, using recipes and techniques brought over from England. To survive the winter months, drying and preserving became a necessity, but when spring arrived and fresh items again became available, they were used profusely. In England, the settlers had learned to prepare gelatins and aspics, which could not be utilized with the new ingredients.

Jelled salads do not preserve fruits and other ingredients for very long periods, but they do maintain them at their peak of savoriness for many days. Also, they add a festive touch to any menu. Either molded or presented in cubes intermingled with diced fruits, these delightful and refreshing salads can be made with virtually any combination of favorite fruits, vegetables, and nuts. Fresh pineapple, however, unless blanched beforehand, has limitations, since its juices inhibit the jelling process; but the canned variety can be used with no problem.

2½ cups raw cranberries
2 cups each, fruit juice and water or ginger ale
½ cup pure maple syrup, honey, or fruit sugar; or ¼ cup, if using prepared fruit-flavored gelatin
2 packages fruit-flavored gelatin, or 2 tablespoons powdered gelatin
1½ tablespoons lemon juice
¼ teaspoon coarse salt
1 unpeeled orange, ground
1 cup diced apples
1 cup diced celery
1 cup chopped pecans or walnuts (optional)
Polyunsaturated oil to rub inside of mold
YIELD: Eight servings

1. Wash and pick through the cranberries; boil in 1 cup of the fruit juice until the skins of the berries pop. Add half the maple syrup and simmer for 5 minutes; allow to cool.
2. Dissolve the gelatin in ¼ cup of the water (or ginger ale), then add the mixture to 1 cup of fruit juice, which as been brought to a boil. Add the balance of the water or ginger ale, the maple syrup, lemon juice, and salt. Allow to chill until the gelatin begins to set.
3. Meanwhile, combine the ground or-

ange with the cranberry mixture and mix well; then add the apples, celery, and optional nuts.

4. Rub the inside of a mold or bowl with polyunsaturated oil. Combine the partially set gelatin with the cranberry and apple mixture; chill in the refrigerator for about 4 hours, or in the freezer for ½ hour, or until firm enough to unmold.

5. To unmold, wrap with a damp warm cloth for several minutes or dip the mold into warm water. Cover with a cold and moistened serving dish and invert. Garnish with lettuce leaves or watercress, and serve with **Slimming Mayonnaise.**

Bonus Ideas: Canned fruits can be used, but will sink to the bottom of the mold. However, interesting layered effects can be achieved by using a combination of canned fruits with fresh fruits that will float on top. The jelled fruit salad has been adapted to the fresh produce available in varying regions of our country; combinations of fresh, frozen, or canned peaches, pears, apricots, or blueberries can be used, as well as bananas, melons, grapes, and canned or cooked pineapple.

CRÈME ST. HONORÉ
(French Confectioner's Custard*)

The use of gelatins for aspics and puddings was well known in the homelands of most of the settlers in this country, and was therefore readily adaptable to newly found produce. The English used gelatin for a custard still referred to as Bavarian cream. The French have favored *Crème St. Honoré,* which utilizes egg whites to achieve its distinctive fluffy consistency.

1¼ cup each, white rye flour and cornstarch or rice flour
5 teaspoons baking powder
3 tablespoons melted polyunsaturated margarine
½ cup pure maple syrup, honey, or fruit sugar
8 egg whites
2 cups skim milk
1-inch stick of vanilla bean
2 teaspoons powdered gelatin
4 tablespoons water
⅛ teaspoon coarse salt
2 tablespoons fruit sugar or ½ teaspoon vanilla extract
YIELD: Six servings

1. Sift the flours and baking powder 5 times. Using a wooden spoon, combine the margarine, maple syrup, and 2 of the egg whites. Scald the milk with the vanilla bean; then gradually stir the milk into the flour mixture.

2. Over low heat, or in a *bain-marie,* cook the combined mixture until smooth and thickened, stirring constantly. Cool, stirring occasionally.

3. Soak the gelatin in the water for several minutes, then heat over low heat or in a *bain-marie* until dissolved. Stir into the cooled custard mixture.

4. Blend the balance of the egg whites with the salt, fruit sugar, or vanilla, and beat until stiff peaks have formed. Fold into the custard and transfer to a serving dish or individual parfait glasses or custard cups. Chill in the refrigerator before serving.

Bonus Ideas: Another French favorite made with gelatin is **Blanc Mange***, or Snowy-White Custard. To serve six, simply mix, then gently heat, 4 tablespoons of powdered gelatin in 1¾ pints of skim milk until dissolved. Add ½ cup of pure maple syrup, honey, or fruit sugar, and 1 teaspoon of vanilla extract, blending thoroughly until smooth. Pour into a mold or individual glasses or cups and chill until firmly set. Unmold, and serve with **Slimming Crème Fraîche** and strawberry or raspberry sauce.

BAVAROIS
(Bavarian Cream)

One of the most versatile custards made with gelatin and egg whites is *Bavarois,* which has been described as an English custard combined with dissolved gelatin.

2 teaspoons powdered gelatin
¼ cup water
1 cup skim milk
3 tablespoons melted polyunsaturated
    margarine
⅓ cup pure maple syrup, honey, or fruit
    sugar
⅛ teaspoon coarse salt
1 teaspoon vanilla, almond extract, or
    your favorite liqueur
1½ cups Slimming Crème Fraîche (page
    305)
5 egg whites
Polyunsaturated oil to rub inside of mold
YIELD: Eight servings

1. Soak the gelatin in the water for several minutes; then add with the milk,

margarine, maple syrup, and salt to the top of a double boiler or *bain-marie.* Cook until the mixture thickens, stirring constantly. When mixture thickens to a consistency that will coat a metal spoon, remove from the heat.

2. Add the vanilla and allow the mixture to cool. Whip the **Slimming Crème Fraîche** and stir into the mixture. Beat the egg whites until they form soft peaks and fold into the cream mixture. Transfer to an oiled 1½-quart mold or individual glasses or cups, and chill for about 4 hours, or until firmly set. Unmold and serve with **Strawberry** or **Raspberry Sauce,** or any favorite crushed fresh fruit.

Bonus Ideas: Bavarian Creams can be varied with an assortment of your favorite flavorings. To prepare **Chocolaty Carob Bavarian Cream***, dissolve 1 tablespoon of carob powder, which has been prebaked for several minutes at 300° F, in 1 cup of scalded skim milk; then proceed with the basic recipe. **Coffee Bavarian Cream*** is made by dissolving 1 tablespoon of instant espresso in the scalded milk. Also you may wish to blend ¾ cup ground hazelnuts, pecans, or walnuts into the gelatin mixture when adding the vanilla or other flavoring.

A festive and popular variation of Bavarian Cream is **Charlotte Russe.** For six servings, line a mold or springform pan with **Italian Sponge Cake.** Prepare any variation of Bavarian Cream to your taste, but omit the beaten egg whites. Pour the Bavarian Cream over the cake and chill thoroughly for several hours in the refrigerator, or ½ hour or more in the freezer. Unmold and cut into 6 or more individual squares or wedges. Top each portion with whipped **Slimming Crème Fraîche,** a maraschino cherry, **Candied Fruits,** or ground nuts.

Slimming Crème Fraîche, the recipe for which follows, can also be used whenever you desire a thick whipping cream with other desserts, or over fresh fruits.

SLIMMING CRÈME FRAÎCHE*

1 can (5½ ounces or ¾ cup) evaporated milk
1 teaspoon powdered gelatin
2 tablespoons cold water
1 teaspoon pure maple syrup, honey, or fruit sugar
⅓ teaspoon vanilla, almond extract, or your favorite liqueur
YIELD: One-and-one-half cups

1. Place the unopened can of evaporated milk into a pan with water to cover and boil continuously for 15 minutes. Using a slotted spoon and heat-resistant gloves, remove the can and open it carefully; pour the milk into a mixing bowl.
2. Dissolve the gelatin in the water, then add to the hot milk, stirring thoroughly. Chill in the refrigerator overnight or in the freezer for ½ hour or longer. Just before serving, beat the mixture with a balloon whisk for at least 5 minutes, or until whipped to a fluffy consistency.
3. Add the maple syrup and the vanilla or other flavoring. If allowed to freeze, thaw thoroughly; then adjust the flavorings before beating with a balloon whisk until desired fluffiness.

BAKED ALASKA WITH FROZEN YOGURT*

This stunning dessert is a surefire conversation piece—so elegant that guests always assume it must be very difficult to prepare, marveling over the fact that the frozen yogurt remains hard and cold during the baking of the covering meringue. It is an American dessert that has been exported to other countries, where it is known as *omelette à la norvégienne* or surprise pudding. Reportedly, it was invented more than 200 years ago by an American physicist named Benjamin Thompson. No doubt it required a physicist to discover that the meringue, brown paper, and board underneath the pudding, being poor conductors of heat, would insulate the frozen mixture within. The dessert became internationally popular and was a perpetual favorite on Delmonico's menu in New York for many years.

Whether you prepare Baked Alaska as a large loaf, or as smaller individual servings, you will find it equally successful and a festive culmination of any meal.

1 tablespoon polyunsaturated margarine
1 1-inch slice of Italian Sponge Cake (page 110), or Angel Food Cake (page 308)
1 quart Frozen Yogurt (page 43)

Meringue:
5 egg whites
¼ teaspoon cream of tartar
1 teaspoon vanilla extract or ½ teaspoon grated lemon rind (optional)
¾ cup pulverized fruit or date sugar
YIELD: Eight servings

1. Preheat oven to 475° F. Line a baking sheet or dampened wooden board with brown paper or aluminum foil greased with the margarine. Cut the cake to form a 6- by 8-inch rectangle, about 1 inch thick, and place on the paper lining.

2. Place the brick of Frozen Yogurt on the cake, allowing a ½-inch border of the cake to remain uncovered. Set aside in the freezer while you prepare the Meringue.

3. Beat the egg whites, cream of tartar, and optional vanilla or lemon rind until foamy. Gradually add the sugar and continue beating until the mixture is glossy and forms stiff peaks.

4. Remove the cake and Frozen Yogurt from the freezer and quickly spread the Meringue to cover the Frozen Yogurt and cake completely. The Meringue must cover all the ingredients and touch the baking sheet or dampened wooden board to provide a complete seal. Decorate by swirling the meringue into a series of peaks, and bake uncovered in the center of the oven for 5 minutes, or until slightly browned. Serve at once on the wooden board or on a chilled platter.

Bonus Ideas: For extra richness, try sprinkling rum or brandy on the sliced cake, or layer with jam or a purée of fresh fruit. Using a pastry bag, you can add piped fluting or patterns decorated with **Candied Fruit.** If preparing individual Baked Alaskas, cut the cake into 3½- by 2½-inch portions. Place one eighth of the Frozen Yogurt on each slice of cake and cover entirely with the meringue. Individual custard cups can be used, but I find them unnecessary; they also detract from the striking presentation of a mounded delight. Although you can prepare Baked Alaska with store-brought cake or frozen yogurt, you will find our slimming recipes for both of these items more healthful and less expensive.

HOMEMADE YOGURT

Homemade yogurt can be produced with inexpensive store-bought yogurts, but this is not essential. All you need is a "starter" —an active culture that can be reused for years—and a constant heating source of between 110° F and 115° F to properly incubate the yogurt and whatever flavoring ingredients you prefer.

Many yogurt makers provide a starter with active bacteria; however, you can test any unpasteurized yogurt to determine whether it contains a live culture. Simply stir 2 tablespoons of the yogurt into 1 cup of warm milk. Cover and let stand at room temperature overnight. If the mixture thickens into a custardy consistency, you know the culture is alive and workable.

1 quart milk or skim milk
3 tablespoons nonfat dry milk
1½ tablespoons fresh yogurt
YIELD: One quart

1. Combine the milk and dry milk in a glass or enamel double boiler and bring to a boil over low heat, stirring constantly. Do not scald the milk, since any skin that forms must be removed before proceeding with the recipe.

2. Transfer the mixture to a warm bowl and allow to cool to about 110° F. Test by sprinkling some on your inner wrist, as when testing a baby's bottle.

3. Blend the starter into the mixture so that it is evenly distributed, but do not whip or beat. Pour into 4 8-ounce jars with covers.

4. Maintain the jars at the incubating temperature of between 110° F and 115° F for at least 6 hours, or preferably overnight. If using a yogurt maker, follow manufacturer's instructions for the balance of the recipe; if not, try placing the jars in an electric skillet, covering them with a heating pad; or place them on an electric hot tray set at medium-low temperature. When the mixture has reached the consistency of a thin custard, it is ready to be refrigerated overnight before using.

5. Reserve at least 2 tablespoons of the mixture to be used as a starter for your next batch of yogurt. If you prefer flavored yogurt, add ½ cup of your favorite puréed fruit to each quart of milk, and heat but do not boil. When cooled to the incubating temperature, add the starter and proceed with the basic recipe.

ANGEL FOOD CAKE*

The cake is ideal for Baked Alaska and other desserts. However, several words of caution are in order. First, for best results the eggs should be no more than 3 days old and at room temperature (70° F) before using. Second, whether you use a wire whisk or rotary beater to bring the egg whites to soft peaks, it is essential that the utensils and bowl used be absolutely grease free. Last, avoid banging the oven door or having anyone stomp around the kitchen during the baking period. It's worth the extra effort to guarantee an el-

egantly tall and delicate cake.

¾ cup rice or potato flour
¼ cup water chestnut flour
1¼ cups pulverized fruit sugar
2 teaspoons baking powder
12 egg whites
¼ teaspoon coarse salt
1 teaspoon cream of tartar
1 teaspoon vanilla extract
¼ teaspoon almond extract
1 tablespoon lemon juice
YIELD: Twelve servings

1. Preheat oven to 350° F. Sift the flours and baking powder twice and blend together. Sift the pulverized fruit sugar twice. Combine the flour and ½ cup of the sifted sugar and resift 3 times.

2. In a large mixing bowl, beat the egg whites, sprinkling in the salt and cream of tartar, until the whites are just stiff enough to form soft peaks and the mixture is still glossy. Gradually sift in 2 tablespoons at a time of the balance of the sugar, folding it into the whites.

3. Using about ¼ cup at a time, sift the flour and sugar mixture over the beaten egg whites and fold in gently. Fold in the vanilla, almond extract, and the lemon juice.

4. Spoon the batter into an ungreased 9-inch tube pan, preferably with a removable rim, and bake for 45 minutes in the lower third of the oven, until the cake is tan and has pulled away from the sides of the pan.

5. Invert the pan so that the tube is inserted into a narrow jar or inverted funnel and cool the cake for about 1 hour before removing from the pan. Cut with a cake divider and serve plain, with **Praline Custard,** or with fresh or puréed fruits.

Bonus Ideas: Angel Food Cake lends itself to delightful variations. Try adding (in step 3 of the basic recipe) 1 cup of walnut meats, ¾ cup blanched toasted almond slivers, or ¼ cup of grated orange rind with 1 teaspoon of orange extract. You can prepare **Cocoa Angel Cake*** by using ½ cup rice or potato flour, ¼ cup of water chestnut flour, and blending ½ cup of cocoa when combining the sifted flours in step 1. Or you can prepare **Marble Angel Cake*** by dividing the mixture into separate bowls after folding in the sifted sugar in step 3; blend ⅛ cup cocoa into one of the portions. Proceed with the basic recipe, but halving the ingredients to prepare 2 separate batters. Spoon in the batters alternately and bake according to the directions for the basic recipe.

MENU

New England Clam Chowder
Baked Striped Bass with Fennel
Stuffed Beet Cups
Sweet Potato and Nutmeat Pie

NEW ENGLAND CLAM CHOWDER*

Fish and seafood were abundantly available to the first settlers on the Atlantic Coast of our country. To utilize these, they quickly adapted their soup recipes, producing chowders or soupy seafood stews. At first, these chowders included vegetables, especially corn; later, in varying regions throughout the country, meats were added to or substituted for the seafood and fish, and other vegetables were added.

Virtually every American region has its chowder specialty, which indicates the versatility of this dish. You can serve chowder as a sumptuous appetizer or alone as a hearty luncheon dish.

1 quart fresh clams, or 2 9-ounce cans minced clams
¼ pound Canadian bacon, diced
2 onions, diced
3 cups boiling water
3 medium potatoes, diced
⅛ teaspoon ground white pepper or cayenne
3 cups milk, scalded, or 2 cups skim milk with 3 tablespoons nonfat dry milk, scalded
⅛ teaspoon dried thyme
3 tablespoons minced parsley
YIELD: Six servings

1. Wash the clams thoroughly but do not pat dry before cooking in a tightly covered pan over high heat for 10 minutes, or until the clams open. Discard any clams that remain closed. Mince the clams, strain, and reserve the clam liquor. Sauté the Canadian bacon and the onions in 2 tablespoons of the boiling water, until the onions are translucent.

2. Add the balance of the boiling water, the potatoes, and pepper; boil over high heat for 15 minutes, or until the potatoes are *al dente*.

3. Heat the clams with their liquor over high heat until the liquid boils; remove and combine with the scalded milk. If using canned minced clams, you may wish to add additional bottled clam juice.

4. Add the clam mixture to the potatoes and bacon and bring the chowder to

the boiling point; then remove from the heat. Add the thyme and serve in heated cups or bowls with sprinkles of paprika or cayenne and minced parsley.

Bonus Ideas: The more additional clam juice you use instead of water, the heartier and richer the chowder. To prepare **Manhattan Clam Chowder***, add ½ cup diced carrots and 2 tablespoons each of minced celery and parsley while sautéing the Canadian bacon and onions. Add 1 cup of drained canned Italian-style tomatoes, and reserve the tomato juices. Continue cooking for about 5 minutes. Combine the clam liquor with the reserved tomato juice and add additional tomato juice for three cups. Add the liquids to the saucepan with 1 bay leaf, 1 teaspoon coarse salt, and ⅛ teaspoon of pepper or cayenne; bring to a boil, then simmer for 30 minutes. Add the potatoes and cook for 15 minutes until almost tender; then add the clam mixture. Bring the chowder to the boiling point; remove and serve with a dash of dried thyme and additional minced parsley to taste.

Oyster Chowder* is prepared as in the basic recipe for New England Clam Chowder, using 1 quart of oysters. After adding the oyster mixture to the boiling chowder, continue to cook until the oysters curl at the edges.

On the Pacific Coast, fresh abalone is a favorite. To prepare **Pacific Abalone Chowder***, cook 1 pound of fresh or canned abalone in 3 cups of chicken broth until tender; then mince or grind. The chowder is prepared in the same manner as New England Clam Chowder, except that the abalone mixture is added with the potatoes and seasonings and cooked for

15 minutes longer, until the potatoes are tender. Season with thyme and serve hot, sprinkled with paprika or cayenne and minced parsley.

Our coasts and rivers abound with excellent fresh fish, and **Fish Chowder*** is popular in all coastal regions. To serve six, you will need 2 pounds of cod or any white-fleshed fish. If you can get extra fish heads, cover them with water and simmer for an hour; then strain to produce 2 cups of fish broth. Or you can use a combination of boiling water and bottled clam juice. Cut the fish into pieces and simmer in the broth for 15 minutes. Then proceed with the basic New England Clam Chowder recipe, adding the fish and broth after the potatoes are cooked. Bring the chowder to a boil and simmer for 15 minutes; then add 2 quarts of scalded milk. Return to a boil and remove from the heat. Add ¼ pound melted polyunsaturated margarine and ⅛ teaspoon dried thyme. Serve hot, sprinkled with paprika or cayenne and minced parsley to taste.

CIOPPINO*

A perfect instance of the intermingling influences of other ethnic cuisines on our own, *Cioppino* is a favorite along the California coast. It is virtually our American *bouillabaisse*. Some culinary experts insist that it was first devised by Portuguese fishermen working along the California coast; others are as adamant that it is derived from *burrida*, a Genoese fish stew adapted by the Italian fishermen who settled near San Francisco; and still others see Greek and Mexican influences. I spoke about *Cioppino* to some fishermen with varying ethnic backgrounds; most were amused by the theories. After all, they explained simply, it is quite natural for hardworking fishermen to avail themselves of easily available seafood and fish, and to prepare a hearty stew in the Mediterranean style after a hard day's work. In any case, it's a delightfully robust dish, often served with garlic sourdough bread and a hearty red wine.

1½ pounds striped or sea bass
1 pound raw shrimp
1½ pounds Dungeness crab or lobster
1 quart clams, oysters, or mussels
2 cloves garlic, minced
1 large onion, chopped
1 green pepper, diced
4 tablespoons minced parsley
2 cups wine, perferably red
3 pounds tomatoes, or 2½ cups canned
    and drained Italian-style plum
    tomatoes
½ cup tomato purée
1 teaspoon coarse salt
5 twists of a pepper mill
⅛ teaspoon dried basil
YIELD: Six servings

1. Cut the bass into 2-inch pieces; shell and devein the shrimp, but leave the tails intact. Disjoint the crab or cut the lobster into pieces without removing its shell. Scrub and clean the clams, oysters, or mussels and set aside.

2. In a saucepan, sauté the garlic, onions, green pepper, and half the parsley in 2 tablespoons of the wine until the onions are translucent. Cut the tomatoes into bits, and add them to the mixture with the balance of the parsley, the tomato purée, the wine and the seasonings; simmer over low heat for 20 minutes.

3. Add the fish, shrimp, and other seafood, and cook until the shells of the clams, oysters, or mussels open, being sure to discard any that do not. Serve hot with additional chopped parsley as garnish.

Bonus Ideas: For an added Mediterranean touch, you may use ¼ pound mushrooms and a pinch of oregano along with the dried basil. White wine, sherry, or Madeira may also be used, depending upon your preferences.

With the abundance of fresh corn in this country, the early settlers inevitably created **New England Corn Chowder.** To serve six, you will need two cups of fresh, frozen, or canned whole kernels of corn. Sauté ⅓ cup diced Canadian bacon, slices of one large onion, and 3 tablespoons each of diced green pepper and celery in 2 tablespoons of water or consommé, until the onions are translucent. Add 2 cups boiling water and 1 cup diced potatoes with 1 teaspoon coarse salt and 1 bay leaf, and simmer for 30 minutes, or until the potatoes are *al dente*. Add 1½ cups scalded milk, the corn kernels, and ⅛ teaspoon of paprika; simmer until the corn is cooked or heated through, if using canned. Serve hot, sprinkled with parsley.

In some areas of the country, ⅔ cup of mashed potatoes or soda crackers are blended with the milk before adding to the chowder. In our Southern states, four tomatoes cut into bits are added when sautéing the onions.

In still other areas, **Potato Chowder** is made by using two cups of diced potatoes and ½ cup diced carrots instead of the corn. After sautéing the onion mixture, as in the basic recipe for New England Corn Chowder, the potatoes and carrots are added to cook for about 15 minutes until *al dente.* One tablespoon of cornstarch is added during the last moments of cooking to thicken the chowder.

I habitually collect recipes, and one of my personal favorites, Mexican **Sopa de Flores de Calabaza,** or Squash Blossom Bisque, calls for squash or pumpkin flowers. To serve six, you will need 1 pound of either squash or pumpkin blossoms with the hard stems removed. Sauté the blossoms and slices of one large onion in 2 tablespoons of consommé or dry white wine until the onions are translucent. Add 1 teaspoon coarse salt and additional liquid if necessary and cook covered over low heat until the blossoms are tender. Grind the blossom mixture and dissolve in 2 quarts of scalded milk; strain if you prefer a finer texture for the bisque. Prepare a roux by sautéing 2 tablespoons of potato starch or cornstarch in 4 tablespoons polyunsaturated margarine. Just before the roux browns, add the squash blossom mixture, additional salt and pepper to taste, and remove from the heat when the soup has thickened. Serve hot with croutons.

BAKED STRIPED BASS WITH FENNEL

I first savored this memorable dish at the Ritz Hotel in Montreal, on a bitter wintry night many years ago. Simple to prepare, it will nevertheless entice your family or guests with its ceremony of preparation and marvelous aroma of burning fennel stalks.

Striped bass, one of our most delectable fish, is a must in the preparation of this dish. Originally, *loupe de mer* was used in France, but this is no longer fished as deeply as it was and the fish is now more inclined to be too mushy in texture.

Green fennel stalks, which can be grown in your own garden, are also available rather inexpensively in 2-ounce packages from leading herb and spice shops listed in the back of this book.

Here is our slimming version of the recipe used by Executive Chef Renggli of The Four Seasons restaurant in New York City.

1 whole striped bass, about 5 pounds
1 bunch dried fennel stalks, about 1 ounce
1 tablespoon coarse salt
1 leek or 4 scallions, green part only
1 each, carrot and celery stalk, diced
2 tablespoons diced onion
8 stalks fresh dill, or 2 teaspoons dried
1 clove of garlic, mashed
6 parsley stems
5 twists of a pepper mill
2 cups dry white wine or dry vermouth
2 cups fish stock, clam juice, or water
4 tablespoons potato flour or cornstarch
4 tablespoons polyunsaturated margarine
1 teaspoon fresh tarragon, or ½ teaspoon dried
1 cup Slimming Crème Fraîche (page 305) or sour cream
2 tablespoons Pernod
1 bunch fresh parsley
YIELD: Six servings

1. Clean the fish, removing the scales, fins, and any small bones, but leave the head and tail intact. Rinse thoroughly.

2. Place the fish in a large baking dish. Stuff the cavity with half the fennel stalks and sprinkle with the salt.

3. Add the vegetables, dill, garlic, parsley stems, pepper, wine, and stock to the fish. Bring to a boil over high heat; then place in an oven preheated to 500° F to bake for about 20 minutes. When the eyes of the fish turn snowy white, the fish is tender and done.

4. Make a roux by combining the potato flour with the margarine, and place in a saucepan with 2 cups of the strained fish stock, diluting with additional clam juice or water as necessary. Bring to a boil over medium heat, stirring constantly. When thickened and smooth, stir in the tarragon and **Slimming Crème Fraîche** or sour cream and adjust the seasonings to taste.

5. Line a large serving dish with the reserved dried fennel stalks and place the fish over them. Heat the Pernod; then flame and ignite the fennel stalks. After 1 or 2 minutes, extinguish the flames with the bunch of parsley. Starting at the head of the fish, roll back the skin and lift off slices of fish. Season with freshly ground pepper and spoon over the sauce. Serve immediately.

Bonus Ideas: Heated Cognac can also be used to flame the fennel stalks, which should be slightly green so that they do not burn too fast and will aromatically smoke the fish.

At Windows on the World, their version, **Grilled Striped Bass with Fennel,** is considered more authentic. The fish is placed into the bottom half of a fish grill,

and then grilled and flamed over the ignited fennel until the eyes of the fish turn snowy white. No liqueur is used. If desired, the fish can be pregrilled, with some of the fennel stalks in its cavity, until almost done, then transferred to a large serving dish, still on its grill, and cooked until done over flaming fennel sticks.

STUFFED RED SNAPPER*

Two other superior fish indigenous to our shores are pompano and red snapper, both abundant along the Gulf Coast. **Pompano en Papillote,** as we noted previously, originated at Antoine's, the famous New Orleans restaurant. Red snapper may be cooked in the same manner as bass; however, this stuffed version is a particular favorite of mine.

1 whole red snapper, about 5 pounds
½ lemon
1 teaspoon coarse salt
6 twists of a pepper mill
⅓ cup dry sherry, white wine, or dry
   vermouth
1 clove garlic, minced
¼ cup each, minced onions, celery, and
   scallions
¾ cup minced cucumber
3 cups dry bread crumbs or wheat germ
½ cup minced pine nuts, toasted almonds,
   or sunflower seeds
1 teaspoon fresh thyme or ½ teaspoon
   dried
1 tablespoon polyunsaturated margarine
YIELD: Six servings

1. Wash and clean the fish but leave the head and tail intact. Rub the inside of the fish with lemon and season with the salt and pepper.

2. Sauté the garlic, onions, celery, and scallions in 2 tablespoons of the wine until the onions are translucent. Combine with the cucumber, bread crumbs, and pine nuts. Moisten the mixture with all but 2 tablespoons of the wine and stir in the thyme.

3. Stuff the fish, leaving room for expansion; close and sew the cavity. Grease the bottom of a baking dish with the margarine; add the fish and the reserved wine. Bake in an oven at 350° F for 35 minutes, or until the eyes of the fish turn snowy white. Baste occasionally with the pan juices. Serve hot.

Bonus Ideas: Rather than sew the fish closed after stuffing, I prefer to leave the cavity open and cover the stuffing generously with crinkled aluminum foil. The fish is then baked right side up until done, and presented cooked, sitting majestically on its throne of foil.

GEFILTE FISH BALLS

Gefilte Fish, originally brought over by Jewish immigrants, and **Finnan Haddie,** or smoked haddock, which originated in Scotland and then became popular in New England, are other dishes that have influenced American taste. Gefilte Fish can be made either in egg-size balls or as a stuffed whole fish, as in the following recipes.

4 pounds filets of carp or pike, or any 2
    combined varieties of white-fleshed
    fish, and their heads and bones
2 large onions, chopped
1 large onion, sliced
3 teaspoons coarse salt
4 twists of a pepper mill
4 egg whites
1 tablespoon polyunsaturated oil
½ teaspoon honey, pure maple syrup, or
    fruit sugar
¼ cup matzo meal, crackers, or bread,
    soaked in skim milk
2 carrots, sliced
1 each, celery stalk and bay leaf
6 peppercorns
YIELD: Six to eight servings

1. Clean and skin the fish, and reserve the heads and bones; grind the filets with the chopped onions. Add 2 teaspoons of the salt, the pepper, the egg whites, oil, honey, the matzo meal and the skim milk. Mix well until fluffy and set aside.

2. Place the sliced onion, fish heads and bones, carrots, celery, bay leaf, and peppercorns in a large pot with water to cover. Bring to a rolling boil. With wet hands, shape the fish mixture into egg-size balls or *quenelles* and gently drop into the broth. Cover; simmer over reduced heat for about 1½ hours, then permit to cool in the broth.

3. Carefully remove the fish balls and set aside. Strain the broth and chill until it has jellied. Serve the fish balls with the jellied broth, garnished with carrot slices. Freshly grated horseradish and **Beet Salad** are excellent accoutrements.

Bonus Ideas: You may wish to adopt the trick of the trade used by the mother of Alan Lewis, director of Windows on the World. Place several pieces of silverware at the base of the pot when preparing the fish broth for this dish; these will serve as heat conductors, as when preparing **Velvet Chicken.**

I prefer serving **Stuffed Whole Gefilte Fish** using 1 4-pound pike or carp. Clean the fish, remove the skin whole, and reserve it. Grind the flesh and the other ingredients as for Gefilte Fish Balls; then fill the washed fish skin with the mixture. Boil the fish broth, as in the basic recipe, for 15 minutes; add the stuffed fish and simmer covered for about 1 hour, adding water or clam juice as necessary. Remove the fish; reduce and strain the broth. Serve either hot with the concentrated broth, or cold with the broth chilled and jellied.

FINNAN HADDIE RILLETTE*

Although Finnan Haddie is originally Scottish, this delightful appetizer has been influenced by French cuisine, as created by Chef Renggli of The Four Seasons restaurant in New York City.

1½ pounds fresh pike filets, trimmed
2 pounds lightly smoked finnan haddie
¼ pound polyunsaturated margarine
8 egg whites
2 tablespoons polyunsaturated oil
¼ cup Cognac or brandy
¾ cup Slimming Crème Fraîche (page 305) or sour cream
1 tablespoon green peppercorns
½ teaspoon coarse salt
¾ cup minced parsley
5 tablespoons frozen margarine, cut into bits
¼ cup dry white wine or dry vermouth
YIELD: Twelve servings

1. Dice the pike and trim away the skin and any dried yellow parts of the finnan haddie. Dice ½ pound of finnan haddie into ¼-inch pieces and set aside.

2. Grind the balance of the finnan haddie and the pike. Using two equal portions if necessary, combine the ground fish, eggs, oil, Cognac, ¼ cup of the **Slimming Crème Fraîche,** and the peppercorns in an electric blender or food processor. Blend until smooth, while slowly adding the balance of the **Slimming Crème Fraîche.** Transfer to a large mixing bowl.

3. Add as much of the salt as necessary; then fold in the reserved diced finnan haddie. Rub a 3-quart terrine or loaf pan with some of the margarine, and line with ½ cup of minced parsley. Spoon in the fish mixture, sprinkle the top with the bits of margarine, pour over the wine, and sprinkle with the balance of the minced parsley.

4. Cover the terrine with a double thickness of aluminum foil and place into a pan with water reaching two thirds the height of the terrine. Bake in an oven preheated to 350° F for 1 hour. Remove from the oven, but leave the terrine in the water to cool. When cool, cover with plastic wrap and keep in a cook place. Serve sliced directly from the terrine.

Bonus Ideas: You will want to serve this with **Chef Renggli's Horseradish Sauce.** It is simply made by combining in a mixing bowl 2 tablespoons of powdered horseradish, preferably *wasabi* powder (Japanese horseradish), and enough white wine to make a stiff paste. Turn the bowl upside down to prevent the aroma from dissipating, and let stand for 5 minutes. Invert the bowl, then whisk into the paste 2 tablespoons of Dijon mustard, ½ cup sour cream, and 1 cup of **Slimming Mayonnaise.** Beat until completely smooth; then let stand for 2 hours before serving.

STUFFED BEET CUPS

The beet is one of the most versatile of vegetables. It can be prepared in many ways, reflecting the varying ethnic influences of cuisines throughout the world. Its leaves may be cooked; and the bulbous beetroot can be boiled, baked, stuffed, prepared as a salad, served as a hot or cold borscht soup, pickled, made into a horseradish or marmalade. It can even be served as a glamorous hors d'oeuvre stuffed with caviar, as we have seen in the Head Start.

Whether boiling or baking, beets need little attention and require about 1 hour to cook depending upon the size of the beetroot; however, a pressure cooker can do the job in about 15 minutes.

And, if you are really in a hurry, the commercially available beets in cans and jars are of excellent quality; they are usually prepared with the addition of salt only.

6 medium-size fresh or canned beets
½ teaspoon coarse salt
1 tablespoon vinegar
4 tablespoons diced celery stalks with leaves

1 tablespoon minced onion or scallion
½ cup cooked green peas

Pennsylvania Boiled Dressing:
1 tablespoon potato flour or cornstarch
½ teaspoon coarse salt
½ teaspoon each, dry mustard and cayenne pepper
1 tablespoon polyunsaturated margarine
½ cup each, cider vinegar, polyunsaturated oil, and water
6 egg whites
YIELD: Six servings

1. If using fresh beets, wash in cold water; then boil in water to cover with the salt and vinegar for about 1 hour, or in a pressure cooker for 15 minutes at 15 pounds of pressure, until almost tender. Cool slightly and, using your thumb and forefinger, remove the skins. If using canned beets, drain well.

2. Cut a thin slice from the root end of the each beet so that it will stand; then scoop out the center of each, leaving a ½-inch shell. Chop the removed beet pulp and combine with the chopped celery, onion, and the cooked peas; set aside.

3. Prepare the boiled salad dressing by mixing the dry ingredients first, then the balance of the ingredients, except for the oil and egg whites. Place the mixture into the upper part of a double boiler, or into a *bain-marie.* Cook over boiling water until smooth. Beat the egg whites for about 1 minute; then add 1 cup of the hot mixture very gradually, stirring constantly. Gradually add the egg mixture to the dressing in the double boiler and stir constantly until it thickens. Add the oil and beat with a rotary beater. If the dressing is too thick, it can be thinned with lemon juice. You

should have about 1¾ cups of dressing.

4. Moisten the reserved vegetable mixture with some of the boiled dressing and fill the beet cups. Serve cold on a bed of lettuce or curly endive, and serve the dressing separate.

Bonus Ideas: Any combination of mixed leftover vegetables can be used for filling the beet cups. Either **French Dressing** or **Slimming Mayonnaise** may also be used instead of the **Pennsylvania Boiled Dressing.**

In Great Britain, diced cheese or cooked leftover meat is often used in combination with the vegetables for **Hearty Beetroot Cups,** which make an excellent luncheon or cold supper dish, served with your favorite salad dressing.

A variation made in our Western states is **Diced Beets in a Turnip Cup.** To serve six, pare 6 white turnips and boil with ½ teaspoon coarse salt and 1 teaspoon of lemon juice for about 30 minutes, or until *al dente.* Scoop out the centers of the cooled turnips, chop the removed turnip, and mix with 1 cup of diced cooked or canned beets, ¼ cup melted polyunsaturated margarine, and coarse salt and pepper to taste. Fill the cavities of the turnips with the beet mixture. Rub margarine in a baking pan. Cut off a small slice from the bottom end of each turnip and stand them in the pan. Sprinkle with a mixture of 2 tablespoons each of minced parsley and wheat germ or dry bread crumbs combined with 1 tablespoon of grated Gruyère or Parmesan cheese. Bake in an oven at 425° F for about 12 minutes.

New Englanders, on the other hand, prefer **Beet and Cabbage Chutney.** To prepare 2 quarts, use 2 pounds each of shredded red cabbage and cooked or canned beets that have been finely diced, and 2 large finely diced onions. Place the cabbage in a saucepan; add 1 cup of pure maple syrup or honey, 1 quart of wine vinegar, 3 juniper berries, 4 tablespoons mustard seeds, 2 teaspoons peppercorns, and 2 teaspoons coarse salt. Bring the mixture to a boil and simmer for 20 minutes; then add the beets and onions and simmer for 10 minutes longer, until the beets are soft. While still hot, pour into jars and seal; let stand for at least 2 days before serving.

An Eastern Mediterranean specialty is *Pancar Salatasi,* or **Beet and Yogurt Salad.** To serve six, you will need ¾ pound of diced cooked or canned beets. Prepare the dressing by whisking together 2 tablespoons of olive or corn oil and 1½ tablespoons of lemon juice. Add 1¾ cups yogurt, 1 teaspoon minced garlic, ½ teaspoon coarse salt, and ⅛ teaspoon white pepper; thoroughly blend the dressing before folding in the diced beets. Sprinkle with chopped parsley before serving.

UKRAINIAN CHRISTMAS EVE BORSCHT

Borscht, one of the most popular dishes using beets, is associated with Russia and has been adopted by Russian immigrants in many other countries, including our own. On Christmas Eve, the Ukrainians generally serve 12 meatless dishes; this is one of them.

⅔ cup dried mushrooms
2 medium-size beets, fresh or canned
1 onion, chopped
1 teaspoon parsley or celery root, cut into thin strips
4 peppercorns
2 quarts water
1 each, potato and celery stalk, diced
1 carrot, shredded
3 cups shredded cabbage
1 teaspoon lemon juice or beet kvas (page 319)
½ cup tomato juice
½ clove garlic, mashed
½ cup cooked white or lima beans
1 teaspoon coarse salt
5 twists of a pepper mill
YIELD: Six servings

1. Soak the dried mushrooms in warm water for 20 minutes; remove the hard stems and cook the caps in their soaking water until tender. Cut the beets into very thin strips and set aside.

2. Sauté the onions in 2 tablespoons of the water or tomato juice until they are translucent. Add the beets, parsley root, peppercorns, and water, and simmer covered until the beets are *al dente*. Add the potato, celery, and carrot, and simmer covered for 15 minutes, before adding the cabbage. Continue cooking for about 7 minutes, until the cabbage is *al dente*.

3. Gradually add as much of the lemon juice as necessary until the mixture is mildly tart; then add the balance of the ingredients, including the reserved mushrooms and their cooking water. Bring to a boil. The borscht may be strained and served as a clear broth, or as a thin broth with most of the vegetables removed. It is traditional not to add the reserved mushrooms to the borscht, but to use them as the filling for **Vushka,** or tiny dumplings, of which several are added to each serving.

Bonus Ideas: To prepare the dumplings, make a medium soft dough using 1 cup each of potato flour and white rye flour, 2 teaspoons baking powder, 1 teaspoon salt, 2 egg whites and ½ cup of cold water. Knead on a floured board until smooth; then divide into 2 equal parts and let stand covered for 15 or more minutes. Roll the dough into thin layers and cut into 2-inch squares. Place a square in the palm of one hand and add a spoonful of the minced reserved mushrooms. Fold over into a triangle and press the edges closed. Set aside until ready to use on a floured board, covered with a cloth towel to avoid drying out. Drop a small quantity at a time into the boiling broth; simmer for several minutes until they are puffed and ready. Cover and keep hot until all of the dumplings are cooked.

Vushka, also known as *pyrohy,* can be made with other ingredients, including ground meat or fish; part skim cottage cheese or ricotta also makes an excellent filling. Using 2 cups, combine with 2 tablespoons sour cream, ½ teaspoon coarse salt, and a pinch of fresh dill. Blend until smooth and stuff the dumplings as in the basic recipe. *Pyrohy* can also be served with wheat germ or bread crumbs sprinkled with melted margarine as a topping, or topped with minced onions that have been sautéed until golden in margarine.

Beet Kvas is the liquid of fermented beets; it is traditionally used to provide the desired tartness for borscht. Cover 4 or 5 coarsely chopped beets with boiling water in an earthenware or ceramic container. Allow to cool to lukewarm;

then add 1 crumbled slice of sour rye bread to the beets. Cover and keep at room temperature for at least 3 days. Pour the sour liquid into individual jars and refrigerate until ready for use.

Probably the most popular American use of beets is the sweet and sour version called **Harvard Beets.** To serve six, you will need 1½ pounds of baby beets, cooked or canned, and drained. Reserve ½ cup of the liquid. In a double boiler or *bain-marie,* cook until clear ⅓ cup cider vinegar, ⅓ cup pure maple syrup or honey, 1 tablespoon cornstarch, ½ teaspoon coarse salt, and 2 whole cloves or 2 tablespoons of shredded ginger. Add the beets, 2 tablespoons of polyunsaturated margarine, and 1 tablespoon of **Purple Onion and Beet Marmalade,** or any favorite marmalade.

SWEET POTATO AND NUTMEAT PIE*

Americans have been enamored of pies and cobblers since the earliest days on the New England coast. Applie pie has been a continuing favorite, but almost every region of the country has drawn on readily available produce for fillings, creating other noteworthy pies.

While Sweet Potato and Nutmeat Pie is believed to have originated in the South as part of its "soul food," it has found its way to many diversified parts of the country. As we learned earlier, one of Betty Silverman's warmest memories of growing up in Iowa was this pie. Traditionally, it is

made with pecans, but walnuts and other nutmeats can be used as well.

1 Wheatless Pie Crust (page 37) or purchased frozen pie shell
1¼ cups mashed sweet potatoes
½ cup pure maple syrup, honey, or fruit sugar
1 teaspoon cinnamon
¼ teaspoon salt
⅛ teaspoon mace
4 egg whites, lightly beaten
1 cup scalded skim milk with 2 tablespoons dry nonfat milk added
½ cup melted polyunsaturated margarine
¾ cup pecan or walnut halves
1 cup Slimming Crème Fraîche (optional; page 305)
YIELD: One 9-inch pie

1. Prepare the pie crust and place into a 9-inch pie pan; set aside and chill. Combine in a mixing bowl the potatoes, ⅓ cup of the maple syrup, the spices and seasonings, and the egg whites, blending well. Stir in the scalded milk mixture.

2. Pour the combined mixture into the chilled pie shell and bake in an oven preheated to 400° F for 20 minutes.

3. Meanwhile, combine the balance of the maple syrup, the melted margarine, and pecan halves, and mix well. Arrange a circle of the pecans around the edge of the pie and a decorative arrangement in the center. Bake an additional 25 or more minutes, or until an inserted knife comes out dry. Serve with the optional **Slimming Crème Fraîche.**

Bonus Ideas: No discussion of pies in America could possibly ignore the ever popular apple pie, which is prepared throughout the country in a number of interesting variations. To prepare a 9-inch **Tart Apple Pie***, you will need 6 cups (about 2 pounds) of tart apples, peeled, cored, and cut into cubes. Combine the apples with ¼ cup of pure maple syrup or honey, ¾ teaspoon of cinnamon, 1 tablespoon of lemon juice, and ½ teaspoon of grated lemon rind. When well coated, layer the apples onto a 9-inch **Wheatless Pie Crust**, and cover with a second shell which has been pricked with a fork. Brush the top crust with skim milk and/or egg white and bake in an oven preheated to 450° F for 10 minutes; then reduce to 350° F and bake for 35 minutes longer.

If serving with slices of American or Cheddar cheese, you will want to omit the lemon juice and rind from the mixture. A popular way of serving apple pie is *à la mode*, with a scoop of frozen yogurt.

Apple Crumb Pie* is made using only a bottom crust. After spooning in the filling, sprinkle the top with a crumb mixture made by sifting together 5 times equal portions of cornstarch and white rye flour totaling ¾ cups, 2 teaspoons baking powder, and ¼ cup of fruit sugar. Cut in ⅓ cup of polyunsaturated margarine to form fine crumbs. Place the pie into an oven preheated to 450° F for 10 minutes; then reduce to 350° F and bake for an additional 35 minutes.

Dutch Apple Pie* is similarly made, except that the crumb mixture includes an additional ½ teaspoon of cinnamon, and half the crumbs are placed on the bottom of a 9-inch pie plate, with the apple filling arranged over them. The balance of the crumbs are then blended with 1 egg white,

beaten until soft peaks form, and this mixture is spooned over the layer of apples. Using 1 additional pie shell, cut into strips to prepare a lattice topping to the pie. Bake in an oven preheated to 350° F for about 50 minutes.

A traditional fall favorite is **Pumpkin Pie,** which should be baked in at least 2-inch deep pie dish for best results. Brush 1 9-inch **Wheatless Pie Shell** with lightly beaten egg white. Combine 2 cups of precooked fresh, frozen, or canned pumpkin or squash with ½ cup pure maple syrup, honey, or fruit sugar, ½ teaspoon each of coarse salt and ginger, ¼ teaspoon each of allspice and cloves; then beat in ⅓ cup skim milk (¾ cup if fruit sugar is used), 4 lightly beaten egg whites, ¾ cup evaporated skim milk, and ¼ cup brandy. Pour in the filling and bake in an oven at 400° F for 15 minutes; then reduce the heat to 300° F and bake for about 45 minutes, or until an inserted knife comes out dry. Cool to room temperature and serve plain, with Cheddar cheese, or topped with **Slimming Crème Fraîche.**

SCOTTISH TEA SCONES*

The early Puritans necessarily revised Old World recipes to meet the new circumstances they faced. They devised the cobbler or deep-dish pies using a biscuit dough, instead of the more refined pastry dough they had used, and this dough probably influenced that used to prepare Scottish Tea Scones.

**1 cup each, white rye flour, and either
cornstarch, potato, or rice flour
5 teaspoons baking powder
¾ teaspoon coarse salt
⅓ cup polyunsaturated oil or melted
margarine
¾ cup skim milk with 1 tablespoon nonfat
dry milk added
Polyunsaturated oil to coat griddle
YIELD: Eight scones**

1. Sift the flours, baking powder and salt 5 times into a mixing bowl, or aerate in a food blender or processor; then pour in the oil and milk. Stir with a wooden utensil until the mixture is blended but not sticky and separate readily from the sides of the bowl.

2. Turn out on a lightly floured board and knead quickly into two equal-size smooth balls. Roll each ball into a round about ½ inch thick. Cut into quarters and place the pieces on a hot griddle rubbed with polyunsaturated oil or margarine; bake slowly on greased, hot griddle for about 20 minutes, turning frequently. When evenly browned, split the scones open, dab with margarine, and place in the oven until the margarine is melted.

Bonus Ideas: To prepare about 2 dozen 1½-inch **Biscuits,** knead the dough quickly into one large, smooth ball; then roll into a round about ½ inch thick. Cut into 1½-inch rounds with a floured biscuit cutter. Place on a baking sheet close together and bake in an oven preheated to 450° F for about 15 minutes for tall fluffy biscuits.

To prepare **Biscuit Dough for Cobblers,** knead the dough quickly into two smooth equal-size balls; then pat each into rounds ½ inch in thickness. Place the fruit mixture of your choice in an 8-inch baking dish, adding dots of 2 tablespoons of chilled polyunsaturated margarine and sprinkle with ½ teaspoon cinnamon. Cover the fruit mixture with 1 of the rounds of biscuit dough and bake in an oven preheated to 350° F for about 30 minutes.

I prefer to use a dish 2 inches deep and line the bottom and side with one of the rounds of biscuit dough. Pour in the filling, then cover with the second round of dough; press with a floured fork to seal the filling between the layers of dough. Puncture the top layer to permit steam to escape; then bake in an oven preheated to 450° F for 15 minutes before reducing the heat to 375° F to continue baking for 20 more minutes. Serve with **Slimming Crème Fraîche** or frozen yogurt as a topping.

Peach Cobbler* filling can be made by combining three cups fresh or frozen sliced peaches, 3 tablespoons of quick-cooking tapioca, ¼ cup pure maple syrup, honey, or fruit sugar, 2 tablespoons melted polyunsaturated margarine, and ¼ cup of water. Prepare the cobbler either with the biscuit dough beneath the filling, over the filling, or with two patted rounds of dough completely encasing the filling, which is my preference. Puncture the top layer of dough and bake in an oven preheated to 425° F for about 30 minutes.

MENU

**Crab Louis San Francisco
New Orleans Chicken Gumbo
Pennsylvania Dutch Potato Salad
Thomas Jefferson's "Pannequaique"
Crêpes**

CRAB LOUIS SAN FRANCISCO

The Dungeness crab from our Pacific coastline and the blue crab from the Atlantic are only two of the many varieties available in our bountiful waters. Many of these have been developed into regional specialties. With the advent of frozen and canned crabmeat, however, this delightful seafood is readily available in virtually every part of our country.

Crab Louis is associated with San Francisco and has become a staple of restaurant menus there. However, it was originally conceived in Seattle, Washington, where its almost instant popularity spread throughout the country and abroad. A refreshing appetizer, it can also be augmented with additional ingredients for a more hearty luncheon dish.

2 pounds fresh crabs or 2 cups flaked, cooked crabmeat

1½ cups Slimming Louis Mayonnaise:
¾ cup Slimming Mayonnaise (page 152)
3 tablespoons evaporated milk
¼ cup chili sauce
¼ cup each, finely chopped green pepper and onion or scallions
2 tablespoons lemon juice
½ teaspoon each, coarse salt and Worcestershire sauce
2 tablespoons minced parsley (optional)

1 head of Boston or other lettuce
3 tomatoes, peeled and quartered
1 tablespoon chopped chives
YIELD: Six to eight appetizer servings

1. If using fresh crabs, boil in 2 quarts of water with 1½ tablespoons of coarse salt for 20 minutes; dip into cold water to cool. Working from the tail end, remove the shells and use only the flaked meat from the bony tissue and the meat from the cracked claws. If using frozen or canned crabmeat, pick it over, discarding any membranes.

2. Prepare the Slimming Louis Mayonnaise by blending all the ingredients well and refrigerating until ready for use.

3. Place the lettuce leaves, whole or shredded, into a bowl or on individual serving dishes. Mount the crabmeat over the lettuce and pour over the chilled pink mayonnaise.

4. Garnish with the quartered tomatoes and sprinkle with chopped chives before serving.

Bonus Ideas: For a heartier luncheon dish, you may wish to add artichoke hearts or bottoms, sliced avocado, and chopped hard-boiled egg whites. Avocado has a special affinity to crabmeat. Halved and pitted avocados can be filled with the crabmeat and served with **French Dressing Vinaigrette, Dill Mayonnaise,** or **Slimming Louis Mayonnaise** to prepare **Avocado Stuffed with Crabmeat.**

The Georgia specialty, **Green Peppers Stuffed with Crabmeat,** can be prepared to serve six with 2 cups of crabmeat and 6 large seeded green peppers that have been parboiled with a pinch of soda for about 3 minutes. Prepare a sauce with 3 tablespoons each of cornstarch and polyunsaturated margarine, 1 teaspoon each of coarse salt and dry mustard, and 5 twists of a pepper mill. Add 1¼ cups of skim milk with 2 teaspoons dry nonfat milk and stir constantly over low heat until the sauce thickens. Stir in the crabmeat until blended, remove from the heat, and fill the green pepper cups. Top with wheat germ or toasted bread crumbs, dot with margarine, and bake in an oven at 350° F for 15 minutes.

Tomatoes Stuffed with Crabmeat and Caviar are simply made by stuffing peeled and halved tomatoes with equal portions of flaked and cooked crabmeat and red or black caviar. Top with the **Slimming Mayonnaise.**

DEVILED CRAB*

Deviled Crab is popular on both coasts of our country as well as in Alaska. It can be prepared to fill crab shells, individual rameskins, or can be served in the form of crab cakes, as a casserole, or as a filling for broiled lobsters.

2½ pounds fresh crabs or 2½ cups flaked and cooked crabmeat
4 tablespoons polyunsaturated margarine
2 tablespoons cornstarch or potato flour
2 teaspoons lemon juice
1 teaspoon dry mustard
½ teaspoon horseradish
¾ cup skim milk
¼ cup each, diced green pepper, onion, and canned pimientos
½ teaspoon coarse salt
¼ teaspoon each, ground white pepper and cayenne pepper
1 teaspoon each, ketchup and Worcestershire sauce
½ cup wheat germ or dry bread crumbs
3 tablespoons dry sherry
2 tablespoons polyunsaturated margarine, chilled
YIELD: Six servings

1. Prepare the crabmeat following instructions for **Crab Louis San Francisco.** Melt the margarine in a double boiler or *bain-marie,* then stir in the cornstarch, lemon juice, mustard, horseradish, and skim milk. Stir constantly over low heat until thickened.

2. Add the crabmeat and the balance of the ingredients except the wheat germ and sherry, and cook until heated through. Remove from the heat and blend in the sherry.

3. Fill the reserved crab shells, individual rameskins, or a casserole with the crabmeat mixture; sprinkle the top with wheat germ, dot with bits of chilled margarine, and bake in an oven preheated to 400° F for about 10 minutes.

4. If preparing crabmeat cakes, blend with the wheat germ and shape into 6 flat patties. Refrigerate for at least 1 hour before sautéing in polyunsaturated margarine until both sides are golden brown. The Deviled Crab can also be used as a stuffing for broiled lobster, or served on triangles of toast after broiling for 10 minutes.

Bonus Ideas: Bookbinders, the famous seafood house in Philadelphia, serves a similar version as **Baked Deviled Crab*.** For our slimming version to serve six, prepare the sauce as in the basic recipe for Deviled Crab. Then, in a bowl, beat 5 egg whites, 2 tablespoons polyunsaturated oil, and 1 teaspoon each of Worcestershire sauce and ketchup; add the hot sauce gradually to avoid curdling, while stirring constantly. Shape the crabmeat mixture into six equal-size mounds and arrange on a baking pan which has been brushed with melted margarine. Bake in an oven preheated to 350° F for 15 minutes until golden brown. Serve hot.

NEW ORLEANS CHICKEN GUMBO*

The basic stew is probably the most indigenous of all American dishes. Many of our regional stews, influenced by original homeland recipes, have enticing ingredients and techniques of preparation and include such dishes as goulash, ragout, pepper pot, Italian and French fish stews, jambalaya, and gumbo.

The name gumbo is derived from *kombo,* the Chocktaw Indian word for sassafras, an important ingredient of the dish, and in fact gumbos are a result of an interesting blend of ethnic influences. The French pioneer women in New Orleans had already been influenced by the Spanish and other Europeans, but it was the African slaves who generally took over the kitchens and the Choctaw Indians in the area who most influenced the Creole gumbo. Okra or filé (powdered sassafras leaves and herbs) are distinctive ingredients in an authentic gumbo, but never used together in the same dish, as previously noted in Head Start. Whereas okra is cooked with the initial ingredients, filé is added at the last few minutes before serving. Filé is available from the specialty shops listed in the back of this book.

Meat and seafood pies can be considered a refined variation of the basic stew, which has also been subject to a wide range of ethnic influences. Such pies include the British **Shepherd's Pie,** using leftover beef from a Sunday repast, and the Russian **Couilibiac,** filled with freshly caught salmon.

1 4-pound chicken
1 tablespoon each, cornstarch and
   polyunsaturated margarine
½ pound Canadian bacon or ham, chopped
1 large onion, sliced
2 quarts water
1 pound fresh or frozen okra, chopped
   (optional)
2 small red or 1 large green pepper
1 tablespoon minced parsley
½ teaspoon dried thyme
1 teaspoon coarse salt
2 cups skinned fresh or canned Italian-
   style plum tomatoes, drained
2 teaspoons filé powder (optional)
YIELD: Six to eight servings

1. Dip the chicken into cold water; drain, but do not pat dry, and brown in a skillet over high heat. Set aside.

2. In a heavy kettle, combine the cornstarch and margarine and cook, stirring constantly, over medium heat until the roux is dark brown. Add the Canadian bacon and sliced onion and cook until the onions are translucent before adding the water and bringing to a boil.

3. Reduce the heat; add the chicken, okra (if filé powder is not used), peppers, parsley, thyme, salt, and the tomatoes; simmer for 1½ hours until the chicken is tender. Cut the chicken into serving pieces, or discard the bones and cut the meat into cubes; return to the gumbo and serve with rice on the side. If okra was not used above, sprinkle filé powder over each serving.

Bonus Ideas: If you prefer, you can be-

gin by cutting the chicken into serving pieces before browning. As noted, filé is never used in the gumbo whenever okra is used. If you elect to use it instead of okra, do not let the mixture boil, and remove from the heat quickly, since filé can become stringy. Once filé has been incorporated into the gumbo, reheating will cause the same unpleasant effect. If freezing, do not add the filé until after reheating.

Creole Gumbo* can be prepared in the same manner using 2 pounds of shelled and deveined shrimp, 1 pound of crabmeat, and 1 pint of shucked oysters. Add 2 cloves of minced garlic and 1 tablespoon minced celery when sautéing the onions as in the basic recipe for Chicken Gumbo. Add 2 quarts of chicken broth or consommé instead of water and season with ⅛ teaspoon each of Tabasco, cayenne, and Worcestershire sauce; simmer for 1½ hours. Add the seafood and simmer for 30 minutes before serving hot with rice.

One of the most famous of all Creole dishes is Gumbo Z'Herbes*, a masterpiece of Black cookery. You will need a total of 12 cups of 6 or more varieties of such greens as spinach, beet or radish leaves, mustard greens, green cabbage, collards, watercress, lettuce, or parsley. Sauté the moist washed greens for about 12 minutes or until al dente. Drain, chop fine, and set aside, reserving the cooking liquid. Using 2 tablespoons each of cornstarch and polyunsaturated margarine, heat the roux until almost black. Add 2 chopped onions, 2 minced garlic cloves, the chopped greens, ½ pound of diced Canadian bacon or ham, 1 pound of veal brisket, and 1 ham bone. Add enough water to the reserved cooking liquid to make 1½ quarts

and pour into the gumbo. Simmer until the mixture thickens into the consistency of a purée; then season with 1 crumbled red pepper pod or dashes of Tabasco, 2 tablespoons of wine vinegar, and 1 teaspoon each of coarse salt, pepper, and cayenne.

BRUNSWICK STEW*

Both Virginia and North Carolina have Brunswick counties, and both claim to be the originator of the legendary Brunswick Stew. Wherever it started, it was originally prepared with small game such as rabbit, opossum, or squirrel and vegetables in season, especially corn and potatoes. In recent years, rabbit and chicken have been used, and lima beans have become a must among the vegetables.

1 5-pound rabbit or chicken, cut into
    serving pieces
2 teaspoons coarse salt
6 twists of a pepper mill
3 medium onions, sliced
2 cups water
½ cup dry white wine or dry vermouth
½ teaspoon honey, pure maple syrup, or
    fruit sugar
¼ cup diced Canadian bacon
2 cups canned Italian-style plum tomatoes
1¼ cups fresh or frozen lima beans
1½ cups fresh, frozen, or canned whole-
    kernel corn
2 medium white potatoes, diced (optional)
2 tablespoons each, cornstarch and
    polyunsaturated margarine
½ teaspoon each, lemon juice, Tabasco,
    and Worcestershire sauce
YIELD: Six servings

1. Cut the rabbit or chicken into serving pieces; dip into cold water, drain, but do not pat dry. In a heavy Dutch oven or pan, brown the meat over high heat and sprinkle with salt and pepper. Add the onions and cook until translucent.

2. Add the water, wine, honey, Canadian bacon, and tomatoes and bring to a boil. Cover and simmer over reduced heat for 1 hour.

3. Add the lima beans, corn, and optional potatoes. Bring the mixture to a boil; then simmer covered for 30 minutes. Blend the cornstarch and margarine and shape into small balls. Add the balls to thicken the stew, then the lemon juice, Tabasco, and Worcestershire sauce; continue simmering for 30 minutes longer.

Bonus Ideas: If using chicken, you may wish to discard the bones and return the meat to the sauce before adding the margarine and flour balls. If the optional potatoes are not used, you may add 1 cup of wheat germ or toasted bread crumbs.

Kentucky Burgoo*, like Brunswick Stew, was originally prepared in large quantities, using squirrel as the prime ingredient, and was served at political rallies, horse sales, and other outdoor gatherings. To serve eight, Burgoo is prepared by browning a 2-pound chicken and ¾ pounds each of the shanks of beef, lamb, pork, and veal, then simmering for 2 hours in 3 quarts of water. The bones and gristle are then discarded and the meat cut into cubes and simmered, with the same vegetables as those used in Brunswick Stew, plus 1 cup each of chopped cabbage and sliced carrots, for 30 minutes, with the seasonings and optional margarine and flour balls.

Philadelphia Pepper Pot* is as old as the American Revolution: it was first served to Washington's troops at Valley Forge. To serve six to eight, you will need ¾ pound of honeycomb tripe, finely cubed. Sauté in 2 tablespoons of stock or white wine, ½ cup each of chopped onion, green pepper, celery, and beets until the onions are translucent. Blend 3 tablespoons each of cornstarch and margarine and stir into the vegetable mixture. Gradually stir in 6 cups of veal or chicken stock; then add the tripe with either 2 cups of diced potatoes or ½ cup of uncooked rice, 1½ teaspoons salt, 5 peppercorns, and 1½ cups of canned Italian-style plum tomatoes. Bring to a boil, cover, and simmer for 1 hour.

Meat and seafood pies are a form of stew. Using **Wheatless Pie Crust,** you can prepare a wide variety of fillings for hearty and delicious one-dish meals or additions to a buffet. If topping the filling, cobbler style, you may wish to use baking powder **Biscuit Dough.**

Savannah Oyster Pie* has been a favorite since antebellum days. For a 9-inch pie, sauté ½ cup each diced celery and onion in 2 tablespoons of oyster or clam juice until the onions are translucent. Add ¼ teaspoon allspice; then mix in 2 tablespoons each of cornstarch and margarine and 2 cup of skim milk with 2 teaspoons of nonfat dry milk. Blend well, then add 1 pint of drained oysters and a dash of salt; cover with a single layer of pie crust or biscuit dough and bake in oven preheated to 525° F for about 15 minutes.

As we learned from Paul Fitzwater, Louisianans often serve meat pies. A substantial Creole version is **New Orleans Pork and Apple Pie***. Line a deep pie dish or casserole with 1 layer of pie crust and reserve the second for the top. Make a mixture of 1 teaspoon coarse salt and ¼ teaspoon each of pepper, allspice, thyme, and cinnamon. You will need 2 pounds of cubed lean pork and 5 medium-size peeled and sliced apples. Line the pie shell with alternate layers of the pork and apples, sprinkling each layer with a portion of the blended seasonings and equal portions of 3 teaspoons of honey, pure maple syrup, or fruit sugar. Dot the top with 1 table-spoon of margarine and cover with the re-served pie crust. Make several cuts in the crust and brush with a mixture of beaten egg white and skim milk. Bake in an oven preheated to 350° F for about 1½ hours, and allow to cool before serving the pie at room temperature.

Shepherd's Pie* has traditionally been prepared in Britain with leftover meat from Sunday roast: beef, lamb, veal or pork. To serve six, use 1½ cups each of diced meat and seasoned diced vegetables, such as carrots, celery, sliced onions, or chopped tomatoes. Combine the meat and cooked vegetables with 1 cup of leftover gravy or beef consommé seasoned with ⅛ teaspoon of Tabasco and heat through. Transfer the mixture to a deep pie dish or casserole that has been rubbed with mar-garine and cover with a layer of 2 cups hot mashed potatoes blended with some of the gravy or consommé. Bake in an oven preheated to 425° F for 15 minutes, when the potatoes will have browned.

Your favorite meat or seafood pie can also be prepared with a **Sweet Potato Crust***. To prepare a 9-inch shell, sift 5 times ½ cups each white rye flour and cornstarch with 2 teaspoons baking pow-der and 1 teaspoon coarse salt. In a mix-ing bowl, blend 1 cup mashed sweet potatoes, 4 tablespoons polyunsaturated margarine, and 3 egg whites beaten until soft peaks form. Stir in the flour mixture; knead and chill thoroughly before rolling out the dough in a ¼-inch thickness.

PENNSYLVANIA DUTCH POTATO SALAD

Although the potato was not indigenous to our country when the first settlers ar-rived, once it was introduced some years later it was readily adopted by immigrants from many lands. Each ethnic group influ-enced the use of potatoes, but the dish common to most of them was the potato salad, which is now popular in every re-gion from the Gulf States to Alaska.

In spite of the many variations of po-tato salad that developed, there are some striking similarities, particularly in those prepared by the Shakers, the religious sect that started in England in 1747, and the Pennsylvania Dutch, a group of German and Swiss immigrants who settled here at about the same time. Let us begin with our Pennsylvania Dutch version of this versatile dish.

2 pounds potatoes, preferably the waxy
   variety with red skins
2 teaspoons coarse salt
2 tablespoons each diced Canadian bacon
   and polyunsaturated margarine
¼ cup each, chopped onion and celery
½ cup each, water and vinegar
1 teaspoon dry mustard
½ teaspoon each, cornstarch and honey or
   pure maple syrup
⅛ teaspoon each, pepper and paprika
2 tablespoons fresh chopped parsley or
   chives
YIELD: Six servings

1. Cook the potatoes in boiling water
with 1 teaspoon of the salt until tender.
While still warm, peel and cut into thin
slices (about ⅛ inch). Set aside in a warm
place.

2. Sauté in 2 tablespoons of the water
the Canadian bacon, the onions, and celery until the onions are translucent. Add
the margarine and continue cooking until
the ingredients are coated.

3. Add the balance of the ingredients,
except the parsley, to the skillet and bring
to a boil. Pour the hot dressing over the
sliced potatoes and mix gently with a
wooden spoon. Serve hot with the
chopped parsley or chives as a garnish.

Bonus Ideas: Shaker Potato Salad is
the same, except that dry mustard and paprika are not used, and generally celery is
omitted.

Creole Potato Salad is made by sautéing ½ cup of diced Canadian bacon in 2
tablespoons of vinegar, then adding ⅓ cup
vinegar and bringing the mixture to a boil.
One tablespoon of polyunsaturated oil is
stirred in before the hot mixture is

blended with the peeled and coarsely
diced cooked potatoes. Two tablespoons
each of minced parsley, onion, and celery
are gently stirred into the mixture before
refrigerating for several hours until
chilled. It is served garnished with additional parsley, diced pickled beets, and 1
tablespoon of **Slimming Mayonnaise** in
the center.

A wide variety of ingredients find their
way into potato salads in different regions
of our country. Dill or sweet pickles,
beets, diced greenpepper, diced apple,
chopped hard cooked egg whites,
pimientos, radishes and pitted ripe olives
are only a few of the many possibilities.
Swedish Sillsallad, to serve six, utilizes 2
cups each of diced pickled herring, cubed
cooked potatoes, and cubed cooked beets.
These are mixed with 1 cup of cubed apples, 4 tablespoons of minced onion, and
seasoned with 1 teaspoon of honey or pure
maple syrup and 3 twists of a pepper mill.
The salad is served chilled with 2 cups of
Slimming Mayonnaise and garnished with
1 cup of sliced cucumber.

Alaska Potato Salad is prepared by
mixing together gently 4 cups of diced,
cooked potatoes, ½ cup minced onion, 4
diced gherkins, and 5 hard cooked egg
whites, minced. The salad is dressed with
4 tablespoons of polyunsaturated oil, 1
teaspoon Dijon mustard, ½ teaspoon
minced garlic, and thinned with 1 cup of
evaporated skim milk. One teaspoon of
coarse salt and 5 twists of a pepper mill
should be stirred into the dressing before
serving the salad at room temperature. I
like to garnish this and other versions of
potato salad with 2 teaspoons of minced
fresh dill.

A personal favorite is **Persian Potato Salad with Yogurt.** To serve six, prepare the dressing with 1 cup evaporated milk or sour cream, 2 cups of commercial or **Homemade Yogurt,** and season with 1 teaspoon each of coarse salt and fresh dill. Gently blend 3 cups of cubed cooked potatoes with 1 cup of chopped dill pickles; then toss with the dressing and thoroughly chill. Serve garnished with an additional teaspoon of fresh dill, or ½ teaspoon dried, and slices of cucumber.

THOMAS JEFFERSON'S "PANNEQUAIQUE" CRÊPES

Griddle cakes, of course, are also known as flapjacks and pancakes; President Jefferson often served sweet crêpes flavored with Cognac, which he called pancakes and his French steward called "pannequaiques."

Whatever it is called, the griddle or pancake is known to most ethnic cuisines and has names such as **Ugnspannkaka** in Sweden, *chun kwen* in China, and *bibingka* in the Philippines. It is made with potatoes by Jewish cooks, with cornmeal in Mexico, with buckwheat groats, or kasha by the Russians, and with puréed pumpkin or squash by South African cooks.

Probably there is no other American dish that has had so many ethnic influences and is so versatile: pancakes can be used in preparing appetizers, hors d'oeuvres, main dishes, and desserts.

¾ cup each, white rye flour and rice flour
3½ teaspoons baking powder
¾ teaspoon coarse salt
5 egg whites
5 tablespoons melted polyunsaturated margarine or oil
2 teaspoons honey, pure maple syrup, or fruit sugar
1½ cups skim milk
1 teaspoon Cognac or rum
YIELD: About sixteen 5-inch pancakes

1. Sift the flours, baking powder, and salt 5 times. Beat the egg whites, margarine, honey, milk, and Cognac with an electric beater or whisk, and add to the flour mixture, stirring only until mixture is moist and thick as a heavy cream. You can also blend all the ingredients in an electric blender.

2. Using a griddle, heavy skillet, or electric skillet which has been given a thin coat of polyunsaturated oil, spoon on enough batter for the desired size of pancake. Brown first one side; then flip over and brown the other side.

3. Place each pancake as cooked on a platter, stacking them after sprinkling with maple syrup. Serve warm.

Bonus Ideas: Try spreading **Purple Onion and Currant Marmalade** between the layers of the pancakes and sprinkling the top one with **Praline Powder.**

Of course, you can use the same batter for the stunningly effective **Crêpes Suzette,** but this cannot be considered a slimming dish from the caloric point of view. Prepare a sauce by blending ¼ pound of margarine with ¼ cup of fruit sugar, then blending in ½ cup of orange juice, the rinds of 1 orange and 1 lemon.

Bring to the boiling point in a chafing dish or electric skillet. Lower the heat and stir in ⅓ cup of Grand Marnier, Cointreau, or Benedictine. Fold the crêpes into quarters and heat through in the sauce until completely saturated. Pour in ⅓ cup of heated Cognac and set aflame. Serve immediately, sprinkled with **Praline Powder.**

Ugnspannkaka, or Swedish pancakes, are made with the same batter, omitting the Cognac or rum. After the batter has set for about 15 minutes, pour into a deep 10-inch pie dish or casserole that has been rubbed with margarine. Bake in an oven at 425° F for about 20 minutes until the large pancake has puffed up and is golden brown. Serve with marmalade or your favorite puréed fruit.

Russian Blinyets, or Blintzes are made with the same batter as Swedish pancakes. Pour 3 tablespoons of the batter on a hot griddle; brown one side only and transfer to absorbent paper. Prepare the filling by mixing together 1 cup of part-skim ricotta or cottage cheese, 1 teaspoon honey or pure maple syrup, 2 egg whites lightly beaten with 2 tablespoons of melted margarine or oil, ½ teaspoon coarse salt, 1 teaspoon each of orange and lemon rind, and ¼ teaspoon of cinnamon. Spread a portion of the mixture on the browned side of each pancake; then roll up with the ends tucked in. Rub polyunsaturated margarine on a griddle or in a skillet and brown the blintzes on all sides. Serve hot, garnished with marmalade.

In many countries including our own, the batter for Swedish pancakes, minus the honey, is used with a wide variety of leftovers for fillings; these make excellent luncheon and supper dishes. Your only limitation is your own imagination. Leftover meats, poultry, game, fish, and seafood can be blended with an appropriate gravy or sauce and other ingredients, such as leftover spinach, mushrooms, mixed vegetables, and soft cheeses. Brown one side of the pancake, fill the browned side and roll up with the ends tucked in. Brown in a skillet on all sides and top with additional sauce or gravy.

Israel has its **Matzo Pancakes,** made by soaking 6 matzos in cold water, draining, then pounding into a paste. Four beaten egg whites, 6 tablespoons of melted polyunsaturated margarine, ⅓ cup of matzo meal, and 1 teaspoon of salt are mixed together, then blended with the matzo paste. Spoon the batter on a griddle initially rubbed with margarine, brown on both sides, and serve as an accoutrement to a main dish or as a dessert.

German Potato Pancakes are made by blending 1 teaspoon each of coarse salt and honey, 3 cups of skim milk, 1¼ cups each of white rye flour and potato flour in an electric blender. Transfer to a mixing bowl and stir in 3 cups of grated potatoes; fold in 5 egg whites beaten into soft peaks. Spoon onto a griddle rubbed with margarine, brown on one side, then add minced onions before turning to brown the other side. Serve hot with meat dishes.

South African Pumpkin Pancakes can be made in the same manner as German Potato Pancakes, using fresh or canned puréed pumpkin instead of the potatoes and omitting the milk. Blend the ingredients well and ladle 2 tablespoons of the batter into an ovenproof dish layered with polyunsaturated oil that has been heated in an oven at 450° F to 375° F. Brown on each side, then transfer to absorbent paper, and pat dry. Serve sprinkled with **Praline Powder** and marmalade.

BLUEBERRY PANCAKES

It is only fitting that for our final recipe we return to the United States. This is our perennial favorite—for breakfast, dessert, or a supper snack.

¾ cup each, white rye flour and rice flour
3½ teaspoons baking powder
¾ teaspoon coarse salt
5 tablespoons melted polyunsaturated margarine or oil
2 teaspoons honey, pure maple syrup, or fruit sugar
1½ cups skim milk
5 egg whites
1 cup fresh, frozen or canned drained blueberries
YIELD: About sixteen 5-inch pancakes

1. Sift the flours, baking powder, and salt 5 times; then blend the balance of the ingredients except the egg whites and blueberries in an electric blender until the mixture is moist and thick.

2. Beat the egg whites until soft peaks form. Stir the blueberries into the batter; then fold in the beaten egg whites.

3. Rub a griddle, skillet, or electric skillet with margarine; then spoon on enough batter for the desired size of pancake. Brown first one side, flip over, then brown the other side. Serve hot with maple syrup, honey, marmalade, puréed fruit, and/or frozen yogurt.

Bonus Idea: If you vary the ingredients with 1 cup of minced apples, you will have prepared **Apple Pancakes.** You can also use 1 cup of drained peaches, pineapple, or cherries, or ¾ cup shredded Cheddar cheese for very delightful and very American variations.

ON BEING
A CAPTIVE DINER
ABOARD AIRPLANES
AND SHIPS

When dining away from home, most of us have a wide variety of choices, of restaurants or other eating facilities, so that we can select the kinds of food we prefer or need to suit our particular mode of living. However, there are special problems whenever we are part of a "captive audience"—and have little or no choice in the selection of the food that is served or how it is prepared. This is the situation aboard a ship, in a private club, an in-house feeding facility where we work, and especially when we travel aboard commerical airliners.

Most of us can manage with the menus of most captive eating places, selecting items such as broiled fish or lean meat, and others that are closer to our slimming or any other particular mode of eating. Aboard an airplane in flight, however, there are fewer options—unless one has had the foresight to order a kosher or other type of specially prepared meal. In such a truly captive situation, our choices are to consume the food that is served or not eat at all. Some critics—notably Craig Claiborne, who has written about this often—suggest that passengers on transcontinental flights carry aboard a box or basket of their own food, which can be as luxurious and satisfying as one wants, and could conceivably include roast quail, pâtés, and caviar. But for the regular traveler, particularly those traveling on business and often on short notice, this is hardly practical. Also it defeats the airline's obligation to serve well-prepared food that meets our needs and preferences.

This widespread problem increasingly affects a greater percentage of the population, as air travel throughout the world keeps growing by leaps and bounds; and for that reason we have investigated some of the problems and attitudes involved in the serving of food on airplanes.

During our tour of Italy, we met with Alitalia Airlines' executive chef, Leonida Morini, and a number of Alitalia's key executives in charge of their commissary and in-flight catering services throughout the world. From their headquarter offices at Fiumicino Airport in Rome, these executives direct the preparation of food, and are responsible for establishing the standards, budgets, and types of service for all of Alitalia's first class and tourist passengers on all their planes. We also visited the catering kitchens in several major cities that prepare the food for national, international, and transcontinental flights. Alitalia's operations are representative; their methods of food preparation and service are not unlike those of other major airlines throughout the world, whether they be Pan American, TWA, Air France, Swissair or Japan Airlines.

Alitalia's Vice-President Guido Raimondi explained that his airline's worldwide commissary division comprises three departments: planning and administration, in-flight service, and field catering activities. It is the responsibility of the planning division to establish standards of catering, general concepts (but not menus), and the budgets—consistent with Alitalia's image, marketing, and operations—on all flights. The first class and tourist menus and food service fall under the aegis of Executive Chef Morini and Traffic Senior Vice-President Paolo Conti, who is in charge of the commissary departments in all locations. One third of all the food on Alitalia's airplanes, we learned, is prepared in Italy in their own kitchens, while two thirds are prepared by outside caterers. In keeping with Alitalia's image, a principal variation from the menus of other major airlines is that a pasta dish is always included in each meal. Sixty percent of the meals are served on long-haul flights, the balance on medium-range flights; for instance, from Rome to Paris. Chef Morini is instrumental in determining the menus for all flights, and the field catering department decides on the necessary food service equipment.

In order to maintain standards of quality and service, Alitalia, like other airlines, has prepared its own Commissary Manual, which includes more than 2,000 recipes, instructions for their preparation, and even diagrams for arranging entrées, condiments, and eating utensils for both first class and tourist passengers on every type of airplane that is part of their fleet. Menus and service vary for Boeing 747s, DC-10s, and so on. The manual covers recipes for appetizers, main dishes, side dishes, sauces, and desserts, and for preparing dozens of different kinds of cocktails. In-flight Service Manager Delio Franca told us they are equipped to prepare special meals in most of their stations, in addition to standard menus, for passengers who request Indian food, kosher or vegetarian dishes, salt-free food, or baby food. "In defining menus for a particular station," Chef Morini said, "we must evaluate the foods available, determine the normal capabilities of the supplier, the sophistication of the cuisine capability, and the price. For example, on our long-haul flight from Rome to India, and then to Singapore, we will first serve veal prepared in Rome. However, since and serve with **Sauce Birgarde** (Orange Sauce), **Brown Sauce with Olives, Sauce Poivrade Verte,** or **Sauce with Green Peppercorns,** and with **Golden Fried Grapes.**

Bonus Ideas: At Windows on the World, Chef René does not mature the duckling. Instead, he makes several fork punctures through the skin, seasons the cavity with coarse salt, pepper, and rosemary, and roasts the duckling in an oven at 350° F, which, he says, maintains the meat's moistness while at the same time draining off the excess fat. He serves it with the natural duck juices, flavored with green peppercorns. This dish is garnished with **Three Purées** of vegetables in contrasting colors.

Sauce Birgarde, or Orange Sauce, can be easily made to serve six by deglazing the pan juices, after roasting the duckling and removing the fat from the pan, with ¼ cup of white wine or dry vermouth and 2 tablespoons Cognac. Add 1 cup of orange juice and ⅓ cup of lemon juice and reduce the mixture over medium heat until most of the liquid has evaporated. Add 2 cups of **Quick Brown Sauce Espagnole** and simmer for 10 minutes, strain and pour over the duckling, or serve separately.

Quick Brown Sauce Espagnole is prepared by cooking 8 tablespoons of polyunsaturated margarine in a saucepan until it browns. Gradually add 6 tablespoons of cornstarch and stir until the mixture is a smooth roux. Add 2 cups of hot beef stock and stir with a wooden spoon until the mixture is well blended. Season with salt and pepper to taste, and simmer over low heat for 10 minutes. Add 1 teaspoon of tomato paste and ¼ cup of red wine and

simmer for at least an additional 10 minutes to yield 2 cups. If the sauce is too thick, add hot stock; adjust seasonings.

Brown Sauce with Olives is excellent with roast duck. Simply boil ·1 dozen stoned olives for 5 minutes, drain them, and simmer in 2 cups of **Quick Brown Sauce Espagnole** for 10 minutes before serving.

Sauce Poivrade Verte, or Sauce with Green Peppercorns, is made by sautéeing 1 sliced onion, 1 shredded carrot, and 2 sprigs of parsley in 2 tablespoons of dry white wine or consommé until the onions are translucent. Add 1 bay leaf, a dozen green peppercorns, ½ teaspoon dried thyme, and ¾ cup of wine vinegar. Boil over high heat until the liquid is reduced by half; add 2 cups of **Quick Brown Sauce Espagnole** and cook over high heat for about 10 minutes longer. Thicken with 1 teaspoon of cornstarch dissolved in 1 tablespoon of water or consommé; add ¾ cup of red wine and simmer, covered, for 30 minutes. If black peppercorns are used instead of the green, you will have prepared **Sauce Poivrade Ordinaire.** For **Duckling au Poivre Verte,** I prefer pressing the peppercorns into the skin of the duckling during the last 15 minutes of cooking. When cooked, I flambé the duckling with 2 tablespoons of preheated Cognac and serve **Sauce Poivrade Verte** separately.

Most cooked fruits lend themselves to the flavoring of duckling, and one of the more interesting is fried grapes, as served by Chef Renggli of The Four Seasons.

Three Purées, the garnish favored by Chef René, consists simply of three balls of puréed vegetables in contrasting colors. Any vegetables in season will serve; durby TWA would result in better and more exciting efforts by other great chefs on subsequent flights. "Hardly," commented Vergé. "We can't do this for more than 200 persons at a time, and it takes many days of preparation. And if meals were to be cooked in the United States, it would require another ten days for all of us to be here. You must keep in mind that airlines require 20,000, not 200, meals for flights in major cities, so it just can't be done on a regular basis!"

As to the economics of such a meal, even TWA officials confessed that the cost of the inaugural flight meal was at least double the cost of a standard first class meal. My article concluded that such meals "would be impractical on a general basis, even if one-class service were to be instituted permanently.

In order to assess some of the problems in preparing and serving satisfactory meals aboard airliners, I made it a point to visit a number of kitchens designed specifically to prepare the food, the trays, and first class specialties for a number of airlines. Many of the major airlines have their own kitchens, but all of them use professional caterers in some locations to provide these services, using each airline's own menus and equipment components. After visiting one of these outside-caterer kitchens, you come away with two main impressions. The first is an awareness that the kitchen is a huge assembly line, not unlike those in factories. These kitchens (which are not open to the public) are clean, functional, and equipped with every timesaving device to prepare and assemble the food quickly, place it on trays, stack them in rolling carts, and transfer the food and compo-

nents for service to the individual airplanes, on which the dishes will be heated and/or additionally cooked and served by the in-flight crew. The second impression is that you are also in a high-pressure expediting operation. Whereas the vast kitchen brigade works quietly and efficiently at their individual chores, the expediting arm of the operation is noisy, frenetic, and appears to be struggling with numerous details. One has more of a sense of being in the tower of a busy airport, than in a kitchen operation.

The De Montis Corporation is the outside caterer used by Alitalia in the Linate and Malpensa airports in Milan for both international and transcontinental flights. Since De Montis' kitchens also provide meals for TWA, British Airways, Iberia, MEA, and other airlines, this caterer must prepare foods in keeping with the menus and standards of each of the airlines, and use the trays, utensils, and other components of service provided by the individual airlines—each of which has its own image to maintain. The expediting arm of the operation, therefore, must be in constant communication with each of the airlines in terms of schedule changes, delays due to weather, or other problems, and must consider every factor that has a bearing on properly expediting the food for placement on the respective airplanes involved.

George Lang's description of the expediting arm of a catering kitchen is particularly relevant here. "The problems of a catering kitchen like Marriott's kitchens in Heathrow or Frankfurt are typified by the enormous electronic board you will see in each location. Let's say they are serving five major airlines and six minor ones, which is probably average; they may have contracts with TWA and Qantas, and then with some of the smaller airlines like Aeroflot. The major airlines may have five to seven flights a day, and each with different menus for economy and first class. The damn board keeps flashing as the reservations and cancellations come in: flight 206 Qantas now becomes 289—and there's only a half hour loading time. So either they have stuff prepared beforehand in the freezer, or they will do it any way they can to meet the emergency. Actually, you are talking about a kitchen equivalent to one serving 60 restaurants, all with different menus and serving requirements, and each changing by the second. Passengers don't understand this problem when they complain about the horrible catering of food aboard a plane. It is; but so would it be if they were traveling to the moon, or down 10,000 feet beneath the earth, or to any place with that kind of built-in difficulty. One of the answers is the suggestion of my friend Craig Claiborne—to take along your own food. It's a very good answer, and I do it very often."

Another problem is the variety of the cooking ovens aboard the various types of aircraft used by the airlines. Generally, an instruction card accompanies each serving of food, so that the cabin attendants can set the proper temperature and time to heat or additionally cook each dish. However, the ovens—like too many in our home kitchens—can produce temperatures other than those set on the oven dial. I have discussed this problem with stewards and stewardesses on a number of different airlines and types of planes in many parts of the world, and most have told me that they usually have to make compensations

in timing the ovens, depending on the efficiency of the particular ovens available and the number of trays or items the oven will hold at one time.

On Alitalia's airplanes, Chef Morini told us, pursers know the problems of each kitchen and will check each oven and indicate whatever compensations may be necessary to the cabin attendant. Once the cabin attendant sets the temperature and timing required, he is responsible for checking halfway through the cooking period to be sure each dish is properly prepared. "You see, we want our passengers to have the best food we can prepare for them, cooked properly and served well," the chef said. "Once we place the food on a plane, it is either consumed by the passenger, or it is destroyed. Everything has been timed for its proper consumption."

Some airlines, such as Laker in Great Britain, are offering reduced airfares and accommodations without serving food. We discussed this concept with Joseph Baum and Ruth Epstein of Windows on the World. "I really can't answer whether I think people should be given the option to purchase or bring aboard their own food. I haven't worked on the problems of airline food, but I would say most attempts to improve it have really been only cosmetic," said Mr. Baum.

Ruth Epstein suggested that Mr. Baum had never considered people as a captive audience, which is the situation on an airline. But Joseph Baum remembered being on a national airline's tasting board, and told us of the experience. "I was asked to come up to an office on Third Avenue and sit in a mock-up of an airplane, and to be served a meal. It was lunch on a 'flight' to San Francisco, and we went through the

ON BEING A CAPTIVE DINER

motions of an actual flight. They served a Bloody Mary, then appetizers and so forth, and then wine. Then at the end of it, they came around with cordials. This was first class service, but it could be any class. I asked the president of the airline, who was there, how much that extra booze might cost, since even if it were only fifty cents, that was a lot of money, compared to the overall budget for the meal. Then I asked him if he really thought they had to serve an after-luncheon cordial, which nobody drinks as a rule. He asked his assistants about this; then they brought out the charts and told him just what each of the other competitive airlines did on the question of serving cordials after lunch. The president then said, 'Do you know how many people call to find out what we serve, and how much business we would lose if we didn't serve that after lunch drink and another airline did?' They really check on one another." Mr. Baum was on this board as a result of something that had happened to him in San Francisco, which was something of a joke. "I had had a very rough night and didn't get to bed until about 5:00 in the morning. At 7:30 A.M. the telephone rings and it was the airline wanting to know which choice of sandwiches I wanted for lunch on the plane. You know, this whole situtation gets so ridiculous."

Mr. Baum reasons that the entire concept of in-flight food service has to change. Taste, preferences, evidence of choice—these values require examination, especially in connection to the way people have changed, or now look at things differently. "What do we enjoy, or enjoy more?" he wondered. "Are we willing to wait twenty minutes for gratification—or do we have to have it with the first course?"

Later we chatted with Alan Lewis and Barbara Kafka of Windows on the World about the problems of airline food. "I am disgusted with the problem," Alan said, "because they haven't taken the matter in hand, and they try to do things that they are not equipped to do. I think that for the average time an average red-blooded American is on an airplane, if you gave him a bowl of soup and a halfway decent sandwich, on decent bread with real fillings, and a good cup of coffee—the passenger would kiss you. Instead they are trying to give you Maxim's service—there was a time they wanted The Four Seasons' service—and there's now a restaurant in New Orleans supplying food; but none of them supply 'their' food." Barbara Kafka observed that one of the popular in-flight dishes is veal cordon bleu, which becomes chicken cordon bleu on cheaper flights. It is virtually impossible to make it properly, however, for an airline meal. The ground veal they use is mashed into a patty, then prosciutto and cheese are added, and then they freeze it. On board the plane, it's stewed in a sauce to heat it through. "Now, what relationship does that have to any food that we know anything about?" she asked.

Our discussion touched on food as a love gesture. We observed that the airlines seemed to be overfeeding people as a psychological comforter during flight. Alan Lewis and Barbara Kafka agreed. But the quesion, as Alan pointed out, is what makes a passenger feel comfortable? "Certainly not a cold jello salad," said Miss

Kafka. "And I'm sure that a good cup of hot soup would make them far more comfortable psychologically."

Another complaint voiced by Alan Lewis concerned the wine served on planes. The food can be abominable and the service virtually nonexistent on some flights, but on top of that, he said, they give you bad wine. "They advertise that they are going to give you this great meal with champagne, and then they serve you cheap American sparkling wine most of the time. Now we probably sell more American wines at Windows than anybody else in the country, but we select only the good American wines; and there are plenty of them available. With the airlines, it's a matter both of ignorance and cost. These are responsible for the problems." Mr. Lewis had also been invited to be on the wine-tasting panel for one of the major airlines, and his choices, he said, were consistently the opposite of those of everyone else. The others on the panel were office people, such as clerks, stenographers, and middle executives. "Later, I asked the guy who arranged for the wine tasting why he had had me and the other people on the panel. He replied, 'That's the average American audience.' Well, I disagreed with him then, and I disagree with him now. Whatever you do, it should be done the right way; how can you quibble with excellence? How can something be average good or halfway excellent; if it's half good, then the other half is bad."

Do the airlines make such decisions regarding food service because they don't know any better, or do they believe their public doesn't? Alan Lewis suggested that they just don't have the right attitude toward the intelligence of their passengers, and they are insecure themselves because the people in charge really understand so few of the problems involved. Barbara Kafka added that she had once been retained by the president of a national airlines as a consultant on the selection of wines for their flights. "Everything went along well, until the president got involved with other problems and the project was run by a brand-new guy in a pale blue BanLon suit. All I can tell you is that there was no chance of getting anywhere. I had made a fantastic wine selection with special half bottles from California vineyards, which they had agreed to do for the first time. Do you know how he finally picked the wines? He consulted the American frequency chart of the most consumed bottled wines—and that is what he bought!"

When we spoke with Charles Bell of Hilton International, which is related to TWA airlines, he chuckled and said, "I don't think I'd better get into that subject, but I would be happy if I could get a good cup of coffee." I mentioned that this has been a problem for many years, and recalled traveling as a consultant with a top executive of American Airlines in connection with the planning and design of new offices for the firm in California; over 25 years ago he was concerned with their inability to provide an adequate cup of coffee on their flights. At that time, the American Airlines executive attributed the problem to the variations in the quality of water in different stations along their routes. "They should be able to get decent water in New York and Chicago," Charles

Bell suggested. "If you place a spoonful of freeze-dried coffee in a cup of hot water, you get a better cup than you get on most airlines. Maybe they ought to give everyone on board a package of freeze-dried coffee and a cup of boiling water and let the passengers mix it; at least they won't complain if they mix it themselves."

Paula Galusha, whom we met on our tour of the United States, believes that airline food has improved a great deal, although the difference in food quality between first class and tourist is extensive. She found out recently that you can order a particular meal ahead of time. "I call and ask what they are serving on our flight, and if it's not exactly what I want, I'll order a chef's salad. Most of the meals I have had on planes have been acceptable; but, of course, you can't expect anything special."

When we met with George Lang, we were able to expand our inquiry to cover the problems of feeding a captive audience on luxury ships. On ships, as in other situations where there is a captive audience, special consideration, Mr. Lang thought, must be given to the nature of "the human animal versus the *animal* animal." He pointed out that whereas animals dislike the unexpected, preferring a rigid regime, especially where food is concerned, people prefer a certain amount of variety. "My cats would be very upset if they were fed something they are not used to, because they are absolutely attuned to a certain regime. The human animal is totally different: he gets upset mentally, rather than physically, when his regime is changed. Actually, he would be infinitely better off physically if he got the same type of food,

and approximately the same amount, at roughly the same time each day. When they did studies on geriatrics in Russia, Armenia, and elsewhere, they found that among the people who lived the longest the only common denominator besides yogurt and apricots—which I personally don't believe were that important—was that these people had lived the most regimented life from the day they were born until they died. Now, physically, it would be terrific if every day at 12:30 P.M. a member of a private club were to eat a shrimp cocktail, a broiled piece of veal with fresh vegetables, and a piece of cheese with a fresh pear. Depending on the person, however, he would revolt by the third day or third week, no matter how fresh and well prepared everything was. People don't like repetition; they prefer variety, and how much variety depends on the age group, the culture, the intelligence, the upbringing, and the background of the particular people involved. An Italian will want to have a pasta at every meal; and a New Yorker, sure as hell, is not going to order onion soup tomorrow if he ate it today."

Mr. Lang applied this analysis to the practical problems of providing food service in a club or on a ship; you have to "build in" a variety, or a seeming variety, and that is not an easy thing to achieve. It is particularly difficult in clubs, because the members frequent them repeatedly, year in and year out. I have been involved with several luxury ships with my associate Alan Reyburn—who previously was head of the Cunard Line; we worked on the *QE 2* and such other luxury liners as the *Daphne*. Our biggest problem was the extreme difficulty of bringing in top cooks, chefs, and dining room personnel. This depends on the nationality of the ship, for you have to engage a large percentage of a particular nationality, in accordance with the prevailing laws of the country of origin. For instance, by law, a minimum of 85 percent of the personnel on a Greek ship must be Greek; otherwise the ship cannot sail under the Greek flag. "This causes problems, because you are certianly going to have the greatest *moussakas* and *mezes* in the world, but you will have very great difficulty when you try to serve a simple but good *consommé*," Mr. Lang said.

The second problem you face on ships is arranging for food supplies in such a way that wherever a ship goes, a purchasing agent can obtain the freshest fish, vegetables, fowl, fruits, and cheeses from that country. Mr. Lang has had limited success doing this, since it is a very difficult thing to achieve. Luxury ships don't always put into ports on a routine basis where such special purchasing is possible; so they have to use a great deal of frozen and canned food and only a minimal amount of top-grade fresh food. The third problem, he said, is that the restaurant industry has moved out of the old concepts of the hotel field since World War II, while ship cuisine has never moved out: "It's still as a hotel kitchen used to be conceptually: the same ideas, the same selections, the same tired, nine-times-removed, bastardized versions of classic French and international cuisines. Unfortunately, those who really tried to move out, like the S.S. *France*, and to some degree the *Michelangelo*, went out of business." Ship cuisine

could be re-created, he thought, in the same way that the restaurant industry was redone, through various specialty restaurants, but it will take not only talented restaurateurs, but those who are familiar with working at sea, which is a very different world altogether. "Remember, everything is miniaturized, including the galleys; and there are a lot of built-in problems that have to be solved. But presuming you had such a restaurateur, with our consulting organization we could do it. We would have to have certain conditions, like an owner who believes in it and enough business to support it."

Our discussions then returned to the problems of catering airline food, which George Lang thinks are different from those of the luxury ships. "Here's a classic case where I could argue for all three sides," he said, "the passenger, the airline, and the caterer. Sometimes the caterer and the airline are identical, as in the case of American Airlines; more often than not, they are not the same. The airlines generally go to a caterer to supply them, and, furthermore, it's not always the same caterer who will supply them in every station. This may be partly because the caterer may not have a kitchen in Athens or Madrid, and partly because the airlines play one caterer against the other, depending on what kind of deal they can make. So you have the first problem of a single airline which may have a mix of catering its own meals in some places and using various caterers in others. The second problem involves the nature of the regulatory procedures imposed on the airlines—to a great degree correctly, but not always completely so. In fact, I'd venture to say that these procedures would spoil, literally, any precooked food, no matter how well it was originally prepared. If you want to transfer food aboard a twelve o'clock flight, it has to be maintained under refrigeration for a specified number of hours, in order to cool down to certain temperatures, before it can be put on the plane to be reheated. Already, with most foods, you are way behind the eight ball. In addition, you have the problem of cooking the food either the day before or at three o'clock in the morning; otherwise you don't have the required six- to eight-hour cooling period."

George Lang has represented many organizations involved with catering food to airlines, including Marriott, which is the world's largest caterer in this field. He still works closely with Marriott, sometimes going into a problem kitchen in Heathrow or elsewhere, to solve a problem, whether it be the cooking, the wrong food, or the procedures. Sometimes he works on creating a new menu for the caterers and makes presentations to the airlines; at other times he works directly for the airlines. He pointed out that there have been thousands of studies concerning what a passenger really wants to eat aboard an airplane. "I can tell you that they believe that on a short flight it would be lovely to give you a nice cold plate with good meat, cheese, and fresh fruit; but the problem is, I've seen 9 million market studies which say that the passengers want a hot, gray meat with a hot brown gravy, served with insipid vegetables. If the passengers don't get it, they complain that they are *not* getting their money's worth. Of course, it also depends on whether you are talking about

the businessman who travels regularly, or tourists; but not coming up with the right ideas may put you out of business!"

George Lang than pinpointed the main problem, which is that the airline industry "vacillates violently up and down in its approaches," as he put it, "in ways that make it impossible to create anything that is really significant." If one were to make a chart of the airline industry, he pointed out, one would see sudden cuts in special service, perhaps making the menus much cheaper whenever the economy wavers, fuel costs increase, or because of competition. Then, suddenly, two years later, when conditions are better, one airline begins by putting out a full-page ad announcing that they are serving champagne on all its flights. A second airline then announces, competitively, that it is going to carve your meat at your tableside; suddenly, all the airlines are following the new trends. And just as suddenly, they cut back their services, and it keeps going back and forth. "There just is no such thing as a steady development process in the airline industry," Mr. Lang concluded. "Nor do they really have the proper training programs, test kitchens, experimental kitchens, or any of the techniques required for really looking into new ways of solving their problems with an awareness of the new eyes and the new stomachs of their new passengers, whose lifestyles keep changing every few years."

At the risk of sounding like a traitor to the industrial design field, in which I worked years ago with Russel Wright, I wondered whether an important aspect of the problems might not be that the design approach was neglected. The design of the plastic food trays and the components of the food service have not truly changed over the years, except possibly in their color or decoration.

"You are absolutely right," George Lang replied, "and I can show you a file cabinet twice as thick as I am which contains presentations I have made to a number of major outfits. Each of those presentations expresses exactly what you just said and presents alternatives involving a complete rethinking of all dining aboard an airplane. Instead of flat trays, we created trays with different levels that would pull out in an absolutely different concept. However, the financial investment involved in throwing out everything they now use is a very large one—and that is what has to be done, since the current concept of their trays cannot be modified. At this point, I have not been able to find a single airline that would say go on experimenting, will pay for the development stage after the presentation, and then develop the molds and produce the new concept of trays. What we are doing today, even in first class, is a barely modified version of cafeteria eating."

And so, it appears that for some time to come, we will have the same options when it comes to dining aboard an airplane. We can consume whatever food is prepared and presented to us, with an attitude that we can't expect anything special —but at least with the foresight of having ordered in advance specially prepared kosher, vegetarian, or other meals more to our liking. We can refuse to eat the food at all, change our reservations to other airlines that possibly come a bit closer to our particular needs and preferences in the kinds and quality of food that they serve, or, we can take Craig Claiborne and George Lang's advice, carry along our own food.

The problem of eating out is far from a new one. As the Chinese epicure Li Liweng cautioned the Chinese eating away from home many centuries ago, "If you like good food, cook it yourself."

EXPLORING THE ADVANTAGES OF FRUIT SUGARS

When I was in the process of writing my first slimming cookbook, *The New French Cooking,* which utilized sugars only found in fresh fruits and vegetables as sweetening agents, I was interested in exploring the crystallized form of those sugars, which I had occasionally found available in some European countries. At that time, the only crystallized fructose I could find in the United States was date sugar, which, because of its coarse texture and brownish color, was not ideal for some of my recipes. I therefore began investigating further, contacting first the Division of Nutritional Scientists at Cornell University. I also contacted sugar foundations and associations, former clients of mine in the interior planning and design field who were involved in the manufactur of sugar and sugar products, and European friends and business associates.

At first, it seemed that even the experts on sugars were not aware of the existence of crystallized fruit sugar, which my European friends confirmed was available aboard. However, my inquiries had stimulated sufficient interest on the part of some of the experts that in subsequent weeks, one by one they got back to me with more specific information. I learned that although many of our American firms have the capability to produce crystallized fruit sugars, and do supply liquid fruit sugars to the manufacturers of many canned, frozen, and packaged food products, they have not seen fit to mass-produce this more concentrated, and less harmful, form of sugar for our consumption in a crystallized form. Professor Carole Bisogni at Cornell was particularly helpful and put me in touch with the United States Sugar Company in Buffalo,

New York, which did produce a blend of crystallized fructose and sucrose sugars that are available at some supermarket chains. Subsequently, I found crystallized fruit sugar available in Canada, and learned that Finland and Germany had perfected the crystallization process required to supply many countries abroad. John Arvonio is a personal friend and an expert in human chemistry. It was he who was most helpful of all, both in clarifying the advantages of fructose as opposed to sucrose for consumption by human beings, and in seeking out commercial sources of crystallized fruit sugars at that time. Today, these sugars are available in many health-food stores, and can be ordered by mail from sources indicated in the back of this book.

I have discussed the availablity of fruit sugars with the executives of many leading firms specializing in providing fruit sugars in liquid form for use in prepared food products; but although there is increased interest on their part in crystallized fruit sugars, they have not reached the stage at which they see a sufficient demand to warrant their venturing into its production. Nonetheless, I am convinced that it is simply a matter of time and further education before crystallized fructose will be more readily available at prices competitive with those of ordinary sugar.

For the time being, the cost of the crystallized fructose sugars that are available is higher than that of sucrose sugars, and much higher than it would be if fructose were competitively produced by manufactures. However, one should bear in mind that because of the greater concentration of sweetening power in this crystallized form of fructose (as well as in honey and such liquid fruit sugars as pure maple syrup), one uses fruit sugars only in one half to three quarters of the amounts that one would use sucrose, which does minimize the currently higher costs.

You will note that whenever sweetening is required in any of the recipes in this book, I have recommended the use of crystallized fruit and date sugars, pure maple syrup or honey, instead of sucrose (cane or beet sugars). In a sense, we are returning to the more healthful attitudes evidenced historically in virtually every culture of the world in their cuisines up to the sixteenth century, when cane sugar was developed, and the nineteenth century, when processing beet sugar became a reality. The ancient Romans, the Greeks, the Persians, and the Chinese, among others, used honey and the sugars found in fruits and vegetables as sweetening agents in their cookery; and medical experts tell us that the many harmful effects due to the use of sucrose were unknown to them.

For several years now, I have used these fructose sugars successfully in the preparation of my slimming and bonus recipes of the new cuisine. In many of these recipes, the addition of manufactured fruit sugars is not necessary, since the ingredients for a specific dish may well include fruits and vegetables, such as carrots, corn, raisins, and onions, which contain high percentages of natural sugar. Many do not realize that the onion is particularly rich in natural sugar. Chemically, the fact that onions become golden brown when cooked in hot oil or margarine is because of the carmelizing of that sugar, which produces color. A dramatic example, using no other ingredients but the natural sugar and the moisture in the onion itself, is the recipe for **Purple Onion and Fruit Marmalades.** The sugar-producing process in that recipe is a variation of what the British refer to as "sweating onions." It does take about two hours for the fruit sugar in the onions to caramelize, but the end product is a delightful marmalade using only natural and safe fructose sugar.

The new international cuisine is not intended as a dietary regime or a health fad, but rather as a refocusing of cooking techniques, eliminating potentially harmful ingredients which are not essential to the delicious flavor and appeal of the completed dishes. In keeping with the principles of this concept of cuisines, which is more suited to our contemporary mode of living, we avoid the use of butter, cream, saturated fats, and egg yolks, which are high in saturated fat and harmful for those who are concerned with the intake of serum cholesterol. Wheat flour is not used because its original nutritional values have been bleached away and harmful or questionable additives processed into it; equally important, however, is the fact that wheat flour is one of the most difficult foods for the human being to digest. As one medical expert put it, "No one should consume wheat flour, unless he has been blessed with multiple stomachs, like a cow —and even then it would be difficult to digest wheat properly."

Again, this chapter is not intended as a medical treatise; we assume that our readers are familiar with medical precautions concerning obesity and a high ingestion of saturated fats, which can contribute to heart attacks from coronary artery disease. In 1970, *Circulation* published the following recommendations, which appeared that year in a report of the Inter-Society Commission for Heart Disease:

Americans should be encouraged to modify habits with regard to all five major sources of fat in the U.S. diet—meats, dairy products, baked goods, eggs, table, and cooking fats. Specifically, a superior pattern of nutrient intake can be achieved by altering habits along the following lines:

- *Use lean cuts of beef, lamb, pork, and veal, cooked to remove saturated fat, and eat moderate portions*
- *Use lean meat of poultry and fish*
- *Use fat-modified (reduced saturated fat and cholesterol content) processed meat products (frankurters, sausage, salami, etc.)*
- *Use organ meats (e.g., liver) and shellfish in moderation since they are higher in cholesterol than muscle of red meat, chicken and fish*
- *Avoid fat cuts of meat, additions of saturated fat in cooking meat, large meat portions, and processed meat high in saturated fat*

Preventive Approaches

- *Use low-fat and fat-modified dairy products*
- *Avoid high-saturated-fat dairy products*
- *Use fat-modified baked goods (pies, cookies, cakes, sweet rolls, doughnuts, crullers)*
- *Avoid baked goods high in saturated fat and cholesterol*
- *Use salad and cooking oils, new soft margarines, and shortenings low in saturated fat*
- *Avoid butter, margarine, and shortening high in saturated fat*
- *Avoid egg yolk, bacon, lard, suet*
- *Avoid candies high in saturated fat*
- *Use grains, fruits, vegetables, legumes*

We find this advice excellent and consistent with our basic principles of the new international cuisine, with one exception: there is no mention of avoiding sucrose, which is found primarily in processed cane and beet sugars. The reason, of course, is that while the above recommendations are those of medical experts concerned with heart disease, the dangers of excessive sucrose intake are the concern of another medical specialization—endocrinology.

Since our concept of cuisine precludes the use of artificial ingredients, we cannot recommend artificial sweeteners, such as saccharin, sucaryl, or sorbitol. These have not been researched and tested sufficiently to warrant whole-hearted endorsement by most nutritionists and medical authorities; in fact, many experts have advocated banning these artificial sweeteners for human consumption.

To sum up, we are concerned with the dangers of sucrose (dextrose) to human beings, and advocate fructose (levulose), found in fruit sugars, for human consumption. According to the National Academy of Sciences and other reputable sources, the average American consumes one third of a pound of sucrose daily, or approximately 100 pounds each year. Many concerned specialists believe that the general population has reached a serious point of addiction. One of the problems is that more than 75 percent of the average sugar intake is often consumed without awareness, since it is contained in processed foods and beverages purchased in our supermarkets.

But it is not my intention to moralize about the excessive use of sucrose; let me simply summarize some of the reasons why fructose, as found in honey and fruit sugars, is preferable as a sweetening agent in the slimming and healthful recipes, especially the desserts, in this book. Essentially, there is no difference in the caloric count of either type of sugar, except that the greater concentration of sweetness found in fructose permits using less of it, thereby reducing the number of calories ingested. John Arvonio—who has proved to be the most articulate expert on human chemistry that I have met—puts it this way: "When we consume sucrose sugars, such as processed cane and beet sugars, they trigger the pancreas to secrete insulin into the bloodstream. Continuous and excessive use can trigger low blood sugar, hypoglycemia, diabetes, and in some extreme cases causes shock. Fruit sugars, however, are composed of a combination of fructose (levulose) and sucrose (dextrose). Chemists, particularly those in Europe, have learned how to separate the fructose and produce it in a crystallized form. It is this crystallized fructose, or fruit sugar, that is considered to be 76 percent more effective and concentrated as a sweetener than sucrose. More importantly, fructose is ingested and excreted without stimulating the production of insulin and its possible harmful concomitant effects."

You may wish to discuss this question further with your personal physician, and read some of the many excellent authoritative books on the subject. The more that you do, I am confident, the more you will agree with my recommendations to use fructose in the forms of crystallized fruit or date sugar, pure maple syrup, and honey, as sweetening agents in the slimming and bonus recipes in this book.

COMPARATIVE MEASUREMENTS AND CONVERSION TABLES

COMPARATIVE MEASURES:

American/English		Metric
1 ounce	—	32 grams, or .035 kilograms
1 pound	16 ounces	454 grams
2.2 pounds	—	1,000 grams, or 1 kilogram
—	3 1/2 ounces	100 grams
1 teaspoon	1/6 ounce	5 grams (5 milliliters)
1 tablespoon	1 dessert spoon, or 1/2 ounce	15 grams (15 milliliters)
4 ounces	1/5 pint	1/10 liter
8 ounces	2/5 pint	1/4 liter
16 ounces	—	1/2 liter
20 ounces	1 pint	—
32 ounces	—	1 liter
34 ounces	1 3/4 pints	—
68 ounces	—	2 liters

veal is not available in Bombay, we serve beef, and occasionally baby lamb in first class, on the leg of the flight to Singapore. On the return flight to Rome, we have far more choice, since Singapore is an outstanding center for fresh fish, vegetables and meats, including excellent veal from Australia; in other words, the menus are always different for each stretch of the trip. But there is always one typical Italian dish, such as lasagna. We include this on flights from Bombay, because we know that there is a fine Italian executive cook who can make lasagna in keeping with Italian standards."

A large percentage of Alitalia's passengers are naturally Italian nationals, including immigrants to countries like the United States, Canada, Argentina, and Ethiopia, which have sizable Italian populations. This fact is kept in mind whenever typically Italian dishes are included on the menus, since it becomes important to prepare and present the food in keeping with traditional Italian standards.

Another important factor is the consideration of passengers traveling the full route of a long-haul flight, as well as those boarding at each transit station. "We must consider first the transit passengers, in terms of what they are expecting," said Mr. Franca, "without forgetting the needs and schedules of the passengers who have been on board. You see, normally, one has six hours between meals; but on planes we have to serve every four-and-one-half hours. For example, from Australia to Italy one travels east, so it isn't a problem; but flying west toward the sun is a problem. On an actual nine-hour flight, with the three-hour time lapse, there is a twelve-hour time differential. Therefore,

the long-term passengers may be ready for dinner; but the new transit passengers, with the three-hour time differential, expect to be served lunch. We solved this problem, as long ago as 1960, by serving a brunch-like combination.

Probably the most publicized attempt to improve on airline food and service was the inaugural flight of TWA's 1011 Lockheed Tristar to London in the spring of 1978, which featured *nouvelle cuisine* prepared by the noted chefs Paul Bocuse, Roger Vergé, and Gaston Le Nôtre. As I wrote in an article for the Gannett newspapers ("Food, All Night, in Flight," August 27, 1978), "The flight was going to be an example of what could be done to improve food preparation and service aboard commercial airlines. However, as Bocuse pointed out, all the food was prepared ahead in France. It was frozen and shipped to the United States because it would have been too difficult to prepare it here. Vergé added that it had been very hard for the chefs to adjust to the fast cooking speed of the new quartz-tube ovens used on the plane."

I wondered what was accomplished on this flight in the interests of airline dining, and thought the illusion of great chefs cooking aboard a commercial airliner especially for the passenger was a myth to begin with. As I pointed out in the article, open fires of any kind were not permitted. The limitations of precooking, freezing, reconstituting, and "cooking" aboard in airplane ovens were problems, even for the experts. One thing was apparent, however—that food can be prepared in advance and a memorable meal can be frozen ahead.

I also wondered whether this attempt

CONVERSION TABLE:

Celsius **into** ***Fahrenheit:*** multiply Celsius temperature by 9, divide by 5, and add 32.

Fahrenheit **into** ***Celsius:*** subtract 32 from the Fahrenheit temperature, multiply by 5, then divide by 9.

Ounces **to** ***grams:*** multiply ounces by 28.35.

Grams **to** ***ounces:*** multiply grams by .035.

SOURCES
FOR HARD-TO-GET
INGREDIENTS

Special ethnic ingredients are increasingly more easily available throughout the country. If a particular ethnic market is not available in your area, then quality food markets, gourmet food shops in leading department stores, and health-food stores will often have these items in stock —or their shop managers will help you obtain the specific items you need.

For your convenience, the following sources will provide you with catalogues and honor your mail orders. Most of these sources have retail shops available on the premises.

EAST COAST:

H. Roth & Son
1577 First Avenue
New York, New York 10028
    Middle Eastern, Russian, Indian, Indonesian, Hungarian, French

Iron Gate Products Co., Inc.
424 West 54th Street
New York, New York 10019
    Veziga, squab, game, and seafood

Katagiri & Co., Inc.
224 East 59th Street
New York, New York 10022
    Japanese, Chinese, Indian

North Nassau Dispensary
1691 Northern Boulevard
Manhasset, New York 11030
    Fructose natural fruit sugar, crystallized

SOURCES FOR HARD-TO-GET INGREDIENTS

Paprikàs Weiss Importer
1546 Second Avenue
New York, New York 10028
    International herbs, spices, and teas;
Indian, Russian, Middle Eastern,
Turkish, Spanish, and South American

Wing Fat Co.
35 Mott Street
New York, New York 10013
    Chinese, Japanese, Filipino, Thai

MIDWEST:

American Tea, Coffee & Spice Co.
1511 Champa Street
Denver, Colorado 80202
    Greek, Middle Eastern, Russian,
Turkish, Indian

Kam Shing Co.
2246 South Wentworth Street
Chicago, Illinois 60616
    Chinese, Oriental

SOUTH:

Antone's Import Co.
4234 Harry Hines Boulevard
Dallas, Texas 75219
    Indian, Caribbean, Greek, Hispanic

Central Grocery
923 Decatur Street
New Orleans, Louisiana 70116
    Herbs, spices, teas

WEST COAST:

Shing Chong & Co.
800 Grant Street
San Francisco, California 94108
    Chinese, Oriental

Kwong On Lung Co.
686 North Spring Street
Los Angeles, California 90012
    Chinese, Oriental

CANADA:

S. Enkin, Inc.
1201 St. Lawrence Boulevard
Montreal, Quebec H2x 2S6, Canada
    Indian, Chinese, European, and
Filipino

Leong Jung
999 Clark Street
Montreal 128, P.Q., Canada
    Chinese, Oriental

GENERAL INDEX

INDEX OF NAMES

COMPARATIVE MEASUREMENTS AND CONVERSION TABLES

OVEN TEMPERATURES:

Temperature	Fahrenheit	Celsius	Regulo	
Extremely Hot	500°F	260°C	No. 10	*Très, Très Chaud*
Very Hot	450°F	235°C	No. 7	*Très Chaud*
Hot	400°F	215°C	No. 5	*Chaud*
Moderate	350°F	175°C	No. 3	*Assez Chaud*
Slow	325°F	160°C	No. 2	*Moyen*
Very Slow	275°F	135°C	No. 1	*Four Doux*
Cool	225°F	105°C	No. 1/2	*Très Doux*

VOLUME:

1 teaspoon = 5 grams (.5 deciliter)

1 tablespoon = 15 grams (1.5 deciliters)

1 fluid ounce = 30 grams (3 deciliters)

1 quart = 900 grams (.95 liter)

1 gallon = 3.60 kilograms (3.8 liters)

1.06 quarts = 954 grams (1 liter)

1 cup = 200 grams (237 milliliters)